THE MOSCOW
ART THEATRE
LETTERS

by the same author

Stanislavski: An Introduction
Stanislavski: A Biography

by Constantin Stanislavski

An Actor Prepares
An Actor's Handbook
Building A Character
My Life in Art
Stanislavski on Opera
Stanislavski's Legacy

THE MOSCOW ART THEATRE LETTERS

Selected, edited and translated
with a commentary by

JEAN BENEDETTI

A THEATRE ARTS BOOK
Routledge
New York

First published in Great Britain in 1991
by Methuen Drama, Michelin House,
81 Fulham Road, London SW3 6RB
and in the United States of America
by Routledge, a division of Routledge, Chapman and Hall, Inc.,
29 West 35th Street, New York, NY 10001, USA.

Library of Congress Cataloging-in-Publication Data

The Moscow Art Theatre letters / selected, edited and translated with
a commentary by Jean Benedetti.
    p. cm.
Translated from Russian.
ISBN 0878 300848
1. Moskovskiĭ khudozhestvennyĭ akademicheskiĭ teatr–History.
2. Moscow (R.S.F.S.R.)–Intellectual life. 3. Theater–Russian
S.F.S.R.–Moscow–History–20th century. 4. Actors–Soviet Union–
Correspondence. 5. Theatrical producers and directors–Soviet
Union–Correspondence. I. Benedetti, Jean. II. Moskovskiĭ
khudozhestvennyĭ akademicheskiĭ teatr.
PN2726.M62M6664 1991
792′.0947′312–dc20   91–19730
                                                                CIP

Photoset, printed and bound in Great Britain

CONTENTS

List of illustrations   vii
Editor's note   ix
Acknowledgements   xi
Introduction   xiii

PART ONE: PROLOGUE 1897

1 Beginnings   3

PART TWO: THE FIRST DECADE

2 The First Season   13
3 *Uncle Vanya*   48
4 *Three Sisters*   72
5 Petersburg   102
6 Changes   113
7 *Julius Caesar*   151
8 *The Cherry Orchard*   170

PART THREE: DISSENSION

9 Dissension   193
10 The Struggle for Control   237
11 The Theatre and the System   264

PART FOUR: THE REVOLUTION AND AFTER

12 America   315
13 Stalin   329

Biographical index   361
Index   367

ILLUSTRATIONS

1. The Slavyanski Bazar.
2. Nemirovich-Danchenko's visiting card.
3. Konstantin Stanislavski.
4. Vladimir Nemirovich-Danchenko.
5. Savva Morozov.
6. The Art Theatre company in Yalta in May 1899.
7. Chekhov reading *The Seagull* to the actors and directors of the Art Theatre.
8. The building at Pushkino where the Art Theatre rehearsed the first summer (1898).
9. A posed photograph signed by members of the Art Theatre.
10. Vsevolod Meyerhold.
11. Olga Knipper.
12. Evgeni Vakhtangov.
13. Michael Chekhov.
14. Anton Chekhov.
15. Leonid Andreiev and Leopold Sulerzhitski.
16. Maksim Gorki.
17. Mikhail Bulgakov.
18. Proscenium arch and curtain of the Art Theatre.
19. The auditorium.
20. The poster for Tolstoi's *Tsar Fiodor Ioannovich* (1898).
21. The production.
22. Chekhov's *The Seagull* (1898), Act I.
23. Close-up of the same production.
24. Gorki's *The Lower Depths* (1902).
25. Maeterlinck's *The Bluebird* (1908).
26. Isadora Duncan.
27. Craig's design for his production of *Hamlet* (1909).
28. Edward Gordon Craig.
29. The poster for Bulgakov's *Days of the Turbins* (1926).
30. The production.

EDITOR'S NOTE

Many of these letters were written in a hurry, sometimes late at night, or during breaks in rehearsals. They are in many cases personal scribblings without too much attention to style. There are frequent abbreviations and inconsistencies of usage e.g. variously Act Two, second act, Act II. These have been preserved.

In general, names have been transliterated using a modified form of the international system except in the case of well-known names, usually musicians, where an accepted spelling exists.

ACKNOWLEDGEMENTS

The bulk of the letters in this volume are taken from published sources, with the exception of Stanislavski's letters to Stalin. I would like to thank Laurence Senelick for permission to use material from his *Gordon Craig's Moscow 'Hamlet'* to which interested readers should turn for a full account of the correspondence connected with that production. I would also like to thank Mr Arthur Vitz for allowing me to use material from *Pis'ma v Kholivud*, edited by K. Arenskii, privately printed in California. Finally my thanks to Dr Anatoly Smelyanski, Literary Manager of the Moscow Art Theatre, for his assistance and advice on the Stalin and Bulgakov correspondence.

INTRODUCTION

The Moscow Art Theatre is a legend. Many of its practices – long careful rehearsal, research and preparation, specifically designed sets and costumes, the imaginative use of light and sound – have passed into normal practice. In the West it was an inspiration to those who dreamed of creating an ensemble theatre, even for those who had never seen it in performance. It was assumed that all its members were selflessly dedicated to the image of an ideal theatre painted by Stanislavski in *My Life in Art*. That was an illusion but it was a useful illusion.

In Russia the Art Theatre never enjoyed unconditional admiration. It was attacked as old-fashioned as early as 1902, a mere four years after it had opened. Its long rehearsal periods were greeted with derision even as late as the early thirties and the Stanislavski System, which had been the official working method of the theatre since 1911, was rejected as insufficiently 'materialistic'.

It was not until 1938, after Stalin had in turn destroyed Meyerhold's theatre and the Second Moscow Art Theatre, (which despite its name had little in common with the first), and the RAPP (Revolutionary Association of Proletarian Writers) Theatre, that the Art Theatre was transformed into the model for all Soviet theatres as part of Stalin's policy of centralized control. *All* theatres were expected to approximate to the organization and practice of MXAT (as it came increasingly to be known in a world of acronyms and abbreviations). And this at a time when Stanislavski had declared the theatre to be stagnant. As a corollary, the Stanislavski System was imposed as the official method to be taught in all state theatre schools. Stanislavski's open, constantly changing practice was codified, standardized, sterilized and given the status of religious dogma. Nothing was allowed to tarnish the image of the perfect harmony of the theatre where all worked for Art and Country with all the idealism of heroes in a second-rate socialist realist novel. History was rewritten and material which did not fit the bright image suppressed. Both the Art Theatre and Stanislavski himself are paying a heavy price in an era of *perestroika* for being included in the Stalinist pantheon.

The truth was less shiny. A mixture of such fiercely individual talents as Stanislavski, Nemirovich, Chekhov, Knipper, Meyerhold, Gorki, Craig,

Bulgakov cannot but be combustible. It was vitality of conflict that kept the theatre moving; only when there was no energy to defend a point of view passionately or to advance a new idea, or when innovation was blocked in the name of stability and security, did the theatre stagnate.

This book is an attempt to convey what it was like to live and work in the Art Theatre during the first forty years of its life through the letters of those involved. It does not claim to be a comprehensive history of the theatre itself – that would require several volumes – nor does it deal with the history of the studios, which again would require a separate study. It is concerned with the personal reactions of key figures to events and the interplay of their personalities.

In selecting material from the thousands of letters available, in the main only those passages relating to the professional, creative life of the theatre have been retained. The purely personal, as, for example, in the relationship between Chekhov and Olga Knipper, has been omitted. Some letters have been included to give an indication of the financial problems which were often a determining factor in the theatre's policy. While we retain the image of a highly privileged, massively subsidized theatre it must be remembered that for the first twenty years of its life and for a short period under the New Economic Policy (1921) the Art Theatre was a commercial undertaking which had, at least, to break even. It was only in the mid-thirties under Stalin's patronage that it was promised unlimited resources.

The letters are not, unfortunately, evenly spread throughout the period under consideration. If absence makes the heart grow fonder, it also creates the need to write. Much of the correspondence occurs when the key figures were separated. Chekhov's enforced 'exile' in Yalta meant that he had to discuss his plays and keep up to date with the progress of rehearsals by letter. Furthermore, it is the first ten years, the most constructive period in the theatre's life, which are the most rich in letters. Thereafter, with the death of Chekhov, the disaffection of Meyerhold, the departure of Gorki and the growing conflict between Stanislavski and Nemirovich-Danchenko, correspondence becomes more sparse. For the crucial period 1926-8 there is almost nothing: Stanislavski was too busy supervising the production of nine plays and five operas to find time to write and, in any case, all his close collaborators were at his side. After the Revolution the letters deal less with questions of artistic philosophy than with the problem of the theatre's survival, its capacity to find a new role. Some key letters are lost or perhaps have been buried in the archives and await discovery.

If there is a central core to this book, it is the complex, turbulent relationship between Stanislavski and Nemirovich-Danchenko. The two worked in harmony for the first four years, the pioneer years, and spent the next thirty-six in a state of almost continuous conflict, at times so bitter as to threaten the very existence of the theatre they had created.

In the popular mind Stanislavski and the Art Theatre are synonymous. The fact that he left the Board of Directors in 1908 and consistently refused a managerial role thereafter is little known. Equally, few people know of his isolation within the company, his reputation as a muddle-headed idealist, full of impossible dreams and schemes – of which the System was one – which threatened to disrupt the good order Nemirovich had established. That such facts should not be part of the accepted history of the Art Theatre is hardly surprising since both Stanislavski in *My Life in Art* and Nemirovich in *My Life in the Russian Theatre* were careful to conceal the true depth of the differences between them. They conveyed a false impression of harmony with only a hint of more discordant notes. The angry, often vitriolic exchange of private letters, often sent from office to office within the same building, which took place between 1902 and 1917, was suppressed. Stanislavski's contributions to this exchange were not included in Volumes 7 and 8 of his *Complete Works* and Nemirovich's letters only appeared in 1979. In the interim, eighteen letters were published without authorization in the magazine *Istoricheskij Arkhiv* in 1962. The issue was seized and the magazine closed down. Stanislavski's appeal to Stalin in 1935 has only recently come to light. Material for the period 1928-38 still has to be classified and released.

I hope that by bringing this albeit limited selection of letters together some insight may be afforded into the arguments, passions, compromises and difficulties that talented artists encounter when they come together in good faith and attempt to create an 'ideal' theatre. No one is absolutely right all the time and no one is absolutely wrong. In that respect it is to be hoped that a fuller reading of the correspondence surrounding the production of Chekhov's plays will dispel some of the more simplistic legends that, by use of selective quotation, have been put into circulation, often by commentators who have no direct experience of the inner life of a working professional theatre.

What is important in this collection is the juxtaposition of disparate and conflicting points of view. Readers must make their own judgement as to where if not the truth then, at least, their sympathies lie.

PART ONE

PROLOGUE
1897

ONE

BEGINNINGS

In the spring and early summer of 1897 both Stanislavski and Nemirovich-Danchenko were at a turning point in their lives. Stanislavski was thirty-four and Nemirovich thirty-nine. After much soul-searching and encouragement from colleagues, Stanislavski had decided to form a professional theatre company. Already, as a so-called amateur, he had surpassed his contemporaries as an actor and director. It had been impressed on him that he was probably the one person in Russia who could set new standards for work and create a theatre to match the Maly in its days of glory and so carry forward the traditions that had been forged in the forty years Mikhail Shchepkin had worked there. His dream was also to take theatre to a wider, more popular audience but without the condescending disregard for quality which often accompanied notions of 'popular' theatre.

Nemirovich-Danchenko had similar concerns and saw himself too as someone who could reform the Russian stage. He had pursued a successful career as a dramatist, winning the Griboiedov prize for best play twice. In 1891 he had taken over the drama department of the Philharmonic School. Early in 1897 he submitted two plans to the government: the first for the creation of a popular or 'open' theatre, the second for the reform of the Maly which was in terminal decline. He was fully aware of the obtuseness and ineptitude of the government officials with whom he would have to deal and came to the conclusion that he might be able to realize his dreams through a private theatre – the sort of theatre that, as was common knowledge, Stanislavski was about to create.

In June 1897 Nemirovich-Danchenko attempted twice to contact Stanislavski whom he had never met but whose work he had reviewed favourably. Stanislavski had been abroad and then gone straight to his country estate in Liubimovka. It was only on a chance visit to his Moscow home that he picked up Nemirovich's second message. He replied by telegram. The result was the legendary meeting at the Slavyanski Bazar which started over lunch at two in the afternoon on June 22 and ended over breakfast at Liubimovka at eight o'clock the following morning.

The two men were strikingly different: Stanislavski tall (about six foot six), a member of the Russian *haute bourgeoisie* whose family fortune at this period equalled that of the Rockefellers, the Vanderbilts and the Nobels; Nemirovich short, the son of a military family, with no other source of income but his pen; Stanislavski a heavy smoker but otherwise abstemious, essentially puritanical in outlook, frowning on heavy drinking and extra-marital sex; Nemirovich with a taste for good living, for women other than his wife and for gambling. In the early years Stanislavski had more than once lent Nemirovich money to cover his debts. Yet the two men came together as soul-mates, discovering complete unanimity in their dream of a new theatre. The memory of that eighteen-hour meeting and the chemistry it produced were to sustain them through more than forty stormy years.

By the morning of the 23rd they had reached agreement on basic questions of policy and ideals, and had some idea of the composition of the new company: actors were to be selected not only on the grounds of talent but of capacity for work and dedication, what later came to be called the 'ethic'. Yet many questions of a practical but nonetheless critical nature were left unsettled. These had to be decided over the summer, by letter, with Stanislavski at Liubimovka and Nemirovich several thousand miles away in Yalta. Both men had gone away from Liubimovka on the morning of the 23rd with tacit assumptions which did not in fact match. Over the next few months they reached a modus vivendi but their failure to explore certain problems in detail in the early days sowed the seeds of future conflict. On the other hand, had they known more about each other they might never have gone ahead at all.

The differences between the two men concerned both the financial and managerial structure of the new company and its artistic priorities. Nemirovich wanted to create a new company that would run itself in the provinces before confronting Moscow audiences. Stanislavski took it for granted that the new company would be an extension of his own company at the Society for Art and Literature, and that it would build on the work he had done over the previous ten years. Nemirovich on his side assumed that Stanislavski would create and finance a private theatre over which they would have absolute control; Stanislavski insisted on a public company. This meant bringing in other people, third parties. Nemirovich was in constant fear that one day aesthetic values would be sacrificed to commercial interests. He trusted Stanislavski's artistic integrity but was suspicious of anyone else from that class. This suspicion extended, in the first instance, to Savva Morozov, a railway magnate and friend of Stanislavski. Attempts to raise private capital for the new theatre had encountered a wall of hostility from the good bourgeoisie of Moscow. It was Morozov who put up a substantial proportion of the launch capital and subsidized the theatre over a period of five years. Nemirovich accepted this arrangement but detested it. He wanted his own relationship with Stanislavski to be exclusive at every level. He attacked anyone who might exercise any influence over Stanislavski and come between them artistically. He was violently antipathetic, for instance, to his own former pupil Meyerhold, to Stanislavski's personal assistant Sulerzhitski, and later to Stanislavski's more talented and rebellious students, Vakhtangov and Michael Chekhov.

The company structure was a constant source of argument but potentially less damaging than the basic disagreement over the nature of theatre which soon emerged. For Nemirovich, a writer, critic and dramaturg of genius, the theatre was the handmaiden of literature. It existed to serve the writer as literally as possible, as a kind of living illustration of text; actors were the instrument of his own perception and appreciation of the author. He regarded Stanislavski, too, as an instrument, a director of flair and imagination who would provide vivid stage images to express his own dramaturgical understanding. Stanislavski, on the other hand, came more and more to see the theatre as an art in its own right, a specific creative medium. He had great respect for authors but he demanded that what they wrote be theatrical, that they see their text as part of a wider process and allow the actor to make his own individual contribution to the final event out of the richness of his own personality.

In the basic agreement they reached at the Slavyanski Bazar the two men recognized the disparate nature of their gifts and imagined that they could avoid potential conflict by a simple division of power. Nemirovich was to have the last word, the veto, on all matters on the literary side and Stanislavski on the production side. This arrangement held good for their first two or three years but as each man developed it became increasingly meaningless. Nemirovich could not help but see literary considerations as first in the order of priority; everything else had to be subordinate. He saw himself, as emerges clearly from the correspondence, as the true artistic and intellectual centre of the new theatre. He regarded Stanislavski to a certain extent as a brilliant, wilful, wayward amateur who had to be kept under control in the interests of higher literary values. He did not realize that Stanislavski's wilfulness, waywardness and obstinacy were the moving forces behind his creative achievement and capacity for development and change.

Disagreements on these two basic issues led Nemirovich first to try and gain control of all essential management decisions, and then to try and maintain artistic control over Stanislavski as a director, monitoring his rehearsal methods. These two themes run like a thread through much of the correspondence.

1 Nemirovich to Stanislavski

Neskuchnoe Estate,[1]
June 7 1897

Honoured Konstantin Sergeievich,
Are you in Moscow? I drafted a huge great letter to you but as I shall be in Moscow I shan't send it. [. . .] If this letter finds you out of Moscow then I'll send the long one I wrote earlier. But where to?
I shall be in Moscow between June 21 and 26.

Vl. Nemirovich-Danchenko.

2 Nemirovich to Stanislavski

June 17 1897
Moscow

[Written on the back of a visiting card]
Did you get my letter?
I hear you will be in Moscow tomorrow, Wednesday. I will be at the Slavyanski Bazar at one – can we meet? Or let me know at the above address when and where. [. . .]

[According to Nemirovich's autobiography Stanislavski replied by telegram which read: 'Happy expect you June 21 at 2 o'clock at Slavyanski Bazar'. The meeting in fact took place on June 22.]

3 Nemirovich to Stanislavski

July 12 1897
Yalta

[. . .]
It would be desirable to show our capitalists that our enterprise is not ephemeral but based not only on artistic but on commercial considerations. If things should drag on with our capitalist-shareholders then we should carry on for the first couple of years at our own personal risk. Our theatre will only really need capitalists in its third year.

1. Estate belonging to Nemirovich's wife.

4 Stanislavski to Nemirovich

July 19 1897
Moscow

[. . .]

You write further that should there be any delay in people taking up
the shares we might run the business at our own personal risk.
Remembering our agreement to speak our minds openly, I must spend
some time on this point in your letter and state my views clearly and
precisely. Bitter experience has led me to swear that never again will I
take on a theatrical enterprise at my own risk, as I do not have the right
to do so, partly because I am not rich enough (my capital amounts to
some 300,000 roubles, all tied up in the business), and, secondly, because
I have a family and am of the opinion that this money does not belong to
me alone but to all the members of my family. How can I risk other
people's money? Naturally, I will take up shares for 5 or even 10,000 and,
under the circumstances, as shareholder in the business, am prepared to
lose that amount if the worst comes to the worst. The losses of a private
entrepreneur or business are always unpredictable. Apart from this, a
private venture smacks of speculation in the public mind and that would
lend a completely different character to our affairs. A public company is a
social, educational venture; a private concern is just profit-making. That's
how people will judge it in my view.

[. . .] Schultz, Barnay's impresario for the Lessing Theatre of Berlin,
etc., came to see me today. He's renting the Paradiz Theatre for the
winter, rebuilding it, i.e., renovating it, cleaning it up, putting in electric
light. Réjane will be playing for him from October 14th to the 22nd, from
the 22nd to November 15th the theatre is free, from November 15th to
December 1st Coquelin is playing, from December 1st to December 12th
the theatre is free, from the 1st to the 22nd the Lessing Theatre company
is playing. From the 22nd onwards and during the festivities the theatre is
free. Then, with gaps, Matkovski, Sonenthal and others are playing. He
(Schultz) has offered the theatre to our society during the periods,
indicated above, when the theatre is free; the conditions are very
favourable to the society . . . At first glance one might imagine it was
some kind of German trick [*Schwindel*], he's being too considerate, the
conditions are too favourable, surely he's having us on. But he gave me a
perfectly understandable explanation, namely: 'It's bad business to put
one touring company on straight after another with nothing in-between.
You can wear the public out. So I asked myself whether to fill the gaps I
couldn't invite Cherepanov's company, the Little Russian Theatre, or the
second-rate operetta company that's just been thrown together? I have
no alternative. But these flash-in-the-pan affairs are of no advantage and

damage the theatre's reputation, as the whole touring system is only of
interest to genuine audiences. That's why I am suggesting giving you the
theatre with no advantage to myself because you will bring me the kind of
audience I want to attract to my theatre and with the help of your Society I
can give the whole affair an air of respectability' . . . He wants, among other
things, to put on [Gerhart Hauptmann's] 'The Sunken Bell' and 'The
Assumption of Hannele' with us. Our Society wanted to produce these two
plays but had to hold off because the Sporting Club stage is so minute. It
would be a good idea perhaps if, parallel to the productions at the Sporting
Club, we were to stage the Hauptmann plays at the Paradiz (or the
'International Theatre' as it is to be known this year). Think it over, isn't this
the place to begin? Shouldn't we engage actors like Petrovskaya and
Kosherov to add to the existing core of the company of the Society?
Shouldn't we turn the fact that we have the use of quite a good theatre, are
under no obligation to perform every day, and can show a few well-
rehearsed and directed plays for one winter only, to our advantage? – and at
the same time kill three birds with one stone, 1) augment the core of the
company with two very important members, an amateur and a dramatic
actress who, perhaps, given the size of the theatre, can be properly paid;
2) prepare a repertoire of plays on the Sporting Club stage for summer tour;
3) demonstrate to the whole of Moscow how well we can produce and
perform plays. It seems to me Moscow will be more impressed by this than
by a success in the back of beyond about which they will only see scanty
reports in the press and which, more than likely, they will find it difficult to
credit, not having seen the productions themselves. Moscow's response will
be: they've been successful in the provinces, yes, but here, that's quite
another matter . . .

5 Nemirovich to Stanislavski

August 2 1897
Moscow

I cannot entirely agree with you (although I bow to your judgement
without reserve) as regards 'personal risk' and 'a shareholders' company'.
For the simple reason that what attracts me in this matter is the social,
educational side, not a money-making concern. The fact is that on that
side – the social, artistic side – I believe in myself and have found a man
in whom I can also believe – you. But shareholders by their very nature
carry with them the intrinsic notion of profit and I am afraid that a
shareholding company, created initially for educational purposes, may
ultimately degenerate into a purely commercial company . . .
If the undertaking starts (I am talking of the initial risks) as a

shareholding company it will dictate the programme to you. But if it is launched by you then the company will be formed to support your initiative. The crucial difference is this, whether you set up a public company to launch a business or to support something that has already been started. You must understand that the character of the people who acquire the shares plays no part in this. It's a question of the shares themselves, which can change hands, not of people.

That's why the more I think about it, the more I incline towards an open and not simply an art theatre.

6 Stanislavski to Nemirovich

August 19 1897
Moscow

Respected Vladimir Ivanovich,

[. . .] The major difference between us, in my opinion, is that you are just embarking on something which is new for you whereas I have been active for ten years. You want to bring a company together and create an ensemble out of them. Possibly I am being carried away by my own enthusiasm but it seems to me that I already have a seasoned, if small, company. Confident in that conviction I am trying to push forward something that is already under way and develop it here, in Moscow itself. If I have got that wrong, then I must admit that I have miscalculated everything and your plan is the right one: the creation of a company in the provinces. It would be impossible not to concur that your plan is more than likely right but, nonetheless, as I have already told you, I could only participate indirectly. At present I cannot possibly entertain the notion of abandoning my office and spending the entire winter in the provinces without something on a sound business footing. I might for a public company but not for a provincial venture.

[. . .] Moscow society will neither trust in a private undertaking nor take it seriously, or, if it does, it will be too late, when our pockets are empty and the doors of the theatre have been boarded up. Moscow will label my participation in a private scheme – witness Mamontov – cheap commercial tyranny. Whereas the creation of a limited company and, what is more, a popular price theatre, will endow me with the merit – that is what they will call it – of being an educator, of serving an artistic and educational charity. I know the businessmen of Moscow. In the first instance they will boycott the theatre *on principle* and in the second case, *on pure principle* they will stump up a pile of money to support *something they have created.*

I learned recently that Mamontov has drawn up statutes for a popular-price opera-dramatic theatre and wants to submit them to the ministry. Needless to say I lost no time in engineering an apparently chance meeting with him. He has promised to send me the statutes in the next few days. It would appear that public companies are the latest thing.

PART TWO

THE FIRST DECADE

TWO

THE FIRST SEASON

During the first few months of 1898 Stanislavski and Nemirovich got down to serious planning. Both men had for many years been committed to the idea of an 'open' theatre, one which ordinary people could afford to attend. In the first instance they formed the Society for the Establishment of an Open Theatre with the intention of raising private capital on the one hand and a government subsidy on the other. They avoided the use of the word 'popular' as this would immediately provoke official hostility. 'Open' or 'accessible' were safer words. In the event they found it difficult to persuade private investors and their request for support from the Moscow City Council was referred from committee to committee before it was finally turned down in the autumn of 1899, a year after the theatre had opened.

Dreams of an 'open' theatre and of giving free performances for working-class audiences were dashed within a matter of weeks – the official censor saw to that.

In the lengthy exchange of letters between Stanislavski and Nemirovich there was an intensive discussion of repertoire and of the balance between established classics and contemporary works of quality. There was also a discussion of the desirability of including light pieces such as Rovetta's *In the Meantime* which had been adapted from the Italian. Stanislavski's tastes were decidedly more catholic than Nemirovich's and he always considered light comedies and vaudevilles good training for actors. Nemirovich tended to be more serious-minded and, in the end, his view prevailed: the projected repertoire for the first season included plays by Aleksei Tolstoi, Gerhart Hauptmann, Sophocles, Ibsen and Shakespeare.

One major author remained. Nemirovich was determined to involve his colleague and friend Anton Chekhov. The two men were on intimate terms and addressed each other in the familiar 'thou' form (whereas in over forty years of working together Nemirovich and Stanislavski stuck to the more formal 'you'). Nemirovich wanted *The Seagull* but he had to persuade a reluctant Chekhov who, though he was willing to let it be performed in the provinces, refused to have it done in Moscow, even though the Maly Theatre claimed to have an option on it. Chekhov was haunted by the memory of the première of *The Seagull* at the Aleksandrinski Theatre in Petersburg. The audience had come expecting to see a favourite comedienne in a gala benefit performance. Confronted with Chekhov's play which they did not consider 'a good night out' they hooted and shouted their derision. Subsequent favourable reviews did nothing to efface Chekhov's experience and he certainly did not wish to see it repeated in Moscow. He feared nothing so much as ridicule. Nonetheless by May 1898 Nemirovich had broken down Chekhov's resistance. *The Seagull* was scheduled for the first season.

In the summer of 1898 a group of mainly young actors – some former pupils of Nemirovich's classes at the Philharmonic School (Meyerhold, Knipper), others members of Stanislavski's Society of Art and Literature – gathered at Pushkino, a country town just outside Moscow, as there was no suitable rehearsal space in town. They lived as a community, sharing domestic duties and household chores and rehearsing intensely, since they had to prepare four or five plays to make the season viable. Meyerhold wrote a series of vivid though not entirely uncritical letters to his wife Olga, describing their life there. It was at Pushkino that Meyerhold's lifelong devotion to Stanislavski was forged. For the first month the company was entirely in Stanislavski's hands as Nemirovich was absent at his wife's estate in the south, completing a novel.

It had been agreed that Stanislavski would write detailed production plans which Nemirovich would then rehearse, altering it where essential. As soon as one production plan was finished Stanislavski would go on to the next, leaving Nemirovich to work on the actors. Nemirovich arrived at Pushkino in the last week of July and saw the work which had been done. Stanislavski left shortly afterwards for the estate of his brother, Georgi, just outside Kharkov, where he was to write the production plan for *The Seagull*.

For Nemirovich, work on *The Seagull* represented, and continued to represent, the ideal. Stanislavski was bewildered by the play. Nemirovich spent two days going through the text, analysing and explaining. The *concept* therefore was his; Stanislavski's staging was an embodiment of that concept. That was how Nemirovich conceived their working relationship: himself, content; Stanislavski, form. It is significant that in all his correspondence with Chekhov, Nemirovich refers to himself as the director.

For all his doubts and hesitations Stanislavski came up with a production plan for *The Seagull* which Nemirovich later described as 'a masterpiece of *creative instinct*'. There was a disagreement as to which role Stanislavski should play. Nemirovich wanted him to play the doctor, Dorn, because the part needed an experienced actor. Stanislavski, however, found it dull; he preferred the writer Trigorin. After much correspondence, and after Chekhov had seen some early rehearsals, (although without Stanislavski being present), it was agreed that Stanislavski should play Trigorin.

7 Nemirovich to Chekhov

Moscow
April 25 1898

Dear Anton Pavlovich

You already know of course that I have launched into a theatrical venture. For the moment we (Alekseiev[1] and I) are creating an exclusively art theatre. To that end we have taken the Hermitage[2] (in Karietni Row). What we have in mind to put on are 'Tsar Fiodor Ioannovich', 'The Merchant of Venice', 'Julius Caesar', 'Hannele', a number of plays by Ostrovski and the best part of the repertoire of the Society of Art and Literature. Among contemporary authors I have decided to cultivate *only* those who are most talented and as yet insufficiently understood . . . And Russian theatre-goers still don't know you. You must be presented in a way that only a man of letters with taste, who can appreciate the beauty of your works, and who is at the same time a capable director, can present you. I consider *I am* such a person. I have made it my business to demonstrate what I think are the wonderful pictures of life in works like 'Ivanov' and 'The Seagull'. The latter play particularly arouses my enthusiasm and I am more than ready and willing to maintain that the hidden drama and tragedy in *every single* character in the plays, given a production which is skilful, not trite, and extremely well thought through, will excite the enthusiasm of the audience as well. It may be that the play will not provoke gales of applause but what I can guarantee is that a genuine production, with a *freshness* of quality, *free from all routine* will be an artistic triumph. What is holding us up is your permission.

I should tell you that I wanted to put on 'The Seagull' as one of the final-year plays at the [Philharmonic] School. I was all the more attracted to the idea by the fact that my students adored the play. But I was stopped by Sumbatov and Lenski who said they intended to produce it at the Maly . . . I retorted that the best actors at the Maly were stuck in a certain mould and were not capable of presenting themselves to the public in a new light, nor of creating the atmosphere, the flavour and mood in which the characters in the play are bathed. But they insisted I should not put 'The Seagull' on. But they still haven't done 'The Seagull' at the Maly. Thank God for that – I say that because I idolize your talent. So give me the play. I assure you, you will not find a director who idolizes you or a company that admires you more. I can't pay you much because of the budget. But believe me I will do everything I can to satisfy you on that score.

Our theatre is beginning to provoke strong . . . antipathy from the

1. Stanislavski's real name was Alekseiev.
2. The Hermitage Theatre, not to be confused with the Hermitage Pleasure Gardens.

imperial theatre. They know that we are starting a battle against
theatrical routine, cliché and the established geniuses, etc. And they
sense that all forces are being marshalled here to create an *art* theatre.
That is why I would be very sorry if I could not get support from you.

                          Your Vl. Nemirovich-Danchenko

A quick answer is essential; just a note saying you give me permission
to do 'The Seagull' when it's convenient.

8 Nemirovich to Chekhov

                          May 12 1898
                          Moscow

Dear Anton Pavlovich

You sent me a promise through Marya Pavlovna [Chekhov's sister] that
you would write to me but I am afraid you will delay and I need to know
right away whether you will let me have 'The Seagull' or not. I will stage
'Ivanov' even without your permission but with 'The Seagull', as you
know, I can't do that. But we start rehearsals in mid-July. I have to work
out full details of the repertoire during May.

If you don't give it to me it will be a real blow as 'The Seagull' is the
only contemporary play that excites me as a director and you are the only
contemporary writer who presents any great interest for a theatre with an
educational repertoire. I am not at all sure if you got my letter in which I
explained everything in detail. If you wish I will come and see you before
rehearsals and discuss 'The Seagull' with you and my plans for its
production . . .

9 Nemirovich to Chekhov

                          May 12 1898
                          Moscow

My dear Anton Pavlovich

I sent you a letter just today and now I have received yours.[1] You
won't allow a production?

But 'The Seagull' is being done everywhere. Why not put it on in
Moscow? The play already has a great number of admirers. I know them.
There were wonderful reviews of it in the papers in Kharkov and Odessa.

What is it that worries you? Don't come to the first performance, that's
all there is to it. Aren't you just forbidding any performance ever *in*

---

1. Chekhov's letter has been lost.

Moscow alone when, after all, it can be done everywhere without your permission? Even all over Petersburg. If you are really worried about the play then give it up as a bad job and send me a note saying you have nothing against a production of 'The Seagull' on the stage of the 'Society for the Establishment of an Open Theatre'.[1] That's all I need.

Why offend only Moscow in this way?

Your arguments are on the whole inconclusive unless you are hiding the most basic one – that you don't believe I can do a good production. If you believe I can, you can't refuse me.

For God's sake answer me soon, that is, rather, change your mind. I must get the set-models ready and order the scenery for act one right away.

How's your health? Greetings to all.

Your Vl. Nemirovich-Danchenko

10 Chekhov to Nemirovich

May 16 1898
Melikhovo

My dear Vladimir Ivanovich, I take you at your word. You write, 'I will come and see you prior to rehearsals to discuss'. So, please, do come! Come, there's a good fellow! I can't tell you how anxious I am to see you and just for the pleasure of seeing and talking to you I am ready to give you all my plays. So, do come. [. . .]

Your A. Chekhov.

11 Nemirovich to Chekhov

May 31 1898
Neskuchnoe Estate

My dear Anton Pavlovich

Your letter reached me here in the Steppes. So, I am to direct 'The Seagull'. Because I shall come and see you without fail. I intended being in Moscow on July 15 (the rehearsals for the other plays are starting without me) but in view of your kind request I will come earlier. Therefore expect me between the 1st and 10th of July. I will write to you in more detail later. [. . .]

I am going through 'The Seagull' and keep trying to find those little bridges over which a director must take his audience and lead them away

1. The name originally taken by the organizers of the Art Theatre.

from their beloved routine. Audiences still can't (and maybe never will) surrender to the mood of the play, it must be put over very firmly. We'll do what we can!

Goodbye.

Greetings to you all from my wife and myself.

Your Vl. Nemirovich-Danchenko

12 Nemirovich to Stanislavski

June 5 1898
Neskuchnoe Estate

Dear Konstantin Sergeievich,

I wrote huge letters to you twice but on reflection decided to send neither.

It's terribly difficult to fix a definite repertoire and a running-order in view first of the performances at the club[1] and second because we don't know some of them really well and I am not confident about them. And so I am looking into who will play what and the order the plays will come in so that 1) we maintain interest in the theatre and 2) don't fire off all our guns at once – that would be a great mistake and 3) don't drag in novelties and 4) don't work some actors to death while others are doing almost nothing, etc., etc.

I've been busy with this and nothing else for ten days, stuck at my desk for eight hours a day. I still haven't got down to the novel. And it's not over yet.

I now have a clear picture of the whole repertoire. I really can carry through a well-considered plan until the end of November. Of course it's not my intention to suggest the whole repertoire *on a daily basis* for the whole season. We must be ready in that sense for the unexpected. *The order* the productions come in must *to a certain degree* be worked out. And I must say that if *all* the plays to come are done entirely in the way I want then it's obvious none of them should be done at the club. Otherwise some of the actors will be playing ten days running etc.

I'll finish the complete plan in a couple of days and send it to you. [. . .]

I've decided to do 'The Lady from the Sea'. All right?

I would ask you to send me 'The Lady from the Sea' by registered post. Please! [. . .]

I've had a letter from Chekhov. He's giving us 'The Seagull'. He made it a condition that I go and spend two days with him. 'For that pleasure I will give you all my plays', he writes.

Of the other plays we didn't discuss recently I mention: [. . .] I read

1. Stanislavski wanted to stage performances at the Sporting Club, where his Society for Art and Literature had performed, as well as at the Hermitage. The idea proved impractical.

through 'In the Meantime' in 2 acts from the Italian. With an excellent leading role for you. The staging is very interesting and *new*. One set. Not difficult . . .

My wife and I read 'Fiodor' aloud the other day and bellowed like a couple of idiots. What a marvellous play. It's heaven-sent.

But how do you play Fiodor?

I have a very serious request to make of you. For this play let me, not Kaluzhski or Schoenberg, but *me* take the actors through their parts separately. I know of no other work of literature, not excluding 'Hamlet', which is so very near to my heart. I will try to instil in the actors all the feelings and ideas this play stirs up in me. [. . .]

A very important question – make up your own mind – which will you play (in turn with the others) Shuiski or Godunov? [. . .]

13 Stanislavski to Nemirovich

June 12 1898
Moscow

Most Honoured Vladimir Ivanovich,

[. . .] Here is my report on what we have been doing.

1. The theatre [in Pushkino] is ready and has turned out well but cost more than we anticipated. The unexpected cold spell gave us a fright. The inside walls had to be covered with card, hessian and then with wallpaper to hide the eyesore. Outside, the heat had caused the boards to split and crack so that they had to be painted. We didn't consider using housepainters as they turn out to be very expensive. We did it the cheapest way by buying our own material. Burdzhalov supervised the plastering, Arkhipov bought the material. This came to about 200 roubles. In our original costing we had forgotten the upholsterer: the material for the pavilion . . . Curtains for the terrace, otherwise you can't use it on sunny days. Curtains for the theatre windows (otherwise you bake in the sun). We were very economical here, too. We bought scenic canvas that could perhaps be used for the sets . . . The material cost 40 roubles (I bought it myself). The furnishing – furniture, tables, sofas, cupboards proved too dear to buy (up to 200 roubles) so I decided to rent them from Gennert for 75 roubles (20 for the transport alone). We had to buy brushes, combs, a samovar, tablecloths . . . I think this will come to 50-75 roubles. We have gone over budget without wanting to. We must cover the amount by our performances at Pushkino.[1]

2. The paint-shop caused us a lot of trouble. Everything finally was rented. We had to take Kupichskaya's dacha (for 300 roubles). Although

1. Originally it was intended to stage performances at Pushkino prior to the Moscow opening. This idea was abandoned.

you can barely lay one canvas flat in it. We have to construct a frame on two floors. We've started work on it. Simov can start work on June 17.

3. Material on Russian history costs an exorbitant amount of money, for example a complete edition of Solntsev is 550 roubles. I preferred to take on a graphic artist for 35 roubles, who has already sketched all the elements we need. He is also relieving me of the job of sketching the costumes and props which I can't do.

4. We think it would be advantageous to take on a props man here rather than to order them outside. We have found and taken on the best props man in Russia who will make wonderful things for us for 50 roubles a month. I consider this type of expense a saving and not an increase in the estimates.

5. 'The Merchant of Venice' is ready. It should be very effective. Simov's models are ideal: just what I had in mind.

6. Almost all the models for 'Fiodor' are ready. I've never seen anything more original or more beautiful. Now I am easy and can guarantee that such an authentic Old Rus has never been seen in Russia. This is the *real* past and not what they have dreamed up at the Maly Theatre. [. . .]

11. The production of 'Fiodor' is beginning to take shape and I think will be very interesting and, most important, not clichéd. [. . .]

15. I read through Shylock with Darski. Magical voice and personality but no art . . . Pity that he's bone-idle with limited imagination. He tries to find major characters in pathos. We have to get him away from this idea, then he will be a splendid actor; if not it will be rubbish and he won't come near our tone. I'm relieved that he seems sharp and picks up what you say quickly. Only he has little confidence in himself . . . Something holds him back . . . He's tense about submitting to new influences . . .

16. 'Tartuffe'? I hate this play. I don't think we have a Tartuffe in the company. Wouldn't it be better to replace it with 'Les Femmes Savantes'? [. . .]

19. 'In the Meantime': I know the play. It may be worth doing but it will need a lot of money to stage. Without proper staging I'm afraid the play will be boring. Let's talk about it when we next meet as we can't start on the play until the important plays in the season are ready. [. . .]

22. [. . .] Do you know what one hears on all sides: our theatre is good because of its repertoire. 'Antigone', Fiodor', 'Merchant', 'Hannele' give it its profile and these plays are interesting and sound. [. . .] Won't we harm that profile by staging [. . .] 'In the Meantime' etc? Perhaps you are right and that without these plays the repertoire will be boring for the masses. I say this because the thought crossed my mind.

23. [. . .] Apart from 'The Merchant of Venice' and 'Antigone' we are beginning read-throughs of 'Fiodor'. That's essential for everyone: the production managers (to establish the moves and check them), the designers (to establish the plans for the sets and check them), wardrobe (to

know which costume suits which actor) and the props men. You are right: you can't grasp a role until you have tried out the actor. So we must start on 'Tsar Fiodor' as soon as possible.

24. I would be very happy if in 'Tsar Fiodor' and indeed in other plays you would take the individual actors through their roles initially. I don't like it and can't do it. But you are a master at it. And there's something I would like: let me shape, sketch in the play as it comes . . . independently . . . You can correct things later if I have done something stupid . . . I am always afraid of falling under any kind of influence. Then my work becomes uninteresting and cliché-ridden. There are occasions when I can't give shape to something I am dimly aware of, for some time. It is often the case that these places turn out the best of the lot. If I am stubborn and let them linger in the unconscious because my instinct tells me I should, then be patient, allow time for my thoughts to clarify and achieve more comprehensible form. It's these touches which, instinct suggests, give a play its special colour. I feel there will be many of them in 'Fiodor' and that we will get away from the routine that we are so accustomed to in the interpretation of Russian plays. For me it is unbearable they should be played in that way . . . we must get further away from it. That needs time. Until you arrive we will do no more than explore 'Tsar Fiodor' and get an idea of the general colour. I won't cast until the actors have been tried out. The main question is, who is to play Fiodor? For the moment the only one I can see whom it suits is Meyerhold.[1] The others are too stupid for it. [. . .]

Your K. Alekseiev

14 Meyerhold to his wife Olga

June 14 1898
Pushkino

[. . .]

I arrived in Pushkino yesterday (without my things of course) at midday. Moskvin travelled with me (we'd arranged it earlier). Darski and Sudbinin were on the same train. We were just out of the carriage when we saw a bewildered Savitskaya, laden with boxes and baskets and other nonsense looking for someone. We went up to her. We discovered that no one could find the cart. 'Go and look', we answered, no less confused in a district totally unfamiliar to us and resembling at first sight, at the station, a town rather than the country – heavy traffic, drivers, roads, shops. 'Go and look, then,' we said soothingly to Savitskaya and went on our way. To our discomfiture this piece of 'virtue incarnate' helped us out

1. In the event six actors read for the part. It was finally played by Moskvin.

of a difficult situation, directing us to Burdzhalov's dacha which has been taken specially for the actors. We went on. We had still not reached the dacha when we met Burdzhalov who was on his way to the station to meet the 'honoured guests' who had been invited to attend the religious service. Lanskoi was with him. We introduced ourselves. I joined up with Burdzhalov. Lanskoi and Moskvin went off towards the dacha.

We weren't at the station long. The 'honoured guests' did not arrive. So as the service was fixed for 2 o'clock at Arkhipov's dacha we got a move on. We arrived early. The actors had not all gathered. There were no more than five people. I lost no time looking at our summer home, a fair-size wooden hut divided into two almost identical parts. One part is for the stage, the other for the auditorium. The stage is on tall trestles, quite large, not high. The curtain is made out of the sort of material peasants use for their shirts. The footlights will be lit by kerosene lamps. In the part of the hut where the stage is there are two rooms on different sides: these are the men's and women's dressing rooms. The auditorium doors give out onto the veranda. This is our temple of Melpomene.

When we arrived everything was ready for the ceremony. There was a table in the auditorium covered with a white cloth on which were icons, water and everything needed for the service. On the veranda there were two tables with hors-d'oeuvres and 'pies for tea'. [. . .]

15 Meyerhold to his wife Olga

June 17 1898
Pushkino

[. . .]

After the service Alekseiev gave a speech of great warmth and beauty, it's just a pity that the head of the Association, created with a specific educational aim – to found an open theatre in Moscow – can't get away from the slogan, 'art for art's sake'. After Alekseiev's speech, which was greeted with loud applause, the actors were invited to have tea. After tea the meeting was opened. Alekseiev took the chair. Mainly there was the reading of telegrams from those who were not able to take part in the 'opening'. There were telegrams from Nemirovich-Danchenko, from the directors but only one from the other actors, from Katya [Munt]. The meeting was all rather formal: deciding on answers to the telegrams, the reading of the minutes, etc. The unofficial part of the meeting was the announcement of casting ('Antigone', 'Merchant of Venice' and 'Hannele'). With that the meeting closed. [. . .]

16 Nemirovich to Stanislavski

June 19 1898
Moscow

Dear Konstantin Sergeievich

Two days ago, i.e., by return post, I sent you another letter but I am
writing now in haste so that there shall be no delay over certain crucial
questions.

I am very grateful to you for finding the time, when you have an
enormous amount of work, to write to me in such detail.

Your expenses don't worry me at all. *I believe* in the financial success of
our venture, whatever the mishaps, I have faith in your intelligence, your
taste and your love for this affair. The budget is going up but the heavy
outlay is being covered by income. The difficult period will be September
when, without a doubt, we shall have to *borrow* 10,000. I'll borrow it
myself. I think that preferable to bringing in another shareholder. There
will, in any case, be no deficit, even with expenses up to 106,000. As I
thought, everything is turning out all right. [. . .][1]

17 Nemirovich to Stanislavski

June 21 1898
Neskuchnoe Estate

There's an important passage in your letter. A few words thrown out
almost in passing but which require clarification.

If we put on 'In the Meantime', etc., won't these plays fly in the face of
the rest what our theatre is doing, 'Fiodor', 'Antigone', 'Merchant',
'Acosta', 'Hannele' etc?

As far as I am concerned that question was settled a long time ago.

If the theatre devotes itself exclusively to the classical repertoire and
totally fails to reflect contemporary life then it will be quickly on its way
to an academic graveyard.

The theatre is not an illustrated book which can be taken off the shelf
at will. By its very nature the theatre must cater for the spiritual needs of
contemporary audiences. The theatre either meets their demands or
directs them towards new goals, new tastes, once the way has been
opened up for them. Among an audience's needs is the opportunity to

1. For details of the budget of the first season see Laurence Senelick's chapter,
'Foundations of the Moscow Art Theatre', pp. 414–17, in *National Theatre in Northern and
Eastern Europe 1746–1900*, ed. Senelick, Cambridge University Press 1991.

respond to what we call 'eternal beauty' but – and especially in the case of contemporary Russian audiences whose minds are riven by doubts and questions – to an even greater degree there is a need for answers to their private sufferings.

If the contemporary repertoire were as rich and varied in colour and form as the classical, then the theatre could put on only contemporary plays and its mission would be broader and more fruitful than with a mixed repertoire.

New plays attract audiences everywhere because they discover in them new answers to the problems of living. [. . .]

And so, a good theatre should put on either those plays among the classics which reflect the most valuable contemporary ideas or those in the contemporary repertoire in which life is reflected in an artistic form.

We are not in a position to stick to the first kind only, because we do not have the means or the actors. We cannot stick to the second because of the absence of a worthwhile repertoire of contemporary plays. So we chart a course between Scylla and Charybdis. And in particular in Moscow, where both kinds of play are put on so badly, and especially in the first year, when we have to establish ourselves.

'Fiodor' and 'Antigone' fall into the first kind splendidly. I don't count 'Acosta' where you provided a new *form* but not content. I don't count 'Merchant' because 'Merchant', as it appears in our theatre, will be regarded as a creation of *pure* art and, believe me, will have nothing to say to the heads and hearts of modern audiences, who cannot *wholeheartedly* respond to the beautiful romantic story of Portia (and so I think that this play is most suitable for charity performances with their sleek, contented audiences who try to avoid any display of contemporary life on stage). [. . .]

The remaining classical plays we selected, like 'Much Ado', '12th Night' or 'The Taming of the Shrew' or Molière – with the exception of his wonderful 'Tartuffe' – can only appear serious, all of them, in the eyes of the young who have still to learn about social questions that are part of personal life. For the adults who come to the theatre these plays are a good substitute for the vaudevilles of Sardou and Rostand. [. . .]

I must hold to my opinion that these plays are trivia, artistically and beautifully executed but nothing more. We need them because there is more craftsmanship and talent in them than in the trivia audiences usually enjoy and because they develop an audience's taste for good art, but they are still trivia and it would be a crime to devote all one's creative imagination and energy to them. Even the most serious of these plays – 'Tartuffe' – is stuffed full of such excesses that, in our opinion, it is merely the most intelligent and serious of this trivia.

You actually agree with me because in the productions of 'Much Ado' and 'Twelfth Night' you saw no necessity to hold your imagination strictly in check, within acknowledged limits, but let yourself go 'to your heart's content'. And you did well.

But it is essential, in my view, that it be taken as read that for a modern theatre with pretentions to any kind of significance the plays of Hauptmann and even of the less talented Ibsen are of greater seriousness and importance than trivia by poets of genius like Shakespeare and Molière. That's why I am so anxious to include 'The Sunken Bell', 'Hannele' and even 'The Lady from the Sea', 'Ghosts', 'Doll's House' in the repertoire. [. . .]

My 'merger' with you is all the more valuable because I see in you the qualities of an artist *par excellence* which I do not possess. I am quite far-sighted as far as content and its significance for contemporary audiences is concerned but I tend towards the conventional in form, although I value originality keenly. I have neither your imagination nor professional skill in that regard. And so I think we will do our best work on plays which I value because of their content and which give you opportunities for creative imagination. First among these is 'Fiodor'. [. . .]

18 Meyerhold to his wife Olga

June 22 1898
Pushkino

[. . .]

Rehearsals are going very well and entirely thanks to Alekseiev. He just captures your imagination with the way he explains things, creates the mood, the way he demonstrates things and gets carried away himself too! What artistic flair, what imagination!

'The Merchant of Venice' will be done à la Meininger[1] with due attention to historical and national accuracy. Old Venice will rise like a living thing before the audience. On one side the old Jewish quarter, dark and dirty, on the other, the square before Portia's palace, beautiful, poetic, with a view over the sea that delights the eye. Darkness here, light there; here, dejection and oppression, there, brightness and gaiety. The set alone expresses the idea behind the play. Simov is responsible. We saw the models he had made which Alekseiev brought to the read-through.

The casting is good. Alekseiev and Darski will alternate in the role of Shylock.[2]

1. The company of the Duke of Saxe-Meiningen toured Russia twice. Stanislavski saw them on their second tour in 1890.
2. Stanislavski never actually played Shylock.

And how, you will ask, is Darski behaving himself at rehearsals, after all his endless touring and eight years in the provinces? Is it possible for him to knuckle under to unaccustomed discipline. The fact is that not only does he submit to outside discipline but he is completely reworking the role of Shylock which he has been playing for so long. Alekseiev's understanding of Shylock is so free from clichés, so original that Darski hasn't dared protest once but dutifully, though not slavishly (he's a clever man) is relearning the whole part, getting rid of everything that's conventional and overblown. He's played this part several times a year for eight years. No, Darski really deserves our respect.

Alekseiev plays the part better, of course. He has been perfecting it for years.

19 Stanislavski to Nemirovich

June 26 1898
Moscow

Most honoured Vladimir Ivanovich,

We are rehearsing 'Antigone', 'The Merchant of Venice', 'A Law Unto Themselves' and 'The Governor' (for Pushkino) with all our might. I have been reading 'Fiodor' with Knipper and Meyerhold since yesterday. The next reading will be with Moskvin, Platonov and Lanskoi (from whom I expect nothing but don't want to dampen his ardour, although I felt cool towards his urgent request).

Here are my opinions regarding the company.

1. *Darski*. At the first reading he went through the part in his own (so-called) interpretation which I and everyone else found deadly. You know what kind of actor this Darski is in the provinces: a parody of Petrov, that's the model he's trying to emulate. I can't think of anything more senseless and anti-artistic. You can't judge what an artist is capable of when he replaces his voice with whistles and hisses and genuine energy with hideous grimaces and a diction in which [consonants] crackle in your ears. I didn't sleep for two nights. He put me in such a rage that my nerves got the better of me and I went to the opposite extreme and started reading the part in a realistic manner (far more than was necessary). The result was rewarding. The other actors, including Darski, felt the truth of the way I read. I know that after this reading (his downfall) Darski was morally very low. At first he argued, more with the others than with me. He stated that this was an oversimplification of the part, that you couldn't take centuries-old figures off their pedestals . . . He gave Schoenberg [Sanin] a particularly difficult time in rehearsal, defending all his caterwauling but in private he was actually working seriously in the direction I had indicated. Poor man, he got thin, wan, was in despair but . . . one successful line, simply delivered, pulled him in

another direction and now he is no longer the Darski he was. Now he is a
schoolboy afraid to take a single step on stage without me or Aleksandr
Akimovich [Sanin]. A more industrious, attentive, hard-working actor I
do not know. He turns up at every rehearsal (even when he is not
involved). He pays attention to the notes given to others and despite the
blow to his pride in front of young people, learns his abc. He has
recovered the self-esteem he lost in front of the other actors – good for
him. I am very pleased with him. Whether he will succeed in acquiring
this method of acting, which is new to him, is difficult to say: whether he
will master it completely enough to become creative in it and not just an
imitator . . . difficult to say, too. But what I do say is that anyone who
saw him in the provinces would not recognize his Shylock. I have
succeeded in destroying his former Shylock so completely that he will
never offer it again. One concern: he should spend less time being clever
and do more work on the part at home. He has an unusual and damaging
habit of underlining everything and worrying at every single detail.
Intelligence is to the fore and feelings get smothered. I think I am using
the right method with him. I am making him act almost over- realistically
. . . so that he will forget these idealized images he has. Then we'll look
for a middle way. He unquestionably has personality (if he doesn't let it
wither). Can he play anything else besides Shylock? Yes . . . He will be
an outstanding character actor. He knows how to characterize. We just
have to develop his facial expression. His face has two or three fixed
expressions. Cut down the gestures [. . .] Unless I am wrong, I think that
we will find more work for him in our venture than we imagine. [. . .]

Knipper. [. . .] Gave a flat reading as Irina but the part will be all right
[. . .]

Meyerhold is my darling. He read Aragon delightfully – a sort of Don
Quixote, conceited, stupid, haughty, lanky with an enormous mouth and his
words sort of chewed up. Fiodor surprised me – the warm-hearted passages,
bad, routine, without imagination. The strong passages, very good . . . I
think I can't avoid giving Fiodor to him, although alternating with others.

Moskvin . . . What a dear . . . He works his guts out. Only in places he
is too common for a nobleman but that will come (Salario). (He read the
clerk in 'A Law Unto Themselves' wonderfully). [. . .]

Lanskoi. Stupid but nice. [. . .]

The *general* mood is one of excitement. Everything is new for the
actors. The common living quarters (a dacha Schoenberg and Burdzhalov
rented at their own expense for their colleagues. A charming dacha and a
very agreeable place for them all to live), a clean pretty little building
belonging to the theatre. The tone is good. Rehearsals are serious and,
most important, a way of working and acting they have not known
before. Here, for example, is Moskvin's opinion: 'When I was given

the role of Salario and I read it through I found it boring but now it is my favourite but also my most difficult role.' The first rehearsals provoked long discussions in the common quarters. It was agreed that this was not a theatre but a university. Lanskoi cried that he had heard and taken in less in three years at school than in one rehearsal here (that, of course, doesn't say much for the Petersburg school). In a word the young people are astonished . . . and they are all a little alarmed and frightened by the new method of work. Discipline during rehearsals has been exemplary (and, happy to say, without unnecessary schoolmasterish imposition from above) and comradely. If there hadn't been a duty rota we would have had total chaos as at first we had no staff (Kuznetsov who had been taken on disappeared the day of the opening). The people on duty clean the rooms, put on the samovar, set the tables and do it all very diligently because I was the first one on service and did everything very carefully. In a word the general tone is good. Rehearsals are going very slowly because they are all new people (although we've had about 22 already).

'Antigone' has been read as cast. The production plan is finished and will be rehearsed complete on stage.

'The Merchant of Venice' has been read as cast a number of times. The production plan for the first four scenes is ready. We are still far from harmonizing everything.

'A Law Unto Themselves' has been read. The production plan for the first three acts is ready.

'The Governor' has been read. The production plan isn't started yet. [. . .]

20 Meyerhold to his wife Olga

June 28 1898
Pushkino

[. . .]
  Alekseiev is not talented, no. He is a director and teacher of *genius*. What a wealth of erudition, what imagination. [. . .]

21 Stanislavski to Nemirovich

End June, beginning July, 1898
Moscow

[. . .]
  2. So, as far as rehearsals are concerned we make do without you. What can go badly wrong is the business side because nothing has been set up. Not only is Manassievich doing *absolutely nothing* – he [hands over] even minor purchases to other people, neglects the bookkeeping,

and even gets muddled in the accounts (which could lead to serious losses). We must *get rid of him as soon as possible.* Without you my hands are tied, there's nothing I can do . . . With the best will in the world I can't take on the business side as well; on the one hand I have rehearsals and on the other the sets, cutters, props men, the hunt for costume material, the purchase of minor items for 'Fiodor' and 'Merchant', I have all that to carry and have to do it quickly. [. . .]

12. I am very very worried about the way the problem of the censor is dragging on. 'Hannele', 'Fiodor', 'Antigone', 'In the Meantime' have still not been passed but we are in rehearsal and spending money on them. What if there's a misunderstanding? What (as often happens) if Litvinov suddenly says in August, 'Yes . . . it's an open theatre . . . ah! that had slipped my mind'. Then we are lost. Or the translator won't let us have 'In the Meantime'? We are starting our venture with a lot of trouble. What if Korsh or Pogozhev play a dirty trick on us concerning 'Fiodor'? They are capable of anything. It's much more convenient to keep the authorized copy of 'Fiodor' in your briefcase. There are other problems with 'Fiodor' too. How has it been cut? Are the religious characters still in? There's a whole army of them. If they stay, then there's one cast-list, if not, the whole thing has to be changed round. [. . .]

22 Meyerhold to his wife Olga

July 8 1898
Pushkino

Yesterday evening we started rehearsals for 'Tsar Fiodor'. Alekseiev read the play and showed us the models for the sets. You couldn't go any further in terms of beauty, originality and truth. You can look at the sets for hours on end and still not get tired. And what is more you love them like something real. The set for the second scene of Act One, 'A Room in the Tsar's Palace', is especially good. You feel at home there. It's good because of its comfortable feel and style. Among the original sets are 'Shuiski's Garden' and the 'Yauza Bridge'. 'Shuiski's Garden' was Alekseiev's idea. Have you any idea what's original about it? There are trees right across the front of the stage, parallel with the footlights. The action takes place behind the trees. You can imagine the effect. The steps up to Shuiski's house are visible through the trees. The stage will be moonlit. Apart from Fiodor I shall be playing V. I. Shuiski (the traitor). So when Platonov is playing Fiodor I shall play Starkov and Moskvin will play Shuiski. And when Moskvin is playing Fiodor, I shall play Shuiski, and Platonov, Starkov.

23 Meyerhold to his wife Olga

July 22 1898
Pushkino

[. . .]

Today Alekseiev read 'Hannele' to us to the accompaniment of music specially written for it and played by the composer, Simon.

I wept . . . But oh, how I wanted to get out of there. You know all they can talk about here is form. Beauty, beauty, beauty! Here they pass over the idea in silence and when they do talk about it it's to its detriment. Dear God! Can these over-fed people, these capitalists, gathered together in the Temple of Melpomene for their own private pleasure, for that and nothing else, really understand the thought behind Hauptmann's 'Hannele'? Perhaps they can, the trouble is they'll never, never want to.

When Alekseiev had finished reading, Katya and I just sat there while the actors talked about stage effects and effective moments in their parts, etc. [. . .]

24 Meyerhold to his wife Olga

July 25 1898
Pushkino

[. . .]

Nemirovich-Danchenko arrived today and attended daytime rehearsals ('Hannele') and evening rehearsals ('A Law Unto Themselves'). In the morning there was the read-through and first rehearsal of 'Hannele'. The evening rehearsal took on something of the character of a celebration and it was only put on so Nemirovich-Danchenko could see it and determine just how ready it was. He appeared to be pleased.

[. . .] I was happy, first because I am used to Nemirovich-Danchenko's demands and tactics as a director, and second because it's very, very difficult to play a role like [Fiodor] for Alekseiev. Together with his considerable virtues, such as a dazzling imagination and technical awareness, he has one huge and unpleasant shortcoming as far as actors are concerned, the overbearing way he thrusts the interpretation of a part at you.

This overbearing manner is tolerable when all a part demands is technique, but it is unacceptable when a part demands psychological analysis and is absolutely to be lived, like Fiodor. [. . .]

25 Meyerhold to his wife Olga

August 9 1898
Pushkino

[. . .]

My interpretation of Tiresias pleased Nemirovich both in concept and
performance. He said, 'splendid'. He wasn't happy with the Prince of
Aragon. Alekseiev, on the other hand, is enthusiastic about it and has
long since stopped giving me notes. Actually there was a rehearsal of
'Merchant' today and my interpretation provoked great gusts of laughter.
All in all 'Merchant' is ready. Today we rehearsed for the last time.
'Antigone' and 'A Law Unto Themselves' are also ready. 'Hannele' will
be ready by the 14th. After that Nemirovich is starting new rehearsals.
Rumour has it he'll be starting with 'The Lady from the Sea'. Apparently
I'll be playing a sick artist. An interesting part at last. [. . .]

26 Nemirovich to Chekhov

August 21 1898
Moscow

I have already participated in read-throughs and discussions for 'The
Seagull' [. . .]

Let me devise the sets differently from the way you indicate. Alekseiev
and I have spent 48 hours on 'The Seagull' and we put our heads together
to see how we could best reinforce the *atmosphere* (and it's so important
in the play). The first act especially. Rest assured, in any case, that
everything will be done to assure the play's success.

The first discussion with the actors went on for more than four hours
and then that was only for the first two acts (just the *general* lines).

Bit by bit I succeeded in stimulating their minds so that our talk took
on a lively not to say passionate character. I always begin a production
with a discussion so that all the actors work towards a common end. [. . .]

I managed to meet Koni and we talked a lot about 'The Seagull'. I am
sure that you won't experience anything with us similar to what happened
in the Petersburg production. I will consider the 'rehabilitation' of this
play one of my greatest achievements.

Your Vl. Nemirovich-Danchenko

27 Nemirovich to Chekhov

August 24 1898
Moscow

Dear Anton Pavlovich,

Today we had two read-throughs of 'The Seagull'.

If only you could have been here, invisibly, then . . . you know what?
. . . You would have lost no time writing a new play!

You would have been a witness to such growing excitement and
interest, to such profound inwardness, to such interpretations and such
nervous energy all round that, for this day at least, you would have loved
yourself.

Today we felt unbounded love for your talent, for the delicacy and
sensitivity of your soul.

We are at the planning stage, trying out the tones or rather the half-
tones in which 'The Seagull' must be done, we are discussing the right
theatrical means of ensuring that the audience is caught up in the play
just as we are.

I am not joking when I say that if our theatre gets on its feet then
having given us 'The Seagull', 'Uncle Vanya' and 'Ivanov' you must write
another play for us.

I have never been so in love with your talent as I am now, when I have
had occasion to go to the very heart of your play.

I am writing this short letter having returned home after this evening's
read-through. I wanted to write to you.

Your Vl. Nemirovich-Danchenko

28 Stanislavski to Nemirovich

August 30 1898
Andreievka near
Kharkov

[. . .] I was very interested by what you had to say about 'The Seagull'.
I am beginning to read through the part of Dorn but for the moment I
don't understand it entirely and am very sorry to have missed the
discussion on 'The Seagull'. Not being familiar with, or rather, not being
steeped in Chekhov, I cannot approach it in the proper way. The part
interests me, if only because it's a long time since I played a character
part but, you see, I don't understand, or better, feel why I, rather than
Kaluzhski for example, should be Dorn, why all the people you say think
I am right for the part. I am irritated by the fact that I do not understand
what people expect of me in the part. I am afraid I will be just worthy in

it and no more. I am afraid I don't see the part properly. I can see myself,
for example, as Shamraev, or Sorin or even Trigorin, i.e., I can feel how
I would transform myself into these characters but I can only play Dorn
tolerably, rather flatly and nothing else. Initially one always has the
impression one can do well in any part except the part one has been
given. That is always the way with me at first. I will do some reading.
You have no time but perhaps someone else, Meyerhold maybe, who, as
you say, is steeped in 'The Seagull', can give me a summary of what was
said about Dorn during the discussion and how he imagines the character,
what he looks like. He would do me a great service and then I could
prepare the part along the lines you have set down. For the same reason,
i.e., because I am not steeped in Chekhov, it may well be that the
production plan I have sent you is quite unusable. The work on it was
quite haphazard . . . I am stuck on the last act. Nothing comes to mind
and I don't want to force it. I will read the play again in the hope that the
three acts I sent (registered) will keep you busy for a long time. [. . .]

Respectfully yours
K. Alekseiev

29 Nemirovich to Stanislavski

September 2 1898
Moscow

Not much news, dear Konstantin Sergeievich!

Tomorrow, the 3rd, we start rehearsals again. They won't allow us to
rehearse the crowd scenes at the club. They say it disturbs them playing
cards. In consequence we rehearse without the crowd scenes, these are
done *at the school*. Not much room there but what else can we do?

I received the first three acts of 'The Seagull' you sent. I've given a lot
of thought to act one, but two and three I've only gone through quickly
(but carefully).

Do you mind if I don't try to stage certain things? There is much that is
incomparable, things I would never have thought of. Bold and interesting
things which give life to the play but which, in my view, must cut
somewhat across the general tone and work against that subtlety of mood
which, as it is, it is difficult to maintain.

You see 'The Seagull' is written in delicate pencil and demands, in my
view, great care in the staging. There are passages which could easily
create an awkward impression.

I thought I should take out anything which disposes the audience to
unnecessary laughter so that they may be ready to receive the best
passages in the play. So, for example, during the performance of
Treplev's play the rest of the cast should not act full out. Otherwise it will

be all too easy for the house to focus on the onstage audience rather than on Treplev and Nina. At that point Treplev and Nina's tense, decadent, sombre mood must dominate the frivolous mood of the other characters. If the opposite occurs then we shall produce the same blunder that sank the play in Petersburg.

Don't imagine that I am against all humour and boldness in such places. I understand that *a shift of mood* can only reinforce the mystical-tragic effect. It is only one or two details which worry me. Let's take for example the 'croaking frogs' during the performance of Treplev's play. I want precisely the opposite, total, enigmatic *silence*. The striking of the bell somewhere in the graveyard is another example. There are times when it is inappropriate to distract the audience's attention, titillate it with some detail of everyday life. Audiences are always stupid. You have to treat them like children.

It was difficult on the whole for me to rework my plan but I have looked thoroughly at yours and made it my own [. . .]

Your Vl. Nemirovich-Danchenko

30 Nemirovich to Stanislavski

September 4 1898
Moscow

Dorn. Why exactly do you have to play him? I am not wrong. Not so very long ago Lenski, Sumbatov and I were discussing 'The Seagull'. Sumbatov is enthusiastic about the play but says it absolutely requires very strong actors, i.e., the kind they have at the Maly. I suggested, i.e. without contradicting him outright, that the play needed *talented* actors because that's what every play needs, and I disputed the view that more than anything 'The Seagull' needed experienced actors. In the first place 'The Seagull' was in the hands of great and experienced actors (Davidov, Sazonov, Varlamov, Diuzhikova, Komissarzhevskaya etc.)[1] and what did they do with the play? In the second place why do Nina and Treplev – the main roles – need exceptional experience? They must, above all, be *infectiously young*. Better still inexperienced, but young.

'But what about Dorn? Dorn?' exclaimed Sumbatov.

'Yes, Dorn is the only one who requires assurance and self-possession because he is the only one who stays calm when everyone else around him is getting into a state. His calm – that is the special feature of the whole play. He is intelligent, gentle, kind, beautiful, elegant. He does not have a single sharp or jerky movement. His voice spreads a note of calm amid all the nervous and neurotic noise in the play.'

1. Members of the original cast at the Aleksandrinski in Petersburg.

'Yes, and how are you going to keep a young actor under control?!'

'We have K.S. to play the part.'

'Ah! That's another matter.'

Then we came to the fact that the end of the play requires enormous self-possession from Dorn. He comes out of the room where Kostya has shot himself, no doubt white as a sheet, but he has to maintain a calm expression and even hum . . . Quite a character!

It seems to me that this quick discussion explains your particular task. Dorn says little but the actor who plays him must dominate everything with his quiet yet firm tone. You notice that the author cannot conceal his admiration for this elegant figure. He is a hero to all the ladies, his speech is high-flown, he is wise and understands that you cannot live for yourself alone, he is sweet and gentle in his relationships with Treplev, with Masha, he is the soul of tact with everyone.

Viewed in this light, Dorn can't rock in the rocking-chair as you indicate in Act Two.

31 Nemirovich to Chekhov

Early September 1898
Moscow

Dear Anton Pavlovich,

Nothing from you but I am rehearsing 'The Seagull'. There is much I want to ask you about. I would come in person but I really do not have the time.

I have started the *mise-en-scène* of the first two acts and tomorrow will start work on them without the book.

Sumbatov has talked to me a great deal about 'The Seagull' and advanced the opinion (which it seems you share) that it is one of those plays which demands strong, experienced actors and can't be saved by a director.

A curious point of view! I argued with him strongly and with conviction. Here is my opinion (accept mine as you accepted Sumbatov's).

First, the play was in the hands of strong actors (Davidov, Sazonov, Varlamov, Komissarzhevskaya, etc.) and did they make the play a success? The precedent hardly supports Sumbatov's argument. Second, in the leading roles – Nina and Treplev – I always prefer the *youth* and artistic innocence of actors to their experience and acquired routine.

Third, the experienced actor in the generally accepted sense is certainly an actor in a recognizable mould and, therefore, quite clearly it is more difficult for him to convey a new kind of character to an audience than for an actor who has not yet become a master of the theatrically commonplace.

Fourth, Sumbatov, evidently, understands directing only as giving moves while we go to the depths of every individual character and – what is more important – of every passage, of the general mood, which, in 'The Seagull', is the most important of all.

There is only one character who requires great stage experience and confidence – Dorn. That is why I have given the part to an outstandingly technically accomplished actor like Alekseiev.

Finally I am told 'you must have *talented* people'. That always makes me laugh. As if I have ever said that you can put on a play with people who have no gifts. Saying an actor needs talent is like saying a pianist needs hands. [. . .]

Here is our casting:

Arkadina – O. L. Knipper (the only one of my women pupils to graduate with highest honours. [. . .]). Very elegant, talented, educated young lady, only 28 years old.

Treplev – Meyerhold, graduated with highest honours. There have only ever been two like that. The other was Moskvin (he is playing Tsar Fiodor for us).

Nina – Roksanova. A young Duse as Iv. Iv. Ivanov calls her . . . Young actress with much nervous energy.

Dorn – Stanislavski.

Sorin – Kaluzhski, number one actor in Stanislavski's company.

Shamraev – Vishnievski, provincial actor, refused an engagement in Nizhni at a salary of 500 roubles to come to us. By chance he was at the same school as you.

Masha – weak for the moment. I will probably replace her with someone else.[1]

Polina Andreievna – Raevskaya, not bad.

Trigorin – very gifted provincial actor; I have suggested he plays *me* but without my whiskers. [. . .]

The *mise-en-scène* of Act One is very daring. I want very much to know your opinion.

Your Vl. Nemirovich-Danchenko

---

1. N. A. Levina was replaced by Stanislavski's wife, Lilina.

32 Stanislavski to Nemirovich

September 10 1898
Andreievska

[. . .]

I repeat, I don't know if the plan for 'The Seagull' is good or completely useless. I only know that the play is talented, interesting but I don't know at which end to start. I've come at it haphazard so do what you like with the plan. I am sending Act Four with this letter. I understand and am in agreement with your remarks that when Treplev's play is being performed the minor characters should not kill the major. It's a question of method . . . As is my wont, I provided a comprehensive sketch of each character. When the actors are on top of things I start taking away what is superfluous and select what is really important. I go about things this way because I am always afraid that actors will only come up with superficial ideas, of no interest, out of which you get nothing but commonplace puppets.

Consider this, I put frogs in during the play scene to create total quiet. Quiet is conveyed in the theatre not by silence but by noise. If you don't fill the silence with noise you can't create the illusion. Why? Because people backstage (stage management, unwanted visitors) and the public in the auditorium make noise and break the mood on stage. Take, for example, the end of Act One of 'The Sunken Bell'. I think I conveyed the quietness of nature . . . and yet how much noise there was! [. . .] There were five men in different parts of the stage whistling, puffing and blowing into various instruments making bird-song. I chose frogs partly because I possess an instrument which imitates them convincingly. Besides, it seems to me that the soliloquy, which deals with animals, is more effective with living creatures calling in the background. Perhaps I am wrong. It would be a shame if you altered your own plan out of tact so as to adhere to mine.

Perhaps we should ask which one is better. I hope at least that you don't attribute any petty pride to me as a director, still less as an actor. In this particular play the cards are in your hands. You know and feel Chekhov better and more strongly than I. [. . .]

Respectfully, K. Alekseiev

33 Nemirovich to Stanislavski

September 12 1898
Moscow

SOCIETY FOR THE ESTABLISHMENT
OF AN OPEN THEATRE IN MOSCOW

[. . .]

I have now received [the] 'Yauza' [scene][1] from you and am starting on it with real excitement.

[. . .] We worked over three acts of 'The Seagull' but . . . the results were not all that reassuring. Here are the details. Your *mise-en-scène* proved to be a delight. Chekhov was in raptures over it. We only altered one or two details concerning the interpretation of Treplev. That was Chekhov not me.

Of the other characters for the moment only one is faultless and absolutely right – Knipper.

Roksanova runs her a close second. She handles the soliloquies splendidly, is almost completely on top of the 'play' scene and produces a considerable impression. The rest is still a bit wishy-washy and the general outline is not clear.

Kaluzhski and Vishnievski have caught the tone quite well but for the moment only quite well.

Meyerhold at the beginning was all nerves and hysteria, which does not fit Chekhov's ideas at all, but now he has toned it down and is on the right track. The main trouble was that he was playing Act Four in Act One. You know?

Gandurina [Levina] is completely impossible. No energy, no voice, feeble. I have already read through the part with Kosheverova and am working with her.

Platonov [Trigorin] is very weak. He is full of fire and passion in emotional roles but he is simply incapable of being calm and gentle and interesting at the same time. He knows he is being boring and is very low.

Faced with these two the moment seemed right to take a break and make a decisive switch of roles.

Chekhov came. I asked him to rehearsal three days ago. He quickly understood how your *mise-en-scène* reinforces the effect. He saw two acts and gave me, and then the cast, his comments. He finds our rehearsals pleasant, an excellent company that works well.

Another day (without Chekhov) we made changes following his notes (I did stand firm in one or two places) and in the evening he saw it again.

---

1. The penultimate scene of *Tsar Fiodor*.

He found many things better. But he was still naturally not happy with
Platonov and Gandurina. Then he started asking for you to play Trigorin. I
said, would Trigorin achieve his *full* stature? Chekhov answered, 'more than
adequately'.

So you see I have done you wrong in keeping this part from you. The
whole company, it appears, was expecting you to play Trigorin.

I also heard Vishnievski read. He reads Trigorin better than Platonov and
is bursting to play it but it can't be. He doesn't have the intelligence –
natural, broad intelligence and simplicity.

We can swap the roles like this: Trigorin, you; Dorn, Kaluzhski; Sorin,
Artiom.

Yesterday *Suvorin* visited rehearsals. Yes!

Suvorin came with his Fiodor (Orlenev) and Irina (Destomb). They wired
me earlier asking to attend a rehearsal of 'Fiodor'. I answered that
rehearsals of 'Fiodor' have been suspended until we moved to the theatre.
They came just the same and barged into the theatre, etc. I was extremely
amiable, told them how we were staging 'Fiodor', let them look at the
costumes (they in any case will not be stitched), etc.

Our people were very much against my telling Suvorin about our
production but I was guided by the following reasons:

1. If 'Fiodor' is a success in Petersburg that can only serve the play's
   interests in Moscow and vice versa.
2. If 'Fiodor' is interpreted *stupidly* there, the censor can take it off *in
   Moscow as well*!!!
3. The success of 'Fiodor' in Petersburg is no competition for us.
4. In any case they will not stage it like us in a million years.
5. Generosity is never a waste.

In a word, our object is to *help* 'Fiodor' to be a success in Petersburg. The
press is already saying that they came to learn from us. They were all out of
their minds at the way you are staging 'Fiodor'. Suvorin called you a 'genius'.
And, if you can believe it, in Petersburg the play is nearly ready, they had 6
rehearsals, starting at 11 o'clock and by one-thirty they had completed *the
whole tragedy* (all 11 scenes). Can you imagine?

Yesterday Suvorin insisted on coming to a rehearsal of 'Seagull' and was
amazed that this play could provoke such ridicule in Petersburg. He was in
raptures over the scene with Treplev's play and over the whole *mise-en-
scène*.

Then he was with Chekhov almost until midnight and praised our
enterprise. And Vishnievski, without much thought, urged him to build a
theatre for us in Moscow. And he urged him so warmly that he said if there
were a space he would contribute 100,000!!!

Further.

I didn't want to write and worry you. Schoenberg [Sanin] attempted his suicide after the second rehearsal with the actors. Impossible to restrain him. Then I insisted that he stay home and rest and got Burdzhalov to rehearse the scenes he had agreed on with Schoenberg. I took 'Antigone' myself.

We did the 5th act of 'Fiodor' without a *mise-en-scène*. Moskvin staggered us with his naturalness and fire. Knipper speaks naturally and weeps. Roksanova is still not rehearsing in full voice and is intimidated by Moskvin's acting.

The chorus for 'Antigone' has been turned over to Vasiliev.

The orchestra has also nearly been assembled.

Today, Sunday 12 September at 2 o'clock, I am assembling the whole administration at the Shchukin Theatre to introduce them to the theatre: 1) Me, 2) Kaluzhski, 3) Schoenberg, 4) Zolotov, 5) Aleksandrov, 6) Simov, 7) Gennert, 8) his assistant (very nice), 9) Kazanski (accountant), 10) his assistant, 11) Marya Nikolaevna Tipolt, my *belle-soeur* whom I have instructed to take charge of all our costumes and supervise the cupboards, cloakrooms, skips and protect them, etc., etc. – in a word to manage the costume department together with 12) M. P. Grigorieva, 13) Kalinnikov, 14) Vishnievski whom I shall probably make *our* secretary, 15) Shchukin. I have divided the theatre into sections with someone in charge of each.

Today we rehearse the crowd scenes with the soloists.

This is our first rehearsal in the theatre. Yesterday Shukin gave his last show and today starts with us.

Ilinski has written an overture for 'Tsar Fiodor' (*gratis*) which will open the season.

There are still probably more details which for the moment I can't remember. I am in such a rush.

There's something else important. I must go down to Odessa which I shall use to take six days' rest (including the journey), as I am already not sleeping at night and feel a rush of blood to the head. [. . .]

34 Stanislavski to his wife Lilina

September 1898
Kharkov

[. . .]

Dear, I have done nothing, just read through the part of Trigorin, which I like better than Dorn. At least there's something in it whereas in the other, absolutely nothing, and they expect God knows what of me. I don't like that. [. . .]

35 Stanislavski to his wife Lilina

September 19 1898
Moscow

I got home to find a whole array of shoes for 'Fiodor'. I was very happy
that they were already finished, I hadn't expected it. It was announced in
all (or some) of the newspapers that I would be home today so that I had
hardly arrived when I received a telegram from the theatre asking me to a
rehearsal of 'Fiodor' which they were putting on specially for me. At first
I didn't want to go but then I thought it would be worse and more nerve-
racking to sit at home and do nothing. It's easier to go and see what's
happening for oneself and calm down. The first impression of the theatre
was not encouraging. Total chaos, rebuilding, cleaning up and so on . . .
The first scene I didn't like and I almost got depressed (I arrived for the
scene between Boris and Shuiski); the second was better and the rest very
good. Moskvin (although I was told he was not on form) brought tears to
my eyes and I just had to blow my nose. Everyone else in the house, even
the helpers, were blowing their noses too. Splendid fellow!

The crowd scenes (still naturally in a rough state) are all blocked . . .
The 'Yauza' scene is blocked, rough of course. Two or three rehearsals
and I think 'Fiodor' will be ready.

I left the theatre very cheerful, especially when I learned of Suvorin's
and Chekhov's enthusiasm. I came home, had a sleep and in the evening
went to see the sets for 'Fiodor' which have been set up for the last time
as the electricity is to be switched off for a week or so for repairs. Not
all the sets are exactly outstanding but they are all interesting and good.
With the exception of two scenes 'Fiodor' is ready as well as the furniture
and props etc. So we shan't have the usual hassle at the dress rehearsal as
in the past. The costumes have been ordered. I'm told they're already
made. They'll be tried on tomorrow. A number of conversations and the
hopes of the actors and the fact that two performances are sold out meant
I came home in a happy mood. I was in bed by twelve and deliberately
read some book or other for an hour and went straight to sleep. I woke
up about ten this morning feeling good; I think I shall feel better about
things here than in Andreievka. This is how I think things will go: until
the first play is on there will be nothing but nerves. There will be clashes
but appreciably less than at the Sporting Club. When we have conquered
the big ones – 'Fiodor', 'Merchant' and 'Hannele' – then everything will
go like clockwork. That's what I think.

36 Chekhov to Dr Ivan Iordanov

September 21 1898
Yalta

[. . .] If you should happen to be in Moscow, then go to the Hermitage
Theatre where Stanislavski and Vl. Nemirovich-Danchenko are putting
on plays. The *mise-en-scène* is outstanding, nothing like it has been seen
in Russia. Among other things they are doing my ill-fated 'Seagull'. [. . .]
Your A. Chekhov.

After the success of *Tsar Fiodor* the next four productions were comparative
failures. Hauptmann's *The Sunken Bell*, Shakespeare's *The Merchant of
Venice*, Pisemski's *A Law Unto Themselves* and Goldoni's *La Locandiera*
failed to excite any interest. Takings were poor. The Art Theatre faced
bankruptcy by the end of the year. Everything now depended on the success
of *The Seagull*, which nobody in their wildest dreams imagined would be a
'smash'.

37 Nemirovich to Chekhov

December 18 1898
Moscow 0.50 a.m.

Telegram

Just finished playing 'The Seagull', colossal success. After the first act
such applause that a series of triumphs followed. At my statement after
the third act that the author was not present the audience demanded a
telegram be sent to you on their behalf. We are delirious with joy. We all
embrace you, will write in detail.

38 Nemirovich to Chekhov

December 18-21 1898
Moscow

Letter

You know already from my telegram of the external success of 'The
Seagull'. To give you some idea of the first performance I will say that
backstage after the 3rd act there was a mood of intoxication. Someone
aptly remarked that it was exactly like Easter Sunday. Everyone was

kissing each other, throwing themselves in each other's arms, everyone was caught up in the feeling of a resounding triumph for truth and honourable work. You will gather all the reasons for such joy: the artists were in love with the play and each rehearsal revealed ever new artistic pearls in it. At the same time we feared that the public, little versed in literature, with little culture, corrupted by cheap stage effects, not accustomed to extreme artistic simplicity, would not appreciate the beauty of 'The Seagull'. We put all our soul into the play and all our calculations at risk. The two directors, i.e., Alekseiev and I, applied all our strength and all our ability to make sure that the astonishing moods of the play came off theatrically. We had three full dress rehearsals, looked into every corner of the stage, checked every electric lamp. I lived in the theatre for two weeks, dealing with the sets and props; I went to antique shops, looking for objects that would give colourful touches.

For the first performance, as in a jury, I took a 'lead' to make sure the audience consisted of people capable of appreciating the simplicity of truth on stage. But I was true to myself, and did nothing to arrange a wild success in advance.

At the first dress rehearsal there was the kind of mood among the cast which promises success. And yet my dreams *never* went that far. I expected that at the very best it would be a success worthy of note. And instead . . . I can't fully convey to you the impression. Not one word, not one sound was lost. The audience got not only the general mood, not only the *story*, which in this play was so difficult to register as the unifying factor, but also every idea which you created both as artist and thinker, everything, everything, in a word, every psychological change, everything got across and was grasped. And all my fears that only a few would understand the play vanished. There were scarcely ten people who didn't understand something. Then I thought that external success would express itself in a few friendly curtain-calls after the 3rd act. But this is what happened. After the first act the actors were given five calls by the whole house (we don't rush the curtain for calls), the house was rapt and excited. But after the 3rd act not one person left the auditorium, they all stood up and applause turned to a noisy, endless ovation. When there were cries of 'author' I explained that you were not in the theatre. A voice called out, 'Send a telegram'. [. . .]

After the 4th act there was another ovation. [. . .]

We played in order [of merit]: Knipper – wonderful, ideal Arkadina. She got so deep into the part that she lost nothing of the actressy elegance, the beautiful frocks, the enchanting vulgarity, the *meanness*, etc. Both scenes in the 3rd act with Treplev and Trigorin – especially the first – were the most successful things in the play and rounded off with the final, unusually staged farewell scene (without the superfluous people).[1] After Knipper comes

1. Chekhov had objected to Stanislavski's idea of bringing a group of people with mothers and crying children into the farewell scene.

Alekseieva [Lilina] as Masha. A spellbinding characterization. Spirited and extraordinarily affecting. They had a huge success. Then Kaluzhski as Sorin. He acted like a good solid artist. After that Alekseiev. He successfully captured the soft, spineless tone. He delivered the speech in the 2nd act particularly splendidly. He was sugary in act three.

Weakest of all was Roksanova who was confused by Alekseiev, who directed her to play like some idiot. I got angry with her and demanded that she go back to the earlier lyrical tone. That confused her. Vishnievski did not quite get into the gentle, intelligent, observant, all- sensitive character of Dorn but his make-up was very successful (like Aleksei Tolstoi) and concluded the play excellently. The rest provided a harmonious ensemble.

The overall tone was calm and extremely *literary*.

The way the play was listened to was amazing, as no play has ever been listened to.

Moscow is buzzing. The Maly Theatre is ready to tear us in pieces. But here's the rub. We had to put off the second performance to another day. Knipper was ill. We also cancelled the 3rd which was due to take place yesterday, Sunday. It doesn't affect the play but we have lost a lot of money.

The production – you would ooh and ah at the 1st [act] and, in my opinion at the 4th. [. . .]

Your Vl. Nemirovich-Danchenko

Can we have 'Uncle Vanya'?

39 Marya Chekhova to Chekhov

December 18 1898
Moscow

Your 'Seagull' was on yesterday. The staging was beautiful. The first act was fully understood and interesting. The actress, Treplev's mother, was played by a very, very sweet actress, Knipper, who is extraordinarily talented and pure delight to see and hear. The doctor, Treplev, the teacher and Masha were outstanding. I didn't especially like Trigorin and the Seagull herself. Stanislavski played Trigorin limply and the Seagull is a bad actress but in general the staging is so lifelike that you completely forget that it's a stage. There was silence in the theatre, people listened attentively.

In the general euphoria that followed the success of *The Seagull*, only one jarring note was heard. That was supplied by Meyerhold, who was becoming

more and more impatient with Stanislavski's dictatorial methods as a
director and apparent anti-intellectual attitudes.

40 Meyerhold to Nemirovich

> January 17 1899
> Moscow
>
> 1. Discussion – a bonus for the
>   success of the play.
> 2. Discussion – a bonus for the
>   intellectual and moral life of the
>   actors.

I looked forward to taking an active part in the *discussion* on 'Hedda
Gabler' that was set for today. Only there was no discussion.

To discuss the general significance of a play, to argue about the nature
of the characters, to enter the spirit of a play of moods through
challenging debate – that is not one of our principal director's principles.

He, in the event, prefers to read the play through himself, sketching
the staging as he goes, positions, moves, marking the pauses. In a word,
for social drama, for psychological drama the principal director uses the
same directorial method he worked out years ago and has guided him
whether it's a play of mood and ideas or something spectacular. Do I
have to prove this is wrong?

Are we the cast really supposed to do *nothing but* act? We also want to
think while we're acting. We want to know *why* we are acting, *what* we
are acting and who we are teaching or criticizing by our acting.

To do that we want and need to know, we want and need to be clear
about the social and psychological import of the play, the characters –
positive and negative, which society or which members the author
sympathizes with or does not sympathize with. Only then, in a word, will
the actors be able *consciously* to express the author's ideas and only then
can the audience also *consciously* relate to the play.

It may well be that the principal director with his great artistic flair can
stage the play without investigating the author's ideas. I believe he can.
But suppose he can't?

That's possible.

Here is our director's literary preparedness, expressed in two or three
remarks thrown out before the reading:

M[arya] F[edorovna] – I have translated a few passages from an essay
in German on 'Hedda Gabler', which might be of interest to us. I have
also found a Russian article.

Al[ekseiev] – if it's anything like Lemaître's articles I don't intend to read it. I only read criticism which expresses the same views that we hold. [. . .]

Vish[nievski] – The play will be a great success.

A[lekseiev] – After seeing the play all the society ladies will be wearing frocks and hairdos like M[arya] F[edorovna]. [. . .]

Now Ibsen castigates the conditions of contemporary social life which make possible the appearance of women like Hedda. Hedda is an extreme type, a type that looks into herself, focusing all the negative aspects of many of our society ladies who are intelligent but do not consciously relate to the phenomena of life, nice but egotistical, with a gift for love but not able to sacrifice their freedom for it.

Ibsen skilful[ly] gathers together a million negative aspects in Hedda with the express purpose of showing more clearly that the moral foundation of our society is shaky and that the absence in people of conscious attitudes towards life and themselves leaves the way open to the influence of decadence and that the product of such a corrupt society is revealed in Hedda Gabler. If society ladies who attend the play are not horrified but rather want to copy her, Ibsen won't thank us for it. He is not writing in order to corrupt the masses, he is not writing so that we shall remain indifferent to the negative phenomena in society. You know that Ibsen, more than anyone else, can be considered the proclaimer of human values and the standard-bearer of the ideal of civic mindedness.

Whoever stages Ibsen's play just for the parts in it and not because of its ideas will give the public the opposite impression to the one the author intended.

I am getting carried away. I'm sorry. It is not my wish to prove the bankruptcy of a generally accepted directorial method (a reading or general read-through without preliminary discussion) when we are dealing with the staging of exclusively literary plays, but to start a debate. Excuse me.

The object of this letter is 1) to ask you not to waver in your principles, as only your method (discussion) can help ensure the success of *literary* works and their interpreters; 2) don't deprive the actors in your company of their only opportunity to break the mould which is propagated by a hack attitude towards the stage and is inevitable when the same play is repeated for the fortieth or tenth time, or for them to use their wits when they have no work; we don't have time to look at the papers.

41 Marya Chekhova to Chekhov

January 22 1899
Moscow

[. . .] I went to the performance of 'The Seagull'. I sat in the stalls. Full house, sold out for 9 performances already. In the third act Roksanova was good but bad in the last act. The Doctor, Sorin and Knipper delightful as before. I saw and heard the play with pleasure. I shall go again.

42 Marya Chekhova to Chekhov

February 5 1899
Moscow

[. . .] I went to see 'The Seagull' for the third time yesterday. Watched it with even more pleasure than the first or second time. Everyone played very, very well, even Roksanova was good. Vishnievski visited us a while ago and invited me backstage and introduced me to all the artists. If you only knew how happy they were! Knipper got very excited and I passed on your greeting. Alekseieva, who plays Masha, asked me to tell you that you couldn't write a better part for her and she thanks you. Everyone sends their greetings. They play your 'The Seagull' with such love!! Fedotova was there and wept the whole time and said: 'Tell him my dear, that an old woman was enchanted by his play and sends him a deep salutation.' Then she bowed very low. She sent for me in every interval and wept and wept. [. . .]

THREE

UNCLE VANYA

The first night of *The Seagull* marked the true birth of the Art Theatre. 'Tsar Fiodor' had been impressive and spectacular. 'The Seagull' was unique. When, in 1902, the company moved into its own building an emblematic seagull was sewn onto the front curtain as the theatre's symbol.

Having, as he put it, 'rehabilitated' a failed play, Nemirovich assumed that the theatre would be invited to include *Uncle Vanya* in the next season. Chekhov had after all promised him all his other plays. Both he and Stanislavski were shocked when they learnt that *Vanya* was to be done at the Maly. They felt morally betrayed and they were also acutely aware that a new Chekhov production was a sure box-office success.

Much concerning this painful incident is obscure. No clear, unequivocal explanation was offered by anyone involved. Stanislavski's claim that Chekhov refused to give him the play on the grounds that he had not yet seen *The Seagull* is nowhere corroborated. In fact, when Chekhov did release the play, in late April 1899, he had still not seen *The Seagull*.

Chekhov was evidently embarrassed but considered he was committed to the Maly by a long-standing, albeit verbal, agreement. The Maly, on its side, having failed to exercise its option on *The Seagull* was determined not to let *Vanya* slip through its fingers. The General Administrator, Telyakovski, noted in his diary on February 4 that anything that could be taken from the new theatre should be. For Chekhov, as for other writers, a production at the Maly still represented official recognition. The Art Theatre had done magnificently but it was still only a few months old. The Maly had been Moscow's premier theatre for three quarters of a century. There were also financial considerations. Chekhov was a professional writer, earning his living from his pen. He had a healthy respect for money. His sister Marya, who took charge of his affairs, wrote to him regularly, detailing the royalties and payments she had received. The Art Theatre had paid him comparatively little. The Maly, as Chekhov pointed out to his doctor friend, Ivan Orlov, could offer better.

In the end it was the officials of the Maly who ruined the theatre's chances. They demanded radical rewrites in a very high-handed manner which Chekhov refused. Nemirovich saw his chance and seized it.

The production of *Uncle Vanya* together with Chekhov's growing affection for Knipper, whom he later married, created an intimate relationship between author and company. Chekhov was highly critical of Stanislavski's performance as Trigorin which he detested – a fact which has been blown up out of all proportion as though it represented the whole of the Stanislavski/Chekhov relationship – but he had great respect for Stanislavski as a director. He also gave his full backing to the philosophy which lay behind the Art Theatre's working methods. While the theatre was for him, on the one hand, a source of dread, he was on the other fascinated by the mechanics of staging and production. He wanted to know how everything worked; he insisted on being involved with the daily life of the company and even when he was obliged to be out of Moscow demanded news not only of what was happening to his own plays but also to other works in the repertoire. He advised the young Gorki to go and sit in on Art Theatre rehearsals and watch the company at work so that he could learn more about the process of play-making.

The second season was planned on much the same lines as the first. It was to open with Aleksei Tolstoi's *The Death of Ivan the Terrible* and, apart from *Uncle Vanya*, would include *Twelfth Night*, and two plays by Hauptmann, *Drayman Henschel* and *Lonely People*.

43 Chekhov to Nemirovich

February 8 1899
Yalta

[. . .] I haven't written anything about 'Uncle Vanya' to you because I don't know what to say. I gave a verbal promise to the Maly Theatre and now it is rather awkward. I would look as though I were spurning the Maly. Be a good fellow, make enquiries:[1] has the Maly decided to do 'Uncle Vanya' next season? If not then, of course, I will declare my play *porto franco*. If they are, I will write another play for the Art Th. Don't be offended; there have been discussions with the Maly about 'Uncle Vanya' for a long time. [. . .]

1. Nemirovich was still officially a member of the repertoire committee of the Maly although he no longer attended meetings.

44 Chekhov to Ivan Orlov[1]

February 22 1899
Yalta

[. . .] Next season my play [Vanya] is being done at the Maly: a bit of cash, you see. [. . .]

45 Marya Chekhova to Chekhov

March 26 1899
Moscow

Vladimir Ivanovich Nemirovich-Danchenko has just been to see me about the following. He is still a member of the theatre committee [of the Maly Theatre] but has not attended meetings for a long time. He heard from Veselovski and Ivan Ivanovich Ivanov that your play 'Uncle Vanya' has been approved for presentation at the Maly but on condition that you make changes to it, i.e., one or two places in the play and then submit it for approval once more. As the Art Theatre was very upset that the play was being done at the Maly, Nemirovich has reached the following conclusion: there is no need to rewrite the play and he will put it on at his theatre without rewrites as he finds it excellent, etc. Stanislavski likes it better than 'The Seagull'.

The minutes will be slow in getting to you so Nemirovich asks you to send a telegram to the committee enquiring: has the play been approved and in what way? And then, if you are agreeable to giving it to the Art Theatre, send a wire to Nemirovich as soon as possible as the repertoire and casting have to be decided this spring.

I saw how sad all the artists of the Art Theatre were at not being able to do the play when I spent an evening at Fedotova's home.

Nemirovich begged me to write to you as soon as possible, he thought that would get better results. Please give him an answer.

He is in a great state.

Olga Knipper's relationship to the Art Theatre was often a difficult one. She had very decided ideas about what she could or would or would not do. This led to frequent clashes, particularly with Stanislavski. The first example occurred in 1899 when Knipper decided she did not wish to be exposed to possibly unfavourable comparisons in the role of Hanna in Hauptmann's *Drayman Henschel*.

1. A doctor friend of Chekhov.

46 Stanislavski to Knipper

June 24 1899
Moscow

Most honoured Olga Leonardovna,

I only received your letter yesterday on my return to Moscow. Please forgive the lateness of my reply which I did not want at all.

If we knew each other better I would venture to speak openly to you about the role of Hanna[1] but for the moment I am afraid to do so for the following reasons.

If the Hannas in other theatres, that is the Maly or Korsh's company or touring theatres, were to please audiences more, you would have grounds for reproaching me for having advised you to take this role since unfavourable comparisons would be undesirable after your first successful season.

On the other hand if you don't take the role then it will have to be played by my sister.[2] A brother's situation in such circumstances is very ticklish. Allow me to let Vladimir Ivanovich decide as I do not have the right to change casting without his full agreement. I will write to him about it today and give him your address. I think he will give you a quick decision.

I take this opportunity to share one or two of my ideas about the role of Elena in 'Uncle Vanya'. Arkadina and Elena are both women of the world and their personality, in both cases, could lead the actress playing them to repeat herself. That is not what's wanted . . . As the greatest difference between the two characters I would present Elena – naturally in moments of calm – as having greater indolence, suppleness, laziness, reserve, sophistication, but at the same time bring out the force of her personality more . . . I throw out this thought, which came to me after the last rehearsal, for you to try. If only you knew how difficult it is! There is a good role in Ibsen's 'Pillars of Society' but like Arkadina it's not young. But it is undesirable for you to play, two years running, before it's right, roles which do not match your age. I will give the matter thought as soon as there's time. [. . .]

1. Hanna Schäl in Hauptmann's *Drayman Henschel*, which was in production at Korsh's theatre, and opened on August 31. A production at the Maly opened immediately after, on September 2. The MXT production followed just over a month later on October 5.

2. Anna Schteker who used the stage name Alekseieva. The role of Hanna was finally played both by Anna Alekseieva and Roksanova.

Stanislavski's workload became a matter of concern. He was working full out as actor and director while still continuing to run the Alekseiev factories. Frequent attempts to relieve the pressure on him came to nothing.

47 Nemirovich to Stanislavski

July 23 1899
Moscow

[. . .]
These last few days during our directors' meetings the most basic feeling Schoenberg [Sanin] and I experienced was affection for you . . . I raised a number of fundamental questions with Kaluzhski and Schoenberg, which I settled with one concern in mind: your health and strength. We came to a series of decisions which we discussed over two whole days. I will write to you in individual detail about these decisions. We decided that you cannot go on working as you have been working during the spring without a break. You can't and that's that. [. . .]

48 Nemirovich to Stanislavski

July 30 1899
Moscow

[. . .]
'Lonely People'. I read it. The play is superb, we absolutely must stage it, honour and glory to you for having found it. Shame on me for never having once mentioned it: when I got your letter I really banged myself on the head.
The translation is very bad, I can't see the characters. Efros could translate it in a week, for 250 r. On one hand it would be good to give Efros this fee, on the other it is *quicker* to correct the existing translation with the original in one's hands . . . He knows the play and praises it but says it is rather too gloomy and pessimistic. [. . .]
Johannes – Meyerhold, although Johannes is more beautiful and *more inwardly mobile* than Treplev. Johannes is vital, greatly inclined to gaiety and unbounded love. It seems to me his face often lights up with a joyful, child-like smile. It is only all the conventions, all that obsolete morality, which so oppresses the spiritual freedom of a man in search of new ideals, which drive the joy out of him. [. . .]

49 Nemirovich to Stanislavski

August 21 1899
Moscow

Dear Konstantin Sergeievich,

I enclose your work schedule. I want to discuss it a little because, while there may be alterations, it is helpful for the general run of things if a recognizable system is worked out. Besides, as the final preparations for 6-7 plays have been accomplished in just one month it will be all the easier to create chaos. Things could come to a bad end; either the cancellation of the first matinées could emphasize the uncertainty of the repertoire, an uncertainty that would be unforgivable for the second season and after ten months' rehearsal; or a delay in opening the season would reveal a certain lack of seriousness of mind and amateurishness; or, finally, the removal of certain plays from the basic programme which would destroy the programme itself.

You hold great power in your hands. You can support the overall plan, you can easily give it a shake, or you can even destroy it. That is why I think it important to explain the system to you.

The programme depends on 9 plays. It is impossible to have them all ready for the opening. Those we should set aside are 'Hedda Gabler', 'The Sunken Bell' and, in part, 'Uncle Vanya'. The first two because you are involved in them and rehearsals in September will in any case be a distraction to you on at least 6 occasions. The third, partly and essentially because I believe the sets will not be ready.

That leaves 6 plays which need to be ready for the opening. Among them 'The Seagull' needs more work, requires one – more, one and a half days' rehearsal for the actors and one morning to take in the new pavilion (3rd act) and set the lights.

That means that all the work comes down to 5 plays. You've got to prepare Ivan to perfection, get Astrov absolutely ready, direct 'Ivan' in its entirety, tighten up 'Henschel', bolster up 'Twelfth Night' and run over 'Antigone' and 'Fiodor'.

How can one divide up the work of an actor who wants to be free to concentrate on one of his roles and of a director who focuses his attention on *everything* (and even on one occasion showing himself to be an efficient manager).

Difficult.

In my view the best thing is probably this: to begin with you work on just one role and nothing else. You must prepare and master it in a given time. The most difficult one while you are still strong and fresh. That is Ivan.

When you have prepared that you switch over to directing.

And it is essential not just for you but for the other directors and actors and the props men, etc., to finish one play and then go on to another.

In this way we can complete the remaining part of 'Ivan', also complete 'Henschel', put the finishing touches to 'Fiodor', 'Antigone' and almost to 'Twelfth Night'.

At the same time you can do some work on Astrov.

When things come to a stop you can breathe freely and say to yourself: now I belong to the role of Ivan for a while, for the second time and finally.

The season is upon us, you must act-rehearse all-out. Now nothing must be allowed to disturb you. So, in the last as in the first week of performances, you rehearse one or two days; you play Ivan. And, for your amusement, you can glance at 'Twelfth Night' and administrative matters.

So, you have three periods in September:

1. Just the role of Ivan, in rough outline, in finished form, this scene and that, then in its entirety. You work, dig into it and discuss it *with the most benevolent* and experienced audience – me, then work on it again.

That should take about ten days.

2. You turn director – some time on Astrov. Ivan, as a role, is put under wraps.

3. You finish that off and get down to being an actor who needs calm and unflurried dress rehearsals.

I went through tens of possible schemes but finally settled on this one as being, in my opinion, the most *psychologically* proper.

I still have to find a time for 'Lonely People'.

I will hold on to the female roles as long as possible.

I will send Marya Petrovna a separate list of 'Uncle Vanya' rehearsals.

In any case I will draft the schedule for later performances after October 14.

50 Knipper to Chekhov

> September 26 1899
> Moscow

[. . .]

We set to work on the whole play without Astrov, with Nemirovich. We went through individual scenes, discussed a great deal, fussed over it the way we fussed over 'The Seagull'. I am worried by Alekseiev's remark about the scene between Astrov and Elena: in his opinion Astrov approaches Elena like an ardent lover, snatching at his own feelings like a drowning man clutching at straws. It seems to me that if this were the case Elena would walk away from him and would not have the spirit to answer him – 'how amusing you are!' He most probably speaks to her with the utmost cynicism and even laughs at his own cynicism. Is that right or not? [. . .]

51 Meyerhold to Chekhov

September 29 1899
Moscow

Dear and respected Anton Pavlovich,

I am writing to you with a small request and I ask your pardon in advance if it is lacking in modesty. My request is this. I have been given the role of Johannes in Hauptmann's 'Lonely People'. Would you help me to study this role? Write and tell me what you expect from someone playing the role of Johannes? How do you see Johannes? Just give me the general outline and only if you don't find it too tiring. Rehearsals start next week.

The company gathered for a religious service yesterday but it didn't take place as the Metropolitan would not allow it to be celebrated in the theatre. And that was fine. Perhaps because of that (in part at least) our meeting was particularly solemn, free and strong. We defend our independence, like the Boers. Konstantin Sergeievich read the prayers and we sang. Vladimir Ivanovich made a little speech thanking us for seven months' work. Then we had tea. The solemn atmosphere was increased by the fact that our meeting, I don't know why, was particularly calm and concentrated. No speeches, not a commonplace word. Vladimir Ivanovich suggested sending a telegram to the Governor-General of Moscow. Some people greeted this suggestion with enthusiasm, others said nothing. As to the suggestion that we send you and Hauptmann telegrams, that was adopted not just unanimously but with wild delight.

I have not felt in such a dynamic mood for a long time. And I know why. The theatre has understood and openly declared that its strength depended on the closeness of its relationship to contemporary dramatists. I am happy that my secret desire has been fulfilled.

We are counting on you to be at the première of 'Uncle Vanya'. I count on a quick answer (write to the theatre) [. . .]

52 Chekhov to Knipper

September 30 1899
Yalta

[. . .]

You say that in that scene Astrov approaches Elena like an ardent lover – 'he snatches at his feelings like a drowning man clutching at straws'. But that's wrong, absolutely wrong. Astrov finds Elena attractive, she captivates him by her beauty but in the last act he already knows that she is lost to him forever – and he speaks of her in this scene in exactly the same tone as he speaks of the heat in Africa and he kisses her simply because there doesn't seem anything else to do. If Astrov plays this scene emphatically it will ruin the mood of the whole fourth act, which is quiet and muted. [. . .]

53 Chekhov to Meyerhold

Beginning October 1899
Yalta

Dear Vsevolod Emilievich

I haven't got the text to hand and so can only talk about the role of Johannes in general terms. If you send me the part so I can read it through and refresh my memory I can be more precise but for the moment I can only talk about what might be of the most direct, practical interest to you. Above all J is an absolute intellectual; this is a young student who has grown up in a univers[ity] town. Complete absence of bourgeois elements. His ways are those of a man accustomed to the society of decent people (like Anna); there is gentleness and youth in his movement and appearance, like those of man who has grown up in a family, a family which has spoiled him, and is still tied to his mother's apron-strings. J is a German student and therefore correct in his dealings with men. With women, on the other hand, when he is alone with them he becomes soft in a feminine manner. In this respect the scene with his wife where he cannot refrain from caressing her although he is already in love or beginning to be in love with Anna is typical. Now about his nerves. It would be wrong to stress the nervousness to the point where the neuropathology of his personality blocks or overwhelms what is more important, namely his loneliness, that loneliness that only lofty but healthy (in the best sense) organisms experience. Give us a lonely man and only show his nerves to the extent that the text shows it. Don't treat his nerves as a purely individual phenomenon; remember that nowadays almost every civilized person, even the most healthy, nowhere feels more irritation than when he is at home with his own family because the difference between past and present is felt most of all within the family. The irritation is chronic, no display of feeling, no convulsive outbursts. It is an irritation that guests do not notice because its full weight falls most of all on the people closest to him – his mother, his wife – it is an irritation, so to speak, that is intimate, domestic. Don't linger over it but show it rather as *one* of his typical traits, don't overdo it or what will

emerge will be an irritable rather than a lonely young man. Konstantin
Sergeievich will push this nervousness, he'll carry it to excess but don't go
along with it; don't sacrifice the beauty of your voice and diction for the sake
of a momentary effect. Don't sacrifice them because, in fact, the irritation is
a detail, something minor. [. . .]

54 Chekhov to Knipper

October 4 1899
Yalta

[. . .]

Of course you're right: Alekseiev shouldn't be playing Ivan. That's not
his *métier*. When he directs then he's an artist but when he acts he's just a
rich young merchant who wants to dabble in art. [. . .]

55 Knipper to Chekhov

October 15 1899
Moscow

[. . .]

I am playing every night except when 'Henschel' is on; rehearsals every
day for 'Uncle Vanya' which drag on until 5 and at 6.30 I am back at the
theatre again. The atmosphere in the company has been awful and even
now it's not brilliant. 'Henschel' is playing extremely well, a great success
but it's not box-office. The play was thrown out by two theatres, people
don't like it and for us it's a desert out front. Luzhski is exceptionally
good, he plays amazingly simply, touchingly, without tricks or shouting.
And if you could see the staging of Act Four – in a tavern! Stanislavski is
tremendously applauded as a director. The takings for 'Ivan' are good but
it is coldly received . . . This week Meyerhold has stood out. Today we
had a good rehearsal of 'Uncle Vanya', strong, but as Astrov was not well
he did not come to rehearsal. Tomorrow Alekseiev proposes to spend the
whole day on 'Uncle Vanya': rehearse all morning, go to the Slavyanski
for lunch then back to the theatre in the evening. How do you like that,
Mr Writer Chekhov? Marya Petrovna [Lilina] has refused, she is afraid of
tiring herself. In the morning we rehearse Astrov's scenes and then in the
evening a run-through on stage (or else in the foyer) with props. The sets
are still not ready. And we were supposed to play on the 14th. The fault

lies entirely with 'Ivan' and Alekseiev's illness.[1] 'Uncle Vanya' is supposed
to be this season what 'The Seagull' was for us last season. And that will be
essential. But think of us, Mr Writer, be with us in spirit during rehearsals
and wish us luck. [. . .]

Your Olga Knipper

56 Meyerhold to Chekhov

October 23 1899
Moscow

Dear and Respected Anton Pavlovich,
I played Ivan the Terrible for the first time on October 19. I had to
prepare the performance intensively. I was so worried by the impending
performance that I couldn't think about anything. That's why I have
taken so long to answer your kind and friendly letter.

I clasp your hand warmly and thank you for having pointed out what
you thought was typical of Johannes. Only someone like you could be
content to sketch in the general characteristics yet with such mastery that
the character emerges with complete clarity. [. . .] Moreover everything
you indicated . . . immediately suggests a host of details which are in total
harmony with the basic tonality of the portrait of an intellectual who is
lonely, elegant, healthy and at the same time sad.

We haven't started rehearsals for 'Lonely People' yet as all our free
time is devoted to putting the finishing touches to 'Uncle Vanya' which is
due to open on Tuesday, October 26.

I've been playing practically every evening; this morning I was tired
and didn't go to the rehearsals for 'Uncle Vanya' (they often take place in
the morning).

I went to a run-through recently and saw the first two acts (I haven't
seen the last two, which were being rehearsed without sets, so as not to
destroy the overall impression).

The play is extremely well put together. What I note most of all in the
production as a whole is the sense of restraint from beginning to end. For
the first time the two directors complement each other perfectly; one, a
director and actor, has great imagination, although inclined to go too far
in the actual staging; the other, a director and dramatist, defends the
interests of the author. And he seems quite evidently to have the upper
hand. The frame does not hide the picture. Not only are the basic ideas

1. Stanislavski was suffering from one of his chronic bouts of flu with a very high
temperature. An announcement on the first night that he was playing despite illness froze
the audience.

carefully preserved by not burying them in a heap of useless details, they are rather skilfully brought out.

The actors I like most are O. L. Knipper (Elena), K. S. Alekseiev (Astrov), A. R. Artiom (Telegin) and M. P. Alekseieva, Lilina (Sonya). O.L. Knipper is astonishingly truthful, in her portrayal of the Chekhovian tedium of nature. I can't say anything about Vishnievski (Uncle Vanya) until I have seen the third act.

I foresee an enormous success for this play which is being put on with even greater care than 'The Seagull'. A rumour that you are coming to Moscow has reached us. Come as quickly as you can! Don't be afraid of the cold. The love all your many admirers bear you will warm you not only in Moscow but even at the North Pole. [. . .]

During the rehearsals for *Uncle Vanya* the first signs of disagreement between Stanislavski and Nemirovich emerged. Nemirovich's letter written some time before October 26 1899 sounds the first warning note. He makes great efforts to be tactful, although, it must be said, his attempts to be diplomatic were sufficiently heavy-handed as often to appear quite insincere and produced the opposite effect to the one he intended.

57 Nemirovich to Stanislavski

Sunday morning
October 26 1899
Moscow

Dear Konstantin Sergeievich,

I have been here thinking about 'Uncle Vanya'. Hence this letter. In essence what I have to say could be – and really should be – said direct but we have so little time for discussion that one cannot negotiate fully and logically. And we both are aware that it is awkward to disagree during rehearsals. It is embarrassing in front of the actors, don't you think?

The fact is that, thinking about the production of 'Uncle Vanya' and the mood of the public (not the reviewers but the interesting and better part of the public) and the demands they make on our theatre as they are emerging at the present time, in a word, trying to anticipate the nature of the performance, *I feel obliged* to ask you for a few concessions. Obliged by my conscience as a writer.

In such requests, where concessions are concerned I am always scrupulous. You – according to our agreement – are the principal director and it may be that in cases where you do not agree I should give way unconditionally to you. I am always afraid that you will suspect me of moral coercion and obstinate unwillingness to understand your creative thinking. You have had ample opportunity in the last year to appreciate how I bend all my efforts to understand and realize your thoughts. That I have not ceased to recognize your power as principal director is something I have also demonstrated many times in our discussions and in rehearsals with the actors.

But at the same time the severe, niggling attitude of audiences towards us obliges me constantly and unremittingly, from play to play, and with the utmost attention, to seek out where they are right and where they are wrong, what is a reaction to novelties which they will accept in the future and what is the result of our own mistakes. It has never been my habit to listen to anyone and everyone. I listen to *the mood* of every audience, the way it feels as a single living organism, and to those intelligent and far-sighted people in the audience whom I more or less trust. And at that moment I listen to that 'writer's' conscience of mine, which I spoke of earlier. I trust it. It has never let me down. I have many times – I tell you frankly – silenced it. Sometimes it rebels within me, I silence it then am sorry for it, because it turns out it was speaking the truth. Then I decide to be worthy of it, this conscience of mine, and not to silence anything it has to say.

All this is a lengthy prologue and perhaps the trivial examples which have led me to write this letter are not worth such a serious introduction. But this only once again demonstrates the scrupulousness of my attitude towards you as principal director. Well, here then are the concessions my writer's conscience demands that I ask of you:

1) in your own role as Astrov.

I don't want a handkerchief on your head to keep off mosquitoes, it's a detail I simply cannot take. And I can tell you for certain that Chekhov won't like it; I know his tastes and creative nature extremely well. I can tell you for certain that this particular detail doesn't introduce anything new. I'll wager that it will merely be numbered among those 'excesses' which just irritate and bring no advantage either to the theatre or to the work you are doing. This is one of those details that simply 'alert the geese'. Finally, even from the point of view of real life it is far-fetched. In short I cannot find any appreciable argument for it, not one serious argument of any kind whatsoever. And precisely because there is no argument for it I cannot see why you won't give it up when I ask you.

Further. You must learn the text *rock-solid*. It's true it's difficult for you. On the whole it doesn't come easy. But you do your utmost, don't you? Above all this is important from a disciplinary point of view. You see, I have taken Artiom and Samarova severely to task in rehearsal. I have even reached such a point of pernicketiness that I won't allow them to change words around but defend Chekhov's (literary) style. That was nitpicking but I wanted to get the veterans to pay more attention to the text. But they could say to me, the principal director himself is shaky, what do you expect from us?

But infinitely more important than the disciplinary side is the artistic side. There is not the slightest doubt in my mind that you spoil yourself as an actor by the fact that you do not know the text. Not knowing it causes you to take a slow tempo when it is not needed and to make pauses (turning to the prompter and then seeking the mood) when they merely deaden the role. For instance, you half-know the speech about the trees and what happens? It all flows out of you easily. It is easy and simple to listen to. You don't know the scene with Sonya in the second [act] and the scene risks in places being *pointlessly dragged out.* It is a fault in you to try and give life to minor, insignificant sentences as apart from that you speak in a lively, simple manner. You need to be especially aware of such things.

Your second fault – the brutal way you treat props and furniture. I know where it comes from. From a certain period when you not only had no confidence in the actors playing under you as a director but in yourself. You employed a system of abrupt movements to keep your energy going. I like this little trick – as an actor's aid. But our actors did not understand you very well. The less talented the actor the more he makes use of this trick. People like, for example, Tikhomirov. But even you have no real need to resort to this trick. You were so brusque that you had to knock aside a few chairs as you got up and moved from one place to another. Even in a scene like the one with Waffles in the 2nd act! The less you move furniture around, the less often you bang perfectly beautiful chairs, (now *all* our actors do it) the more attractively and appealingly your real qualities come through.

About concessions in other scenes. (I have *said not a word* to the actors so as not to create confusions with the two chiefs).

You interpret the little scene between Vanya and Elena (in the 2nd act) as though she were genuinely afraid about his drinking. That's not what's in the play, on the contrary, for Elena to be afraid in these circumstances is *not at all in keeping* with her character.

– 'You've been drinking again today. What's the point?' The very structure of the sentence gives a much quieter tone, the languid tone which marks Elena's attitude to everything going on around her.

I have nothing against Elena's singing at the end of the 2nd act and – you know – Olga Leonardovna is quite worked up about it. But I don't think anything much will come of it and, probably, we shall have to simplify it. I mean, be prepared for that. Beginning of 3rd act.

Uncle Vanya's 'bravo' and his recovery [of humour] while they are playing shocks my conscience.[1] I think it's out of key. And then we have already used this kind of 'bravo' in 'Seagull' and 'Henschel'.

And, for instance in Elena's speech I stick exactly to your moves (she walks, calculating squares on the floor) although Knipper has not mastered them yet. But I explain it to her because I find your instructions excellent and intelligent.

I still do not understand your two scenes with Elena but I may well ask for some concessions or clarifications in the 4th act.

That's it.

I repeat, I am writing this so that we shall not disagree in front of the actors, so that you can know my thoughts and because I am excessively scrupulous.

V. N-D

58 Nemirovich to Knipper

October 27 1899
Moscow

'Uncle Vanya' 1st performance.
O. L. Knipper.
I said that we have to find one or two actor's 'touches' to put more life into the role. I can now see two. At the end of the 2nd act. 'Go and ask . . . I'd like to play. I might play something . . .' This must either be extremely *tense* or if you can't find the kind of tension that will capture the audience then try to find it in *intensified* sounds and the way they *throb* more.

The second touch could be in the 3rd act speech. Simply in more passionate sounds. It seems to me that one need not be afraid of overacting.

In the *attitudes* you strike and the movement of the hands an element of *posing* can be seen – hardly perceptible but ominous. For example, the way you lay your hands on the 'gymnastic' baluster or on the oval table in the 3rd act (after moving away from Astrov).

When Astrov seizes his opportunity, we get the impression that Elena quickly takes pleasure in the fact that Astrov is about to embrace her.

---

1. In Stanislavski's production plan, Act III opens with Elena and Sonya playing four hands one piano. Vanya enters, takes off his coat and scarf and lays them on a chair, goes to the piano and conducts. When Sonya makes a mistake he corrects the chord. They finish. Uncle Vanya applauds. Elena rises and turns away.

She might almost be the first to put her hands on him. It's only a hair's-breadth away.

V. Nemirovich-Danchenko

59 Nemirovich to Chekhov

October 27 1899
Moscow

Well, dear Anton Pavlovich, we played 'Uncle Vanya'. You will see from the reviews that, probably, we didn't manage to cover up some of the faults in the play. But then, there isn't a play in the repertoire of the entire world that is not without faults. Only these faults could be felt by the house. The faults include: 1) a certain theatrical slowness over 2½ acts, despite the fact that we cut 40 of the 50 pauses you ask for. We cut them little by little during rehearsal. 2) The lack of psychological clarity in Ivan Petrovich himself and the 'weak' motivation in his relationship to the Professor.

This and other things were felt in the house and that produced an inevitable indifference. (I am trying to express it precisely). The curtain-calls, although numerous, were not outbursts of enthusiasm but simply good calls. Only the third act was strongly and whole-heartedly received, as was the end of the play when there were calls and a genuine ovation. And ⁴/₅ of the audience did not disperse during the 15 minutes' applause.

The audience was much affected; the simplicity of the scenes (on the poster I put 'scenes from country life'), the beautiful, gentle staging of the play, wonderful in its simplicity and poetry – language etc. [. . .]

There were some irritating shortcomings in the staging too. Here's how it was. Far and away the best in everyone's mind was Alekseiev, who played Astrov excellently (this is a joy for me, as he did the whole part just as I suggested, literally, like a schoolboy). After him comes Alekseieva [Stanislavski's sister], who had a great success. But she had been even better at dress rehearsal as now she sometimes falls back into her old fault – speaking quietly. Nonetheless, in her Moscow saw a wonderful, lyrical *ingénue*, not having her equal on the stage (except perhaps Komissarzhevskaya). And what is good is that as well as a lyrical quality she gives strength of character.

Knipper caused us great annoyance. At the dress rehearsal people said she was fascinating, enchanting, etc. Today she got flustered and overplayed the whole part from beginning to end. There was a lot of posing and emphasizing with lines coming out like a first reading. Of course she will be all right at the 2nd and 3rd performances but it is not helpful that she had no success at the first at all.

Kaluzhski provoked a lot of argument and indignation but you, as the author, and I, as your interpreter, will accept that with a bold heart. The admirers of the Serebriakovs of this world were incensed that the Professor should come out this way. On the other hand Kaluzhski does need toning down a little. But not too much.

Vishnievski will be criticized. There's no real character. Nervous energy, fire, but no character.

Artiom, Samarova, Raevskaya contributed to the success.

Summing up the performance, as compared to the rehearsals, I find 5–6 details which cluttered up the show. But as they are just details you can assume that some of them will disappear of their own accord without any comment from me. For others a word will suffice.

Unfortunately it has to be admitted that most of this clutter was due not to the actors but to Alekseiev as director. I did everything I could to get him to abandon in this play his fondness for underlining things, for noise and external effects. But something of it remained. That's a nuisance. However, after the second performance that will go too. The play will run and that means none of this is all that terrible. It's just a nuisance.

The first act went well and got 4 calls, although without precise enthusiasm. After the 2nd, the end of which was cluttered up with Elena *singing* – something Olga Leonardovna held out against throughout all 20 rehearsals – there were 5-6 calls. After the 3rd, 11. It created a strong impression but even here, at the end, there was clutter – Elena wailing hysterically – Olga Leonardovna held out against that too. Another piece of clutter, a shot *off-stage* and not on stage (second shot). The third (that is not clutter) Vishnievski could not manage in the tones he achieved at the dress rehearsals but fell to shouting. Still, I repeat, eleven calls.

The fourth act went splendidly, without a hitch or any roughness and received an ovation.

For me the staging of 'Uncle Vanya' has enormous significance for the essential nature of the whole theatre. For me important questions concerning art, décor, props and administration are linked with it. And so I watch the whole not as a director but as the founder of the theatre, looking to its future. And so, in the end, many many problems are apparent to me and I don't feel in quite that state of high euphoria which, probably, was reflected in the telegram I sent you.

I will write to you.

I embrace you warmly.

Vl. Nemirovich-Danchenko

60 Knipper to Chekhov

October 27-29 1899
Moscow

[. . .]

I hadn't intended writing to you today, dear Anton Pavlovich. I feel so terribly down in the dumps.

Last night we performed 'Uncle Vanya'. The play was a resounding success, the entire audience was enthusiastic, no need to go on about that. I didn't close my eyes all night and today I just howl at the slightest thing. I played so appallingly – why? Some of it I understand, some of it not. There are so many thoughts running through my head it's impossible to express myself clearly. I am told I played well at the final dress rehearsal but now I don't believe it. The problem to my mind is this: they wanted me to forget my own conception of Elena because the director found it boring but I had not been able to carry the idea right through. They imposed a different conception on me on the grounds that it was essential for the play. I held out for a long time and was still opposed to it at the end. At the final dress rehearsal I was calm and perhaps for that reason played calmly and evenly. On the first night I was infernally nervous and simply panicked, something which has never happened to me before, and therefore it was difficult to play a conception which had been imposed on me. If I had been able to play the way I wanted, probably the first night would not have worried me so. Everyone at home is appalled by my performance and I shall have a long talk with Nikolai Nikolaievich [Sokolovski]. He sees Elena as I did at the start and I think he is right. God, I feel so infernally low! Everything seems to have fallen apart. I don't know what to hold on to. My head is so useless, I just sit here like a block of stone. It's awful to think of the future, of the work ahead, if I have to resist the director's yoke again. That's why I can't settle down! I'm tearing my hair. I don't know what to do.

(28th)

I didn't finish yesterday, I mean I couldn't. Today's a little better but I still can't face people and am staying at home. I just went to your house, sat for two hours waiting for Marya Pavlovna [Chekhov' sister], returned home, while she, it turns out, had come to see us. Such a pity, such a nuisance! [. . .]

Strange, after 'The Seagull' I suffered physically, now, after 'Uncle Vanya' I am suffering psychologically. I can't tell you how depressed I am by the thought that I performed so badly in your play of all plays! Vlad. Iv. [Nemirovich-Danchenko] says I became too tense and played more aggressively, underlining things, and was too loud, whereas the part demands half-tones – Perhaps even then I don't know, I only know that I didn't play simply and that, for me, is awful. That the papers and the public will condemn me is more than likely, of course, but that is nothing in comparison with what I suffer at the thought of how I treated Elena Andreievna, i.e., you and myself too. [. . .]

Marya Petrovna [Lilina] and Alekseiev played wonderfully; the audience seemed to like Vishnievski.[1]

61 Marya Chekhova to Chekhov

October 31 1899
Moscow

The first performance of 'Uncle Vanya' was not as good, according to the audience and the actors, as the public dress rehearsal. That was something the actors were afraid of as never before. Knipper, when I saw her for the first time, was terribly nervous. Vishnievski too. I was at the second performance. They played so splendidly that I can see why you like Katichka Nemirovich, who turned to the actors and said, 'Today, you played like young gods'. I was moved by the first and second acts and wept with pleasure. I was invited to go backstage. I was met by a glowing Nemirovich and then the rest came out of their dressing-rooms and there were very warm greetings. I couldn't, naturally, express my pleasure at their wonderful acting, especially Alekseiev who is the best of all. Knipper and Lilina are very sweet. Artiom is good – there couldn't be a better Waffles.

I like the third act less, although other people like it. There was too much hustle and bustle. I'll see it again. The fourth act again created a great impression. In a word, it's a huge success. There's not a ticket left for the third performance, i.e., today's. People talk of nothing except your play.

Personally, I don't think Luzhski is particularly good. He plays such a disagreeable, contrary Professor. Most people agree with him. You really must write another play without fail.

Everyone sends greetings and says that if you had been here they would not have been afraid.

1. Lilina played Sonya, Vishnievski Vanya.

62 Chekhov to Knipper

November 1 1899
Yalta

[. . .]

I understand your mood, dear sweet actress, I understand it very well but all the same I wouldn't get myself into such a desperate lather. Neither the role of Anna[1] nor the play is worth tearing your nerves to shreds for. It's an old play,[2] it's already out of date and there are all sorts of defects in it. If over half the players couldn't get into the mood in any way then, of course, it's the play's fault – number one. Number two, once and for all you must stop worrying about success or failure. Don't let such things concern you. Your business is to work step by step, from day to day, softly-softly, to be prepared for unavoidable mistakes and failures, in a word, follow your own line and leave competition to others. To write or to act and at the same time be aware that you are not doing what you ought to be doing is important – it's so essential for beginners, so useful!

Number three, the director wired me[3] that the second performance was wonderful, everyone played splendidly and he was completely satisfied. [. . .]

63 Marya Chekhova to Chekhov

November 5 1899
Moscow

[. . .]

I go to the theatre often. 'Uncle Vanya' gets better as it goes on. One even feels sorry there are only four acts. [. . .]

There's a cricket in the last act . . . Oh, boring, boring. I've seen the play three times and I shall go back again! Nemirovich is now very happy. [. . .]

---

1. Chekhov means Elena. Anna is the character in Hauptman's *Lonely People* which Knipper was playing at the same time.
2. *Uncle Vanya* is a reworking of an earlier play, *The Wood Demon*.
3. Telegram from Nemirovich, October 30.

64 Nemirovich to Chekhov

November 19 1899
Moscow

[. . .]

Currently we are working on 'Lonely People'. It's very difficult.
Difficult because I feel cold towards the petty tricks and external
colouring Alekseiev is planning and because I want to have done with
some of Meyerhold's usual tones and sounds – he is always inclined
towards the hackneyed – and because the cast of 'Lonely People' really
are playing a lot and are tired and because, finally, I can't take the *mise-
en-scène* to my heart. [. . .]

In the meantime the repertoire depends on two plays – 'Ivan' and
'Vanya'; the revival of 'Hedda Gabler' brought nothing in and we must
get a move on. At the same time the greater part of the company are
running around and getting depressed with nothing to do, while
Goslavski's play is still waiting for me to correct it and without that it
can't go on. And we have to think of the future, of the other [new]
theatre. And I have to keep an eye on the humdrum routine of the
theatre. Etc., etc.

Sometimes one gets apathetic, one thinks, 'What the devil am I doing
in this ship?'[1] Suddenly one wants to abandon everything, go away . . .
the Crimea perhaps. The idea of writing attracts rather than busying
oneself with the trivia of theatrical life. Then one begins to find fault with
Alekseiev, to latch on to every dissimilarity in taste and method . . .

At the same time one is tired of everything.

What can one do?

I hear you are writing a play for the Maly. Not for the Maly, I don't
believe it. [. . .]

65 Chekhov to Nemirovich

November 24 1899
Yalta

[. . .]

I am not writing a play. I have a subject, 'Three Sisters', but until I
have finished the stories which have been in my head for a long time I
can't stick at a play. The next season will go ahead without a play by me,
that's decided. [. . .]

1. Adapted quotation from Molière's *Les Fourberies de Scapin*: 'Que diable allait-il faire
dans cette galère?'.

66 Nemirovich to Chekhov

November 28 1899
Moscow

[. . .]
I can't say that I have cooled towards the theatre. But tiredness often gives rise in me to a certain apathy. That's true. You see we've only completed ¼ of the way. We still have ¾ to go. We're only just beginning. We still need (only you understand) 1) a theatre, a building and all its equipment; 2) a few actors who are not completely ruined by clichés but are intelligent and talented; 3) an unlimited repertoire insofar as our capacity and means permit.

I shall be glad when I can finally say *feci quod potui* – because I will always be told that we 'can' do more and more!

And then I am ageing fast, I sleep badly and my nerves don't get the quiet, the calm, pure physical rest, they provoke unhealthy, critical changes of feeling, those changes of feeling, that tension which you only find in a theatrical atmosphere. I am 40 and more and more I think of the end and that disturbs me and drives me, drives me on to work and to satisfy my own ego. [. . .]

67 Chekhov to Nemirovich

December 3 1899
Yalta

[. . .]
Of course, you are right, for Petersburg[1] it is essential to rework Alekseiev somewhat as Trigorin. Inject a little guts into it. In Petersburg where the bulk of our writers live, Alekseiev playing Trigorin as hopelessly impotent will provoke general confusion. Remembering Alekseiev's acting for me is so depressing I can't shake it off,[2] and in no way can believe that Alekseiev is good in 'Uncle Vanya' although everyone writes to me with one voice that he is nonetheless good and even very good.

---

1. A tour was being considered for 1900. It, in fact, took place in 1901.
2. Chekhov refers to the special performance of *The Seagull* which had been given for him in Moscow on May 1 1899.

68 Gorki to Chekhov

January 1900
Nizhni-Novgorod

[. . .]

Not long ago I saw 'Uncle Vanya' in the theatre. It was marvellously
acted (I am not an expert on acting and when I like a play it is always
wonderfully acted). Yet 'Uncle Vanya' has the virtue of making even bad
actors play well, just by itself. That's a fact. For there are plays that no
kind of acting can ruin and others that good acting does ruin. [. . .]

69 Chekhov to Knipper

January 2 1900
Yalta

[. . .]

I won't congratulate you on the success of 'Lonely People'. I still have
faint hopes that you will all come down to Yalta and that I will see
'Lonely People' on stage and will congratulate you properly then. I wrote
to Meyerhold to prevail upon him, in the letter, not to push his portrayal
of a nervous man. A great majority of people are nervous, the majority
of them suffer, a minority feel acute pain but where – either in the street
or at home – do you see them throwing themselves about, jumping up
and down or clutching their heads in their hands? Suffering should be
expressed as in life itself, not with your arms and legs but by a tone of
voice, or a glance; not by gesticulating but by elegance. Subtle
expressions of feeling which are natural to intelligent people and must be
expressed subtly in outward form too. The stage has its demands, you will
say. No demands justify lies.

My sister tells me you played Anna marvellously. Ah, if only the Art
Theatre would come to Yalta! [. . .]

70 Gorki to Chekhov

January 21-22 1900
Nizhni-Novgorod

[. . .]

I went to the theatre and got there in time for the third act of 'Uncle
Vanya'. Again. 'Uncle Vanya' again. And I shall go back and see it and
reserve a seat. I don't consider it a pearl but I see more ideas in it than
other people do. Its ideas are huge, symbolic and its form is original,

incomparable. Pity that Vishnievski doesn't understand Uncle but the rest are all equally wonderful. Stanislavski is not quite right as Astrov. Yet they all play amazingly well. The Maly Theatre is strikingly crude in comparison with this company. Such clever, intelligent people with such artistic sense. Knipper is an amazing artist, a charming woman with a head on her. How good her scenes with Sonya were. And Sonya, also beautifully played. All of them, even the servant – Grigoriev – were excellent, they all knew beautifully and precisely what they were about and, by heaven, you could even forgive Vishnievski his mistaken interpretation because of his acting. Generally this theatre gave me the impression of a sound, serious-minded undertaking. The way they do things, no music and a curtain which parts and does not rise. You know I could not for a moment imagine such acting and such staging. Bravo! How sorry I am I don't live in Moscow. I would be at this wonderful theatre all the time. [. . .]

FOUR

THREE SISTERS

Three Sisters was Chekhov's first completely new play since 1896. *Uncle Vanya* was a revised version of an earlier work, *The Wood Demon*. *Three Sisters* was also specifically written for the Art Theatre and with a definite casting in mind, even if this was not followed. Chekhov could not resist, however, playing cat and mouse, refusing to acknowledge for a time that he was writing a new play at all.

Success had not diminished Chekhov's fear of ridicule. On the contrary, if anything it was worse. His moods were increasingly volatile – an effect of his tubercular condition. He could be savage. As Gorki wrote in his short *Memoir*, on a bad day Chekhov hated everyone.

He also resented being labelled as a pessimist. He kept announcing his intention to write something light and amusing and seemed to imagine that he had done so. He insisted that *Three Sisters* and, later, *The Cherry Orchard* were comedies or even farces. No one else in the company – including his wife – nor his sister agreed with him. Gorki, perhaps, came nearest to the truth when he said that Chekhov diagnosed his characters like a doctor. They were what they were. One was supposed to learn from them not weep for them. Such an approach can be seen very clearly from Chekhov's letter to the young Meyerhold, written in early October 1899, in response to a request for advice on how to play Johannes in Hauptmann's *Lonely People*. Chekhov offers less a literary and dramaturgical analysis than a pathological description (see letter **53**, p. 56-57).

Chekhov's touchiness not only with regard to interpretation but also to advance publicity was not helped by the fact that his health only allowed him to spend limited periods in Moscow, mainly in the summer when the theatre was not working. He could attend early rehearsals but as soon as the weather turned cold he had to return to Yalta, his Devil's Island as he called it, or, as during the rehearsal for *Three Sisters*, go abroad. He rarely saw his plays in their completed state and had to rely on reports from his sister Marya, from Knipper, both before and after their marriage, and friends. This has provided a rich but not always objective correspondence.

The theatre in the meantime had decided to move into premises of its own as soon as possible. They needed a modern building with up-to-date equipment. The problem was how to finance such an ambitious project. The only person who could put up the money was Savva Morozov. He was now heavily subsidizing both the theatre and the actors. His natural curiosity and interest led him to take an ever greater part in the daily running of the company. Nemirovich reacted badly to this, suspecting a loss of control. He wanted Morozov out but Stanislavski was determined that he should stay.

71 Nemirovich to Chekhov

February 1900
Moscow

Yesterday I finally went to see Marya Pavlovna, spent half the evening finding out about you. 1,000 r have been remitted to you. Apart from which 400 r odd were paid to her and the second instalment is about 250 r.

We have much to do at the theatre as before and, as before, there is little system or organization in our work. Takings are excellent. From December 26 to today there were only two performances that weren't full because of the cancellation of 'Lonely People' but otherwise completely full. But, alas, in all that's 975 r. A bit of a nuisance. And a worse nuisance is that we are often obliged to take the path of compromise, in view of our personal agreement with Morozov, who is rather rich and who is not satisfied simply to be connected with the theatre but wants to have an 'influence'. We have much work on the future of the theatre: Petersburg, the spring, rehearsals, reorganizing the repertoire, the company, our inter-relationship (me, Alekseiev, Morozov). It's awful to think how much there is to do. And then I want to write something for the theatre. And there's still the school.[1]

We are thinking a great deal about coming to Yalta to play specially for you. We have worked out the following plan:

25 February - 15 March – Petersburg.

18 March - Holy Week – rehearsals in Moscow.

From the third day of Easter and the whole of April – ditto.

May: Kharkov (4 performances), Sevastopol (4 performances) and Yalta (5 performances).

June and July – for the majority, rest but for the *really good minority* rest in Yalta on condition that there are daily rehearsals from 7 to 9 in the evening.

August – Moscow, rehearsals.

1. The Philharmonic School.

Etc.

Such a plan should please you.

The repertoire is as follows: 'Snowmaiden', 'The Mayor', 'Enemy of the People', your play, mine, Goslavski and one other? Two? Of the old stuff 'Ivan', 'Fiodor', your two plays, 'Bell', 'Lonely People', 'The Heart is not a Stone' remain.[1]

Of course, I know nothing about your new play, i.e., is there to be one or not? There absolutely must be. Of course the earlier the better but be it in the summer or the autumn!

72 Marya Chekhova to Chekhov

> February 2 1900
> Moscow

[. . .]

Nemirovich was here and asked you to give a definite answer and, of course, I hope a positive one otherwise they, i.e., the Art Theatre, are sunk. Are you writing a play for next season? The management will agree to all your conditions. Your plays continue to be good box-office. I beg you to write a play or the season will be boring. [. . .]

73 Nemirovich to Stanislavski

> Mid February 1900
> Moscow

[. . .]

Did I start this business with you for some capitalist (Morozov) to come along and think he can turn me into – how shall I put it? – some kind of secretary?

74 Stanislavski to Nemirovich

> Mid February 1900
> Moscow

Dear Vladimir Ivanovich,

I give you my word I am writing this letter quite calmly but I am so shattered and I feel so awful that I am beginning to fear for my sanity; during the day I am over-excited, my nights are *absolutely* sleepless. I am

---

1. Neither the Goslavski play nor Ostrovski's *The Heart is not a Stone* was staged.

living on bromide and drops of laurel-water. So put yourself in my place and try not to be harsh. Letters such as your last one I am *all too* familiar with. I had letters like that 12 years ago and that was the beginning of the end for the Society of Art and Literature. [. . .] I think you have convinced yourself that I can sacrifice anything for the sake of this enterprise of ours. For its sake I try, as much as I can, to suppress my own ego. For its sake I put myself into quite strange and sometimes ludicrous positions. I am prepared to share my labours and successes with anyone, treading a mid-path between people's pride, trying discreetly to stop up the cracks; not only do I give up money but, so as to have the right to work in an enterprise I love, I carve 10,000 roubles out of my budget, put my last penny in the business, deny my family and myself the most necessary things, try to get by somehow while I patiently wait for all debts finally to be settled so that I can get back what is mine by right. When all the egoism and the ambitions of the shareholders break out and they start to talk of their hurt pride, their rights, etc., I hold my tongue and take on board the results of their disputes, i.e., the financial losses. Prokoviev goes broke and I quietly pick up the consequences. I reconcile myself to the fact that (often) I neither play in nor direct things I long to do but act what I have to, not what I want to. In short, I am ruining myself financially and mentally, without complaint as long as my nerves are not stretched to breaking point. That's the stage we have obviously reached now and, as you can see, I have started to kick. In fact, I'm sick and tired of the fact that everyone else seems to have the right to talk about themselves *except me* and that's unfair.

So while I am ready for any kind of sacrifice there's one thing I will not agree to *under any circumstances*. I won't play the role of the idiot. But I am now close to doing just that. You and Morozov can't or won't get on. It seems as though there are going to be quarrels and squabbles and I am supposed to stand in the middle and take the beating. No, that won't do and my nerves won't take it. I won't stay in the theatre if you go. We started it together and we should lead it together. I recognize in you, of course, as in any human being, certain failings but, at the same time, *I value your many good qualities highly* and especially the good relationship you have with me and my work. Without Morozov. [. . .] I cannot remain in the theatre *under any circumstances*. Why? Because I value Morozov's good qualities. I have not the least doubt that he is heaven-sent and help like this only comes along once in a lifetime. Finally because I have been waiting for such a man since I started in the theatre (as I waited for you). Remember I have no money, I am a family man and have *no right* to take risks with that part of my assets. [. . .] I believe . . . in Morozov's honesty blindly. My confidence in him is so rock-solid that I have no written agreement with him. It's superfluous. [. . .] If two people driven by a common purpose cannot reach an agreement by word of mouth how can paper help? In the future I have no intention of playing a double game, trying to reconcile Morozov with Nemirovich and vice versa. If conflict is inevitable then let it happen quickly and our enterprise be wrecked while it will still be missed, let us Russians prove once more that we are rotten to the core and that personal egoism and petty ambition will destroy anything worthwhile. In our case that will be more than amply demonstrated since in the history of the theatre there has never been a more glorious page than the one we have written in the last two years. If it should happen then I spit on the theatre and on art and will go and make gold thread in the factory. The devil take that kind of art! [. . .]

75 Chekhov to Nemirovich

> March 10 1900
> Yalta

[. . .]
   Am I writing a new play? It's pecking through the shell but I haven't started writing yet, I don't want to, we have to wait until it's warm [. . .]

76 Chekhov to Knipper

> March 26 1900
> Yalta

[. . .]
   I have no new play, the papers are lying. In any case, the papers never tell the truth about me. If I were writing a play you would, of course, be the first to know.

77 Stanislavski to Nemirovich

> August 9 1900
> Alupka

[. . .]
   I am writing to you in terms of the utmost secrecy. Yesterday I managed to drag out of Chekhov the fact that tomorrow he is going to Gursuf to write. He will be back in Alupka in a week and will read what he has written. He hopes to be able to deliver the play on September 1 with the proviso that it is good and that it comes quickly. He is writing a play about the life of military men. I know that we can expect good roles for

Meyerhold, Knipper, Zhelyabuzhskaya, Vishnievski and Kaluzhski. *I repeat I gave my word that for the moment all this would be of the utmost secrecy*. But you need to know. I think it will be easier to release you at the beginning of the season rather than before its opening. We will have to think and give you an opportunity to rest and finish your play. [. . .]

I will come to the essentials quickly, that is to the production plan for 'When We Dead Awaken'. You want to change the décor as it stands? Of course, change it, if the plan is interesting and the whole staging is moving in the right direction, i.e., not towards the conventional but towards life. I don't consider my production plans faultless particularly in the case of 'Dead' to which I hardly gave much thought [. . .]

After the completion of 'An Enemy of the People' I said to myself: 'Vladimir Ivanovich is busy with the play he is writing, he must be left in peace; with so little time before we have to start rehearsing "Dead" we could suddenly wake up and find ourselves without a production plan.' With that in mind I started the first act and it's now written. What shall I do with it? I'll send it to you and you can do what you like with it. There can be no pride here. There's no place for it in our theatre. If the production plan doesn't work, put it aside but don't tear it up. I am collecting all the work I have done, I need it for my production notes which I am writing up. Above all I want to say that I liked the plan you sent me very much. It has been created with a great deal of imagination, but I find one or two things in it that are not practical. [. . .]

78 Chekhov to Knipper

August 17 1900
Yalta

[. . .]

I am writing a play but our guests are an infernal nuisance . . . They arrived, installed themselves in the study and now they are drinking tea . . . I abandoned the study and have come to my bedroom and am writing in a corner. [. . .]

79 Meyerhold to Chekhov

August 18 1900
Moscow

Dear Anton Pavlovich,

If it's not too much trouble can I ask you to help me with advice in the following matter. This summer I translated Hauptmann's drama 'Vor

Sonnenaufgang' ('Before Sunrise') from the German. On my return to
Moscow I gave it first of all to Vladimir Ivanovich to read with the idea
the theatre should do it. Vladimir Ivanovich read the play and found it
very interesting although written by an inexperienced hand (this is his first
play). He's afraid that the play will not get past the special theatre censor.
He finds it too daring to be reproduced onstage because it is ultra-
naturalistic. The play is evidently written by someone with an enthusiasm
for Zola.

He advises me to publish it first.

Advise me, Anton Pavlovich, what to do. There are only two places, I
believe, where I can send it; either to *Zhizn* . . . or include it in the
complete works Balmont is editing. [. . .]

I got back to Moscow on July 31.

Rehearsals started on August 1. At the moment we're rehearsing
'Snowmaiden', 'Enemy of the Peope' and 'When We Dead Awaken'. I'm
just a walk-on in the last two and I'm terribly bored. We are all wildly
impatient for your play. When will you finally send it to us, Anton
Pavlovich? Are you writing?

Have you decided to come to Moscow? [. . .]

80 Chekhov to Knipper

> August 20 1900
> Yalta

[. . .]

The play seemed to get off to a good start but I have gone cold on it, it
seemed vulgar and now I don't know what to do. The point is a play has
to be written continuously, non-stop, every morning – I mean early
morning when I am alone and there's no one to interrupt. [. . .]

Of all the great stars of the Moscow Art Theatre Vasili Ivanovich Kachalov
(1875–1948) was the only one not to have been a member of the original
company. At first Stanislavski did not take to him. He was rather flamboyant
and concerned to show that he was a Real Actor. Invited by Nemirovich to
audition for the parts of Boris Godunov and Ivan the Terrible in *The Death
of Ivan the Terrible* in March 1900 he arrived in a bright orange overcoat.
Stanislavski was not impressed and wrote to him politely saying that he was
not sure they both spoke the same language or that the theatre could make
use of his gifts. Kachalov spent a few weeks attending rehearsals of
Snowmaiden, observing and learning the company's method. His good

sense finally paid off when in May he was offered the part of Tsar Berendi as there was no one in the existing company who was suitable.

81 Nemirovich to Stanislavski

August 21 1900
Moscow

[. . .]
Kachalov is our biggest hope. When you get to know him better in rehearsal you will see how outstanding his gifts are, simply outstanding. A splendid, well-proportioned body, lacking any kind of vulgarity in gesture, a distinguished face out of which you could create the make-up of an intelligent and inspired man, a *heavenly* voice. And – this is new for you – an undoubted, warm personality. With such gifts this is the young actor out of which we can make an outstanding lead. [. . .]

Since this morning they have been rehearsing 'Enemy' and Kaluzhski wants to play it your way but Meyerhold, his. I will attend the next rehearsal. Meyerhold came to see me yesterday complaining about my making him read or rehearse the Burgomaster. He didn't want to but I insisted. [. . .]

82 Chekhov to Knipper

August 23 1900
Yalta

[. . .]
Alekseiev came yesterday. He stayed until 9 in the evening then we went (or rather I took him) to see the headmistress of the girls' high school. [. . .]

I am writing the play but I am afraid it's turning out to be boring. I'll write it and if I don't like it I'll put it to one side until next year or to a time when I feel like writing. One season without a play by me is no great misfortune. [. . .]

83 Chekhov to Vera Komissarzhevskaya

August 25 1900
Yalta

[. . .]
I am writing the play all the same and will most probably finish it in September and then I will come to see you. In September I shall go to Moscow and then go abroad – for a long time. [. . .]

84 Chekhov to Knipper

August 28 1900
Yalta

[. . .]
The play is in my head, it's already starting to come, it's improving and
longing to be on paper but I am scarcely at the paper before door opens
and some ugly mug or other slips in. I don't know what the outcome will
be but the beginning has turned out all right, or so it seems . . . I see
nothing of the Alekseievs or Mme Nemirovich.[1] [. . .]

85 Nemirovich to Knipper

August 1900
Moscow

I hesitated a long time between speaking to you or writing. Writing
won. Perhaps it's for the better since I am too angry and may speak to no
purpose.

My dear Olga Leonardovna! What do you think you are doing to
yourself? Take a look at yourself *as an actress*. Make an effort with
yourself. There have now been four rehearsals[2] at which you have given
me an appalling time. I tried to see if Marya Petrovna [Lilina] could have
some influence on you but nothing came of it. In rehearsals you either
look as though you have been condemned to solitary confinement or you
use your free moments to shut your eyes out of sheer exhaustion or you
cannot resist a tired yawn. And you do no work at home *whatsoever* or
show the least artistic enthusiasm.

I shake with indignation merely at the thought that while your
comrades are straining every nerve, when all our efforts are needed for
work, when it is essential that you love this work, you are trampling your
talent underfoot with a disgraceful lack of concern and are preparing a
new role and a new play with a negligence worthy of a provincial actress.

I would rather not use such harsh words. I have that right since
there is not one of those around you who, if they could enjoy your artistic
stature, would use it so.

1. All in Yalta at the time.
2. Of Ibsen's *When We Dead Awaken*.

I would rather not say too much about how profoundly insulting it is that we should be talking about a play on which I am working with such enthusiasm.

86 Meyerhold to Chekhov

September 4 1900
Moscow

Many thanks, dear Anton Pavlovich, for the part you played in my plans for the publication of the play I translated. [. . .]

The theatre is humming. We are rehearsing morning noon and night. Lots of people and activity. 'Snowmaiden' is almost ready. The production of this play is amazing. There is enough colour for ten plays. Grechnaninov, who has written the music for 'Snowmaiden', has surpassed Rimski-Korsakov in naïve simplicity and stylishness of colour. There are moments in the music when the people listening suddenly break into gales of laughter. And, note, the cause of this reaction is not the dialogue but the music itself. Try and be here for the opening of the season (September 20) so you can hear this wonder.

Maksim Gorki is staying with us. He is at every rehearsal and is in raptures. [. . .]

Are you really not going to give us your play this year? I would be very sorry. Because, you see, I hope to be given a part in your play. I admit it. First of all it's bad enough to have nothing to do but, apart from that, playing a character in a Chekhov play is as important and interesting as playing Hamlet in Shakespeare. [. . .]

Chekhov's state of tension, his quickness to react to anything he considered adverse criticism is well illustrated in his response to an article by Nikolai Efros which suggested the title *Three Sisters* was provisional. Trivial though the incident was it stuck in Chekhov's mind.

87 Chekhov to Knipper

September 8 1900
Yalta

[. . .]

Is Gorki writing a play or not? Where does the news come from in *Novostni Dnia* that the title 'Three Sisters' is unsuitable? What rubbish! It may not be suitable but I have no intention of changing it. [. . .]

88 Gorki to Chekhov

September 11–15 1900
Nizhni-Novgorod

[. . .]

Now to 'Snowmaiden' – quite an event! A great event, believe me. I have no great understanding but in general I infallibly feel what is beautiful and important in the realm of art. These artists stage this play wonderfully, excellently, astoundingly good. I saw a run without sets or costumes but I left . . . enchanted, shedding tears of joy.

Such playing from Moskvin, Kachalov, Gribunin, Olga Leonardovna, Savitskaya! All are good, each better than the other; they are like angels sent from heaven to reveal to men the depths of beauty and poetry.

I shall go to Moscow on the 20th for the première come what may. I'm not well, I caught dry pleurisy in the right lung. but that's a trifle. You're the one who shouldn't go to Moscow, you'll be ill. But for 'Snowmaiden' one should go to the North Pole. And if you could come on the 20th it would be so good!

89 Chekhov to Knipper

September 28 1900
Yalta

[. . .]

Ah, what a part there is for you in 'Three Sisters'. If you give me ten roubles you can have it otherwise I'll give it to another actress. I won't release 'Three Sisters' this season, let the play lie awhile, mature or, as bourgeois ladies say about a pie when they put it on the table, 'give it a little breathing space'. [. . .]

90 Meyerhold to Chekhov

October 1 1900
Moscow

[. . .]

The season opened a week ago. 'What I have lived through yet what have I not felt . . .'[1] 'Snowmaiden' which cost so much of the actors' strength, so much nervous energy, so much imagination from the director and so much money was a complete flop. All concerned are depressed and go on working with heavy hearts, dejected . . . Audiences are indifferent to the beauty of the play and the subtlety of its humour and continually pick holes and repeat opinions taken from different 'papers' and 'rags'. Takings are down already. Everyone is uneasy. What's the reason for all this?

It's quite evident 'Snowmaiden' is old hat. It's quite evident that in times like ours, when everything is falling down about our ears, an appeal to pure beauty is not enough. [. . .]

Is it just the fickleness of a public that's off its head or is it its blind faith in the press? How can we explain it? . . . M. Gorki believes, I don't know why, that the press and the public are ignorant.

Our critics are ignorant, that's true. But the public? It may be credulous but it hasn't lost its instinct. Isn't the play simply beautiful but irrelevant?

Our principal director will have to shoulder part of the blame; once again he's been too clever by half. You'll see when you come. It's impossible to say everything on paper . . .

Yesterday we played your 'Uncle Vanya'. It's the first time this season we've done your play. Though it was Saturday there were more people than for the other revivals ('Lonely People', 'Death of Ivan the Terrible'). Everybody played well and both the play and the actors were enthusiastically received.

On Thursday we play 'The Seagull'. At last! We were beginning to droop. [. . .]

91 Knipper to Chekhov

October 1 1900
Moscow

Yesterday we performed 'Uncle Vanya', my dear! With what delight, what joy! The audience greeted the first play of the season with such

1. From Gorki's *The Song of the Petrel*.

warmth, such friendship! . . . I cannot describe to you how wonderful it was to perform yesterday. I thought of you, my sweet! I wanted you to be there, for you to see how much the audience and the actors love 'Uncle Vanya', how happy they were at your success. Everyone played well yesterday. After the first act Nemirovich came back-stage, excited, and said that we were all playing with delicacy, subtlety and style. You see how much they love you. After the first act the applause was like thunder. I now play the opening of Act Two differently – tense, excited, holding back the voice, not loud and I think that it is better and nearer to the intentions of my dear, modest writer – right, my joy?

92 Nemirovich to Chekhov

October 10 1900
Moscow

Telegram

I am not writing to you as I expect you in person any day. After your telegram I expect you even more confidently. Take yourself in hand and finish the play. Bring it and we will discuss in a friendly way whether to put it on or postpone it. The theatre loves you as before but it is beginning to suspect that you have cooled towards it. Give us news of yourself more often.

93 Chekhov to Knipper

October 15 1900
Yalta

[. . .]

I learn from the papers that you start performances on September 20 and that Gorki may be writing a play.[1] Look, write to me without fail how you are getting on with 'Snowmaiden', tell me what sort of play Gorki is writing, if he really is writing one. He is a man whom I like very much, very much and whatever people write about him, even nonsense of all kinds, is a source of pleasure and interest. As far as my play is concerned, whether it will be finished, now or later, in September, October, November perhaps, and whether I decide to put it on this season, who knows, my baby baboon. I have not decided because in the first place it may be the play will not be finished – it might just lie there on the desk, and secondly it is essential for me to be present during

---

1. *Small People.*

rehearsals, essential! I can't just hand over four crucial feminine roles, four young, intelligent women to Stanislavski, for all my respect for his talent and understanding. I have to keep even half an eye on rehearsals. [. . .]

94 Chekhov to Gorki

October 16 1900
Yalta

[. . .]

I had a terrible time writing 'Three Sisters'. Just think: three heroines who all have to have their own special qualities and all three, general's daughters! The action takes place in a provincial town, rather like Perm, among officers, artillery. [. . .]

95 Chekhov to Vera Komissarzhevskaya

November 13 1900
Moscow

[. . .]

'Three Sisters' is finished but its future, or at least its immediate future for me is shrouded in mystery. The play turned out boring, awkward because, for example, there are 4 heroines and the mood, to coin a phrase, is all gloom and doom. [. . .]

96 Knipper to Chekhov

December 12 1900
Moscow

I was busy the whole day today. We rehearsed 'Sisters' from 12 onward and 'himself' [Stanislavski], with more than a little bad grace, didn't come as he is rather ill. Vlad. Iv. gave Sudbinin a dressing down because he did not know Act One and because as usual he is insolent with it – all very provoking! In my opinion he is not right for Vershinin – he's coarse-grained. He really feels uncomfortable in the part and treats it in an offhand manner. [. . .]

They say we played 'Dead Awaken' quite well. Masha was there and watched with interest. Are you really bored with the theatre? [. . .]

97 Knipper to Chekhov

December 13 1900
Moscow

[. . .]

Today, my dear, we had a glorious rehearsal of 'Three Sisters' – we are beginning to get the general feel for Solyony, Chebutykin, Natasha, Irina and me. Marya Petrovna has decided that I am the very picture of a daddy, Irina of a mummy, and that Andrei, a father role, is, by nature, a mother.

I have found the gait, I talk in low chest tones, which you know, you find in these aristocratic women with a kind of elegant abruptness, if I can so express it. But don't worry I'm not overdoing it. Tomorrow we start to break down Act Two and on the 23rd we have the first general stagger-through. Lilina is in raptures over her role, she calls it bashfully-cheeky. I still have no clear picture of Olga and Vershinin, played by Sudbinin. But that will all come. Yesterday we played 'The Seagull' in aid of the war veterans. There was a lot of laughter. We had a four-year-old boy in the audience who made comments all the time. Looking at the set for Act One he said for the whole house to hear, 'Mummy let's go into the garden and run about!' Of course the audience laughed.

'There's the samovar' – 'She's drinking water' (me in Act Three), etc., – those of us on stage could hardly contain ourselves.

98 Chekhov to Knipper

December 15 1900
Nice

[. . .]

I am rewriting my play and I am amazed at the fact that I am able to write this farce and at the reason I am writing it. [. . .]

Now I am going to the sea and will sit there and read the papers. Then I shall come back to the house and get down to writing – and tomorrow I shall send Act III to Nemirovich, and Act IV the day after – or perhaps both together. I have made a few changes in Act III, added a little but not much. [. . .]

99 Knipper to Chekhov

December 16 1900
Moscow

[. . .]
Today we roughly blocked the 2nd act. Tomorrow we go through it
with Konst. Serg. I think it's going to be very interesting. He's put in
things of his own, of course – a mouse scratches during the scene between
Masha and Vershinin, the stove hums – but that comes from the author's
comment presumably. Tuzenbach swoops down on Andrei, sings '*Seni
moï seni* ', everyone dances – Irina, Chebutykin. Then, when Tuzenbach
plays the waltz, Masha leaps forward and dances, alone at first, then
Fedotik catches hold of her but she pushes him away (he can't do it) and
Irina dances with Rodé and into all this racket walks Natasha. [. . .]

100 Chekhov to Nemirovich

December 18 1900
Nice

[. . .]
In Act III the last words Solyony pronounces are essential: (*looking at
Tuzenbach*) Cheep, cheep, cheep. Extend this, please. [. . .]

101 Stanislavski to Chekhov

December 15–23 1900
Moscow

Most Respected Anton Pavlovich,
Countess Sofya Andreievna Tolstaya, with her husband's approval, is
organizing a charity concert and I have been asked to read a newly
completed story by L. N. Tolstoi, 'Who is in the Right?' As they do not
wish for readings of contemporary writers apart from yourself, the
Countess would, of course, very much like some scenes from 'Three
Sisters'.
I am sorry to say I was so overawed by the presence of Lev
Nikolaievich that I could not bring myself to say no to this request. I only
said that I didn't have the right to allow the presentation of extracts from
an as yet unperformed work without your permission.
Now you are my only hope: don't agree to it! Or provide something in
place of 'Three Sisters'. Your play, which I love more and more as I
rehearse it, is such a complete whole that I cannot extract single scenes

from it to be read on a concert platform at a charity event. Imagine an ordinary, everyday conversation among two or three people reading, dressed in tails, in the middle of a huge hall in front of an audience of high society folk in décolleté. The impression produced by such a presentation of the play can be disadvantageous, and, of course, such a reading should not be allowed until the play has been properly addressed by the public and the press. So, for God's sake, don't agree and find some other way out. Forgive me for having dealt with this so clumsily . . . I was scared! The Countess expects a quick answer, not to say a wire.

On December 23rd we have a very sketchy run-through of the first two acts. It seems, God willing, that the play is not going badly. I think Luzhski, Vishnievski, Artiom, Gribunin, Moskvin, my wife, Marya Fedorovna will be good. Savitskaya has still not stopped whining. Olga Leonardovna has found a beautiful tone. If she works on it she will play beautifully, if she waits for inspiration to come–? Meyerhold has still not found the correct tone but is working very hard. Gromov and Sudbinin are not getting there (even as understudies). Schoenberg [Sanin] is being ingratiating and has understood that he has overlooked a treasure, as the role of Solyony is a real jewel for an actor. He'll probably play it. If you agree I'd like to try out Kachalov as understudy instead of Sudbinin. He will be pleasant and agreeable, but Sudbinin won't even do as Vershinin's batman. [. . .]

102 Chekhov to Knipper

December 28 1900
Nice

[. . .]

I was in such a rush over the last act I thought you needed it, all of you. Now it turns out that you won't start rehearsing it until Nemirovich gets back.[1] If only I could have kept this act 2 or 3 days more, then it would have been richer, you know. [. . .]

103 Chekhov to Knipper

December 30 1900
Nice

[. . .]

I had a letter from Vishnievski yesterday in which he told me he was

1. Nemirovich was in France with his sister who was ill.

splendid in the run-throughs of the first two acts. Have you left the house
and gone to rehearsals? You know the changes I made to Acts III and IV
but do you know Act II? Have they rewritten the parts for you? Or are
you still working from the old copy-books? Vishnievski writes that Sanin
is playing Solyony and Kachalov, Vershinin. The latter won't be bad and
if Sanin doesn't ham it up he will be more or less all right. [. . .]

104 Chekhov to Stanislavski

> January 2 1901
> Nice

[. . .]
   As regards that old play 'Three Sisters' it must not be read at the
Countess's soirée under any circumstances whatsoever otherwise you will
cause me great distress.
   I sent off Act IV some time ago before Christmas addressed to
Vladimir Ivanovich. I've made many changes. You write that when
Natasha is doing the rounds of the house at night she puts out the lights
and looks for thieves under the furniture. But it seems to me that it would
be better if she went across the stage in a straight line not looking at
anything or anyone, à la Lady Macbeth with a candle – it's quicker and
more frightening. [. . .]

105 Chekhov to Knipper

> January 2 1901
> Nice

[. . .]
   Describe one rehearsal of 'Three Sisters' for me at least. Is there
nothing that needs adding or cutting? Are you acting well, my darling?
And look here don't put on a gloomy face, not in one single act. Angry,
yes, gloomy, no. People who carry sorrow within them, and have become
accustomed to it, just whistle and sometimes become pensive. The way
you often become pensive on stage during discussions. Understand?
   Of course you do, because you're bright.

106 Knipper to Chekhov

> January 4 1901
> Moscow

[. . .]
   Today Fedotova came to the theatre to greet us on the new century,

and saw part of the second act, only we were rehearsing in the buffet as
the décor for Act 4, which I like very much, was set up on stage for
viewing. Tomorrow we will run all three acts. I like my Masha very much
but I don't know about the 4th act from the new angle. [. . .]

107 Knipper to Chekhov

January 7 1901
Moscow

[. . .]
   On the 14th there will be a daytime run of the 3rd act of 'Sisters'. For
the moment I don't like Sanin at all, I don't know what will happen on
the day. I don't like Meyerhold either – no gaiety, no strength, no life –
dry! [. . .]

In January 1901 Nemirovich returned to Moscow from France. Stanislavski
had been directing Chekhov alone for the first time. He was understandably
nervous. The production now needed an objective eye. Nemirovich,
treading very carefully, began to tidy up the staging.

108 Knipper to Chekhov

January 11 1901
Moscow

[. . .]
   We ran the third act 2 times. Nemirovich watched it and altered a great
deal. Stanislavski had created a tremendous commotion onstage with
everyone running about and getting excited. Nemirovich, on the other
hand, advised a great deal of noise offstage and onstage a feeling of
emptiness with slow playing, which will be much stronger. Everyone has
captured the tone and we have reason to hope that the play will go well.
Yesterday Stanislavski talked to me for more than two hours at a stretch,
examining the kind of artist I am, giving me more lectures on my inability
to work, telling me that I had already appeared in public far too often
and that I was never ready by the 1st performance only by the 15th . . .
Our discussion was difficult; he feels that as an actress I don't put myself
absolutely and entirely in his hands and that puts him on edge. It's true, I
don't have blind faith in him. [. . .]

109 Stanislavski to Chekhov

January 1901
Moscow

Most honoured Anton Pavlovich,

Of course, I mixed things up. Natasha doesn't look for thieves in the third but in the second act. Tolstoya's concert did not take place. You were needlessly upset. I wrote to the Princess in such a way to give the most agreeable of refusals to her request. Rehearsals for 'Three Sisters' would be going well were it not for the influenza and my considerable exhaustion, or rather, my total exhaustion. I can say with absolute certainty that the play gains from being staged and if we don't make a success out of it we deserve to be whipped. Today we showed and read through the plan for the last, the 4th act and I started on the role of Vershinin. If Olga Leonardovna, please God, brings off the last act it will be very impressive. The set is ready and is successful. Sudbinin has finally been taken out, even as an understudy, as Kachalov is much more gifted. Schoenberg [Sanin] is playing Solyony. Up till today he has been very obstinate and tried to play it like some Calabrian bandit. I have now got through to him and he is on the right path. What can I say about the actors? Kaluzhski (slow as ever but right). Meyerhold is working but wooden for the present. Artiom (a little tight in movement but will find the tone and is near it), Samarova (ditto), Gribunin (ideal), Rodé (bright but is playing himself), Tikhomirov (ditto), Schönberg (too soon to tell), Kachalov (very nice), Vishnievski (ideal and not overdoing it), Marusya (will play well), Marya Fedorovna (very good), Savitskaya (good, playing herself), Olga Leonardovna (was ill, have not seen her since her illness).

The run of the 2nd act took place and was a joy. At all events the play is marvellous and works well on stage. The tempi can be defined, or rather, turned out like this:

1st act – joyous, lively,

2nd act – Chekhovian mood,

3rd act – terribly tense, works on speed and nerves. Towards the end energy has run out and the tempo slackens,

4th – not sure yet.

Olga Leonardovna promised to write to you in detail about the ending. I'll tell you in a couple of words. The final speeches of the sisters, after all that has happened, capture the attention and have a calming effect. If the body is then carried across the stage there is no calm at the end. In your text you write: 'The body is carried across in the distance', only in our theatre we don't have any distance and the sisters would have to see the body. What are they supposed to do? In rehearsal, though I like the idea of the body being carried across, I began to wonder whether it would not be to the play's advantage to end with the speeches. Perhaps you are afraid that will be too much like the end of 'Uncle Vanya'? Ask yourself the question: how do we go about it?

Your K. Alekseiev

110 Knipper to Chekhov

January 13 1901
Moscow

[. . .]

Stanislavski asked me to ask you about the end of the 4th act. Is it possible to dispense with carrying Tuzenbach's body across, as to do so would mean a crowd scene and that could break in on the trio of the three sisters and above all would make the set wobble, since, as you know, our stage isn't big. For the moment we are rehearsing without it. Reply this minute for heaven's sake. Don't delay. Of course the sisters can't sit there indifferent if a body is brought into the house. What do you think?

Tomorrow there is nothing but a run-through of three acts at 12 noon – that means getting up early. The tram-tram[1] is causing a problem. Nemirovich thinks these signals should be sung, like buglers, with mimed actions of course. If they are simply spoken they could come out either as crude or incomprehensible. Write about that too. [. . .] I have just come from the theatre where we have played the 99th performance of 'Fiodor'. It's 2 in the morning, I'll read through 'Sisters' as I've hardly rehearsed the 1st and 2nd acts – I've been ill. Nemirovich is having talks with all the company about next season. Sanin says they'll raise me 400 roubles. I'm not greedy but it's only just as I have to spend more than all the others on clothes for my work, so it's not all that much. At all events I shall persuade them the cost of all clothes should be borne by the management. For the rest I have to resign myself to the fact that there are no [new] parts for me next season. Well, we shall see. [. . .]

111 Chekhov to Nemirovich

January 14 1901
Nice

[. . .]

Why don't you write anything about 'Three Sisters'? How is the play

---

1. 'Tram-tram' is a secret signal between Masha and Vershinin.

going? You write about Sanin and Meyerhold but not one word about the play. And I suspect that my play is already a disaster. And when Nemirovich-Danchenko and I met here it was very boring and it seemed to me that the play was an unmitigated disaster and that I would write no more plays for the Moscow Art Theatre. [. . .]

112 Chekhov to Tikhomirov

January 14 1901
Nice

[. . .]

Here are the answers to your questions: 1. Irina does not know that Tuzenbach is going to fight a duel but has a feeling that something happened the previous day which might have serious or even tragic consequences. And when women have those feelings they say, 'I knew it, I knew it'.

2. Chebutykin only sings the words 'Will it not please you to accept this date . . .' These words come from an operetta, which they put on at the Hermitage. I don't remember the title but, if you like, you can ask the architect, Schechtel (private house near the Yermolaev church). Chebutikin should not sing more than that otherwise it will drag out his exit.

3. Solyony really does think he looks like Lermontov; but of course he doesn't, it's silly even to think of it . . . He should make up like Lermontov. The resemblance to Lermontov is enormous but only in Solyony's mind. [. . .]

Nobody writes anything to me about the play. When he was here Vladimir Ivanovich said nothing and I got the impression that the play bores him and won't be a success. Thank you for your letter which did something to relieve my melancholy.

113 Knipper to Chekhov

January 15 1901
Moscow

[. . .]

Point of disagreement with Nemirovich – Act III – Masha's confession. I want to do Act III in a state of tension, in fits and starts, that means the confession is strong, dramatic, i.e., the darkness of the surrounding circumstances gains the upper hand over the joy of love. But Nemirovich wants the joy of love, so that Masha, looking at everything, is full of that love which does not repent and confess. The 2nd act is full of this love. In Nemirovich's interpretation Act IV is the culminating point, in mine it's Act III. What's your answer?

114 Chekhov to Stanislavski

January 15 1901
Nice

[. . .]
Of course you are a thousand times right, it is not right at all to show Tuzenbach's body; I felt that when I wrote it and spoke to you about it, if you remember. If the end echoes 'Uncle Vanya' that's no great misfortune. After all, 'Uncle Vanya' is my play and not somebody else's and when you echo yourself in a work people say that's how it should be. [. . .]

115 Chekhov to Vishnievski

January 17 1901
Nice

[. . .]
Of course you can appear in a formal, double-breasted jacket in Act III, yes; but why in Act II do you go into the drawing-room in a fur coat? Why? On the other hand, it might be right. As you know. [. . .]

116 Chekhov to Knipper

January 17 1901
Nice

[. . .]
Of course the third act must be taken quietly so as to get the feeling that people are exhausted and want to sleep . . . Why have noise? Off-stage the ringing of a bell is indicated.

117 Knipper to Chekhov

January 18 1901
Moscow

[. . .]
What nonsense to think of failure! God help you! The play is terribly

interesting to see. We don't yet fully understand it. Everything is going well for everyone, only Meyerhold still lacks *joie de vivre* and Sanin still hasn't fully captured the tone. Today we did really good solid work on the 2nd act. I'm writing very little because I still don't see everything quite clearly. You, after all, don't like talking about what you're working on and I don't want to chatter. Don't be cross, my darling, and don't worry.

This evening Nemirovich and I worked on Masha, I came to understand her, made it stronger; I love the part enormously. It plays itself really, doesn't it?

I shall play the repentance[1] in a quiet voice but with strong inner drive and feeling, and with a hint of happiness if I can so express it. Almost no movement, the eyes . . . oh, I'm chattering on like an actress and you can't understand at all. In the 2nd act Nemirovich insists that Vershinin and Masha should not be alone but there should be the impression that they have discovered each other and experience the joy of love. Finally Stanisl. has decided that Irina and Rodé should dance to the waltz Tuzenbach is playing while Masha becomes immersed in a Russian waltz at the words 'The baron is drunk'; Fedotik catches hold of her but she pushes him away and spins all alone. In the 3rd act I'm not comfortable with the fact that Stanisl. has Masha take care of Irina, who is sobbing hysterically and, on Andrei's entrance, has the sisters take her behind the screen because she doesn't want to see him. But that, I think, will change and the sisters will stumble down-stage on the beat.

The décor is charming. A wonderful pathway lined with fir-trees, a house with a large terrace, and a porch where officers pass and Masha and Vershinin part. Does it matter if I make a small cut in my final speech? If I find it difficult to deliver? Does it matter? I really like the shaping of Masha in the 4th act. The whole role is a marvel. If I ruin it I'll give myself up as a bad job. Marya Petrovna is a perfect Natasha. Andrei, a little officer, Ferapont is good; Fedotik still a little but not completely false.

Petrov causes a lot of good-hearted laughter when he is at rehearsal, 'our military professor' as we call him. He's apparently decided that we can't do without him and is chipping in not only about the uniforms but also about the acting. Luzhski, a bit of a joker, does a wonderful imitation of him saying in very thoughtful tones: 'Now what can "we" do about Solyony – it's not working for some reason!' What a character!

---

1. Masha's admission in Act Three that she loves Vershinin.

118 Chekhov to Knipper

January 20 1901
Nice

[. . .]

Noise in Act III . . . Why noise? There's only noise in the distance, offstage, muffled noise, confused, but on stage itself everyone is weary, half-asleep . . . If you ruin Act III the whole play goes for nothing and in the twilight of my years I will be hissed off the stage. In his letters Alekseiev praises you highly and also Vishnievski. And though I can't see you I praise you too. Vershinin delivers 'tram-tram-tram' to you in the form of a question and you, in the form of an answer, and to you this represents such an original joke that you speak this 'tram-tram' with a smile . . . She says 'tram-tram' and begins to laugh, but not loudly, just a very little. We don't need a character, in this instance, like the one in 'Uncle Vanya' but someone younger, more vital. Remember, you are easily amused, easily angered. [. . .]

I already said that Tuzenbach's body musn't be carried across the stage during your scene but Alekseiev insisted that nothing could be done without the body. I wrote to him that the body should not be carried across but I don't know whether he got my letter. [. . .]

119 Chekhov to Knipper

January 21 1901
Nice

My dearest, Masha's confession in Act III just isn't a confession but simply a candid conversation. Do it tensely but not desperately, don't shout, even smile from time to time, mainly try and feel the weariness of the night. And for people to feel that you are cleverer than your sisters, you must think that you are cleverer at least. As far as 'tram-tram' is concerned, do it your way. You're intelligent . . . I am writing, of course, but without any kind of pleasure. 'Three Sisters' seems to have worn me out or I am simply sick of writing and getting old, I don't know. Perhaps I won't write for five years, travel for five years then come back and settle down.

So 'Three Sisters' won't be done in Moscow this season. You're doing it for the first time in Petersburg? By the way, just remember, you will have no success at all in Petersburg . . . In Petersburg there'll be fights but success not a whit, please believe me. [. . .]

120 Nemirovich to Chekhov

January 22 1901
Moscow

Telegram
Give permission make cuts long speeches three sisters end play.

121

Letter

At last I can give you an answer concerning 'Sisters'. On my return I first of all saw each act twice and questioned Konstantin Sergeievich about whatever I did not understand in his conception. Since then I have approached the play as the theatre's manager and have been working all the time, every day. Konst. Serg. has done a great deal of work on the play and has produced a beautiful and in places astonishing *mise-en-scène* but by the time I arrived he was very tired and has relied entirely on me. At first, the play *seemed* to me overloaded both by the author and the director, cluttered by talented ideas, executed with talent, but embellished with a superabundance of detail. I realized that the actors were not yet at home with them but all the same they seemed to me too much. I am talking about all the moving around, the noises, the exclamations, the external effects, etc., etc. It seemed to me almost impossible to create a harmonious whole out of the tonalities of the different episodes, the thoughts, moods, traits, changes in every character without damaging the stage-worthiness of the play, or the clear expression of each of these details. But little by little, after removing as many details as possible, the overall aim started to come clear as did our ultimate goal.

Today we finished work on three acts – in their essentials. The fourth is still not corrected but if three are going well the fourth will come of itself.

This is how the play looks at the moment:

Plot – The Prozorov house. The life of the three sisters after the death of their father, arrival of Natasha, her taking control of the entire household and the isolation of the sisters. Their individual destinies and especially that of Irina represent the basic theme: 1) I want to work, be happy, lively, healthy; 2) her head is aching from work and she is unsettled; 3) her life is in pieces, youth is passing and she agrees to marry a man she does not love; 4) destiny takes a tumble and her fiancé is killed.

The plot unfolds as in *epic* works, without those surprises which were thought essential by older dramatists – life as lived in the midst of simple, truthful squabbles. Name-days, parties, a fire, departures, stoves, lamps, a piano, pies, drunkenness, night, housemaids, parlourmaids, chambermaids, winter, spring, summer, etc., etc.

The difference between the stage and life lies only in the author's world-view – all *this* life is life seen through his world-view, the feelings, the personality of the author. It receives that distinctive colouring which is called poetry.

I am writing quickly but I hope you get my drift.

All this, i.e., life and poetry will be achieved and the story will unfold. The details, of which there initially seemed to me to be an enormous number, have now merged to form the kind of background which provides the lifelike aspect of the play and against which passions, or at least their outward expression, erupt.

The actors have mastered the tone. Kaluzhski [Andrei] is a sweet, not unintelligent little fat man in the first two acts, tense and wretched in the 3rd and especially dear to my heart in the last.

Savitskaya [Olga] – a born high-school principal. All her opinions, morals, delicacy in her relationships, her withered feelings – everything is fully and truthfully expressed. She cannot end as anything other than a principal. A certain actor's energy is still missing but that's the last thing to worry about. It will come.

Knipper [Masha], very interesting in tone, which she has captured very well. She still has not got control of her strong temperament but she is close to it. It will be one of her best roles.

Zhelyabuzhskaya [Irina] is about to repeat what she did in 'Lonely People' but she is touching and sweet and makes a great impression.

Alekseieva [Lilina, Natasha], no praise is good enough. Original, simple. She underlines with particular clarity the idea that attractive people can sometimes get into the clutches of a completely ordinary, common woman. And even feel no horror.

Samarova [Anfisa] cries real tears.

Alekseieva (Olga)[1] a typical housekeeper.

Vershinin . . . Sudbinin has been replaced. Kachalov is pleasant enough but ordinary. He would make a good Tuzenbach if you would allow me to give it to him. But as Vershinin he's not very good, just wishy-washy.

Alekseiev read the part over for me. Very interesting. He's coming into the play tomorrow.

Meyerhold is sweating blood, poor fellow, to convey merriment and get away from theatrical cliché. Hard work can overcome anything. He will be good in the end.

Solyony has not worked out at all. For all his efforts Sanin couldn't give

---

1. Stanislavski's sister-in-law, née Polyanskaya.

anything. I had not seen Gromov before. I worked with him today and think he will be good.

Artiom is beyond my expectations.

Vishnievski is simply playing his unadorned self but he brings great richness of feeling and so is good.

Today I am in spirits and have confidence in the play.

About the 4th act. It needs cutting. I have just sent you a telegram but, to give a few details, three long speeches for the three sisters is not a good idea. It's both out of key and untheatrical. A cut for Masha, a big cut for Irina. Only Olga can offer some consolation. Yes? [. . .]

122 Knipper to Chekhov

> January 23 1901
> Moscow

[. . .]
Now Stanislavski has joined the play. Vlad. Iv. says Kachalov should play Tuzenbach. What do you think? Why have you written nothing about Tuzenbach's corpse?

123 Chekhov to Knipper

> January 23 1901
> Nice

[. . .]
I received the news from you that in Act III you all lead Irina by the hand . . . Why? Is that really in keeping with your mood? You shouldn't move from the sofa. Doesn't Irina come to you? Honestly! The colonel [Petrov] wrote me a long letter complaining about Fedotik, Rodé and Solyony; he complained about Vershinin and his immorality. If you please, he is going astray with someone else's wife! . . . He's full of praise for the three sisters and Natasha I am happy to say. He praises Tuzenbach, too. [. . .]

124 Chekhov to Vishnievski

> January 25 1901
> Nice

Dear Aleksandr Leonidovich, after the sentence: 'The most important thing in any life is its form' add the words, 'Our headmaster said'. Responses to your performance are favourable, enthusiastic, too.

125 Knipper to Chekhov

January 26 1901
Moscow

[. . .]

Tomorrow there's a run-through of 'Sisters'. I find the 4th act very moving, I cry my heart out. I'm told – sincerely. In the 3rd act I talk to my sisters or, as I put it, I repent, holding back, jerkily, with pauses, it's really hard to express it, not loudly. I only really shout, 'Oh, you're so silly Olya! I am in love, that's my fate . . ., etc.', then, once more, not loud, tense. She sits motionless, her hands clasped on her knees until the offstage 'tram-tram'. Then she lifts her head, her face lights up, she jumps up nervously, takes leave of her sisters. I decided that by 'tram-tram' (in your version *she* calls, *he* answers) she is saying that she loves him and will belong to him, i.e., the admission he has been seeking for so long. I sit at the desk down by the footlights, face out front and agitatedly scrawl something with a pencil. When he signs, she looks, smiles, turns away, i.e., bends her head and asks, 'tram-tram'. After his response she says, even more anxiously, 'tra-ta-ta' and finally, decisively, 'tram-tram'. If this is all done with a smile, lightly, it could not be vulgar, seeing it's a mere *rendez-vous*. Because up to that night their relationship has been pure, yes? I think that everything is going well now. I'm told the fourth act, starting with the parting of Masha and Vershinin, creates a very strong impression. I will write about the run-through the day after tomorrow. Today was the 100th 'Fiodor'. Everyone's getting presents, Moskvin got a writing-set, with a wonderful document-case in light-coloured skin with an inscription in oxidized silver, from the management. For his jubilee Sanin has been given a whole library. There will be an address. I'll write everything. [. . .]

126 Marya Chekhova to Chekhov

January 28 1901
Moscow

Dear Antosha! yesterday we had the first dress rehearsal of 'Three Sisters'. I was at the theatre and wept, particularly in the third act. The production and acting in your play are outstanding. The three sisters play very well, one can't find any fault at all with them. The scene among the three of them is very touching. Savitskaya [Olga] is terribly engaging. The only one I'm not entirely happy with is Lilina, it seems to me she overacts somewhat. . . . If you knew how interesting Act One is, how merry! My greatest problem was to persuade Olya [Knipper] to get rid of her red wig, which doesn't suit her at all and makes her head look big. She's going to play with her own hair from now on. I know, I feel that the play will have a huge success. [. . .]

FIVE

PETERSBURG

Sooner or later the Art Theatre had to confront the fashionable and snobbish Petersburg public. The 'provincial' Muscovites would be weighed in the balance and, almost inevitably, be found wanting. True to form the press was hostile to the company, making an exception for Stanislavski, whose genius as an actor could not be denied. Knipper was particularly upset. However, audience reaction was more positive and the tour left its mark.

During 1901 the Art Theatre was holding its breath waiting for the new Chekhov play. It was waiting, too, for Gorki's first play. After much persuasion and prodding, particularly from Chekhov who sat him in the theatre for a whole week and made him watch, he had decided to try his hand at drama. He was in fact working on two plays simultaneously, *Small People* and *The Lower Depths*. *The Lower Depths* proved the more difficult to write and even *Small People* was not finished until late in the year, too late for inclusion in the Moscow season. As a result the decision was taken at the last minute to put on Nemirovich's new play *In Dreams* as it would be easy to mount. The play was less than a total success.

127 Knipper to Chekhov

February 21 1901
Petersburg

[. . .]

We have just played 'Uncle Vanya' for the second time. The public was receptive but the papers roasted us shamelessly. Oh, did they not! They absolutely tore me to pieces. The reviews were illiterate, stupid and contained such wicked venom. But we are not hanging our heads, we go on acting. At the first performance we were all infernally nervous, like schoolchildren. 'Lonely People' was roasted all ways, the play and the acting.

. . . Sanin showed me all the papers – the roasting went to the very

limit – there are no actors, only Stanislavski and Sanin were praised.
Meyerhold and I were completely chewed up, so were Andreieva and
Moskvin. In a word, terrible, my dear! I was in terrible torment all night.
You cannot conceive how disgusting, how insulting the attitude is towards
our theatre. I am sick at heart. [. . .]

128 Gorki to Chekhov

> February 28 1901
> Petersburg

[. . .]
  'Three Sisters' is on – wonderful! Better than 'Uncle Vanya'. Music,
not acting. [. . .]

129 Chekhov to Knipper

> March 1 1901
> Yalta

[. . .]
  As for me I'm giving up the theatre altogether. I'll never write for the
theatre again. You can write for the theatre in Germany, in Sweden, even
in Spain but not in Russia, where dramatic authors aren't respected, get
nothing but kicks and are forgiven neither for their success or their
failure. You have been the object of abuse for the first time in your life,
that's why you are so sore, but it will pass in time, you'll get used to it.

130 Chekhov to Knipper

> April 22 1901
> Yalta

[. . .]
  Sometimes I feel a strong urge to write a four-act *vaudeville* or comedy
for the Art Theatre. And I will do, if nothing else gets in the way but I
won't give it to them before the end of 1903. [. . .]

131 Knipper to Chekhov

August 23 1901
Moscow

[. . .]

I forgot to write to you yesterday: Nemirovich and Sanin told me that
they want to put on 'Ivanov'. You won't be against it will you? You may
need to make a few minor changes but a production would be a very good
thing. [. . .]

132 Knipper to Chekhov

August 23 1901. Midnight.
Moscow

[. . .]

Tomorrow Nemirovich reads his play [*In Dreams*]. It seems he's
nervous . . . Stanislavski, I hear, is very enthusiastic about Vl. Iv.'s play
and has already written the *mise-en-scène* for the first act. We'll hear and
see if it's interesting. It really will be dreadful for Vlad. Iv. if people don't
like his play . . . What will he do? You, on the other hand, are
philosophical about it and see nothing terrible, right?

133 Knipper to Chekhov

August 30 1901
Moscow

I read through Nemirovich's play today. The hero, who is supposed to
be a strong character, who leaves the wife he loves and who loves him,
and quits his university post in the city, turned out, for me at least,
wishy-washy, i.e., you don't feel his strength, you just see someone full of
high-sounding phrases, coldly reasoning. The heroine is not a very rich
character either. She is very much in love, wants to be everything for the
man she loves but that only emerges in her words; she gives her husband
Platonic love and gets angry when he gives her the same in return. There
is a lot of bankrupt feeling in the play. A lot of interesting discussions.
2nd and 3rd acts very interesting but the 4th act changes and he comes
out rather wet. If you had seen how nervous he was yesterday, Vl. Iv., I
mean! It would be interesting to have a discussion soon and see who
would speak out. Meyerhold and Roksanova sat frosty faced.

134 Chekhov to Gorki

October 22 1901
Moscow

Dear Aleksei Maksimovich, five days have passed since I read your
play [*Small People*] and I haven't written to you before for the good
reason that I just haven't been able to lay my hands on the fourth act, I
waited then couldn't wait any longer. So I have read only three acts but
that, I think, is enough to make a judgement on the play.

As I expected it is very good, written in the Gorki manner, original,
very interesting and if we start with what's wrong, there is only one fault
which is as irreparable as a red hair on a red-head, its conservatism of
form. You make new, original people sing songs with new notes in
outworn shapes, you have four acts, the characters moralize, one can feel
the fear of being long and boring, etc., etc. But all this is not important, it
is all drowned, so to speak, in the play's qualities. Perchikhin is so alive!
His daughter is charming, so are Piotr and Tatyana and their mother is a
perfect old woman. Nil is strongly drawn, he is extraordinarily
interesting. In a word, the play carries you with it from the first act. Only,
for God's sake, don't ask anyone except Artiom to play Perchikhin and
Nil must be played by Alekseiev-Stanislavski. These two characters will
do what is necessary. Piotr – Meyerhold. Only the role of Nil, a splendid
role, should be two or three times as long, it should end the play, it
should be the lead. But don't set him up against Piotr and Tatyana, let
him be self-sufficient as they are self-sufficient, they are all remarkable,
excellent people, independent of each other. When Nil tries to appear
superior to Piotr and Tatyana in his asides about being a fine fellow then
he loses the element which is native to our steady, working people –
modesty. He boasts, he quarrels but even without that we can see what
kind of man he is. Let him be merry, let him be mischievous for the
whole of the fourth act, let him eat a lot after work, that is enough to win
the audience over. Piotr, I repeat, is good. You probably don't suspect
how good he is. Tatyana, too, is a rounded character, all it needs is: 1. for
her really to be a teacher, teaching children, coming home from school
bringing textbooks and exercise books, and 2. there must be mention of
the fact in the 1st or 2nd act that she has already tried to poison herself;
then, knowing this, the poisoning in the 3rd act will not come as a
surprise and be in place. Teterev talks too much, people like that just
need to be shown fleetingly, *en passant*, for people like that are always
episodic, in life as on stage. Have Elena lunch with everybody in the first
act, let her sit down and be pleasant because we see her too little and she
lacks definition. Her conversation with Piotr is bold; on stage it will stick
out too much. Make her a woman of passion, who is lovable even if not

loving. You still have time before it goes on and you have time to revise
your play ten times over. What a pity I am leaving. I would attend the
rehearsals of your play and would have written everything that was
needed to you. [. . .]

135 Knipper to Chekhov

> October 27 1901
> Moscow

[. . .]

'Kramer'[1] is on . . . There was not much feeling of success in the
house. In my opinion the audience behaved disgustingly, coughing,
blowing their noses, fidgeting. I think that at first the audience was only
really caught by the scene between the father and the son in the 2nd act.
Not many curtain calls but after the third act, a lot of applause and then
insistent calls for Stanislavski . . . They say he lost heart after the 2nd act.
I didn't go back and see him. Marya Petrovna was well received. Moskvin
very well received. For the moment it is still difficult to sort things out in
my head, I will write tomorrow. [. . .]

136 Knipper to Chekhov

> October 30 1901
> Moscow

[. . .]

Yesterday I went to a rehearsal. Sanin is in charge of the play [*In
Dreams*]. Vlad. Iv. isn't in the theatre. I take part unwillingly, very
unwillingly. Sanin is in the middle of dealing with the 'crowd' scene, i.e., the
chorus of students in the 1st act . . . I don't know how 'Kramer' went
yesterday . . . It seems to me Moskvin is not getting the praise he deserves.
What was your impression when you read the reviews? . . . Efros isn't going
to write anything, he doesn't like it but let fly in the office . . .

137 Chekhov to Knipper

> October 30 1901
> Yalta

[. . .]

Balmont came to lunch today . . . Tell Nemirovich that Balmont is

1. *Michael Kramer* by Gerhart Hauptmann.

writing something for the Art Theatre and will finish it without fail around the spring; I'm happy about it as I think it will be a fine, original piece. I received a play from Fedotov, a dark-haired man who came to see us and you didn't like . . . It's for the Art Theatre, too. I spent the whole day reading newspapers which have been piling up on my desk in my absence; I find something about myself in every one . . . To judge by the provincial press the Art Theatre has created a complete revolution in the theatre. [. . .]

138 Chekhov to Knipper

November 1 1901
Yalta

I knew you would be in Nemirovich's play. That is not a reproach just a reply to your letter. Judging from the papers 'Kramer' didn't have the success I anticipated and that is painful to me. What our audiences want are shows not plays. And as for Alekseiev losing heart, as you write, that's stupid and terrible; it means that Alekseiev is not aware of how well he has done. [. . .]

139 Knipper to Chekhov

November 1 1901
Moscow

[. . .]
Now Nemirovich has asked me to convey the following to you: as you are only writing some sort of short story please send it to him a.s.a.p. He wants to arrange a matinée on behalf of our needy students at which Chalyapin and Sobinov will sing and he will read your story, tickets all fixed at 10 roubles. A good idea. Write if you agree.

140 Chekhov to Knipper

November 2 1901
Yalta

[. . .]
Gorki will soon be on his way to Moscow. He told me he would be leaving Nizhni on the 10th. He has promised to change your part in the play [Small People], i.e., to make it bigger; he promises quite a lot, which makes me very glad because I think with the changes the play will emerge better, not worse, than before. [. . .]

141 Chekhov to Knipper

November 9 1901
Yalta

[. . .]

Roksanova playing in 'Seagull' again? The play was taken out of the repertoire until they got a new actress and now suddenly we've got Roksanova again! How appalling! I gather from the repertory list that 'Ivanov' is in rehearsal. In my opinion that is a wasted, a futile effort. The play will be a flop because it will be done in an uninteresting way for slack, limp audiences.[1] I shall persuade all our best authors to write something for the Art Theatre. Gorki has already written something; Balmont, Leonid Andreiev, Teleshov are already writing things. I ought to get a fee, say a rouble per person. [. . .]

142 Chekhov to Knipper

November 12 1901
Yalta

[. . .]

'In Dreams' – a good title, gentle and pleasant. I would be more than happy to send Nemirovich the story but everything I am writing at the moment, I mean everything, is rather long and unsuitable for public reading and also what I am currently writing is almost entirely censored and hardly permissible for reading in public. So ask for me to be excused. [. . .]

143 Chekhov to Knipper

November 27 1901
Yalta

[. . .]

Nemirovich's play will be a success. Don't lose heart. Only it would be a good idea to rehearse 'Small People' at the same time otherwise after Christmas you will have nothing to play except the Nemirovich.

But Alekseiev is apparently losing heart. He's been spoiled by success and that means that anything less than complete success is like a sharp knife through him. [. . .]

---

1. *Ivanov* was planned as an extra but got no further than three rehearsals.

144 Chekhov to Knipper

December 13 1901
Yalta

[. . .]

I read the last act of 'Small People'. Read it but didn't understand it. I laughed twice, both times it was funny. I liked the end, only this is the right end for a first or second act, not the last. He'll have to think up something else for the last act.

Your role in the last act is not worth talking about. [. . .]

145 Nemirovich to Chekhov

Wednesday December (14?)
1901
Moscow

Dear Anton Pavlovich,

Olga Leonardovna whispered to me that you have definitely started on a comedy. And I have been intending to write to you all this time to say: don't forget us! The sooner we have your play the better. There will be more time for discussion and putting things right. On our side we, you know, do our best to compensate you. If a performance is not always what it should be there is nothing to be done: theatre! Theatre means performances every day. Nothing gets done without compromises. If we were only to give performances of the highest artistic quality it would mean reducing them by half and being even more dependent on patronage.

As to the financial side, things look very good for you. I can guarantee that after this winter, when Lent is over, you will receive not less than 7 thou. from the Art Theatre.

You will get the programming and then you will know when your plays are on. Takings are excellent. They rarely fall below 900 and a bit. Your plays make about 1,100 r. They are always performed with pleasure.

In short, write plays! Write plays!

The theatre itself is on the move. The most certain of all is that we are taking the Omon Theatre (on Gazetni Street) for twelve years and are rebuilding it to suit our requirements. I conduct discussions, keep a watch on things and spend my spare time with architects, etc.

My play [*In Dreams*] is going well. We play in one week. I'll send you a telegram about its success (or failure). The production turned out more complicated than we thought and rehearsals were seriously interrupted because of illness and also 'Enemy of the People' which took up a week's rehearsal.

I'm expecting a play from Gorki. Get him to send the play as soon as possible, please . . .

146 Chekhov to Knipper

December 18 1901
Yalta

[. . .]

I'm writing nothing, nothing at all, and doing nothing. I've put everything off until next year. You see the lazybones you married?

How did Nemirovich's play go? It must have made a stir. Moscow audiences like him. I'm thinking of writing a funny play in which the devil appears as a dragon-fly. I don't know if anything will come of it. [. . .]

147 Knipper to Chekhov

December 22 1901

Telegram

Success, writing.

148 Knipper to Chekhov

December 22 1901. Night.
Moscow

[. . .]

We played 'In Dreams' last night. In my view a middling success . . . They liked Kachalov as the prince and praised me. Today Samarova told me that the whole of the Maly Theatre was buzzing about me and Kachalov. In one of the press notices they mentioned, i.e., singled out Knipper and Lilina . . . Rokshanin in his article didn't single anyone out, only said 'I cannot pass over Knipper's sparkling performance in silence. She is an outstanding actress who has only played "atmospheric" parts up till now but has now advanced to the ranks of the finest contemporary artists, displaying a mastery of acting' – something like that. I'll send you the cuttings. Efros, of course, either said nothing or tore people to pieces. The audience listens to my words and laughs. Colleagues praise me and tell me that in the provincial theatre I could earn 700 r per month. Nemirovich got calls but not very warm ones, received two garlands

yesterday and two today. So yesterday there was a presentation back-
stage and we gave him a most artistically worked blotting pad and an
elegant writing set. He was quite embarrassed but didn't show it. Then
quite a large group of us went to the Hermitage [Gardens] but not the
Alekseievs. We had supper and chatted about our lives, didn't want to
break the party up and decided to wait for the papers . . . At 7 in the
morning the papers arrived, we read them out loud, stayed till we were
satisfied then started to split up. Moskvin got a bit drunk, was very nice,
talkative and forced himself on me for morning tea with Geltser, Lika
and Aleksandrov. Vlad. Iv. got very angry and decided to go home and
get some rest but they came to my place nonetheless, had tea, coffee and
a snack, chatted and laughed until 10.30 in the morning, I got rid of them
at 11 and went to bed but did not sleep and got up at 3 and went to lunch
with mamma and then went on to the theatre.

How do you like this crazy life? [. . .]

Audiences either like the play or tear it apart. They say the exposition
is long, spread over two acts. There is no intimacy. They like Kachalov
very much in the 3rd act. Today the play was down, well received but not
much energy. [. . .]

149 Chekhov to Knipper

> December 24 1901
> Yalta

[. . .]

I received your programming for the festive season. Samarova doesn't
appear once in my plays, in 'Three Sisters', Stanislavski doesn't play
once, Lilina not once. Overall my plays are being neglected. I can't abide
N.N. [Ekaterina Munt] and she's in 'Three Sisters' every time. [. . .]

150 Knipper to Chekhov

> December 26 1901
> Moscow

[. . .]

Today we discussed 'Small People'. At first everything was very flat,
nobody said anything. Vladimir Ivanovich delivered the opening address
but he seemed *distrait* and what he said was flat. Sanin, as usual, spoke
well, going through the whole of Russian history and literature in a grand
sweep, speaking poetically about Perchikhin and Tatyana – a weeping
willow. Mikhailovski wittered, Tikhomirov spoke. Nil was the object of

disagreement. Everyone has his own interpretation. The majority said that he was not a new type, that in the future he would be a petit bourgeois, even, if you please a slightly better version of Bessemenov. In my opinion he's a quite ordinary worker, like thousands in the west, although perhaps he's new in Russia. He has no special needs, is striving, if you like, for freedom but for freedom in the bourgeois sense. What do you think? A good role for an actor perhaps but presenting little interest for an actor who is a creative artist. Who will play him we don't know. Luzhski has turned it down. It's said Konstantin Sergeievich will play Teterev.[1] I don't know what's going to happen. Most of the casting still hasn't been decided, we are just discussing among ourselves.

151 Knipper to Chekhov

December 28 1901
Moscow

[. . .]

We had a reading of Gorki's play. Vlad. Iv. read with a voice full of cold. The reading was frequently interrupted by bursts of laughter . . .

Tomorrow there will be a discussion. I will write in the evening. Casting is still not known. The play is good but doesn't arouse enthusiasm, there are some interesting character-types. You know, I like the role of Polya terribly. I like Elena too but I still don't feel her. I shall have to do a lot of work and let my imagination wander – I have to carve a likeable lower middle-class woman out of myself. Don't worry about your plays, they're doing fine. Lilina played yesterday. Natasha will be played by a newcomer. [. . .]

1. Presumably on account of Stanislavski's tallness. Teterev is described as a huge man.

SIX

CHANGES

The year 1902 marked a watershed in the affairs of the Art Theatre. It was the year in which the company established its supremacy in Russian theatre; it was also the year in which a serious rift appeared between Stanislavski and Nemirovich-Danchenko, a rift which was to determine the history of the theatre for the next thirty-five years.

When the theatre was founded Nemirovich had foreseen a time when it would become an actors' collective, when each member of the company would hold shares. This idea came to fruition early in 1902 but not in a way he approved. It was Morozov who picked up the idea, suggesting that he should lend money to the less well-off actors to enable them to buy in, providing that he was the majority shareholder with a right of veto over any subsequent reorganization. Since it was he who was also putting up the bulk of the money for the purchase and refurbishment of new premises, Morozov became in essence the owner of the Art Theatre.

The reorganization of the company had its less pleasant side. Only selected members were to be invited to become shareholders. This meant that Meyerhold, among others, was excluded. He had acquired, rightly or wrongly, a reputation as a troublemaker. Certainly it would appear that Stanislavski thought this to be the case for, although he refused to discuss the matter directly with Meyerhold, he refers in a letter written in the summer to 'troublemakers'. Chekhov, who also accepted an invitation to become a shareholder, was incensed at the way Meyerhold had been treated and wrote a letter of protest to Nemirovich now unfortunately lost.

152 Knipper to Chekhov

January 1 1902
Moscow

[. . .]
Well, I'll tell you what I've been up to for the last two days. Yesterday, during the day, we discussed the play [*Small People*] again, not very interesting, we talked about the characters from the actors' point of view.

The male parts are badly cast: the old folks, Luzhski and Muratova (good), Tatyana – Roksanova (so-so), Piotr the student – Meyerhold (?), Nil – Sudbinin, Teterev – Sanin (dreadful!), Perchikhin – Artiom and Moskvin (good), Polya – Adurskaya, the rest not are not important. Savitskaya has unexpectedly been asked to understudy me as Elena. She is in a terrible state and really offended, she says they're laughing at her. [. . .]

153 Chekhov to Stanislavski

January 4 1902
Yalta

Dear Konstantin Sergeievich, the municipal library in Taganrok (it's also a museum) has come to me with a request that I should get a photograph of you as founder and director of the Art Theatre. Please be so kind as to help me meet this request. [. . .] I got your most recent telegram, thank you!

[. . .]. Gorki was here with me [. . .] we spoke at length about his play [. . .] We discussed the cast list which Nemirovich sent him. It seems to me that Nil is a part for you, that it is a wonderful part, the best in the entire play. But Teterev who goes on at length about the same thing doesn't seem right for you. He's not a living, rounded character. On the other hand, I may be wrong. Give Marya Petrovna [Lilina] my greetings for a happy New Year and my heartfelt wishes for her health and success. I am infinitely grateful to her, she cannot imagine how grateful I am and how fond I am of her.

Your A. Chekhov

I was unwell for a month and a half but am all right now.

154 Chekhov to Knipper

January 5 1902
Yalta

[. . .]

It seems to me that the actors, all of you, have not understood 'Small People'. Luzhski must not play Nil; this is an important, heroic role, just right for Stanislavski's talent. Teterev is a role which is difficult to make anything of over four acts. Teterev is the same in every act and says the same thing, not a real live thing but cobbled together. [. . .]

155 Meyerhold to Stanislavski

January 6 1902
Moscow

Konstantin Sergeievich, dear sir,

In view of the *exceptional importance* for me of the meeting I requested, of which you are aware from the card I left at your home in the evening of the 5th, I beg you to allow me the possibility to speak to you in the presence of Savva Morozov and Marya Andreieva.

156 Knipper to Chekhov

January 9 1902
Moscow

[. . .]

Today we went through the 1st act with Konst. Serg., Luzhkski – Bessemenov, his wife – Muratova, Adurskaya – Polya, Shishkin – Tikhomirov and I have found the tone. If Roksanova will just say Gorki's words that's all that's needed. Not complicate things and get clever. As Teterev, Sanin is hopeless throughout. Meyerhold (student) is still not happy and so far we've heard nothing from Sudbinin as Nil. Artiom is funny but we don't need that. Yet that's what he's doing. Tomorrow I will come off the book and test the ground. I'm going to speak with a slight Ukrainian accent, to hide my own intonations, to make it sound simpler. The most difficult thing for me is to identify with this petite bourgeoise, so that her petit bourgeois ways don't appear to be stuck on and seem contrived. I will write to you about my work and my success or lack of it. Are you interested?

In January 1902 a key figure made his appearance in the life of the theatre: Leopold Sulerzhitski. His career had been varied. He was a writer, painter, sculptor, had been a merchant seaman but above all was a trusted disciple of Lev Tolstoi. He had accompanied the persecuted religious sect, the Doukhobors, to their new home at Tolstoi's request. A friend of Chekhov and Gorki, he came to know Stanislavski slowly but in 1905 became his personal assistant, the only man, Stanislavski claimed, ever to have understood him fully.

157 Knipper to Chekhov

January 10 1902
Moscow

[. . .]
   A good rehearsal today, intelligent, the shape of the act began to
emerge. In my view Konst. Serg. is not Nil and the role is not interesting
to work on. It might suit Sudbinin, I don't know. Meyerhold, no. I'm sort
of tinkering. Yesterday evening Sulerzhitski came to the theatre, he's out
of hospital. He's going to see Gorki, to recuperate in the Crimea. He'll
come and see you, of course.

158 Knipper to Chekhov

January 13 1902
Moscow

[. . .]
   'Small People' is to my mind a very difficult play and it will be difficult
to act . . .
   Konst. Serg. wasn't at rehearsal today either, apparently he's writing
the plan for the 2nd act. Vishnievski came and told us that Fedotova is
horrified by Gorki's play, calls it a childish play. Now, when we are
rehearsing it!

159 Stanislavski to Chekhov

January 14 1902
Moscow

Kind and most respected Anton Pavlovich,
   I thank you for your wonderful, simple and heart-warming letter, it
moved me and reduced my wife to tears. She will write to you herself as
soon as her nerves are better, they have been in a bad state recently.
What a shame and what a pity that you have been ill . . . we received the
news and were very upset but kept it quiet so as not to disturb Olga
Leonardovna even more . . .
   I am embarrassed and gratified that the Taganrog Library wants a
photograph of me. I hope you won't think me naïve but I simply don't
know what to do in these circumstances. Say I send a simple, ordinary-
size photograph unframed, people will say: 'He's stingy, he couldn't
manage a frame and a big photograph'. If I send a framed picture, they
will say: 'He's pretty pleased to be in the museum'. What should one do?

Tell me what to do in one of your letters to Olga Leonardovna. With or without a frame?

[. . .]

Your statement that I should play Nil has left me no peace for some time. Now that rehearsals have begun and I am working on the *mise-en-scène* I keep special track of this role. I realize that Nil is very important to the play, I realize how difficult it is to play a positive character but I don't see how I could transmute myself into a positive character more or less using my own face and attributes, and without an outer transformation, without a definite shape, without clear characterization. The tone is not natural to me. True, I have played various peasants in plays by Shpazhinski but that was representation, not life. In Gorki you can't represent, you have to live . . . Nil retains certain characteristics of his way of life and yet at the same time is intelligent, well-read, is strong and is a man of conviction. I'm afraid if I do it, it will come out as Konstantin Sergeievich dressed up and not as Nil. For me to play the cantor, Teterev, would be considerably easier as the outlines of his character are much clearer, rougher; it would be easier for me to get away from myself. For the moment I will hold myself in reserve and will play if one of the actors currently interpreting Nil or Teterev doesn't come up to the mark and of course, if one of the parts is right for me.

There is general enthusiasm for Aleksandr Maksimovich's play. Everyone wants to be in it and, of course, the public demands that we should put it on with our strongest and best people. However, not all the actors the public knows and trusts can be in this play. It is possible that Baranov, for example, may impress us all in the role of the cantor. That is why we have created two casts. Each cast is rehearsing the same *mise-en-scène*. One is working with Kaluzhski, the other with Tikhomirov. In a few days' time we shall see both casts, select the best and then draw up the final cast-list. Even then, there might be individual changes. My wife is anxious to play Polya but I'm afraid she is too old for it and she is in all the plays and won't have the strength for rehearsals. The same is true of me. If the play really can't be done without older actors in it, I will suggest putting it off to next year rather than present the public with something which has weaknesses in the casting. In my opinion that would be criminal with regard to Aleksandr Maksimovich, who has confided his first effort to us.

For the moment, everyone is working with great pleasure and gusto, each cast wants to outdo the other. What will come of it? . . .

After the performance of 'Uncle Vanya' the cast celebrated at the Hermitage and at Omon's theatre.[1] It was all very merry in our box but

1. Charles Omon, who presented farces. The theatre was acquired in 1902 and transformed into the Art Theatre.

dreary on stage as it wasn't bawdy enough. The most interesting thing was to see Papa Omon running up and down the corridor between the artists' dressing-rooms, saying to the actresses: '*Mesdames, ne vous décolletez pas trop!*'. It was touching. You probably know the details of that evening. [. . .]

160 Chekhov to Knipper

January 20 1902
Yalta

[. . .]
I've had a letter from Konstantin Sergeievich. He writes at length and courteously. He seems to suggest that Gorki's play may not, perhaps, be done this season . . .

By the way, Gorki intends to start work on a new play, about life in a doss-house, though I have advised him to wait a year or two and not rush things. An author should write a lot but not rush things. [. . .]

161 Knipper to Chekhov

January 20 1902
Moscow

[. . .]
There's nothing to tell Gorki for the moment and no need to worry him. At the moment there's not the faintest sign of Nil or Teterev. In my view Konst. Serg. should play Teterev and Vishnievski Nil because of his temperament and because he is a sound, promising actor and Sudbinin can't cope, barring a miracle. Luzhski will play the old man well. I don't know what to say about Meyerhold, I wonder about him. Roksanova, nothing except hysterical shouting, delivery same as in 'The Seagull'.
[. . .]

162 Knipper to Chekhov

January 25 1902
Moscow

[. . .]
The theatre's long-term future is being decided, Anton. Vlad. Iv. came to see me during the 3rd act and explained everything and we have a meeting fixed for Sunday. The board will consist of Stanisl., Nemirovich,

Luzhski, Vishnievski, Samarova, Lilina, Andreieva, Knipper – that's all it seems. We are all shareholders in the theatre. Ostensibly we put in 3,000 roubles, i.e., we give a promissory note. Morozov is rebuilding Lisanov's theatre, will give us 10,000 and 30,000 roubles subsidy. We shall be the owners. I tell you roughly what I am able to understand. I'll chew it over, discuss it and write to you about it clearly. They think of you as one of the shareholders, they really do want you. Vlad. Iv. will write to you. You can imagine how worried we all are?! How it will be settled! Of course, you won't say anything about it for the time being. For the moment not everything is clear, you know what an utter fool I am in business. Vishnievski is convinced that in the new theatre's first year there will be profits of 50,000 – is that possible? Should I believe it? Well, I will write to you all about it, every day, so that you know everything.

I didn't tell you yesterday that Baranov created a sensation as Teterev. The two directors saw the rehearsal and when it was over they asked Baranov to appear without any preparation at all. He's just recovered from a long illness. He did his scenes with wonderful calm and control, was very touching, presented a very rich character. He laughed a good deal, i.e., somehow conveyed every word of the part with ease and was moving in those places where his love for Polya could be felt. Simply splendid, now just let him play it. The drunk scene in the 2nd act was weaker and needs work. [. . .]

163 Meyerhold to Stanislavski

January 26 1902
Moscow

Konstantin Sergeievich, dear sir,

I have waited long enough. Three weeks have passed since I asked you for an appointment. You wrote to me saying that you didn't have a single free moment, yet you have found it possible to give an appointment to pupils from the school, a fact of which I am aware.

I am in no position to wait any longer. I expect an appointment in the course of the next three days (28, 29 or 30 January). I will not wait any longer. The absence of a reply from you will give me the right first to resort to correspondence and then to consider myself free to take other measures.

164 Stanislavski to Meyerhold

January [?] 1902
Moscow

I must request you in the future to spare me letters written in the tone of your last communication and also your monitoring of the people whom I choose to receive at home. I further request you in future to spare me the threatening tone which frightens me very little, as *my* conscience, as far as you are concerned, is completely clear. I will not answer letters of such a kind. Perhaps you might find it more sensible, before resorting to threats, to acquaint me with the matter which seems to have provoked such extreme measures on your part. As for an appointment on the 28th or 29th, which you demand in such a high-handed tone, please understand that I must refuse so as not to appear a coward and also to allow you liberty to act. If you really do need an appointment then you would be well advised to write a more suitable letter and to take cognizance of the fact that at the moment my time is not my own but is at the service of an enterprise of which you are a member and the circumstances of which you cannot be ignorant.

165 Meyerhold to Stanislavski

End January 1902
Moscow

Konstantin Sergeievich, dear sir,

My last letter to you was official and nothing more. It contained no threats of any kind. It was written in the same official tone as my first letter to you at the beginning of the month.

The necessity for such an official tone will be apparent from the following.

You write: 'Wouldn't you find it natural to acquaint me with the matter that has provoked such threats?'

I find it not only natural but essential. Otherwise I would never have made such efforts to get an appointment for a whole month. And if you really do not know the reason for my persistent attempts to talk to you the fault is yours not mine.

On the 5th (?) of January I left my card at your flat asking you to give me an appointment as soon as possible. You did not give me an appointment, explaining that you were very busy. So I began to wait. I waited *three weeks*. This will serve as evidence that I am not ignorant of our social obligations.

If I drew your attention to the contradiction between your words ('I am

busy') and the facts (you found it possible to receive at home a delegation
from the school) that does not mean that I have been monitoring those
individuals whom you receive at home. If I set a limit to the time beyond
which I would not wait that does not mean I displayed a 'high-handed'
tone. Anyone who is being insulted, who demands satisfaction, who is
being fobbed off, it doesn't matter with what, lack of time or some other
reason, would have done the same. [. . .]

Since I am evidently not to be allowed to speak to you *face to face*
soon, I have no other resort but correspondence.

[. . .]

The whole company knows that *you* on January 1st this year in
conversation with some members of the company *stated* that I

1. was an 'intriguer' who should be thrown out,
2. that I had admitted people to the auditorium who had hissed the first
performance of Vl. Iv. Nemirovich-Danchenko's play,
3. that you possessed factual evidence in the form of letters signed by
people you know that I had actively incited someone to hiss the author of
'In Dreams',
4. that I was 'undermining the enterprise' of which I am part.

I humbly beg you to corroborate these remarks made behind my back,
to repeat them to my face with a short response, 'yes, I accuse you' or
'no, I do not accuse you'.

I shall interpret the absence of a response on your part by the end of
the month or February 1st as an affirmative response.

If the accusations made against me are based on letters you have an
obligation to provide me with the names of those who signed them.

If you wish to conceal these names that means you take full
responsibility yourself.

Please, don't be afraid to repeat what you said.

I know full well that outside of artistic matters your opinions are not
always *first-hand*. For that reason I wish to settle accounts not with
you but with those who have led you to think about me as you do, that's
all.

I expect a prompt reply.

*In any case this matter must be made as widely known as possible, and
that I am not afraid of as my conscience is clear. I will stop at nothing to
bring the truth out into the open.*

Vs. Meyerhold

166 Knipper to Chekhov

January 28 1902
Moscow

[. . .]
  Yesterday we were at the Hermitage from 2 in the afternoon to 10 at
night and discussed the future of the theatre. Morozov wrote to you
today, of course infinitely more clearly than I . . . You will think it over
and answer him. We shall be 16 in all: Morozov, Stanisl., Nemirovich,
Luzhski, Vishnievski, Simov, Artiom, Moskvin, Kachalov, Aleksandrov,
Samarova, Lilina, Andreieva, me and you, if you agree, and, it appears,
Stakhovich. But you'll hear it all from Savva Timof. It's true, he's helping
us a great deal and I think our theatre has got off on a firm footing . . .
  I'm told Sanin wants to leave the theatre but I really don't think it will
happen. [. . .]

167 Knipper to Chekhov

February 2 1902
Moscow

[. . .]
  Nemirovich was at the house last night and we talked a lot about the
theatre . . . He said how good it would be if you could only live here and
take an active part in the life of the theatre. Of course that would be
wonderful. There's a meeting today at 3 o'clock when Vlad. Iv. will tell
us about his misgivings. [. . .]

168 Chekhov to Knipper

February 2 1902
Yalta

[. . .]
  I had a letter from Morozov today, I will write to him and say that I am
willing to put 10 th. into this business only in two chunks: 1st Jan. and
1st Jul. 1903. You see how I do things in a big way!

169 Chekhov to Morozov

February 2 1902
Yalta

[. . .]
  I can do it this way, so that my wife and I together have the equivalent

of ten thousand's worth of shares between us (of course, on condition that the income comes to me and the losses are my wife's). It seems to me, or rather, I am sure that the company will make a profit at the Lyanovski Theatre, at least in the first few years, if everything remains as before, i.e., if there is same energy and love of the undertaking. [. . .]

170 Chekhov to Knipper

February 10 1902
Yalta

[. . .]

I have written to Nemirovich[1] that a shareholding company is fine but that their articles of association aren't worth a damn. Why are Stakhovich and I shareholders and not Meyerhold, Sanin and Raevskaya? You don't need names you need rules. It should be established that anyone who has served at least 3 or 5 years and has received a salary not less than such and such should be a shareholder. I repeat, you don't need names but rules otherwise the whole thing will fall apart. [. . .]

171 Knipper to Chekhov

February 12 1902
Moscow

[. . .]

Today we rehearsed my scene with Teterev in the 3rd act then there was a meeting until 5.30. We went to a ballot on the 'doubtful' members of the company. It was not pleasant. Sanin and Meyerhold informed the management, officially, of their departure from the theatre. We all decided to ask them to stay as we need them in our work. Roksanova, Munt, Abessalomov and someone else, I can't remember, yes, Sudbinin were voted out. The whole proceeding was revolting. I am tired and my head is splitting. [. . .][2]

1. Letter lost.

2. Meyerhold formed his own touring company, which included his sister-in-law, Ekaterina Munt, and Roksanova. In a letter to the press he denied any financial motive behind his departure.

172 Nemirovich to Chekhov

After February 20 1902
Moscow

[. . .]

You say that writing a play doesn't attract you. And yet my ideal for
the coming season would be to open it on October 1 with your new play.
It could be done this way: the play would have to be completely finished
by August 1. You would stay in Moscow for August and September and
all discussions and rehearsals would take place with you present. In
October and part of November you would follow a series of
performances. [. . .] Is that really impossible?

Sanin and Meyerhold were not included in the shareholding members
because Morozov (and Alekseiev) didn't want them. As a result both, it
appears, are leaving the theatre. The conditions were drawn up by
Morozov himself and the members did not argue very much. And even
when I provoked an argument about §17[1] and refused to accept it, even
though the majority agreed with me, when it came to a vote, I found
myself alone. Then the whole thing nearly fell apart because on one side
Morozov declared §17 a *sine qua non* and because, on the other, without
my participation there was no chance of getting things started.

You are somewhat mistaken in your remarks. You always confuse the
Association with the Association of three years ago. We may in the future
create another, special association. Then your remarks will be useful.

Your presence will be generally welcomed. We expect to see you in
Moscow after Easter.

Farewell. I embrace you.

Your Vl. Nemirovich-Danchenko

The second Petersburg tour in 1902 was a triumph. The company were
showered with gifts. Less agreeable were the problems of censorship,
particularly when it came to *Small People*, which was premièred. Gorki's
notoriety caused the police to mount a huge security operation, which was
turned into a farce by those very aristocrats it was designed to protect, since
they vied for seats at what was supposed to be a 'private' showing to enable
the authorities to decide just how subversive the text was. *An Enemy of the*

1. It was under Paragraph 17 of the new articles of association that Morozov was given a
power of veto over all future reorganization of the company and the nomination of
shareholding members – 'sociétaires' in Nemirovich's expression, like the Comédie
Française.

People, which created a sensation, also suffered from last-minute censorship.

173 Knipper to Chekhov

March 11 1902
Petersburg

[. . .]
  There was absolute uproar at 'An Enemy of the People' last night. Konst. Serg. was carried in triumph, the audience climbed up onto the stage and some madmen kissed his hands. Prince Shakovskoi was there and gave Stanislavski something and gave the ladies magnificent baskets of fruit and sweets. Then came a curious incident. The fruit and sweets were given backstage to Raevskaya, as the doyenne, and she imagined that the sweets were for her personally. It was awkward explaining things to her and she was beside herself when everyone fell upon 'her' refreshments so unceremoniously. And also in the dressing-room there was a box of chocolates that Kachalov's wife wanted to take to someone after the performance. Raevskaya thought they were a gift from the prince too and gave them to the cast. You can imagine Kachalova's embarrassment and desperation when she had to grab back her own things with her bare hands. Everyone laughed at Rayevskaya terribly. Some girl students brought her some flowers and, poor thing, she thought they were from the prince, too. Shakovskoi heard the word 'revolutionary' onstage and was very angry. He has ordered it to be cut.
[. . .]

174 Chekhov to Knipper

March 16 1902
Yalta

[. . .]
  I am not writing a play and I have no wish to, as there are enough dramatic authors at the moment and work on plays is boring and trite enough. Most of all you should put on 'The Inspector General' with Stanislavski as the Mayor and Kachalov as Khlestakov. That would be for Sundays. And you would be a wonderful mayor's wife. Then, 'The Fruits of Enlightenment', also for Sundays and in reserve. Only you need to take on two or three competent actresses and the same number of actors – competent, too. If, even by choice, leading roles are played by people

like N., [Munt] or even Z., [Litovsieva] then the theatre will founder in 2–3 seasons.

175 Knipper to Chekhov

March 20 1902
Petersburg

[. . .]

You know, dearest, our two directors have a lot to answer for: apart from the censor's excisions, they have cut the play so that there is nothing left. The actors (ignored) were horror-struck after last night's run. Gorki could well be aggrieved at such high-handedness – what do you think? Many of the company are indignant. There is nothing left of Nil. And apart from our changes yesterday Prince Shakovskoi came and made more cuts. I am sure Gorki never gave us his play with this in mind. Did he really give Nemirovich *carte blanche* to do with the play as he thought fit? The big-wigs say the play will be allowed if Kleigels[1] can guarantee that there will be no disturbances. How can you guarantee such a thing?

176 Knipper to Chekhov

March 21 1902
Petersburg

[. . .]

Lilina . . . dragged me off to have lunch with her at home . . . Afterwards we all sprawled out on the sofas in the Alekseievs' big drawing-room and Vlad. Iv. read us Kataiev's play. He has only received one act. Luzhski arrived and we began to chat about the repertoire. We decided on Ibsen's 'Pillars of Society', 'The Fruits of Enlightenment', 'A Month in the Country' in reserve then a play by Chekhov and one by Gorki and we shall be fine. What do you say Mr Shareholder? – We have put a lot of things back into 'Small People'. Everyone says that Meyerhold is bad as Piotr. Lilina praises me and Luzhski the most. [. . .]

177 Knipper to Chekhov

March 27 1902
Petersburg

Yesterday we played 'Small People', my dear Anton. A success. There

1. Governor of Petersburg

was a great deal of applause but less so after the 3rd and 4th acts . . . You
said that the act should end with the poisoning and that the scene that
comes after drops the tone. That's right. Yesterday Vlad. Iv. said that we
must ask Gorki to rewrite the 3rd act for Moscow. The whole romance
between Piotr and Elena is rather uninterestingly presented in the play,
so that to end the act with a love scene between them is a disadvantage.
Right? Yes, and there is too much hustle and bustle in the poisoning
scene for the audience to be entertained by Teterev and Elena talking
philosophy afterwards. The theatre was full of policemen in plain-clothes
and uniform. There were shouts of 'Author' but rather feeble and it was
only after the 4th act that a voice was heard proposing to send a telegram
which we did. No noise, no disturbances, nothing. [. . .]

178 Chekhov to Knipper

March 31 1902
Yalta

Telegram

Gorki's play a success? Well done everyone!!

In the early summer of 1902 Knipper was extremely ill. Stanislavski was
greatly concerned and suggested that she and Chekhov should use the house
at Liubimovka while he and Lilina were abroad. It was during this stay that
Cherry Orchard was mainly conceived. Gorki in the meantime had
completed *The Lower Depths*.

179 Chekhov to Gorki

July 22 1902
Liubimovka

Dear Aleksei Maksimovich, I read your play. It is new and
undoubtedly good. The second act is very good, the best, the strongest,
and when I read it, especially the end, I almost bounced up and down
with delight. The mood is dark, heavy, the audience will leave the theatre
in a state of surprise and you can say goodbye to your reputation as an
optimist. My wife will play Vasilisa, a shameless and wicked woman.
Vishnievski's walking up and down the house, working out the Tartar –
he's convinced that's the part for him. Luka, alas, can't be given to

Artiom, he'd repeat himself and get tired; on the other hand he would do splendidly as the policeman, that's the part for him, his mistress is for Samarova. The Actor, whom you have brought off very well, should be given to an experienced actor like Stanislavski. Kachalov should play the Baron. [. . .]

You have removed all the most interesting characters from Act IV (except the Actor), be careful of the result. This act could seem boring and superfluous especially if only mediocre actors remain after the strong actors have gone. The death of the Actor is appalling; a real slap in the face for the audience and without warning. How the Baron ended up in the doss-house, why he is a Baron is not sufficiently clear . . .

In Moscow they're transforming the Lyanovski Theatre into the Art Theatre, work is in full swing and they have promised to be finished by October 15 but performances won't really be able to begin before the end of November or the beginning of December. I think work is held up by rain, torrential rain. [. . .]

Nemirovich retired, as usual, to his wife's estate for the summer. He was far from happy. His hostility towards Morozov had considerably increased, the more so since Morozov, not content to confine himself to matters of finance, building and management, was championing the cause of a group of young writers, (which Nemirovich contemptuously described as the 'Gorkiad'), and was thus encroaching on his prerogative as final arbiter in matters of repertoire. The enormous success of the 1902 Petersburg tour, particularly the way in which the company had been 'taken up', only served to reinforce the fears he had nurtured from the very start, that the theatre would abandon its artistic ends for fashionable success. It was to Knipper that, not for the first time, he confided his misgivings.

180 Nemirovich to Knipper

> July 1902
> Neskuchnoe Estate

[. . .]

So you are living at Liubimovka and do not know whether you are getting better or not. Anton Pavlovich fishes and rejoices in the northern summer, Vishnievski either says nothing or thinks about full houses or laughs at Anton Pavlovich's every word. Morozov and Stakhovich have been to see you and surreptitiously or even quite consciously try to instil in you a taste for the kind of theatre into which, as a result of their sincerely held beliefs, the Art Theatre will degenerate.

It is glorious at Liubimovka. For me it merges with the strong impression I have of the 'Pushkino' summer. And when I remember the fir-lined paths at Liubimovka, under the mild August sun or that little balcony when I was chilly because it was dawn and we were making far-reaching, passionate plans for the theatre, only breaking off to hear how the stillness of the night was pierced by the church watchman's bell or the whistle of a train, then it seems to me that that summer marked the sunset of my youth and I rushed greedily to enjoy it to the full.

No, what dullness of soul there must be in the man for whom everything comes down to getting as much praise from people as possible. We all enjoy being praised. But we are happy for it as a just appraisal of our efforts, which are so immeasurably dearer to us than the reward itself. But when this reward becomes an end in itself and moreover everything turns into a game for rich, idle people, when you can put your hand on your heart and say it all comes down to that, then it has become simply repulsive.

When I spoke to you this winter of the 'disagreeable cachet' imposed on us by layabout 'sweet, nice' Muscovites, that cachet about which, you will remember, I imparted to you my first, vague, inadequately defined impressions. I can tell you now for certain that it is much more serious. You feel this.

I took a backward look, summed up the last four years fully and from every side and I was appalled to see the point we had reached. Appalled, whatever it was I started to think about or from whatever quarter I came at it.

I took everything in strict order so as not to deceive myself or anyone. I cannot tell you how my heart ached sometimes, and was then overwhelmed by a feeling of indignation and a terrible longing to fight.

There is one question which frightens me more than anything: have I, or have those who with all their heart agree with me, enough strength? Have I the strength to rescue our enterprise from the path it is following and which will surely lead to a shameful 'ignominious' fate? Have I the strength, without creating havoc, to lead the theatre carefully back to its earlier path, bearing with me all the good things that will create a new position for it? Will I have the strength to bite my tongue and be diplomatic so that I can enlist the people who are necessary to our theatre yet vacillate unconsciously? Do I still have the drive which has always helped me get what I wanted? Am I still tenacious enough? Is it too late?

I am speaking to you in general terms because I feel that if I were to start to explain the mass of ideas, conclusions, conjectures, proposals, references, etc., etc., that stand there so clearly before me I would be writing for two or three days.

I've done that already. I spent two days drafting a letter to Alekseiev. But I didn't send it because when I had finished it I saw that such an important and profound matter could not be settled by a letter to Alekseiev.

A new feeling emerged: I fear everyone, that is I fear the powerful people in the theatre. I know that Alekseiev will readily agree with me, and not just in theory, but he will not deal with the question directly but will consult his secret desires to see whether they are in accord with what I want. And his secret desires will tell him that whatever form the theatre may take, he, Alekseiev, must above all be 'the master-artist Stanislavski'. Outside of that the theatre's mission does not interest him. I know that it is possible to lead Morozov along the theatre's earlier path, its path of glory, but, at the same time, the moment he realizes that that particular path means there can be no thought of the theatre being 'fashionable' he adroitly starts a fight with me. And I am afraid to show my hand to Alekseiev or Morozov. I am afraid of the vast majority of the actors because the vast majority of them keep close to the wind and only show sympathy when circumstances are at their most favourable, and avoid a fight.

And that fear leads to depression and a feeling I have not known before like a man who has fallen into a whirlpool and drops his oars and strikes up a song which reminds him of occasions when someone has succeeded in dragging his affairs out of the mire. Happily I can say that in my own career no catastrophe has ever frightened me.

From the campaign I have now planned, and for which I still have finally to prepare myself, out of this campaign against people who themselves do not understand where we are leading the theatre, and when they understand that their perhaps unconscious, hidden desires must be revealed and they must recognize that what they say is not what they really wish – from my campaign against this trend can come only two results: the first, defeat, slow defeat, almost by attrition, my defeat; the second result, victory, but victory without the superficial successes which fill everyone's heads at the moment. The damage began in Petersburg. We experienced the 'joys of victory', which came when we were not thinking about them, and which we then made the whole purpose of our efforts.

Since then we have been going downhill in the sense of superficial success and are sliding down lower in the sense of glory for the Art Open Theatre. Now our situation is highly risky. 'To conquer' for me means being obliged to forget the 'joys of victory' and to work on things which we sincerely consider beautiful. Psychologically this is an enormous task. And I still can't believe in its success and it is so important! But to cultivate these 'joys of victory', that is to strive after them, that means

one or two years of rowdy success and then total, irrevocable
collapse . . .

I beg you not to speak of this letter to anyone (except your husband, of
course). And not even to Vishnievski.

I am still not ready.

Up till now I haven't received Gorki's play although I have been most
careful to keep in correspondence with him. [. . .]

181 Nemirovich to Stanislavski

End of July 1902
Yalta

Yesterday I got your letter written on perfumed paper . . . The letter
came in the evening; we were fighting off the mosquitoes so we had
hardly lit any candles and for a moment I thought that the letter which
gave off such a strong scent had been written by some lady admirer of 'In
Dreams' . . . I am writing to you, dear Konstantin Sergeievich, but don't
know where to address it. You have now probably learned from
Kaluzhski's letter that I am off 'The Pillars of Society' and currently
busy with Gorki's play. Best of all would be to start on the
Chekhov but the story is that he will finish it in August. And in any case
Olga Leonardovna won't be fit enough to rehearse in August.

The production plan for 'Pillars' I have, in any case, finished and the
4th act took me more time that all the other three. (This act should be a
huge success!) But at the same time I have kept up a great
correspondence with Gorki. He has already prepared a lot of
photographs, sketches and even props. He is begging me to go to see him
so we can deal with things that are difficult to write about. He finished the
play, sent it to Petersburg, asked for it back so he could send it to me,
then started to rewrite it. I wired him that he should hang on to all the
material until I arrived and that I would try and get to him on August
9 . . .

I reckon that until you arrive we will discuss the play, try out the sound
of this or that actor, gather material, go only where we have to . . .
sketch what we need or don't need . . . and then you will arrive and we
will load all this onto you.

There is one disagreeable aspect to this: 'Small People', 'The Power of
Darkness' and the new Gorki play . . . a definite and clear trend. That's a
totally undesirable image for the new theatre, undesirable for a multitude
of reasons some of which you probably are not conscious of but surely
feel . . . But there's not much to be done about them at the moment . . .
They are the result of past mistakes . . .

But one thing I must decidedly take issue with and you must agree with me. I mean, rehearsals in your absence, just with the second director, at least without you there as the author of the production plan.

For instance, in his schedule prior to your arrival Kaluzhski arranged several rehearsals of the 2nd act of 'The Power of Darkness'. You then write that you are sending 'Les Aveugles' [Maeterlinck]. That's what I take issue with. This mistake has been repeated year after year and it leads to agonizing results which you somehow do not appear to feel.

I think rehearsals in your absence can be conducted as follows:

a. Going over what has been finally set, when your intentions are finally clear – going over it to keep some technical point in trim or so as not to forget. As, for example, 1, 3, and 4 acts of 'The Power of Darkness'.

b. Bringing in individual characters into plays we have *already performed* following patterns which you have already laid down, with any departures from it as my responsibility. [. . .]

c. Plays totally delegated to the second director – for example 'The Pillars of Society', i.e., plays for which you have not written the production plan. And, with certain necessary conditions, rehearsals of those plays with the author of the production plan so that you can take a look at them, but this should only occur in special circumstances, and it would be better if it did not occur at all.

d. Sorting out the blocking in the production plan, i.e., *maximum* 3-4 rehearsals of a complex act.

e. On those occasions when the second director has rehearsed a play according to your production plan and called you to see an act that had been more or less set, a great deal of annoyance has always been caused with a consequent loss of time.

This is what happens. The director was anxious to do the best he could so you would think the act was ready. He worked intensely; at first the actors were half-hearted, then he got them going. The act is set. You arrive. You whisper to me that none of it is any good but that we must be supportive to the director and the cast. Then you go into your act, one which has caused great disappointment in recent times to directors who are still only apprentices, i.e., you praise them loudly for all their hard work. Then you arrange rehearsals and start to alter everything . . . After two rehearsals nothing is left of all the hard work that has been put in. Revolt wells up in the hearts of Sanin and the actors.

That's how it has always been and I have no reason to think it will be any different with Tikhomirov.

If he starts to justify himself by reference to your own production plan, you answer, 'Yes, yes, yes. It's my fault. Don't let's argue about it. But this isn't right, we must rework it'. Or 'Ah, Dear God! What rubbish I wrote in the production plan. It's clear when you see it in rehearsal.'

But it wasn't rubbish – and that's where the disaster lies. It comes out as *rubbish* because the ideas you wrote down in the production plan have been wrongly understood.

And so we must decide once and for all that immediately after the blocking, until the roles have been learned, rehearsals must take place with *you there*. Then, once an act has been set, the second director can go over it. The exception . . . and then not even an exception, but simply *more frequently*, they can take place without you when I am your second director. Not because there won't be mistakes but because there will be fewer of them and because I will try to replace what is obscure in your plan with other things, decisions other directors cannot take. And because, finally, this way there is less risk of wasting the free time which is essential for you . . .

Unfortunately I find that it is pointless to rehearse in new actors into old plays in August. No kind of orders, fines, heated words can induce these characters to approach the work with energy two months before the revival itself. It lies at the root of the actor's psychology and must be taken into consideration. But when the performance is staring them in the face they do in three days what would have taken them ten. Finally, it is simply more profitable to deal with these roles away from rehearsals, in the study and not with the ensemble – then you can stop over every line.
[. . .]

As part of the 'campaign' which he mentioned to Knipper, Nemirovich addressed the whole company with a thinly veiled attack on Stanislavski. Nemirovich took the opportunity to reaffirm his belief in drama as literature.

182 Nemirovich to the Members of the MXT Association.

End of July, beginning of
August 1902

[. . .]

What is the general purpose of theatre?

Not everyone gives the same answer to this question. The answer at the Maly theatre would be – at least a few years ago – the theatre exists so that actors can develop their God-given gifts. From that point of view one must stage plays in which this or that artist or the whole ensemble can display their talents. This path leads inevitably to productions that seem designed for touring, or to the public losing interest in productions in which their favourite artists do not appear and, in addition, therefore to a decline in the repertoire.

In our theatre, thanks to the outstanding talent of the principal director and to the general increase in the importance of the director we could answer: the theatre exists for the director to display his gifts. Yet whatever the importance of the director may be, this path detracts from the theatre as a whole and reduces it to the activity of one or two, more, three people and makes the theatre a studio-workshop for one, two or three artists.

The really correct answer is: the theatre exists for dramatic literature. However broad its independence, it is totally dependent on dramatic poetry. A theatre of any importance and significance speaks of things which are important and significant. To get itself listened to, it must have talented directors, talented actors, talented designers, etc. Only the well fed come to the theatre. The hungry, the sick, the broken have no place in the theatre as living drama and are hardly likely to at any time while man lives, as the hungry, the sick or the depressed never have a voice. But the well-fed need to be upset and disturbed by important aspects of life as most people know it. Art, even when its devotees are not conscious of it, assumes this primary purpose. All the best works in the world have provoked this unease about life and its different phenomena. When art ceases to serve this end it becomes a plaything for the well-fed.

Form in art is everything. It encompasses content itself. Real art is above all a matter of talent.

The most lofty ideas when clothed in form which has no talent lose their purpose.

It does not follow from this, however, that excellently performed trifles possess any serious significance. Just as lofty thoughts expressed without talent lose their charm and force so trifles remain trifles to the end of time. And when a certain artistic institution or a certain stratum of society, or a whole nation, are content with art which deals with nothing but trifles then that artistic institution, that stratum or that whole nation has come to its last days . . .

The theatre, like any great art, must respond to the positive tendencies of contemporary life. Otherwise, as an institution it is dead. [. . .]

In August Nemirovich replied to a letter from Stanislavski which is now lost. Stanislavski's letter was possibly his reply to Nemirovich's letter written at the end of July [181]. Some of the contents of Nemirovich's letter of

August 7, in particular his account of the theatre's history, are almost identical to passages in his general letter to the company [182], which have been omitted here.

183 Nemirovich to Stanislavski

August 7 1902

[Beginning of letter missing]

I am replying to your letter which I have had constantly before me. Once again it comes down to the question of bias in our repertoire, a bias that has developed independently of our conscious wishes . . .

Now, we have been in full charge of our affairs, you and I, with, for the last two years, Sav. Tim. [Morozov]. The rest followed our lead. If you think deeply about the direction we took the theatre the following is clear: whatever is talented, artistic and independent is typical of us but whatever is talentless, tasteless and hackneyed is not.

This general formula applies to our repertoire, our staging and our relationship with the outside world. We did not give this formula – if you think, I repeat, deeply about it – greater definition or precise shape because we didn't find it necessary. Greater definition and precision in setting our goals might have narrowed rather than broadened them. Neither of us ever spent much time thinking about whether our repertoire ought to be liberal, conservative or popular, symbolist or naturalistic. If we had shown a particular bias it would have tied us down artistically and that is the reason why *everyone* can find something interesting in our theatre and *everyone* can find something they object to.

But in recent years, in my view two, in addition to our efforts to run the theatre in line with this broad artistic policy, new forces have been added which, imperceptibly, have begun to influence the direction we take. It is as though we had started work on a massive building and discovered friends who, seeing our efforts, decided to help us. We were both so taken up with this sudden development and with our own exertions, that sometimes we didn't look ahead enough, assuming that the direction in which we ought to move was clear to all. But our friends, bit by bit, without malicious intent, with their entertaining talk, as it were pushed the building sideways. And when we paused for breath and looked around us we found that we had lost our way . . .

We were so busy that we accepted the help of our sympathisers with pleasure, not noticing that our goals did not always tally with those which attracted *them* towards us and that the help they provided was nudging our affairs in a direction that needed thinking about.

These outside forces expressed themselves in various *trends* that have gradually surfaced in the internal life of our theatre. To get a clear picture of these trends try to remember what the general mood was like, the theatre *up to the Petersburg tour* and the theatre *now*.

The characteristic features of the first period of our theatrical life were 1) boldness to the point of foolhardiness in everything – in the choice of repertoire, in our attitude to the audience, in our staging. The boldness of our staging is all too obvious to you since it is said to be *your* style, it belongs to you personally.

Boldness in the choice of repertoire: 'Fiodor' when there was no one to play Fiodor; 'Lonely People' when there was no Johannes; 'Antigone' with an Antigone scarcely out of high school; 'Hedda Gabler' with an actress who scarcely had any technique; 'The Seagull', which the public would not accept as a play, and without a Seagull; 'Ivan' with an actor little more than 26; 'When We Dead Awaken' with no Rubek, and so on . . .

Boldness in our attitude towards audiences – we saw them as some kind of mob that might crush us but which we wished to tame – a mob that was alien to us with individual elements that simply didn't interest us.
2) Unfamiliarity with the *joys of success,* or, to be more precise, almost not *running after it* at all. We did what we thought we had to; we did it to the limits of our strength. The joy of success (with 'The Seagull', 'Lonely People', 'Enemy of the People') came of itself.

People are stupid, crude, grubby and dishonest. When they get a whiff of personal gain they swoop down and batten on like lice on a young tree. It is their instinct for survival but they manage to preserve an attractive human shape.

That is how we got where we are. *Now* 1) we have known the joy of success and so, as we set down to work let us first examine it with this in mind: does this work give us the same joy we once knew or does it not? 2) We have become timid and apprehensive. We are afraid that Mar[ya] Fed[orovna] won't be up to 'A Month in the Country', that we won't have the time or energy for 'Julius Caesar'. And so, instead of going after plays we considered to be good and which will stretch our actors . . . Of Ibsen's plays we choose not his best, *obscure* (!) works but 'Pillars' because it is similar to 'Enemy'. We have become timid in the creation of the repertoire and in casting. I think that if, right now, by some miracle, 'Tsar Fiodor' were to turn up we would take fright and hand it over to the Maly.

Finally, we have stooped to that monster, the audience. We have begun not merely to pay attention to certain parts of it but tried to bring them into closer contact with us. The Stakhoviches and the Yakunchikovis and such-like *mondains* are now our back-stage friends. And despite my rigorous protests, the necessity for such friendly contact is warmly

proclaimed as is some kind of salon for selected members of the
audience.

All this has provided fertile soil for two main trends in our theatre –
trends which are not healthy – and when I discovered them and thought
around all the aspects of our enterprise, *I was terrified*, faced with the
question: where are we going?

The first trend is sincere – but no less harmful – which I call the
'Gorkiad'. I would say this is Tikhomirov's trend. It has infected almost
everyone, yourself included. The 'Gorkiad' is not Gorki. It is perfectly
natural to attract a great artist like Gorki to the theatre. But the
'Gorkiad' is Nil, Teterev, student demonstrations, Arzamas, elections to
the academy, the 'Gorkiad' is all the ballyhoo surrounding the reputation
of a man who has been rocketed to the top of Russian political life. But
that does not prevent the two of us from realizing very soon that this, in
any case, is of secondary importance. Of primary importance is the fact
that Gorki is a great artist. But as regards the tendency which I call
Tikhomirov's, that's the resounding phrase, the Russian kulak, the tramp
in prison, the rape of a girl's corpse, down with culture! And as regards
Vishnievski's tendency, that's full houses first and foremost. If there were
not the 'Gorkiad' how can we explain this absurd, in my view, way we're
running after Andreiev, Chirikov and Skitalets? Andreiev wrote about
three masterly short stories. Are we to conclude from that he will write
splendid plays? Chirikov is known to everyone. It is my profound
conviction that Goslavski, or even Timkovski are head and shoulders
above him. Skitalets is a nice, boring little talent situated in the tail of the
rocket, i.e., Gorki's talent.

The second trend, which is already undoubtedly harmful and more
powerful is the attempt to make our theatre 'fashionable'. That's
Vishnievski's trend. There you will find Zinaïda Grigorievna [Morozov's
wife], Stakhovich, Yakunchikova, Garderina and others.

By chance, in recent times this trend has merged with the 'Gorkiad'
because that, too, is fashionable. But it leads to the appalling result that in
our theatre *form completely stifles content* and that instead of growing into a
great art theatre with a broad educative influence we are turning into a little
art theatre making splendid statuettes for nice, dear layabout Muscovites.

A detailed review of the last four years, in terms of the figures, plays and
atmosphere gave me a terrible *depression* which I cannot convey – in short I
wanted to play Beethoven. It became clear how many people had battened
on to our undertaking, showering it with flowers and money but at the same
time depriving it of the freshness, cleanness, the real boldness of true art,
which is not required by these trends or by fashion. They always want to
make something out of our theatre which . . . remember I spoke to you
about Koni and Petersburg? . . . We will be glittering, empty souls.

Without dwelling on the consequences, I, naturally, asked myself the following question: 'What is to be done? How can the theatre be stopped in its tracks? I do not doubt that in all major questions I can count on your full support, nonetheless I note that we are already very far gone. We have enormous work to do in our own hearts and minds. We must strip away this patina that has become a canker so as to be, as before, free from the 'Gorkiad', from fashion, from the pursuit of victory and its pleasures, from contempt for intelligent plays, from a resurgence of dreams about full houses, from loss of faith in artistic strength and perhaps from many other things . . .

I am not blaming anyone, you understand . . . I am merely concerned with the Art Theatre as such.

In my depression (now, on the contrary, I want to get up and fight) such were my thoughts. Five or six years ago I dreamed of such a theatre. Now the Art Theatre exists. It is the best of theatres but it is far from the theatre I dreamed of and, to be exact, less like it than it was two years ago. Is it possible that we can just leave the great edifice we began unfinished, occupying only a small part of it and leaving others to accomplish something which was our idea? This is the fate of 'results'.
[. . .]

184 Knipper to Chekhov

> August 20 1902
> Liubimovka

[. . .]
The Alekseievs returned yesterday . . .

K.S. read Gorki's play [*Lower Depths*] today. We went to bed late of course – two o'clock. We talked about the theatre and sat up late. Vlad. Iv. came in the evening too with K.S. and stayed overnight, went to the theatre this morning.

185 Stanislavski to Knipper

> August-September 1902
> Moscow

My dear Olga Leonardovna,
I have put everything aside to write to you, as only by such energetic means will I be able to do something I have wanted to do for some time.

Savva Timofeievich is burning to build the theatre[1] but you know what he's like at such moments. He doesn't give himself time to take breath. I

---

1. Morozov had provided the finance for the conversion of Oman's Theatre.

so admire his energy and effort and am so in love with our new theatre and its stage that I am all in a muddle and can scarcely answer all Morozov's questions. Please God, the theatre will be wonderful. Simple, strong and serious. There will be a room for writers. The foyer will present a gallery of Russian authors which will stand out against the oak panelling instead of a panel. On one wall there will be a glass case for the gifts and messages to the theatre. The corridors will be laid with wide carpets (as in the Burgtheater) and brightly lit. The corridor walls will be in imitation white stone blocks. The other side of the stage, the auditorium, will be done the same way. The auditorium is extremely simple, in the grey tones of the front curtain with broad art nouveau borders at ceiling and floor level. A row of boxes in wood (water-seasoned oak) with candelabra of unusual form like matt bronze. No door curtains. In front of the proscenium arch, in the house, going the whole width of the stage, a very large batten with lights in antique bronze. In them are concealed several dozen lamps, which light the actors from the house and from above. This arrangement enables us to get rid of the footlights. Instead of chandeliers, lights are installed on the ceiling. Rows of oak seats (as abroad with tip-up seats). A reading room and library for the audience. A complicated ventilation system which keeps the theatre at a steady 14 degrees. Under the entire auditorium storage space for props, furniture and costumes. Next to the dressing-rooms a separate stage for students, exercises and rehearsal during performances. Two green-rooms for the artists. A dressing-room for each actor. A large wash-room with hot water for the actors. A three-tier stage . . . A revolve with large sections which can be raised and dropped. A photographic section, a museum of rare objects and a museum of set-models. Separate entrance for the actors and their ante-room, etc., etc. Thinking about this theatre it is terribly difficult to play 'The Power of Darkness' which is making our lives a misery at the moment. Unbelievably difficult. We have worked through the first act but for the moment we have all farmers and no peasants. [. . .]

A small request to Anton Pavlovich. Would it be possible to ask Lev Nikolaievich Tolstoi through someone the following: the 4th act (murder of a child) does not work because it is divided into two small scenes. As soon as the audience has been worked up (scene in the yard) the curtain falls and the alternative version starts again from the beginning. That means the audience have to think back, as both versions happen at the same time, begin at the same moment, and force the audience to make this leap in time in their imagination. Yet it would be easy to merge both scenes into one sequence (without bringing down the curtain). This would be possible by building a special set. Like this:

[Sketch combining the two locations. In Tolstoi's script the first scene is played in a hut with a cellar, the second scene, in a courtyard]

The inner part of the yard and the hut are both on stage. As soon as the conversation in the yard is over and Nikya disappears into the cellar with Matriona and Annisa the scene between Mitrich and Aniutka takes over. This can be done without changing the text but by altering the scene order. Would Lev Nikolaievich approve such a change round? I have not the least doubt that the scene would gain in effect if only because it will not be split by the curtain falling and a long pause. [. . .]

186 Nemirovich to Stanislavski

September-December 1902
Moscow

I've been thinking and thinking and here's the result.

My ideas on Satin.

It's not a question of your needing to create some image or other so that you can drum up some enthusiasm for the role. To me, for instance, the image is absolutely clear, and I can instil it into you but you won't portray it. There are several reasons why you are dissatisfied with your own acting. You don't need a new image but a *new method. New for you.* You have worn your old methods – intensity, inward tension, etc., to shreds. Not in your roles (and so you're not frightened to use them) but when you are working as a director. Good actors, who have worked with you for 4-5 years know them, know them all too well. And you know them all too well too, and so they don't appeal to you.

I won't be at the theatre this evening and I am writing to you in case I do not see you.

What you need . . . I would even say, is just a bit of a rebirth. Satin is an excellent occasion for that as a more complex role would not give the time or the opportunity for rebirth. You must show yourself to be a slightly different actor from the one we have come to know. We need suddenly to see different methods.

I have already given this much thought in practical terms.

Above all, you must know the role like the 'Our Father' and develop a flowing delivery, not one peppered with pauses, something bright and light. So that the words flow from your mouth without tension.

This is the most difficult aspect of a measure of rebirth.

The same applies to movement – lighter.

For example, I can easily imagine Satin at the beginning of the 4th act like this: he is sitting, he does not collapse into a chair as you are doing but leans against the stove, his head clutched in both hands looking out into the audience to the dress-circle boxes. He sits like that for a long

time, immobile, throwing off his words, not once turning to look at the
people who answer him. He gazes at a fixed spot, obstinately thinking
about something but hearing what is being said around him and
answering everything quickly.

That's the first thing.

Then perhaps I should stop you using bursts of energy as a trick and
make you find new methods. Perhaps ones which are diametrically
opposed [to what you are doing].

Reflecting on the psychology of your artistic personality I think you
have great difficulty in just surrendering to a role and that is because,
first, you have no faith in the audience's intelligence, because you think
you have to hit them on the head all the time, and second because you
want to make something out of practically every sentence. It becomes
difficult to listen to you because, as the dialogue progresses I, the
audience, have long since understood from your facial expressions and
gestures what you want to say or act, but you continue to play something
at me which is not going to interest me especially by being prolonged.
This happens not only with individual lines but even in the middle of
speeches and lines. The things I was able to do with Moskvin and the
tone of the whole play are also relevant in equal measure to you.
Suppose, for instance, I were to give you [Luka's] speech, on the just
earth? You would cut it up into several parts and then overdo it. And it
would not reach the audience as easily. But the whole fascination of the
play lies in this *lightness* of touch. And if I am told that this is like a
production at the Maly Theatre I will answer quite firmly – nonsense. On
the contrary, playing tragedy (and 'The Lower Depths' is a tragedy) in
this tone is something completely new on the stage. It needs to be played
like the first act of 'Three Sisters' so that not a hint of tragedy creeps in.

But the absence of such lightness of touch weighs your acting down.
[. . .]

For instance, you delivered your speech, 'Man is truth . . . I understand
the old man', etc., almost by heart, with warmth and pace and made an
impression both times. Then it was *strong* but *light*.

So here is what you should do:

1. Don't thrust the role and yourself on the audience. They understand
both it and you;

2. Don't be afraid the role will disappear in those places where a great
deal of acting is not appropriate to the situation. If there's nothing there
to play then don't do anything, it's easy to wear yourself out prematurely;

3. Learn by heart;

4. Avoid excess of movement;

5. Keep the tone bright, light and vital, i.e., with vitality, *carefree and
vital*.

I do not doubt for a moment that you will do this excellently. Even in your very first lines: 'My head is splitting', 'Why is that man banging my head', even for these lines you need to develop a light, bright delivery, i.e., say the lines quickly even though your head and whole body are aching. As in light comedy.

Your Vl. Nemirovich-Danchenko.

187 Knipper to Chekhov

September 2 1902
Moscow

[. . .]
Today Gorki read his play to us. He was terribly agitated and cried several times. He doesn't look well, is coughing and terribly tense. [. . .]

Morozov told me that you have ceased to be a shareholder. He is very sorry and says that if it is only a matter of financial difficulties then forget it. It is good for you to be a full member and you can have money when you want it. He's afraid that there's some other reason you don't want to be a member of our theatre. Give me an answer, please.

188 Chekhov to Knipper

September 10 1902
Yalta

[. . .]
I stopped being a shareholder in Morozov's company because I didn't receive any credit, and apparently won't do so in the near future or indeed at all. I have no wish to be a shareholder in name and not in fact. You, actress, are getting less than you deserve because you want to be a shareholder on borrowed money but I don't.

189 Nemirovich to Chalyapin

End of November 1902
Moscow

[. . .]
On Sunday December 1 Gorki will give a reading of 'The Lower

Depths' in the foyer of the theatre. The tickets have gone to 40–50 people. The price for the tickets is 25 roubles (many are paying more). So we shall have a very intimate matinée. And I have promised these 40–50 people that you will be at the theatre, will hear the play and that then you will sing something, without ceremony, even in a frock coat. In short I very much hope you won't refuse. It really won't be difficult for you to sing one or two ballads in the theatre foyer. Everything will be over by 4–4½.

I would like to ask Rachmaninov to accompany you. [. . .]

190 Nemirovich to Chekhov

December 13 1902
Moscow

[. . .]
'Depths' has only been rehearsed in fits and starts. In the last two weeks there has not been one rehearsal with everyone present. Samarova, Gribunin and Kachalov have all been ill. Yes indeed! Today was the *last* rehearsal before the final dress rehearsals and we haven't touched the second half of the 4th act. Nonetheless it is all in hand. We have discovered interesting tones and even if they are not interesting they are not stupid and not too inartistic.

We have developed a tone for the whole play which is new for our theatre, clear, fast, tight, which does not clutter the play with unnecessary pauses and details which hold little interest. The actors are largely responsible for that. The excellence of Moskvin and the interesting and amusing tone of your wife's performance are to be noted. Then comes the second category of good performances which include Alekseiev, Vishnievski, Luzhski, Kharlamov and to a certain extent in my opinion Muratova, Gribunin. The 3rd category create misgivings: Burdzhalov, Zagarov, Andreieva. [. . .]

191 Nemirovich to Chekhov

Wednesday December 18 1902
Moscow

I expect a very big success today, not unanimous but noisy. The performance of the play is all right. [. . .]
Gorki is in a state of happy agitation. At the dress rehearsal (no public present) he was delighted that members of the cast who were out front laughed or gave other signs of approval. Vishnievski made a great show

of laughing at the good lines like a real *claqueur* at the Comédie
Française. And Gorki imagined his laughter was genuine. I'm told that
after the performance Gorki is giving a supper which will cost him 700–
800 r. He even gave 200 r to the stage-hands. I urged him strongly not to
do this but he wouldn't have it. 'The wanderer', he said, 'has come with
his psaltery and will sing to us'. [. . .]

What are you doing? Writing? Scribble a line.

I embrace you from my heart.

Your Vl. Nemirovich-Danchenko.

192 Stanislavski to Chekhov

December (after the 19th) 1902
Moscow

Dear Anton Pavlovich,

I haven't written to you for such a long time as I have been very busy
and in a state about the forthcoming première. If Gorki's play had been a
flop it would have meant the end of the whole business. Now, as you
know, the victory is ours and, most important, Gorki is happy. The first
performance was sheer torture for the actors and had there not been such
a noisy reception for the first act I don't know if our nerves would have
held out to the end.

Vladimir Ivanovich has found the right way to perform Gorki's plays.
Namely one must play the lines lightly and simply. It is difficult to
characterize under such conditions and just everyone stayed themselves,
trying to convey the splendid lines distinctly to the audience. All the more
honour then to Olga Leonardovna who alone transformed herself. Of
course the Efroses of this world will not appreciate her but among the
cast she had a huge success and, as we say in the company: 'That was
quite an act!' I am not very happy with what I have done, although I am
being praised.

Gorki was present at two performances and had a very great success.
He was kind and merry all that time, the way he was when I first met him
two years ago in Yalta. He has gone away happy and intends writing for
the theatre. I repeat, that's the most important part of our success.

I have just sent Yegor to buy all the newspapers and I will send them to
you or at any rate, the cuttings (but I won't read them). Gorki's presence
at the performance led to thunderous ovations for him so it is hard to
judge how far they were for the play and how far for the actors. The
press, it appears, is laudatory.

Now comes a difficult time: instead of the great delight of starting to
rehearse a Chekhov play we have to take on a heavy task – study Ibsen.

Take most pity on two artists: Knipper and Stanislavski. They have the heaviest work to do. [. . .]

193 Nemirovich to Chekhov

December 26 1902
Troitse-Sergieva Monastery

[. . .]

I won't write about the success of 'Depths'. You probably know all about it. Thank God the theatre has once more attained the heights it reached with 'Three Sisters' in Petersburg.

I would like to have your good advice on the repertoire for the coming year. You didn't answer the official request. Answer this please. Even if you cannot indicate specific plays, answer in principle. In general what kind of play we should keep. Here is some material to choose from.

Chekhov. New play. Trump card. Your play ought really to reach us in May.

Gorki. Intends writing something.

Naidenov. Gone to Constantinople. Wants to make something out of his 'Lodgers'.

That's the contemporary Russian repertoire.

Not one of these plays is actually in our hands and we have to prepare the production. We'll have to start 'Pillars' all over again. At all events from Lent onwards. We have to think it through and prepare set-models.

Remount 'Seagull' with décor by Surennianets and Lilina as Nina but that doesn't count.

'Julius Caesar'

'Die Verschwörung des Fiesko' (our men are not effective enough for it)

'Macbeth.'

'Faust' . . .

'Inspector General'

'Month in the Country'

'Young Oaf'

'Masquerade' (Lermontov)

'The Governor'

'The Fruits of Enlightenment' (not out of the Maly repertoire)

'Enough Stupidity'

'Lady from the Sea'

Also by Ibsen – 'Rosmersholm', 'Ghosts'

By Hauptmann, 'The Triumph of Compromise' (in the old manner)

New manner 'Poor Heinrich' . . .

There are also plays recommended by the shareholders: a new Mirabeau and 'Dimitri the Pretender' by Khromiakov.

I don't want either of them.

We ought to revive 'The Sunken Bell'.

That's the list I have before me but I catch myself all the time thinking about 'Julius Caesar' and 'Month in the Country'.

Oh yes! And there's 'Miniatures' (Maeterlinck).

Think hard and advise me.

For now goodbye. I embrace you.

Your Vl. Nemirovich-Danchenko.

194 Chekhov to Knipper

January 7 1903
Yalta

[. . .]

Today I received the list of proposed plays for production. Among others there is Ostrovski's 'Enough Stupidity in Every Wise Man'. It seems to me that this play is quite out of court for us. This is just a Russianized 'Tartuffe' . . . So either do 'Tartuffe' or don't do either. What if you were to dig around a little: isn't there anything in Victor Hugo? For a gala performance? It would also be good to stage Gogol's 'Marriage'. It could be done charmingly. [. . .]

195 Nemirovich to Chekhov

January 17 1903
Moscow

You know, dear Anton Pavlovich, one can never get away from the fact that our theatre must, in terms of theatrical (and if possible dramatic) art, be in advance of other theatres. I really mean *must*. If it is on a par with them, then it has no reason to exist. Let other theatres do imitations of other people's creations and manufacture clichés. There's no point in devoting one's energies to a theatre simply to repeat what others are doing. What could we *create* with 'Marriage'? Or with 'The Inspector General'? It seems to me that both have been exhausted as literary and theatrical material. 'Woe from Wit' is another matter . . . If we had a Famusov I would not hesitate for a moment. I can see untapped material in terms of cultural and literary images in 'Woe from Wit'.

'The Inspector General' could be cast wonderfully from the company. If we knew for certain that out of 5 plays – the number we can do in a year – we could live off three then I would recommend 'The Inspector General'. We really need 'bread and butter' plays.

But they are difficult to choose.

I desperately want to do 'Julius Caesar'. I think I already wrote to you about that. But there's no Brutus. Alekseiev doesn't want to play Brutus or to have anything to do with the play.

So we still haven't decided anything. I think I'll call another shareholders' meeting this week. We'll consider what to do for the best.

And then as to what we should do right after 'Pillars', we are having thoughts about 'The Lady from the Sea'. The plan is this: 1) The play isn't complicated. It could be prepared during Lent. Dress rehearsals straight after Easter. 2) Undecided play. Rehearse it during April and May. 3) Read and discuss your play. 4) In summer prepare a large-scale, complex play such as 'Julius Caesar'. August and half of September will be devoted to the first three. From October we continue with No. 4. And at the end of November we set to work on No. 5 (Gorki).

This could be changed. If, for example, you give us the play at the end of Lent then we can prepare it during April and May and the undecided play can be put off until autumn.

I am absolutely convinced that you will come to the theatre with the new play. And I think that if you were to deliver it at the end of Lent you could spend a splendid spring and summer in Moscow.

'The Lower Depths' is doing colossal business. 19 performances, the 20th tomorrow (in one month!) and not a ticket available for the last two days. [. . .]

196 Chekhov to Lilina

February 11 1903
Yalta

[. . .]
They may have weeded out 'The Inspector General', 'Woe from Wit', 'A Month in the Country' but they will have to do them in the end. And it seems to me you could do 'The Inspector General' splendidly. And 'Marriage' too. In any case, to have these plays in the repertoire is far from superfluous. I am beginning to think that 3–4 new plays in a year is already enough and the public on the whole will want not a new repertoire but one of literary quality. I could be wrong of course. [. . .]

197 Nemirovich to Chekhov

February 16 1903
Moscow

[. . .]

We desperately need your play. Not only the theatre but literature as a whole. Gorki is Gorki but too much of the 'Gorkiad' is harmful. Perhaps I haven't the strength to keep up with these movements and am already old, although I am on my guard against becoming conservative but there's this letter from [Countess] Tolstoya,[1] stirring up indignation against me, the like of which I have not experienced in a long time, though I have restrained myself so as not to appear boorish towards her, and, with all that, I feel a nostalgic attraction for the melodies of your pen which are dear to my heart. Were your songs to end it seems to me that my life in letters, my soul, would end too. I am writing in an overblown manner but you know I am very sincere. And that's why, probably, I have never been as attracted to Turgenev before as I am now. I want more balance and stability in the repertoire in that sense . . .

We may be old but we will not refrain from that which is balm to the soul. It seems to me that sometimes you thought privately that the theatre no longer needed you. Believe me, *believe me absolutely*, that is a great mistake. There is a whole generation younger than us, not to mention people of our own age, to whom your new things are extraordinarily necessary. I would so like to persuade you of that!

I hope you don't suspect me of theatrical guile. That could be! You are needed in any case. What a happy event a play by you would be, even if it were simply a reworking of old themes. While the whole theatre is enthusiastic about Gorki, they are still waiting for refreshment from you.

At the moment we are busy with 'Pillars'. What torture it is not to believe in the beauty of the play oneself yet try to make the actors believe in it. I cling to every detail so as to maintain the energy to work. I am quarrelling the whole time and often believe that I will finally emerge victorious from this agonizing business. It was very difficult up to the run on the 9th. But at that run a new impetus was felt which gave me heart. It came from Olga Leonardovna. Somehow she conveyed the inner image of Lona with new affecting notes, drawing Alekseiev after her, and the play began to take on a more serious, profound hue. Then she lost it completely and I did not even have the energy to fight against the tiny external things Alekseiev was trying to do, so tiny they block the psychological.

1. A 'Letter to the Editor' from Countess Sofya Tolstoya, which appeared in *Novoe Vremia* on February 7 1903.

I shall not shed many tears if 'Pillars' is not a success. Pity though to lose two months', no three months' (May) work. If it is successful then it will be a win for the serious and the profound over a thirst for pretty trifles. That will be a very useful win.

A crack has appeared in the business side of our life in the theatre, the sort that appears in walls needing repair. On one side I see Morozov and Zhelyabuzhskaya and I feel that there you will also find those whose first love is financial peace and quiet. On the other side Alekseiev and his wife, me, your wife, Vishnievski clearly form a group. Possibly Luzhski too. Less probably Moskvin. Where Kachalov stands I don't know.

The crack is widening slowly. [. . .]

198 Nemirovich to Stanislavski

March 27 1903
Moscow

Dear Konstantin Sergeievich,

Yesterday the show was dreadful. Daily performances are the obverse side of a theatre with pretensions to art, often they poison its life because performances are bad. When this happens with old plays which are losing their importance for the artistic side of things, somehow you bear it. But yesterday was insufferable because there was a bad performance of the best play in the season, one which has had a good deal of success.

God forbid that you should think I am blaming you. I am writing to acquaint you with the dirty side of things, which you run away from, as it were washing your hands of them. It is absolutely essential that you, the principal manager of the theatre, take a look some time independently at *every* problem in performances, starting with the situation in the administration and ending with what is happening at the box-office and the anti-artistic atmosphere back-stage. Anything more excruciating I do not know. You become very indignant when you see a student in the role of Andrei Shuiski, or Soloviova's extras playing badly in 'The Lower Depths' . . . why should performances like yesterday's remain a secret for you?

Here is the full picture of yesterday's performance.

First, the play which has had a huge success was performed to a theatre that was less than half full. The takings were scarcely more than 700 roubles.

Second, Gribunin was brought in drunk – he had been dining with some friend or other. And although he played well everyone was in a state of terror in case he got up to some tricks. Moreover (and this is to his credit) he didn't want to act and almost had to be put into his costume by force.

More. Baranov didn't turn up *at all*. And Kharlamov played Zob. There was also confusion in the casting of minor roles.

In addition to all this Moskvin and Kachalov are out of all humour at having to repeat the same old words again and again.

And Olga Leonardovna wants nothing more than to have done with Lona.

I would run out of the theatre had the actors not promised in my presence to pull the performance together.

This, clearly, is the worst result of swapping 'Depths' with 'Pillars'.

This is the sort of thing that is happening in the theatre.

This letter grieves me but it's not all roses! [. . .]

SEVEN

JULIUS CAESAR

Nemirovich regarded his production of *Julius Caesar* as an opportunity to demonstrate his ability as an independent director who was as theatrically effective as Stanislavski and as historically authentic as Chronegk and the Meininger company. In July he went with the in-house designer, Simov, to Rome to do research and make sketches.

Nemirovich made it almost aggressively clear from the outset than he would brook no interference with his concept of the play. Everyone, including Stanislavski would have to knuckle under. Everything was to be subordinated to Nemirovich's sense of the play's structure.

Reception was mixed. The production was admired more for its archaeological virtues than for its artistic or political insights. Schoolchildren were brought to see it as a living example of what life was like in ancient Rome.

Stanislavski, for reasons which he never fully explained, was less than enthusiastic about the project from the very beginning and took on the role of Brutus unwillingly. He did, however, provide production plans for the Senate and Forum scenes. He came to dislike the production more and more but kept quiet, doing exactly what was required of him, particularly as he had been so difficult during the rehearsals for 'Pillars of Society'. It was not until three weeks after the opening that he expressed his reservations about the production, thus eliciting a violent reaction from Nemirovich. The strength of the reaction was to some extent due to the fact that Stanislavski's comments sounded uncomfortably close to adverse comments in the press. First, Stanislavski had taken issue even at the planning stage with the costumes, which he found too clean, too perfect. Certain art critics found the production design too picturesque. Secondly, Stanislavski had wanted more psychological depth, more scope to explore the inner life of Brutus. Everything had been sacrificed to Nemirovich's concept of the play as political drama. Efros found the production all surface and no heart – no Brutus. The most important cause of Nemirovich's anger, however, was the fact that Stanislavski expressed his reservations in front of the detested Morozov, to whose ideas on the future development of the theatre he was totally opposed. He immediately suspected a plot, an attempt to diminish his importance in the theatre.

Nemirovich had counted on universal acclaim and he had been disappointed. His mistake was to equate hard work and painstaking effort with artistic merit. How could he be wrong when he had worked everything out in such meticulous detail and, above all, when he understood the play so much better than anyone else? People who did not unequivocally accept his work either had no sense of the true nature of a director's work, like Stanislavski, or had provincial tastes, like Efros.

Stanislavski's elementary psychological mistake was not to realize that what Nemirovich wanted above everything was recognition. A few words of praise would have gone a long way. But Stanislavski, who was always looking for the flaws in his own work, took the good for granted and was permanently on the look-out for the next step forward. His constant fear was that the theatre would get into a rut, that its work and method would become institutionalized.

Julius Caesar was a deeply unhappy experience for Stanislavski as an actor. His performance as Brutus, with rare but distinguished exceptions, was generally regarded as a failure. Worse, he had to go on and do it every night. Added to his nightly misery was the painful realization that he was becoming more and more isolated in the company. If he saw something wrong he said so, whether it was a piece of scenery or bad behaviour backstage, but his concerns were not shared. He felt he was beginning to acquire a reputation among his fellow actors as an overdemanding busybody who created chaos out of order. Nemirovich dismissed this assessment of Stanislavski's position as exaggerated. But the fact remains that Knipper described Stanislavski with brutal frankness as 'a hopeless mess' (see letter **214**, p. 169). In that she was referring to questions of management. It is one of the paradoxes of Stanislavski's character that he rarely applied the management skills he had acquired in his factories to the theatre. He was prepared to delay, rework, scrap, cancel until he got things right. A theatre constantly in the red could not afford to be so rigorous. It was Nemirovich who saw that things happened on time and there was an endless tug-of-war between Nemirovich's sense of sound economics and Stanislavski's perfectionism.

The private griefs of the two men came out in a heated exchange of letters in late October 1902.

In the midst of the dispute the script of *The Cherry Orchard* arrived. Knipper delivered it on the 18th. For Stanislavski it spelled deliverance from the torture of *Julius Caesar*. But even here there were problems. Chekhov took violent exception to an inaccurate outline of the plot which Efros gave in an article in the *Novosti Dnya*. Bitter memories of the comment on the title of *Three Sisters* were revived. The fact that Efros' mistake was mainly due to a slip of the pen Chekhov himself had made did nothing to assuage Chekhov's fury.

199 Nemirovich to Stanislavski

Early June 1903
Rome

Dear Konstantin Sergeievich,

I am writing to you from Rome. I don't much like setting out
impressions in letters but there's nothing else for it. Today I wandered
through the Forum with Simov and an excellent guide. The weather has
been kind to us – not hot – so we don't get tired out. We are sleeping and
resting well. [. . .]

So, when the Forum opened out before us, although at first it was no
more than what every tourist with two hours to spare sees, we suddenly
realized that there were real mistakes in the set-model. So we buried
ourselves in work – on site and in our rooms – and came up with an
exceptionally interesting viewpoint, an original perspective, original
details and historical truth. And we also found ways to make a few
adjustments to the first act. There are quite definite traces of the tribune
from which Mark Antony spoke. The base and four steps have survived.
The tribune was on this 'platform', just like Cicero's *Rostra* which is even
better preserved. With very little violation of historical truth we have
produced the following roughly-sketched plan:

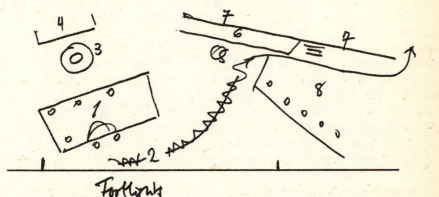

Forum

1. Platform and tribune. Columns. Two statues.

2. The celebrated *via Sacra*. The Forum itself runs into the street – into
the auditorium. The arrows mark the way.

3. (New!) the spot where Caesar's body was cremated. That means we
see through the columns to the pyre which is being prepared, the priests
etc.

4. (New!) *Reggia*, that is the house of the pontifex maximus, Julius

Caesar himself, where he lived. This was a *small house*. From there by a
narrow street to the circular temple of the Vestal Virgins 5. and further
on to their abode, a spacious building 6. Above it the *Palatine* – the
summit – with the gardens, the wall (with gates) built by Romulus when
Rome was founded and the houses of Cicero, Catalina, etc., etc., – and
probably Brutus (on that side of the Palatine). On the right 8. Julia's
basilica, a huge place with columns built by Caesar but completed by
Octavius. The court was there and children's games, etc.

An agreeable, wonderful, highly varied and colourful picture unfolds.

And we have crammed the street in front of the tribune in Mark
[Antony]'s street with chariots, litters for rich Romans and donkeys, etc.

We didn't create this all at once but it is so true and clever that I am
convinced that the great Chronegk was in Rome only long enough to
change trains.

(We'll have to get Vishnievski to address not just the first citizens
standing near him but the whole audience. What if they are embarrassed
at first by this bold appeal! It doesn't matter!) . . .

In the museum we discovered many interesting things for the general
tone – wall-decorations and an opulent picture by Veronese – of a battle
in which there is good armour. We saw some remarkable statues . . .

That's far from being everything!! Goodbye for the moment. I embrace
you.

V. Nemirovich-Danchenko

200 Nemirovich to Stanislavski

July 25 1903
Neskuchnoe Estate

Dear Konstantin Sergeievich,

I don't know where you are, what you are doing, how well you are
resting. I would like to tell you something of our work on 'Julius Caesar'.
[. . .]

I hope that with the work schedule I have worked out things will go
quickly. Above all I must free myself from detailed work with extras. So
on the 5th I will divide up all the work and together with Burdzhalov,
Tikhomirov, Aleksandrov and Andreiev, once the plan has been fixed,
distribute the walk-on parts. The morning and the evening of the 6th I
will bring the crowd into the 1st act (154 people), on the morning of the
7th and of the 8th I will spend time with the individual heads of
department and in the evening I will bring in the crowd to the 1st act and
assign 5-6 extras to individual actors. We shall have to decide costume
and make-up quickly since just as in May every single corner was taken

up by material so now every single corner will be taken up by extras who are being pulled into shape and taught. The 9th they will work without me (I have to have one day a week when I am not rehearsing). The 10th with me again. On the 11th I start on the characters . . . I have the temerity to consider having a run of the 1st act on the 17–18.

My production plan is a complete treatise. God grant (something that is absolutely necessary) that I come up from the country with the plan complete up to the Forum scene. I still haven't started on the Senate. Everything is finished up to that point. But I have glanced at your scene and I like it, the Senate, very much – I am counting on it.[1]

I have prepared everything up to the Senate with great care and intend to dragoon the cast into what I have written with conviction. Including, incidentally, the role of Brutus . . . I know that you find it difficult to take advice and foresee much expense of time and nervous energy but I hope to win. Understand that I have got to know this role so well that it is now extraordinarily dear to me. I find Brutus an outstandingly sympathetic character, I know his tone, his face, his movement. I am equally enamoured of the role of Caesar. Wonderful!

I see the tone and tempo of the second act, especially for Brutus, *absolutely* differently from you. Quite differently too the Brutus scenes, the conspiracy, Brutus and Portia, and Ligarius. And I intend to follow my line without restraint. Portia and Calpurnia, who in Shakespeare are rather similar, are at opposite poles in my version.

The role of Portia came out very well but I really don't know how to cope with Savitskaya. I can't yet see Moskvin either. Kachalov must play Caesar.

One other thing I want to do, which I didn't succeed in doing in 'Pillars' (you were against it). Instil the tone and tempo of the whole act before passing on to individual scenes.

For the moment I think the most difficult will be the Forum and the Senate. It may be because I think that I haven't worked on them. [. . .]

In the meantime, we have to think what we will do if Chekhov doesn't deliver the play at the end of August.

My first choice is 'Ivanov'. Then there's 'Rosmersholm', 'Seagull', 'Bell' or (if we have the means) Turgenev.

'Lady from the Sea' would be good but there would be a delay with the estate.

And 'Ivanov' is terribly out of date.

At all events, we must be prepared for the fact that Chekhov will be late, although Olga Leonardovna wrote to me that he has gone off to the Crimea to work on the play again.

1. Stanislavski had written a plan for the Senate scene.

I still have 7 days in which to work. Less. I must get on with it.
I did the first act in 10 days and then three scenes in 6 days in all.
I really have worked.
I am feeling well but get tired quickly.
Farewell. I embrace you.

Vl. Nemirovich-Danchenko

201 Nemirovich to Efros

October 2 1903
Moscow

Dear Nikolai Efimovich,

I feel the necessity to convey to you my thoughts concerning your article of today [*Novostni Dnya*]. The following reasons cause me to write to you:

When influential newspapers respond negatively to our 'Julius Caesar' what is distressing is not the fact that they disapprove but the fact that they misread the theatre's intentions.

It is more distressing to me if you take a wrong stance concerning the play itself.

So that is why I am writing. I feel that the author of today's article, 'Rome', has not thought of that.

1. He emphasizes the interest the theatre takes in the sets, props and the construction side, but that, from our *very first* steps, never loomed large in our theatre. What emerges from your article is that the theatre took from the play those things which provided material for an external picture. That is a crude and distressing mistake. Crude enemies of the theatre have the impression that the strength of the production is in the 60 thou. it cost (it was twice as little) and the gathering together of European props. I consider such a conclusion concerning our efforts to be simply insulting to the theatre.

2. You have a false view of the tragedy (I thought you would). 'The soul of Brutus' cannot under any circumstances be seen as the centre of the tragedy. That is an absolute delusion. You cannot in that sense range the play alongside 'Hamlet', 'Othello', 'Macbeth', etc., (in that case Shakespeare would have called the play 'Brutus'). In the present play Brutus is the chief conspirator in that he is the only one to be motivated by pure republican feelings. In this play Shakespeare has abandoned his interest in a single human soul or a single passion (jealousy, ambition, etc.). In 'Julius Caesar' he paints a huge picture, in which the main interest is concentrated not on individual figures but on events as a whole: the disintegration of the republic, the degeneration of the nation, the

masterly comprehension Caesar shows of this fact and the *natural* incomprehension displayed by a worthless group, 'the last Romans'. The conflict and the dramatic impetus stem from this. How then is Brutus' soul not more than just one – admittedly one of the leading – figure in this conspiracy? True, Shakespeare makes a number of errors of historical detail but he has grasped *the spirit of a given historical moment and the events related to it* and also the amazing psychology of *human history*. That is the centre of the play and not individual characters.

3. *That was the main task the theatre set itself.* To portray Rome, the decline of the republic and its death-throes.

An old story!

We staged *the power of darkness* not Nikita and Matriona *and not details of peasant life.* We staged an historical picture and not Brutus and Mark Antony and the topography of Rome . . . We wanted to portray the decline of the republic and the birth of monarchy in a nation coming to the end of its history so we could have Brutus and Cassius and Caesar and a true picture of events.

Ideally they should all be there. In practice it's not possible. But above all there must be the overall picture. In this case – the spirit of a great historical event which occurs in the life of any nation: first the commune, then the emperor, then the republic and finally the monarchy which covers its weakness with external might. (Romulus and Remus, Tarquin, the Consuls, Augustus and others.)

These were the ideals we lived by as we staged 'Julius Caesar'. If we succeeded we did something great, colossal, artistic. If not – we are impotent.

If you looked at us more closely, if you, like a good chess player, had more faith in your partner and respected him more, then all would suddenly become clear. But it may well be, and here you are mistaken, that you regard Shakespeare from a somewhat primitive point of view – one that prevails in touring companies – which is fatal to Shakespeare's genius . . .

I hope this letter will not evoke anything other than friendly feelings in you.

Your V. Nemirovich-Danchenko

202 Nemirovich to Chekhov

October 3 or 4 1903
Moscow

[. . .]

I haven't written to you for a long time, I've been so busy recently. The play is finally on but I haven't had a real rest. 'Julius Caesar' emerged as a grandiose, broad canvas, and it is not for me to say but, it appears, painted by a bold and convincing brush. 'There is the breath of hell here' said the critic in a German paper.

That is what I wanted. That elevation of spirit that I experienced in Rome – I wrote to you about it – I wanted to put into the production. Judging by the innumerable curtain calls, I succeeded.

The success of the play or, rather, of the production, has been uneven. Grandiose in places if not in the sense of applause then in terms of the public enthusiasm and artistic influence.

In places less so and certain characters – the first of them I am very sorry to say Konstantin Sergeievich – did not go down well at all.

The audience fluctuates.

But I am absolutely convinced that the show as a whole is a great, a huge theatrical creation, and many details are disliked because they often occur in splendid scenes where not everything is beautiful.

Today's papers are full of big articles in which there is much excitement. They are quite fair. Not all, of course, are sufficiently wholehearted.

The mood in the theatre is good. We have not opened the season with a success like this since 'Tsar Fiodor' ('Ivan', 'Snowmaiden', 'Wild Duck', 'Small People') and at the beginning we are always in a sour, limp mood. Besides a colossal task like 'Caesar' was completed comparatively fast.

Our impatience as we wait for your play is acute. We are waiting, counting the days. For the moment we are reviving 'Lonely People' but that will be done in two, three weeks at most. By that time your play must be read, cast and the production plan written.

Hurry and, most important – *don't think for a moment you can be uninteresting!*

Goodbye!

I embrace you.

Vl. Nemirovich-Danchenko

203 Stanislavski to Chekhov

Monday October 13 1903
Moscow

Dear Anton Pavlovich,

Me angry with you? What right would I have to be? I can't see the reason. You obviously do not know how highly I respect you. If I were to hear that an accusation had been made against you, I would not doubt for a minute that right was on your side. Am I really incapable of understanding that you cannot finish a play on time and to order? To do that you have to be a talentless Krylov and not a genius like Chekhov. I'm not able to contain my impatience to read the new play and start rehearsing it . . . That's true.

I am haunted by the fear that your play will only get on stage at the end of the season and won't be able to create a sufficient stir for the public to form a more appropriate opinion of it once they have swallowed all the nonsense that will be written about it . . . The truth is that since yesterday we have all been longing for your play. Yesterday was a happy day. We have all come to life again after 'Caesar'. We performed 'Three Sisters' after a long break. In rehearsal last year's history repeated itself. We got together to talk through the play, got carried away and played it in full voice, just for ourselves. Yesterday we played it a second time for an audience.

It's a long time since I played with such pleasure.

It was received with enthusiasm and when the play was over there was an ovation at the door. It seems we played well. [. . .]

I must confess to you that I have only recently recovered from my failure as Brutus, which was hard. It depressed and confused me to such a degree that I no longer knew what was good and what was bad on stage. On the day of the performance, at night, I wrote you an account of the first performance but had to tear it up because it was written in such a dismal tone. Now the mood has changed although I am still not clear in my own mind as to where my failure as Brutus lay. My life became sheer drugery: 5 times a week I had to play an unsuccessful and exhausting role in nothing but a shirt and tights. That was difficult, cold, and you have the feeling, 'this is no use to anyone'. I await the play with great impatience.

> Faithfully and affectionately
> yours,
> K. Alekseiev

204 Marya Chekhova to Chekhov

> October 16 1903
> Moscow

[. . .]

I was at 'Julius Caesar' but did not see it to the very end, there were still three scenes to go and it was one o'clock in the morning. I liked it but I was not in raptures about it. In my view Stanislavski played better than anybody (they say he was on form that evening). [. . .]

On October 18 Knipper delivered the manuscript of *The Cherry Orchard* to the theatre.

205 Nemirovich to Chekhov

October 18 1903
Moscow

My very first impression is that as a theatrical work it is greater than anything previous. The subject is clear and firm. As a whole it is harmonious. The harmony is somewhat broken by the slowness of the second act. The characters are new, exceptionally interesting and will give the actors trouble in playing them but are rich in content. The mother is marvellous. Anya is very like Irina, but new. Varya has been developed out of Masha but has left her far behind. I feel there is outstanding material in Gaev but I can't grasp his character as I do the Count in 'Ivanov'. Lopakhin is splendid, new. All the minor characters, especially Charlotta, have come off very well. For the moment the weakest seems to be Trofimov. The most remarkable act in terms of mood, dramatic quality and toughness and courage is the last; in terms of grace and lightness of touch the first is outstanding. What is new in your writing is clear, rich, simple theatricality. Previously lyricism was predominant, now there's real drama which was only felt before in the young women in 'The Seagull' and 'Uncle Vanya'; in this respect there is a great step forward. There are many inspired touches. I am not all that worried but I don't like one or two coarse details, there is overindulgence in tears. From the social point of view the basic theme is not new but treated as new, in a poetic and original manner. I will write to you after the second reading without fail; for the moment I thank you and embrace you warmly.

206 Stanislavski to Chekhov

October 20 1903
Moscow

Telegram
I have just read the play. I am staggered, I can't pull myself together. I am absolutely bowled over. I think it is the best of all the beautiful plays you have written. I congratulate the author with all my heart. He is a genius. I feel and treasure every word. Thank you for pleasure given and greater pleasure to come. Keep well.

Alekseiev

207 Knipper to Chekhov

Morning October 20 1903
Moscow

[. . .]
They're reading 'Cherry Orchard' today. I decided not to go yet I want to.
I still don't know if I'll go. Konst. Serg, it can be said, has gone mad about
the play. The first act, he says, he read as a comedy, the second he found
thrilling, in the third act he was in a sweat and in the fourth he cried the
whole time. He says you have never written anything so powerful. [. . .]

208 Stanislavski to Chekhov

October 21 1903
Moscow

Telegram
Play read to the company. Extraordinarily brilliant success. Listened
entranced to first act. Wept in last act. Wife bowled over as everyone. No
play ever received with such unanimous enthusiasm.

209 Chekhov to Knipper

October 21 1903
Yalta

[. . .]
I had a telegram from Alekseiev today in which he calls my play a work of
genius: that means overpraise the piece and deprive it of the comfortable,
semi-success it will get if it's lucky. Nemirovich still hasn't sent me a list of those
taking part but I fear the worst already. He has already wired me that Anya is
like Irina, quite clearly because he wants to give the role to Marya Petrovna
[Lilina]. But Anya is no more like Irina than I to Burdzhalov. Anya is above all
a child, joyful to the end, knowing nothing of life and never crying, except in act
II, when there are only tears in her eyes. Marya Petrovna really does yearn for
every role she's too old for. Who's playing Charlotta? [. . .]

210 Stanislavski to Chekhov

October 22 1903
Moscow

Dear Anton Pavlovich,
In my opinion 'The Cherry Orchard' is your best play. I have fallen in

love with it even more than my dear 'Seagull'. This is not a comedy, nor a
farce as you have written, this is a tragedy, whatever escape towards a
better life you open up in the last act. The effect is enormous and is
achieved with half-tones, delicate watercolours. There is more poetry and
lyricism, theatricality in it; all the roles, not excluding the bit-parts, are
brilliant. If I were offered the chance to select a role according to my
taste, I would be confused, I am so drawn to all of them. I'm afraid all
this will be too subtle for the audience. They will not grasp all the finer
points quickly. Heavens the amount of nonsense one must read and listen
to about a play. Nonetheless the success will be enormous as the play
carries you along with it. It is such a complete whole that one cannot take
out a single word. Perhaps I'm biased but I cannot find a single fault in it.
There is one: it requires actors of extraordinary stature and refinement to
bring out all its beauties. We won't be able to do that. One thing shook
me at the first reading: that I was so quickly gripped and began to live the
play. That didn't happen with 'Seagull' or with 'Three Sisters'. I was used
to receiving confused impressions at first readings of your plays. That was
why I was afraid that a second reading of the play would not grip me. Not
a bit of it!! I wept like a woman, I wanted to control myself but I
couldn't. I hear what you say: 'Look you must realize this is a farce' . . .
No, for simple men this is a tragedy. I feel a special tenderness and love
for this play. I hardly heard any criticisms although actors love to
criticize. This time they surrendered almost immediately. And if a critical
voice is raised I leave and don't even bother to argue. I feel sorry for the
critic. Someone said: the best act is the 4th and the least successful is the
2nd. To me that's laughable, I don't argue. I just go through the 2nd act
scene by scene and this character is soon confused. The 4th act is good
precisely because the 2nd act is excellent and vice versa. I consider this
play peerless and not susceptible to criticism. If people do not understand
it they are fools. This is my genuine conviction. I will play in it with
delight, all the roles if that were possible not excluding Charlotta. Thank
you, dear Anton Pavlovich for great pleasure given and to come. How I
would like to push everything aside, free myself from the yoke of Brutus
and live in and work on 'The Cherry Orchard' the whole day. I dislike
Brutus, it oppresses me and drains my life-blood away. I hate it even
more now I have my dear 'Cherry Orchard'. I warmly shake your hand
and beg you not to take me for a complete madman.

Affectionately and faithfully
K. Alekseiev

An article by Efros in *Novosti Dnya* on October 19 1903 provoked a furious reaction from Chekhov as it contained inaccuracies concerning the plot. Chekhov sent a telegram to Nemirovich (now lost) and on October 22 Nemirovich sent two telegrams in response explaining that Efros had not seen the actual script but had based his article on information which he himself had given. Despite Nemirovich's explanation Chekhov refused to speak to Efros for several months.

211 Chekhov to Nemirovich

October 23 1903
Yalta

Dear Vladimir Ivanovich, when I gave 'Three Sisters' to the theatre and an article appeared in the 'Novosti Dnya'[1] *we both*, i.e., you and me, got angry. I had a talk with Efros and he gave me his word that it would not happen again. Then suddenly I read that Ranevskaya is living abroad with Anya, with a Frenchman, that the 3rd act takes place in some hotel or other, that Lopakhin is a kulak, a son of a bitch, etc., etc. What was I supposed to think? How could I suspect that you were involved? In my telegram I only had Efros in mind, I accused Efros only and I felt so strange, I couldn't believe my eyes when I read your telegram in which you took all the blame on yourself. It's distressing that you should have understood my meaning in such a way and even more distressing that it should have led to this misunderstanding. We must put the whole thing behind us as soon as possible. Tell Efros I no longer wish to know him and then forgive me if I went too far in my telegram and basta!. [. . .]

I still haven't seen 'Pillars of Society', or 'The Lower Depths', 'Julius Caesar'. If I were in Moscow now I would be in my seventh heaven for a week. [. . .]

212 Nemirovich to Stanislavski

October 26-7 1903
Moscow

Dear Konstantin Sergeievich,

I cannot believe that you are so insensitive as not to have felt how distressed I was during the last half hour at the 'Hermitage'. Strange things are happening. Before 'Depths' we were on the downward path, we were on our way to perdition. 'The Power of Darkness', notwithstanding all the brilliance of a talented director, was being staged in such a way that had I not

1. September 5 1900. See Chekhov's letter to Knipper, **87**, p. 82.

taken a hand in it we should have had a repetition of 'Snowmaiden', i.e., the play's a flop but Stanislavski is great. I worked on 'Depths' almost single-handed during the early rehearsals, i.e., I set the main idea of the entire production; a play must above all be a harmonious whole, the creation of one mind, only then will it take hold of people, but individual displays of talent are never more than individual displays of talent.

'Depths' was an enormous success. The theatre had suddenly achieved its proper heights.

And what did I get from you? Constant reminders that the production of 'Depths' was not truly artistic, that if we went on this way we would end up like the Maly, and that, everyone knows, is the worst kind of insult on your lips.

Never mind, I took it.

Afterwards I buried myself in work in order to make the season a success. I directed 'Pillars'. Nothing is said about it now. You consider my work completely negative.

I'll go into details later.

We decided to do the Turgenev [*Month in the Country*] and then came the moment when you lost heart because no one was helping you. And that in a comparatively simple production.

Then *you allowed me to decide* whether to do 'Julius Caesar' or not. I did decide and took on that enormously difficult task.

I saw it through to the end. Its success exceeded my expectations. The artistry of the production was universally acknowledged as enormous.

I thought that I had proved my ability to be considered a director worthy of the prestigious Art Theatre.

And what happened? I found myself alone with the two principal managers of the theatre, you and Morozov, for the first time. We discussed 'Caesar' *for the first time* and, with an amazement that beggars description, I found myself caught in a cross-fire – of praise and compliments? Oh no! of condemnation and reproach because the theatre was on the slippery slope, putting on productions worthy of the Maly (that word again, and, of course, in the most pejorative sense).

I cannot find words to express the emotions I felt.

So, I am supposed to believe you and Morozov when you say that five months of continuous work into which I poured *all* my spiritual energy, *all* my knowledge, *all* my experience, *all* my imagination, did not result in anything artistic. And I am supposed to believe you and Morozov when you say that I can draw on nothing from within myself which is worthy of that in some way wonderful theatre which you (and, by ricochet off you no doubt, Morozov) have created in your imagination.

Fortunately I have my own fundamental artistic beliefs which neither Morozov or even you can shake. The fact that you have the talent to create this or that particular detail better than I does not in any way alter my confidence in the value of *my* opinions. You don't recognize them. For you it's enough for . . . some pretentious woman in Zinaïda Grigorievna's circle to say there's nothing, alas, extravagant in my work, no whiff of game *faisandé*, for you that's sufficient to forget that the most important, the most essential, the most crucial element in any production is its inner meaning, the strength and beauty of the total picture.

You are always forceful when someone has been bending your ear, and capable of believing that the most important thing in 'Caesar' is not the overall interpretation but the costume of some Gaul. You even think that a good theatre is one which is attacked. That's something I have never understood, although I've given in to you a million times and am prepared to do so again many times but not when the theatre needs to be strong, robust and to fulfil its major task, of being a theatre of quality, with resolution. And not, naturally, when the production is my sole responsibility.

And had the discussion not taken place when Morozov was present, and not at a time when *the least disagreement between us* can play into the hands of his ugly schemes, I would have answered you at greater length.

I controlled myself and kept silent because I did not want to put a trump card in Morozov's hand – a dispute between you and me.

But I beg you to consider very carefully the sort of position I am being put in at the theatre. If someone else were in my place . . . anyone you like, after 'Julius Caesar' the theatre would have surrounded him with such praise that he would have started work on the next play with redoubled energy and love. The exact opposite is happening to me. The theatre's two chief managers, the Chairman of the Board and the Principal Director shifted onto me (despite their agreement to diminish my position), off-loaded onto me almost all their own responsibilities. I was so tired that I was *in tears* from working from morn till night, I suffocated from breathing the air in the theatre from 11am to midnight and after all my huge, my successful efforts they insisted that I am no artist.

How long do you and Morozov think that I can tolerate such a situation?

Let me tell you this: if 'The Cherry Orchard' did not belong to my dearest friend, I would send him a letter tomorrow and say that I cannot possibly *direct* it in two months but will look after the school and routine business instead.

I have no grand pretensions. In certain fields of artistic endeavour no one has more respect for you than I. But I really do wish that the two chief managers would not belittle *my* gifts. If this is not spoken from the heart but it turns out I am 'putting on airs' (I know these tricks), then it's just a silly game and not worthy of grown men and can only lead to my losing all desire to work. But if it is spoken from the heart then it points to profound differences between us and becomes a serious issue.

If this had happened at the end of the season, I would have met it head on. Now, unfortunately, we have work to do and nothing but work. *And must not put the theatre at the mercy of dogs.*

213 Stanislavski to Nemirovich

October 27 1903
Moscow

Dear Vladimir Ivanovich,

What a bolt from the blue! In God's name, what are you accusing me of, duplicity, conspiracy or just plain stupidity? You could only draw such conclusions if you were in the mood to pick on my every word. And one would think that the very fact that I spoke in Morozov's presence, knowing something of his plans, ought to have convinced you that nothing I said was derogatory. On the other hand, you must have a very low opinion of me.

Calm down and remember the sense of what I said. It was most innocent. If I criticized anyone it was myself. You were directing the play and I thrust my advice on you, this inhibited your independence and I wasn't able to carry my ideas right through either, because I was not directing the play. This dual responsibility for productions has worried me in the past and worries me now. I don't think we have found the right way as regards our work in common as directors and continue in that opinion. Didn't I say at the very beginning of the 'Caesar' production that we would have to make compromises and stage the play without artistic realism in the sense that I understand it? I stuck to that and did not press you to dirty the costumes and put patches on them. We decided that *on this occasion* it would be superfluous. [. . .]

I give you my word I do not sense your distress for a moment just as I can't imagine what it was I said that offended you. I was criticizing myself, not you. If I spoke so frankly it was precisely because your role as a director is so clear, firmly established, so evidently acknowledged by everyone that it wasn't you but *me* who was in the background, not me but *you* who took first place as chief director (I don't regret that). Were you really happy about the performance of 'Lower Depths'? Did you really consider it to be a model? How many times have I heard you give a negative answer to that very question. Whose fault is it, the actors' or the directors'? Isn't it our *duty* to raise that question?

Remember how we rehearsed the play, sometimes at top speed (at my suggestion) and others at your suggestion at the very opposite speed. Perhaps our dual responsibility confused the actors? Are such questions and doubts criminal on my side? Neither as far as 'Caesar' is concerned, nor 'Depths', have I ever said anything which could be considered derogatory or possibly insulting to you, on the contrary I have told everyone that it was *you* who found the tone for Gorki's play.

At the same time, you have never missed an opportunity to remind me of the failure of 'Snowmaiden' or 'The Power of Darkness' but, as you see, I have not taken offence.

As for 'Pillars' as you well know, I have always blamed myself for a bad set in which no one could act anything. The only reproach that can be made against you is that you accepted that bad set.

As for my being wilful while I was rehearsing the role of Bernick I was sorry for that and as Brutus tried to be different. [. . .]

So I foisted on you the responsibilities of the chief director? That very chief director whose name has been destroyed in the theatre and removed from the posters.

I took a different view. After the conversation we had when you said you were not satisfied with your position in the theatre and that you were sacrificing everything and getting nothing in return, I considered it my responsibility to hand over to you everything you thought necessary to take from me so as to strengthen your position and for the sake of our enterprise. I dealt with that question very honestly. I didn't sell you short but simply gave you everything that belonged to you by right. If you have the heart to tell me that you are the only one doing any work and that I am doing nothing and if you do not understand what I have sacrificed for the theatre –business, family, health which is in a far worse state than you imagine, then it is not worth living, working or believing in anyone. You work very hard and I honour you for it. It could be I deserve the same of you.

You can and *must* understand what it costs me to take on the unrewarding work as an actor which is laid on me . . .

In conclusion I offer you one thought: for 15 years I was used to being independent. For the past 5 years I have mastered my well-developed sense of pride and controlled myself. I now reconcile myself to many things which I would not have agreed to under any circumstances. I have schooled myself to turn a blind eye to scandalous incidents going on under my very nose. I get on with Baranov and Gromov whereas I cannot, any more than before, endure Shidlovska with whom I was for very long on good friendly terms. I see everything that is going on around me and I am silent.

Do you think I am not aware of the degree to which the theatre has declined? Do you think I cannot foresee in how short a time it will be brought to nothing? Nonetheless, I reconcile myself to the present and the future without bitterness or envy of any kind. I will be reconciled to suffering the fate of Sanin.

One thing I prize greatly. The right to voice my artistic 'credo' out loud. I am beginning to lose that right. You must have noticed how glaringly obvious this has become recently. If I speak to Tikhomirov *as a private individual* about his affairs (Tikhomirov knows my position in the school[1] – it amounts to nothing) I am told that I have made a mess of things and that students have left because of me. If I give any kind of advice everyone shouts 'He's messing things up' and no one takes the least trouble to consider my ideas in any depth. If I ask for someone to be fined – for blatant bad behaviour about which I would have created an uproar 5 years ago and had the whole theatre up in arms – my words are now quietly ignored and nothing is done. If I give any kind of artistic advice, 'crank' is written over everyone's face.

My ideas have produced worthless seed, actors are praised for it and I suffer, witnessing the desecration of everything I hold sacred and dear. But I say nothing. First because I am depressed and lack the energy or strength to carry on, to insist on having my way, and secondly because I shall never again insist on anything in this business of ours. I believe that if I am right the justice of my cause will vindicate me. If I am wrong then the time has come to recognize the fact and for me to devote the rest of my life to something really useful, perhaps in a completely different field.

Now I am resolute, I will not lift a finger to create any kind of new position for myself in the theatre. If I have started on the slippery slope then the sooner I hit bottom the better. I am a very reserved person by nature and say much less than I know. I turn over the theatre without a struggle. If it needs me then let me be treated with care and tact. If not, then let them get rid of me and (if it is inevitable) the sooner the better. Should the latter be the case, I shall no longer speak out so frankly. I shall confide my secrets to you and as for the theatre itself, let it use me and my energy as it thinks fit.

I reserve one right: if I come to the conclusion that my family needs me more than the theatre, I will come and say so (naturally without prejudice to the business) and you must agree to let me go voluntarily and not ask impossible sacrifices of me. The time has come for you to alter your opinion of me. I understand and feel more greatly and more delicately than I am able to express.

Affectionately and devotedly,
K. Alekseiev

If I have offended you in any way I apologize. It was quite unintentional.

214 Knipper to Chekhov

October 28 1903
Moscow

[. . .]

There's a lot of nonsense going on in the theatre. I feel sorry for

1. Attached to the Art Theatre.

Nemirovich. He directed 'Pillars' and 'Caesar' on his own. The plays are successful; he expended enormous time and energy on them, the more so since he is still a learner in this kind of work. But all the time he is made to feel that the theatre is in decline, that these productions are inartistic whereas 'Snowmaiden' – that was brilliant.

Today we had a first meeting to cast 'The Cherry Orchard'. V.I. arrived at the theatre in a very disturbed state. He was with me during the 2nd act and told me things were going badly for him. K.S. is talking the whole time of the decline of the theatre . . . If K.S. has anything against V.I. let him say it face to face and not to the merchant [Morozov].

V.I. has written K.S. a letter in which he sets everything out. He read it to Luzhski, Vishnievski and myself. He was in a terrible state and I can understand him. All this is not at all good. There must be fairness, openness and trust between K.S. and V.I. otherwise it will be impossible to work. Please God things will be smoothed over very quickly. But if Nemirovich goes I won't stay in the theatre. K.S. cannot be at the head of things. He's a hopeless mess. [. . .]

215 Nemirovich to Stanislavski

October 28[?] 1903
Moscow

I am in tears for having made you speak out to the extent you did. Nothing would have happened if Morozov had not been present at our conversation . . . Yesterday's meeting was inimical to me because we were not speaking as people sincerely devoted to the business but with some sort of ulterior motives. *I am very fond of you and value you highly* and it is good for me to work with you but when it *seems* that you are falling under influences which are hostile to my very soul then I become suspicious and everything I hold dear within me takes offence. I did not hear *one single* good word from Morozov concerning the enormous labour I accomplished and I started to shake inside when he took over the discussion.

But what can one do? Pride is so acute in the theatre! . . .

But everything you wrote about your own position is exaggerated *in the highest degree*.

Your V. Nemirovich-Danchenko

THE CHERRY ORCHARD

The Cherry Orchard brought Chekhov and the Art Theatre into serious disagreement. Efros' innocent article still rankled with Chekhov even when the mistake had been adequately explained. This obsession with a minor mistake is a strong indication of Chekhov's state of mind and all subsequent reactions should be judged in the light of it.

Stanislavski was desperate to start work on it. Responsibility for the production was to be his, although Nemirovich was careful to present himself to Chekhov, as always, as the true guardian of his interests. Feelings of personal loyalty or professional solidarity never seem to have prevented him from drawing attention to and distancing himself from the flaws in Stanislavski's productions.

No company set about its task more willingly but there were serious problems. First casting: Chekhov had written the role of Lopakhin for Stanislavski but Stanislavski did not want to play it and Lilina certainly did not want him to play it. Stanislavski had the sense to know that he could not play the 'new men', the Nils and Lopakhins. Gaev was his role, his class. Chekhov had to accept this and other casting which was different from what he suggested. Second and more serious: the problem of the nature of the play itself. Chekhov, having intended to write a farce and break his reputation as a pessimist, insisted that he had done so. No one agreed with him. In his attempts to impose his point he made statements which some critics have chosen to take at face value. His assertion that nobody except Varya actually cries is in contradiction to his own stage directions – Ranevskaya is twice instructed in Act III to 'weep bitterly'. As to his instruction that the last act should 'take 12 minutes *maximum*', that is a physical impossibility.

Chekhov, suffering the final ravages of illness, persisted in his view to the end and the last letter included in this volume is his protest against the play being described as a 'drama' on the posters.

216 Chekhov to Knipper

October 30 1903
Yalta

[. . .]

Stanislavski will be a fine and original Gaev but who is going to play
Lopakhin? The role of Lopakhin is central. If it doesn't come off then the
whole play falls apart. You don't have to play Lopakhin as a loud-mouth.
He doesn't absolutely have to be a merchant. He's a kind person.
Gribunin's not right, he should play Pishchik. God preserve you from
giving Pishchik to Vishnievski. If he doesn't play Gaev, I can't see
another role for him in the play, so tell them so. Look wouldn't he like to
try Lopakhin? I'll write to Konst. Serg. I had a letter from him yesterday.
[. . .]

217 Chekhov to Stanislavski

October 30 1903
Yalta

Dear Konstantin Sergeievich, many thanks for your letter, many thanks
for your telegram. Letters are now very precious to me because, first, I
am all alone here, secondly because I sent the play off three weeks ago
and I only received a letter from you yesterday and I would simply know
nothing were it not for my wife and would imagine anything that came
into my head. When I wrote Lopakhin I thought it was the part for you.
If for some reason it doesn't appeal to you then take Gaev. It's true
Lopakhin is a merchant but he is a decent man, intelligent, not petty or a
trickster and it seems to me, he is the central role of the play and that you
would do it brilliantly. If you take Gaev then let Vishnievski do
Lopakhin. It won't be an artistic Lopakhin but then it won't be feeble
either. In this role Luzhski would be a cold outsider, Leonidov a small-
time farmer. In choosing the actor for this role one must not lose sight of
the fact that Varya loves Lopakhin and she is a serious, religious young
woman; she wouldn't love a farmer . . .

Write and tell me which role you are taking. My wife wrote to me that
Moskvin wants to play Epikhodov. That's fine, the play can only gain
from it . . .

I still haven't seen 'The Lower Depths', 'Pillars' and 'Julius Caesar'. I
very much want to.

Your A. Chekhov

218 Nemirovich to Chekhov

October 30 1903
Moscow

[. . .]

Efros came to see me yesterday. He showed me the telegram in the *Yuzhni Krai* in Yalta[1] which states that the essay in *Novosti Dnya* 'is a crude hoax which bears no relation to reality'. Efros said, 'You understand the situation the paper is in, reassure me that it is not a hoax'. I reassured him with the reservation that when I read the account of the contents of the play in *Novosti Dnya* I discovered some inaccuracies. That evening, on the telephone, Efros asked me to retract that reservation but I refused. Yet today for some reason he did not use my letter. [. . .]

219 Nemirovich to Chekhov

End October 1903
Moscow

Dear Anton Pavlovich, I simply can't find the time to write a detailed letter. I have 20 minutes and I will try and be concise.

I have now read the play through three times.

I absolutely take back what I said about Anya being like Irina . . .

There are one or two little places which are too reminiscent of passages in previous plays. It is difficult to avoid the similarity in Anya's speech at the end of the 3rd act. The rest you can alter or not when I show them to you in 10 minutes, without getting up off your seat.

Simov had already gone to Nara to sketch motifs.

He has already collected motifs of the rooms.

He is in fine artistic fettle and is avid to put all his energy into the sets.

We will have trouble from Konstantin Sergeievich with this play . . .

I would already have started on the play if I were not worn out by boring work – first, all the routine things which, as never before, have fallen to me, second 'Lonely People', third, the school.

But the play must be put on in mid December.

Nothing has yet been decided about casting. We are trying out this and that but nothing definite. But of course *we won't cast without your approval*.

Ranevskaya, your wife. Possibly Marya Fedorovna but she would be too young-looking.

1. Efros' article had been reprinted in the *Krimski Kurier* and the *Odesski Novosti*.

Anya – Lilina preferably. She is not very young but her eyes and tone can be young. Marya Fedorovna is young enough but her eyes and tone won't be young . . .

Varya. Possibles are: Lilina (she's not keen, she's afraid of repeating Masha), Savitskaya (she doesn't meet with unanimity on the board) Litovtsieva – she, evidently, has the best chance. I recommend Andreieva but she doesn't want it, says she will be too aristocratic.

On the whole something strange is happening with this role. I really find it a successful character that will produce a great effect. It doesn't attract actresses as I expected.

This has happened before. Nobody wanted to play Caesar and I said it was a very effective role, I almost had to use brute force to make Kachalov famous.

I think I can see better than anyone what will work on stage. Charlotta, the ideal would be Olga Leonardovna. If not her then I think Muratova. Another candidate is being put forward, Pomyalova. But she is an actress without any artistic aroma. I don't like her.

Lopakhin. Everyone says Konstantin Sergeievich. I'm uneasy. Apparently he wants it. But he himself and his wife say that he has *never* played simple Russian people successfully.

On the other hand everyone's first impression was that Konstantin Sergeievich should play Gaev. Me too.

He is willing to play either. So we may well try out both.

He'll play whichever suits him better.

If he plays Gaev then the best Lopakhin would be Leonidov. That's a good combination. Gribunin can also play real, natural Russians. But people are afraid he'll be insipid.

If Konstantin Sergeievich is Lopakhin then Gaev can be either Vishnievski, or Luzhski or Leonidov. The first will be an imitation Dorn, the second an imitation Sorin.

Vishnievski wants to play Lopakhin but that's absolutely impossible. He's not Russian.

Pishchik, Gribunin. If Gribunin plays Lopakhin then Pishchick can be played by either Luzhski or Vishnievski. The latter is better. But Gribunin would be best of all.

Epikhodov, no one to touch Moskvin.

Yasha, Leonidov. Aleksandrov would be good too. Andreiev is begging to do it.

Trofimov, no one to touch Kachalov.

Dunyasha, Andruskaya, Khaliutina and if Marya Petrovna doesn't play Anya or Varya she would, of course, be ideal.

Those are all the combinations. I have been thinking like a chess-player. Goodbye. I embrace you.

Your Vl. Nemirovich-Danchenko

220 Stanislavski to Chekhov

October 31 1903
Moscow

[. . .]
I have decided on the following: to study and work on two roles –
Lopakhin and Gaev. I can't say which role I want the more. Both roles
are marvellous and to my liking. It's true, I am wary of Lopakhin. The
general view is that I don't succeed in merchants or rather they come out
stagey and calculated. Lopakhin is a decent fellow isn't he – warm-
hearted but tough. He almost buys the cherry orchard by accident and
then is thoroughly confused. He gets drunk because of that, I think,
doesn't he? Gaev in my view should be light, like his sister. He doesn't
even notice what he is saying. He understands after he has said it. It
seems I have found the tone for Gaev. He comes out, as I do it, something
of an aristocrat but a bit stupid. [. . .]

221 Stanislavski to Chekhov

November 1 1903
Moscow

[. . .]
Today we got down to the set-model. The 1st act is difficult. Olga
Leonardovna says there should be vestiges of the former upper-class way
of life. But shouldn't the house be somewhat or even very dilapidated?
Lopakhin says he will pull it down. That means it's no use at all.
Otherwise he would have turned it into a dacha and rented it out the
following summer. Or repaired it and sold it.
Is the house wood or stone? Or perhaps the centre part is in stone and
the wings in wood? Perhaps stone below and wood upstairs? Another
problem. In the third act there is a salon visible but in the fourth act there
is talk of a salon on the lower floor. Which of the two?
This summer I recorded a shepherd's pipe. It was the same shepherd
you liked so much at Liubimovka. It turned out splendidly and now this
cylinder will come in useful. [. . .]

222 Stanislavski to Chekhov

November 2 1903
Moscow

Dear Anton Pavlovich,
I seem to have found the set for the first act. It's been very difficult.

The window has to be down-stage so that the cherry orchard is visible both from the upper and lower parts of the auditorium; three doors; we need to see just a corner of Anya's room, a young girl's room and light. It is a communicating room but one should feel that here (in the nursery) it is cosy, warm and bright; the room has been emptied and one can sense a degree of shabbiness. Above all the set must be agreeable with a number of acting spaces. We seem to have managed that now. Do you remember Simov's showing you last year a model for Turgenev's 'Where it's Thin it Tears'? We decided, with your permission, to use the flats for the last act of your play. I have just looked at the model again and I am convinced that with a few small changes it will be suitable (for the 4th act). If you remember the model, have you any objections? [. . .]

223 Chekhov to Nemirovich

November 2 1903
Yalta

[. . .]

Now as regards the play.

1. Anya can be played by anyone, even a completely unknown actress provided she is young and looks like a little girl and speaks with a young, clear voice. This role is not one of the important ones.

2. Varya is a much more important role, what if Marya Petrovna [Lilina] took it? Without Marya Petrovna the role will seem banal and crude and I shall have to rewrite it, tone it down. M.P. won't repeat herself first because she's a person of talent and secondly because Varya is not like Sonya and Natasha; she is a figure in a black frock, a nun, not very bright, a cry-baby and so on.

3. Gaev and Lopakhin – for Konstanin Sergeievich to try out and choose between. If he were to take Lopakhin and was a success in this role then the play would be a success too. But if Lopakhin is colourless, played by a colourless actor, then both the part and the play will fail.

4. Pishchik – Gribunin. God forbid it should be given to Vishnievski.

5. Charlotta – question mark. It can't be given to Pomyalova, of course. Muratova would be good, perhaps but not funny. This is a role for Mme Knipper.

6. Epikhodov – if Moskvin wants it then so be it. He will be an excellent Epikhodov. I assumed that Luzhski would play it.

7. Firs – Artiom.

8. Dunyasha – Khaliutina.

9. Yasha – if the Aleksandrov you wrote to me about is the one who

works as assistant director then let him do Yasha. Moskvin would make a wonderful Yasha. I have nothing against Leonidov.

10. Prokhozhi – Gromov.

11. Station-master, who reads 'The Sinner' in act III should be an actor with a bass voice.

Charlotta does not speak broken but proper Russian; here and then she replaces a soft by a hard ending and mixes up masculine and feminine adjectives. Pishchik is an old Russian, crippled by gout, old age and too much eating, fat, with long coat (à la Simov), boots without heels. Lopakhin wears a white waistcoat and yellow shoes, he walks in great strides waving his hands, he thinks as he walks, going in a straight line. His hair is not short and so he often throws back his head; when lost in thought he combs his beard from the back forwards, i.e., from neck to chin. Trofimov seems to me clear. Varya – black frock, broad belt.

'Cherry Orchard' has been three years in the writing and for three years I've been telling you to engage an actress for the role of Liubov Andreievna. And now you're involved in a game of patience that has no chance of coming out.

At the moment I am in a ridiculous situation. I am here all alone and have no idea why. You are quite wrong to say that you are working but that nonetheless it is 'Stanislavski's' theatre. It's you they talk about, you they wrote about, while Stanislavski is being slated for his Brutus. If you go, I go. Gorki is younger than both of us, he has his life before him . . . As for the theatre in Nizhni-Novogorod[1] that's a mere detail; Gorki will try it out, sniff at it then forget it.

Be it said that popular theatres and popular literature are both nonsense, both a sop for the people. It's a question not of reducing Gogol to the people's level but raising the people up to his. [. . .]

Why does Marya Petrovna want to play Anya so badly? And why does Marya Fedorovna think she is too aristocratic for Varya? She's playing in 'The Lower Depths' isn't she? Well, I leave them to God. I embrace you. Keep well.

Your A. Chekhov.

On October 31 1903 *Novosti Dnya* published an article by Nemirovich which explained and corrected the errors in Efros' article on *The Cherry Orchard*. It would appear that when Chekhov wrote his first comment on it, on the 3rd, he had not actually read the article.

1. Gorki was attempting to create a theatre with help from Savva Morozov.

1. The Slavyanski Bazar, site of the first meeting between
Stanislavski and Nemirovich-Danchenko which launched
the Moscow Art Theatre.

2. Nemirovich-Danchenko's visiting card, arranging the
above meeting (See letter **2**, p 6).

3. Konstantin Stanislavski (1863–1938).

4. Vladimir Nemirovich-Danchenko (1858–1943).

These photographs were taken about 1898, the time they were co-founding the Moscow Art Theatre.

5. Savva Morozov (1862–1905), principal shareholder of the Art Theatre with Stanislavski and Nemirovich-Danchenko from 1898–1904.

6. The Art Theatre company in Yalta in May 1899.

7. Chekhov reading *The Seagull* to the actors and directors of the Art Theatre (1898). Left to right, standing: Nemirovich-Danchenko, Luzhski, Andreiev, Nikolaeieva; seated: Raevskaya, Vishnievski, Artiom, Knipper, Stanislavski, Chekhov, Lilina, Tikhomirov, Roksanova, Meyerhold.

8. The building at Pushkino where the Art Theatre rehearsed the first summer (1898).

9. A posed photograph signed by members of the Art Theatre, parodying the acting style against which they revolted.

10. Vsevolod Meyerhold
(1874–1940), actor and director.

11. Olga Knipper (1868–1959),
actress, later Chekhov's wife.

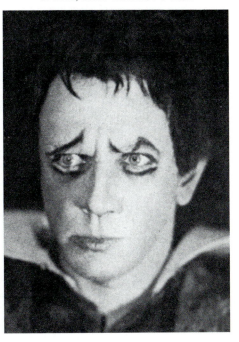

12. Evgeni Vakhtangov
(1883–1922), actor.

13. Michael Chekhov (1891–1955),
actor and director, nephew of
Anton.

14. Anton Chekhov
(1860–1904).

15. Leonid Andreiev (1871–1919),
playwright (left) and Leopold
Sulerzhitski (1872–1916), director and
assistant to Stanislavski.

16. Maksim Gorki (1868–1936),
playwright.

17. Mikhail Bulgakov
(1891–1940), playwright.

18. Proscenium arch and curtain of the Art Theatre, showing its art nouveau decoration and the seagull logos woven into the lower part of the curtain.

19. The auditorium with its stark seating and modest decoration.

20. The poster for the first production by the Art Theatre, Tolstoi's *Tsar Fiodor Ioannovich* (1898).

21. A production photograph showing Ivan Moskvin (Fiodor), Aleksandr Vishnievski (Boris) and Olga Knipper (Irina).

22. Chekhov's *The Seagull* (1898), Act I.

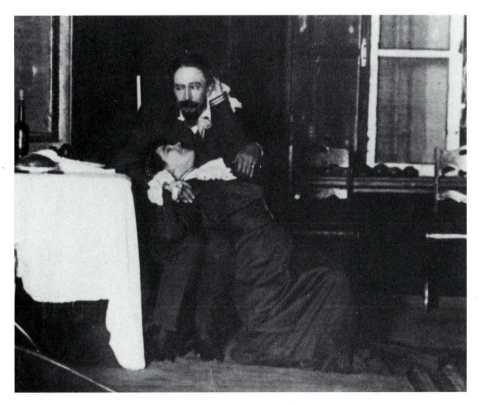

23. Close-up of the same production showing Stanislavski (Trigorin) and
Knipper (Arkadina), Act III.

24. Gorki's *The Lower Depths* (1902).

25. Maeterlinck's *The Bluebird* (1908).

26. Isadora Duncan (1878–1927), creator of 'free dance', at about the time she met Stanislavski in Moscow.

27. Craig's design of massive screens for his production of *Hamlet* (1909).

28. Edward Gordon Craig (1872–1966), designer and director.

29. The poster for Bulgakov's *Days of the Turbins* (1926).

30. The production.

224 Chekhov to Knipper

November 3 1903
Yalta

My little darling, hello! I am coming quickly although I don't believe my play will be done in December. It will be put off till next season, in my view.

As far as Efros is concerned, I won't write any more to you about it, excuse me, my own one. I have the feeling that I had raised a small daughter and that Efros had taken her and raped her. But it is ludicrous for Nemirovich to reply to some provincial newspaper . . . today in the *Novosti Dnya*, as if Efros had given a proper account of the substance of my play. Either Nemirovich didn't read the *Novosti Dnya* or he is afraid of Efros or he had some special reason. Whatever it is, it stinks. [. . .]

225 Chekhov to Knipper

November 5 1903
Yalta

[. . .]
I read Nemirovich's letter in the *Novosti Dnya* and only now understand the origin of the misunderstanding. He says there are no mistakes in the article but that there are many slips of the pen in the play and that in fact the drawing-room is called 'some hotel or other'.[1] If that's the case, tell them to change it, dearest; if they are playing billiards it doesn't mean it's a hotel. Is the text really not clear? But I still don't understand. I don't think Nemirovich would tell a lie just to protect Efros. So write and tell me what's written in my play, hotel or drawing room? If it's hotel then wire me. [. . .]

226 Chekhov to Stanislavski

November 5 1903
Yalta

Dear Konstantin Sergeievich, the house in the play is a large two-storey building. And in the 3rd act they talk of a staircase going downstairs. Although I have to say that this act III worries me greatly. In *Novosti Dnya* Efros gave an account of the contents of the play, then in one of the recent issues corroborated it (with not a little insolence be it said),

1. The word for drawing-room is *gostinaya*; the word for hotel is *gostinitsa*.

quoting Vladimir Ivanovich's letter, published at the same time. According to Efros, act III takes place 'in some hotel or other', in his letter VI. Iv. says that 'in its general, basic outlines the account of the play is accurate'; apparently there is a slip of the pen in the play.

The house should be large and solid; wood . . . or stone, it doesn't matter. It is very old and big, summer visitors don't rent houses like that; such houses are usually demolished and the material taken to build dachas. The furniture is antique, period, solid; dilapidation and debt have not touched the furniture.

When people buy a house like that they say: it's easier and dirt cheap to build something smaller rather than repair this one.

Your shepherd played well. It's just what we need.

Why don't you like 'Julius Caesar'? I like the play so much and will see you in it with pleasure. Probably not easy to play? Here, in Yalta, they are talking of an enormous, unprecedented success and I think you will be playing this play to full houses for a long time. [. . .]

227 Stanislavski to Chekhov

November 5 1903
Moscow

[. . .]

I don't know why but I would like to see the 3rd and 4th acts in the same set. In the last act stripped and ready for the departure. This is not, really, a matter of stupid sentimentality. I have the feeling that it will make the play cosier, because the audience has become used to the house. A second room brings a kind of messiness. Perhaps you need it so as to accentuate past riches even more. But that, it seems to me, comes over this way too. One set for two acts won't be monotonous as the ruin of the house completely changes the mood of the 4th act. We will go on working on the model and perhaps in the meantime you will write a couple of words . . . Another question: can Epikhodov and Dunyasha sit in Lopakhin's presence? In my view, yes. [. . .]

228 Nemirovich to Chekhov

November 7 1903
Moscow

Dear Anton Pavlovich,

We have problems with the casting not because there's no Ranevskaya but because we want to do everything for the best and because there are various back-stage considerations. Only you would be wrong in thinking that I would sacrifice the play to back-stage considerations.

My casting isn't exactly the same as yours – here's how and why. Alekseiev is chary of playing Lopakhin and, besides, Gaev is no less important than Lopakhin. Leonidov and Alekseiev is a better combination than Alekseiev and Luzhski or Alekseiev and Vishnievski.

Anya – Andreieva, in my opinion absolutely not. Anya, Lilina would be better but is a pity because her talent is needed more for Varya or Charlotta. So I have cast: Anya, Varya and Charlotta – a student, Andreieva and Lilina . . . Muratova as Anya would be dreary.

But I am not objecting to your casting. Generally I find one role a little better, another a little worse but that doesn't alter the play's success and interest. Lilina as Anya, Muratova as Charlotta, Lilina as Charlotta, a student as Anya makes no difference. One must remember that Lilina is not reliable as an actress and needs an understudy.[1]

Today we are finally giving 'Lonely People' and tomorrow we start work on 'Cherry Orchard' . . .

We must give Konstantin Sergeievich his head as director of 'The Cherry Orchard'. First, he has staged nothing for the best part of a year and in consequence has built up a great store of energy and imagination; secondly he understands you completely; thirdly he is long since free of his whims. But, of course, I shall keep a sharp eye on him.

The 'Morozovitis' back-stage grates on my nerves but one must be patient. In every theatre someone has to grate on one's nerves. In state theatres it's the bureaucrats, the minister, here, it's Morozov. The latter is easier to neutralize. One's self-esteem sometimes suffers badly but I like myself better when I surrender my self-esteem than when I let fly and create a scene. Fortunately satisfaction is not long in coming. [. . .]

229 Chekhov to Knipper

November 7 1903
Yalta

[. . .]

I have had letters both from Nemirovich and from Alekseiev, both, apparently, are bewildered; you told them that I didn't like my play, that I was afraid for it. Do I really write so incomprehensibly? Up till now I have only been afraid of one thing, that Simov would draw a hotel in act III. That mistake must be corrected. I wrote about that a whole month ago and all I get for an answer is a shrug of the shoulders; they obviously like the hotel.

1. Lilina was frequently ill and unable to perform.

Nemirovich sent an urgent telegram with a request for a response also by urgent telegram, who were to play Charlotta, Anya and Varya. For Varya there were three names, two I didn't know and Andreieva. It should be Andreieva. That's an astute arrangement. [. . .]

230 Stanislavski to Chekhov

November 8 1903
Moscow

[. . .]
We have rehearsals every day. They are working with great energy. One or two have found some interesting notes. There are some interesting hints in Olga Leonardovna's performance. I seem to have found something that's right for Gaev. My wife is playing Anya and has found a beautiful tone for Charlotta. We must get it into Muratova. In my thoughts I thank you every day for this play; it is such a delight to work on it. The rub – 'Caesar'. I want to put everything aside and think only about 'The Cherry Orchard'. I've just got away from everything, just got into the mood when along comes Brutus with a heavy, hot cloak, bare legs, cold armour and long speeches. You act and you feel it's no use to anyone . . . There's only one good thing about 'Caesar'. There's time to write these few lines to you which gives me pleasure but may not amuse you over much. [. . .]

231 Chekhov to Knipper

November 10 1903
Yalta

[. . .]
I had a letter from Konst. Serg. informing me that today, November 10, they are starting rehersals for 'C.O.' . . .
In his letter Konst. Serg. says that there will be one set for acts III and IV. And I am happy, happy about that as it means that obviously act III will not be done in a hotel, which, I think is what Nemirovich and Efros wanted.
[. . .]

232 Chekhov to Stanislavski

November 10 1903
Moscow

Dear Konstantin Sergeievich,
Of course there can be one set for acts III and IV, namely with the hall and

staircase. In general, you know, as far as sets are concerned, please, don't be ashamed. I assure you, I normally sit in your theatre open-mouthed. Without doubt, whatever you do will be beautiful and a hundred times better than I could have imagined.

Dunyasha and Epikhodov stand in Lopakhin's presence, they do not sit. Lopakhin is at his ease, he is a gentleman, says thou to her but she says you to him.

233 Lilina to Chekhov

November 11 1903
Moscow

Dear Anton Pavlovich,

At last we have been given our roles. And I am Anya: because when Vladimir Ivanovich read the play I fell in love with the part at once and started asking for it, something I have never done with any role and when I got it, I took fright because the most important thing in it is youth and I am 37.

Then there was a lot of discussion and the casting was left undecided, and I started to think about Varya and I saw her quite clearly. Blonde, plump, pale, neatly dressed and combed, very active and therefore often flushed and perspiring. She dreams of a monastery as the one place where there is no hustle and bustle. Sincere, honest, affectionate, adoring Anya and especially Ranevskaya, she speaks clearly but very fast, she is always in a hurry. But I am not playing her so it doesn't matter now.

As Anya my first task will be to fool the public and my immediate friends, even Vishnievski, who keeps telling me I must stop playing children. Everything must be young, even the legs; Vladimir Ivanovich laughed in amazement. 'Does it matter what the legs are like?' To my mind they are quite different, i.e., a girl's feet and a woman's feet.

When we read the play many people wept, even the men; I thought it was cheerful and even drove to rehearsals happily but today as I walked, I heard the sound of the autumn trees and thought of 'The Seagull' and then of 'Cherry Orchard' and I realized that 'Cherry Orchard' is not a play but a piece of music, a symphony. And to act this play one must be especially true to life but without the rough edges.

If it's not too much trouble write to me about Anya; how she is dressed, whether she is in love with Trofimov, what she thinks about when she is lying in bed at night. [. . .]

234 Stanislavski to Chekhov

November 15 1903
Moscow

[. . .]

The model for the 3rd act has turned out well. I am beginning to waver because the view of the distance is more interesting in this set. The most difficult model of all was the first act. It is quite simple on the ground-plan. It is designed to give a better view of the orchard. The set depends on the draughtsmanship; if Simov pulls it off it will be splendid, if he doesn't it will be bad. Nothing really definite is coming from the actors yet. But Kachalov is giving something interesting. Artiom, as usual, started with his Kurioukov (from 'Fiodor'). That means in epic tones . . . I am worried about Muratova as Charlotta. Big, with a man's costume, it could be crude . . . You write that your arrival depends on Olga Leonardovna. Unfortunately she is right not to ask you to come. The weather is appalling. Snow melts as it falls. The roads are churned up. Filth, stench. Very soon there will be frost. [. . .]

235 Knipper to Chekhov

November 15 1903
Moscow

[. . .]

We have been working out the 1st act for the last two days; now we are starting to rehearse properly . . . K.S. has come to life again with your play; the general mood is excellent, work will be joyful and good. That should give you pleasure. I am sending you the ground-plan for the 1st act. Understand? There's a big window and the cherry orchard could climb through the window. This comes out well on the model. The set is simple as you can see. A partition against which it appears Nanny sleeps. The entrance is from a suite of rooms. I drink coffee on the old divan No 1; the divan is like the one at Liubimovka, in the little connecting room, next to our dining-room. Remember? You have to climb up onto it. Pishchik dozes sometimes in the old chair, sometimes above the stove.[1] The scene between Anya and Varya: Anya sits on the stove, Varya on the chair near her. It goes very well; intimate, affectionate. You'll like it. I would like to rehearse all day and not leave the theatre. [. . .]

---

1. A ledge was often placed above the stove where people could sleep.

236 Sulerzhitski to Stanislavski

Early November 1903
Moscow

Dear Konstantin Sergeievich,

It is a few days since I saw Brutus for the first time but his image, his face, words, all that deep, rewarding, honest life and the death of a great man stand before us as though in life.

Up till now I 'knew' what Brutus was, I respected this 'type' if I can so express it. He existed only in the mind, in the realm of abstract ideas. You, your performance, transformed that beautiful but cold, classical statue into a living being, you clothed him in flesh and blood, you warmed him with tribulation and brought him down from his inaccessible pedestal and into men's hearts. You gave him the property of life . . .

It seems to me you did the most that an actor can do, achieved the highest goal which theatrical art can set for itself.

Is that not the purpose of art to transfer great ideas out of the realm of thought into the sphere of feeling so as to make them near and dear to every heart?

This was done beautifully.

When Brutus passed a difficult, sleepless night in his garden, I felt pain all over my body with him, there were the sore eyes, the dry, burning hands, there was the tense agonizing travail of soul, so completely, so intimately connected with life, truth and the duties of men.

I could spell out every individual movement, facial expression at every moment, the intonation of every word and yet I have only seen it once. In brief, I do not know a moment when Brutus was not Brutus in the best sense of the word.

It seems to me, dear Konstantin Sergeievich, that this is one of your best roles. I can say that because I know nothing of the actor's technique but that does not put me off. I am one of the audience and therefore have the right to speak . . .

In the theatre I have gained a new treasure – the touching, pure image of Brutus who has occupied his proper place in that far corner of the human soul where Buddha, Socrates, Epictetus and others live.

I am not writing to Alekseiev, whom I do not know at all; I write not as an acquaintance but as a member of the audience, wishing to join the actor in sympathy for Brutus who died as all fine things must die in this life where only lies can triumph. On the other hand eternal, single truth is for us what it was for Rome.

I write to the Stanislavski who more than once already has upheld and strengthened people in their belief in 'man'. Thank you once more for myself and for those who can only express their gratitude by applause.

Your L. Sulerzhitski

237 Sulerzhitski to Stanislavski

November 17 1903
Moscow

[. . .]

I saw it again. [. . .] Beautiful, beautiful . . .

Don't trust, dear Konstantin Sergeievich, anyone who is not enraptured by the performance of Brutus. Sometimes people do not understand themselves. People are incapable of appreciating your acting, your Brutus in the theatre. There is too much splendour, light, 'the real Rome' there, too much noise and movement, fascinating, beautiful movement for which we have to thank Vladimir Ivanovich; but when one goes home to bed then only does Brutus, moving, pure Brutus, emerge against the variegated background of noisy, radiant Rome. He gives one no rest and is a living reproach for everyone who sees him. That feeling is so profound that it is altogether impossible to give thanks for it and even more by applause.

Believe in yourself, we the audience need it. Don't trust me, trust yourself. I am convinced that you yourself feel satisfaction at your performance as Brutus. But you are worn down because you expected great approval.

But not everything receives immediate approval.

You are doing great things, you are doing them superbly, and so onward! Strike, strike, strike people's hearts . . . But it sometimes seems that you are timid and do not trust yourself. That should be impossible for you and Brutus!

L.S.

238 Sulerzhitski to Chekhov

November 17 1903
Moscow

[. . .]

Are they getting ready to do 'Cherry Orchard' at the Art Theatre? Kachalov wants to play Trofimov, the student, 'in a version of me'. I don't know if he will succeed in his intentions. Unfortunately I haven't read the play yet. It seems that unfortunately something is not going well with them at the theatre.

I hear that 'The Cherry Orchard' will not be directed by Vladimir Ivanovich but by Stanislavski. Will that be a good thing? [. . .]

239 Stanislavski to Chekhov

Wednesday November 19 1903
Moscow

Dear Anton Pavlovich,
   Again yesterday there was no time to write. I was busy doing the
second act and finally finished it. Please God the set will work. A little
chapel, a small gully, a neglected cemetery in an oasis of trees amid the
Steppes. The left part of the stage and the centre without masking flats –
just the distant horizon. This will be done with a continuous semi-circular
backdrop with supports to take it into the distance. In one place a stream
glistens, on a hillock a country house can be seen. Telegraph poles and a
railway bridge. Allow us, during one of the pauses, to bring a train with
little puffs of smoke across. That could work splendidly. Before the
sunset the town is briefly visible. Towards the end of the act, mist; it will
rise especially thick from the canal downstage. The concert of frogs and
the corncrake at the end of the act likewise. On the left downstage, a
hayfield with a small stook, in which the scene with the group of walkers
will take place. This is for the actors to help them live their roles. The
general tone of the set in the style of Levitan. Countryside – like Orlov
but not further south than the Kursk district. [. . .]

240 Knipper to Chekhov

November 21 1903
Moscow

[. . .]
   In terms of the set the second act will be splendid – you never saw such
a landscape. Wide, open and picturesque. [. . .]

241 Chekhov to Knipper

November 23 1903
Yalta

[. . .]
   Konst. Serg. wants to bring in a train in act II but I think we must stop
him doing it. He also wants frogs and corncrakes. [. . .]

242 Chekhov to Stanislavski

November 23 1903
Yalta

Dear Konstantin Sergeievich,

Haymaking normally takes place 20-25 June, at that time the corncrake does not cry, frogs also are silent at that time. Only the oriole is heard. No churchyard, there *was* one a very long time ago. Two or three slabs lying scattered about, that's all that remains. A bridge, that's very good. If the train can make its appearance without any noise, not a sound, then go ahead. [. . .]

243 Knipper to Chekhov

November 23 1903
Moscow

[. . .]

Things are going well for Konstantin Sergeievich as Gaev. I like it. Things going well for Kachalov too. Although Kachalov is now so much in fashion people like everything. [. . .]

244 Chekhov to Sulerzhitski

November 25 1903
Yalta

[. . .]

Trofimov isn't like you one iota. [. . .]

245 Nemirovich to Knipper

Before January 17 1904
Moscow

O. L. Knipper.

In my opinion this is how matters stand.

You are wearing out your nerves by performing.[1] Now they have lost their edge and resonance on stage. You are only acting in *preparation* for a role. No matter. In two or three days' time your nerves will have settled and your soul will sparkle and everything will be all right.

But then you must understand *above all* the two contrasting aspects of the role or, rather, of Ranevskaya's soul: *Paris and the cherry orchard.*

1. Dress rehearsal of *The Cherry Orchard* which opened on January 17 1904.

Outward lightness, grace, the *brio* of the overall tone are in evidence *every* time we skim over trifles which do not go deep into the soul. Even *more clearly* giggles, gaiety, etc. Such brightness will make the switch to drama more acute.

You managed to get away from yourself and that is something you must hang on to firmly. You can go forward firmly and boldly in these tones.

Why are you worried because there are 'no tears'? The drama will lie in the contrasts I spoke of earlier and not in tears which do not always reach the audience.

There!

V. Nemirovich-Danchenko

246 Nemirovich to Leonidov

January [?] 1904
Moscow

Lopakhin is healthy, strong: he bawls, the way peasants bawl, he shivers with the morning cold, the way peasants shiver. But you are half-hearted about it.

– 'You'll get about . . . twenty-five thousand.'

Do you have to think before 'twenty-five thousand'?

He has already given the matter some consideration, he hasn't just started thinking about the project.

In the 3rd act he plays the stroppy peasant.

He's afraid of the pause and so drinks straight from the bottle.

'My grandfather and father were peasants.'

He again acts with his eyebrows.

In the hall I want him more tense.

Before 'I could weep for it all', a lengthy pause.

Here's what I finally want to say. And I think it's of the greatest importance for the growth of an artist.

The role is going well at the moment; clear and good. But your acting in this play could get into a rut. After 10 performances you could get bored with playing it and revert to well-organized mechanics. How can you find something interesting?

Of course, partly in perfecting yourself in the technical sense. But that's secondary. Truly speaking, that is the result of other, more important, inward work: work on the image. If you play not just the script but the image, the living man, and not *play* it but *create* it more deeply, more clearly, more subtly then a performance can never lose interest for an actor. In every performance you can find a new character trait in some phrase or other and work on conveying it, embodying it, without changing the pattern of staging. Get to know every trait of this complex character more deeply and you will get farther and farther away from theatrical tricks and finally achieve a character which is not like Leonidov although it has been created by Leonidov.

Find a moment and show this to Konstantin Sergeievich. He will be able to explain it in more detail, with more understanding, as actor to actor.

V. Nemirovich-Danchenko

Gorki's attitude to the Art Theatre was complicated by his affair with a member of the company, Marya Fedorovna Andreieva, who later became his second wife. Andreieva was an erratic actress, often in dispute with Stanislavski who found her a 'ham'. She held extreme revolutionary views. In 1904 she decided to leave the theatre, feeling it had sold out on its original ideals. Later she went underground to pursue her revolutionary activities. Gorki suffered from an inevitable conflict of loyalties.

247 Lilina to Chekhov

February 25 1904
Moscow

[. . .]
This evening I thought I would be able to talk to you about Anya. You say my crying out is better now – fine; and so I say 'Farewell house! Farewell old life!' I say it with tears in the voice. I tried it out twice with a note of cheerfulness but it didn't work. How do you think it should be said? Tell Olga Leonardovna and she will pass it on to me. [. . .]

248 Nemirovich to Stanislavski

March 15 1904
Petersburg

[. . .]
Yesterday I went to see Gorki. He'll finish the play [*Summerfolk*] in a few days. He read a lot of the play to me. I formed one or two ideas. It's

still rough. He'll certainly have to rewrite. But there's a lot that's interesting already. Good female characters. Six young ones, that'll please the actresses.

And then he wants to start on another play right away. He thinks both will be ready by the autumn.

We spoke very frankly on the whole. Among other things he told me there was a period when he was thinking of breaking with the Art Theatre completely but Marya Fedorovna [Andreieva] persuaded him that he should not sever his connection with the theatre because of her. (He doesn't conceal his closeness to Marya Fedorovna, at least not from me.)

I was bored at first when I was with him because we both felt a wall between us and because of the presence of a third person (he had a guest) we couldn't remove the wall. But once we were alone we were able to discuss things . . . I left him late at night by the last train and will see him on Wednesday. He's coming to Petersburg. We parted on very good terms. [. . .]

249 Chekhov to Knipper

March 29 1904
Yalta

[. . .]
[Your brother and his fiancée] went to see 'The Cherry Orchard' in March; they say that in act IV Stanislavski plays disgustingly, that he drags it out painfully. That's simply appalling. An act which should last 12 minutes *maximum* takes 40 in your production. All I can say is Stanislavski has ruined my play. Well, I leave him to God. [. . .]

250 Nemirovich to Chekhov

April 2 1904
Moscow

Telegram

To date, not since I have been connected with the threatre have I ever known an audience react to the least detail of a play, the genre, the psychology, as they have today . . . The success in terms of general delight is enormous, greater than for any of your other plays. I can't decide how much of the success is due to the author and how much to the theatre. The overall mood backstage is contented, happy and would be complete were it not troubled by events in the East.[1] I embrace you.

Nemirovich-Danchenko

251 Chekhov to Knipper

April 10 1904
Yalta

[. . .]
Why do they persist in calling my play a drama on the posters and in press announcements? Nemirovich and Stanislavski absolutely do not see in my play what I actually wrote and I am ready to give my word in any terms you wish that neither of them has ever read my play attentively.
[. . .]

252 Kuprin to Chekhov

May 1904

[. . .]
I found you downcast, worried, bored, exhausted by the staging of 'Cherry Orchard'. Olga Leonardovna, who, she said, had to act as a buffer between you and the director was not in the happiest state of mind either. [. . .]

1. Japan attacked Port Arthur in February 1904.

PART THREE

DISSENSION

NINE

DISSENSION

The spring of 1904 marked the moment when the latent conflicts that had been developing over a period of two years burst into the open. It was a difficult time. Chekhov was gravely ill and died of tuberculosis at the end of June. *The Cherry Orchard* was the last play he wrote for the Art Theatre. He imagined that he had a natural successor, Gorki, and indeed nothing would have been more obvious than for Gorki to become the Art Theatre's own dramatist. An unfortunate letter from Nemirovich (letter **253**, pp. 194-200) destroyed all chances of that.

Nemirovich had expressed his reservations after seeing a rough draft of *Summerfolk*. Stanislavski, too, had his doubts but reserved judgement. When Gorki read the play to the company on April 18 1904 reaction was far from enthusiastic. Nemirovich could not resist the temptation to write a long letter of criticism the following day. Gorki never forgave him for it. He broke with the theatre and it was only out of friendship for Stanislavski that he subsequently allowed the Art Theatre to do *Children of the Sun*.

As a result of Gorki's break with the theatre Morozov, in his turn, withdrew his support, transferring his funds to Gorki who was trying – unsuccessfully in the event – to launch a People's Theatre in Nizhni-Novgorod. Morozov doubtless saw Nemirovich's letter as another shot in the war over the 'Gorkiad'. Only in the autumn of 1904 did he agree to maintain a minimal investment.

With Chekhov dead, Gorki alienated, Morozov's patronage withdrawn, both Stanislavski and Nemirovich realized they had to take positive steps to keep the theatre in the forefront. They needed to confront the new drama, mainly the Symbolists – Chekhov had already done his best to persuade them to stage Maeterlinck. It should have been the moment when the two men worked closely together. Unfortunately the crisis divided them, for while they agreed on the problem they could not agree on the solution.

The 1904-5 season was a comparative failure. Nemirovich's production of *Ivanov* was efficient but unremarkable, although it stayed in the repertoire for over a hundred performances. Stanislavski finally staged his evening of short stories, his miniatures, but not in the form he would have wished. His original idea had been to employ a 'cinematic' technique. He intended creating a small inner stage around which props and costumes would be placed in order to be able to effect changes and make the transition from one piece to another without interruption, thus building a specific rhythm. Nemirovich poured cold water on the idea and Stanislavski backed down, opting for a more conventional presentation. The evening, completed by Nemirovich's production of *At the Monastery* by Yartsev, was a failure.

It was at this moment of doubt and uncertainty that Meyerhold returned from the provinces, full of ideas and creative energy. It was agreed that he should resume his original role as Treplev in the planned revival of *The Seagull*. It was to Meyerhold that Stanislavski turned for artistic refreshment, thus precipitating a crisis.

The turbulence inside the theatre was matched in the world outside by a disastrous war in the Far East and the first rumblings of an impending revolution.

253 Nemirovich to Gorki

April 19 1904
Petersburg (?)

That the play, as read, was a failure is, I am afraid, beyond question.[1]

I will try and analyse why this is so.

The author is angry. This can be a distinct advantage when the object of his anger is worthy of indignation and when it is clear what exactly the author loves. But when the author's heart remains an enigma, when its beatings cannot be heard, when his sympathies are not clear or, what is worse, when his sympathies encounter no response and when the object of his anger cannot command attention then the listener remains indifferent.

'Summerfolk' was a matter of indifference to those who heard it for the whole four hours it took to read (!) and commands attention, at most, in four or five places.

The author is angry, generally speaking, because people have no capacity for life, they fear it, confine it, diminish its beauty, they rob and swindle each other and cover their rottenness of soul with the rags of fine phrases; moving in an atmosphere of aimless whining they admire only what is contemptible, fearing above all anything which leads to freedom and strength of spirit.

All that is fine. Bourgeois society – and society is still bourgeois – may not agree with the author. But when an author gives it a sound thrashing using artistic forms, any society succumbs to the magic of his artistry, surrenders to it, is rendered incapable by it.

1. For text see *Gorky: Five Plays* (Methuen 1988).

But we have none of that. The author's indignation does not emerge in artistic forms. Such a thing can occur for three reasons and all three reasons are present in 'Summerfolk'. The first is the vagueness of the author's beliefs. I do not know what he himself believes in. His beliefs do not emerge freely from the structure, they are not revealed in the individual characters, they do not percolate through the colours in which he has drawn these figures. The second reason for the loss of artistic quality is apparent at the point where I, the listener, begin to suspect that the author believes in the very things he is inclined to condemn, or is drawn towards those things he is most indignant about. Then his work loses its greatest strength – the strength of sincerity and clarity in his world view. The third reason is the ordinariness and flatness of the means used. The more banal the means the less interesting the work.

If I can develop these reasons further, I find that the author has no real love for any of his characters or, rather, cannot work up any affection for them. I am not speaking of these people as artistic images who appear as characters in a play. Gogol cannot possibly feel any love for the average town mayor but he cannot help but love Skvosnik-Dmukhanovski [the Mayor in *The Inspector General*] as an artistic type. Gogol cannot possibly feel any love for a miserly landowner who blights the lives of his wife and children by his avarice but Pliushkin is near to his heart and every feature of this type is dear to him . . . Without this love, this tender, affecting love towards one's artistic images, like the enormous, tender love found in a father's heart for his children, without this love there can be no work of art. Gorki could not possibly feel any love for Baron Butberg [the prototype for his baron] who is a drunkard and rotten to the core but he loves the baron as he appears in 'The Lower Depths' as his own son, as an artistic creation, as God loves even the most depraved people, and his love communicates itself to the audience, infects it and binds it to the work and its ideas.

Going through the dramatis personae and the stage directions I detect all three reasons.

Basov. He is not original. We have seen a lot of his kind on stage. He is a stock character and the author's negative attitude towards him is, of course, clear. But the author has not found anything new or independent for this character. He repeats the old and the hackneyed. This character is principally found in the creations of women authors or of dramatists who wish particularly to appeal to women. All his dialogue can be found in a large number of plays which have had a transient success on the stage of the Maly Theatre over the last 25 years. He is still uninteresting in Act Three although he is a little reminiscent of Kulygin [in *Three Sisters*] . . .

Varvara Mikhailovna. If one uses the painter's term 'to catch' then this character is 'caught' in the correct perspective. She is splendid in silence, splendid as she moves around with her hands behind her back, answers her husband intelligently and concisely. As with Basov, she is not new and many dramatic actresses have played such characters on our stage beginning with Ermolova. But there something about her the author is afraid of. He imposes scenes of unnecessary, really unnecessary, dialogue on her because he is afraid the audience won't pay sufficient attention to her. But that makes the character less distinct. Personally speaking, she is not a complex figure and she could remain silent right up to her splendid long speech on wasted souls in the 4th act . . . But the author forces her to talk unnecessarily. But despite the fact that this character is not very original it is possible to like her. Not as the heroine of a play – such a play would be superficial – but as a character in a large scene. But the author can't bring himself to like her enough to protect her from rattling on.

Still, she doubtless enjoys the author's sympathy. You are obliged to take notice and listen when you discover the author's own soul. And then comes a critical moment from that point of view: the scene between her and Marya Lvovna in Act Three and Varvara Mikhailovna's powerful dialogue.

'How afraid we are to live! We have a year ahead of us, perhaps six months' – etc.

I prick up my ears and, I admit, I am embarrassed. A 37-year-old woman, a wonderful person, an intelligent person, sees very clearly that she can expect nothing from her relationship with a crazy 25-year-old youth except six months of burning kisses. This 37-year-old woman, is saying, touchingly, marvellously, that she is simple and ordinary, that she has greying hair and three false teeth, and that she fears that her womanly pride will be humiliated; yet Varvara Mikhailovna, also a woman, who has the author's sympathy, is of the opinion that there is no cause for alarm here, that what she means is that she is 'afraid to live'!! Have it your way, but such a theory cannot count on having the least success. Society wants you to show it things that make its life better and more agreeable. Saving one's womanly pride. Marya Lvovna is the image of purity and goodness. And for that quality in her she, for all time, while the world exists, enjoys and will continue to enjoy people's sympathy. And if she is suddenly seized by a wild passion for a glamorous 25-year-old youth, the better part of mankind can only regard it as an enormous disaster, the kind which fills people with pain. And Marya Lvovna understands that perfectly well. And I am profoundly grateful to the author for not making her obey either Varvara Mikhailovna nor her stupid daughter Sonya, but for letting this beautifully strong character end as she should.

But from that moment Varvara Mikhailovna loses my sympathy as a person of distinction. And, truth to tell, as an artistic creation. Because I do not feel a harmony in three characteristics that go to make up this woman: the principle of 'the time is my own', indignation against a friend whom she accuses of neglecting her children, and a capacity for solitary and concentrated thought. In my view these characteristics do not come together in a single whole. The character is also spoiled by the scene with Shalimov . . .

Fortunately the scene is on the whole insipid. It can be found in the serialized novels of second-rate authors . . . And it depicts Shalimov as a vulgar individual, the kind portrayed by men in general and, as I said before, in particular by women-writers and women dramatists.

So, the author does not like Varvara Mikhailovna sufficiently not to sully the character with dubious traits.

Marya Lvovna is a rich, splendid character; in climactic moments her psychology is boldly, beautifully drawn. But the author can't bring himself to like her. It seems to me that he vacillates a great deal in his feelings towards her. But at least he does not belittle her with the platitudes with which the men in the play characterize her. Here, perhaps, emerges the general weakness of the play, the artistic weakness: on stage they talk too much, they all explain too much, demonstrating their opinions, be they intelligent or stupid, strong or weak and this results in such a plethora of judgements about life and people that it is difficult, not to say impossible, to distinguish one from another. Any feeling of art disappears when clear boundaries are lost in the mist. If a character is clear in itself, by its behaviour, its words and actions, the less it is talked about the more quickly it achieves the beauty of letters. But the author of 'Summerfolk' gives them too much liberty to exercise their tongues. It would be no bad thing if he were to shout at one or two of them, 'Stop arguing!'.

I called Marya Lvovna's daughter stupid but only with regard to the advice she gives her mother about Vlas. In herself, her tone, she is pleasant and her scene with her mother is touching. But I cannot escape the impression that over the question of how to deal with Marya Lvovna's all-consuming passion, whether to fight it or give in to it, that where that question is concerned, he does not achieve the stature of a great poet whose voice rings out loud and clear in the present age almost to the whole world. I cannot escape the impression that at this point in his play the author's soul is not free, that it has been precipitate in its desires. I cannot dismiss the hope that when the author rewrites these scenes, his enormous talent, which makes him such a wonderful human being, will prompt him with the real truth and that this truth will manifest itself quite differently and that people will receive this truth with joy and not perplexity.

Far be it from me to consider my convictions infallible or to be immodest enough not to listen to what Gorki has to say but all the same I believe that the 'good', in the profound, universally human sense of the word, does not lie in 'desires' but somewhere near or above them.

But in these scenes the author supposes the supreme good to lie in desires. I don't believe him. And when, after the scene with her mother, Sonya takes leave of Zimin and assures him that she will be faithful to him, I don't believe her . . . In Zimin's absence she will meet another student and discover a new lullaby with which to kill the memory of that farewell scene with Zimin.[1]

Another thing, I am not always happy with Sonya's witticisms. In fact I can't really call them wit. Like Vlas, she can't let a word pass without playing on it. That is wearisome.

Superiority of Kaleri. On the artistic side this is the character which pleases me most. And not just because she has the best passages in the play, because both of her poems are the best passages in the play, but because of her behaviour and disposition.

She is new because the author, unlike dramatic writers hitherto, has not turned this 30-year-old poetess into a cheap caricature. She is strong because she has been rescued from chatter and because everything she says is simple and sincere and accurately and aptly portrays her. She is attractive because the author – perhaps unconsciously – likes her, she rests in the sincerity of her soul. She is, in fact, original.

The author's pusillanimous attempt, in one scene (with Riumin), to make innuendoes against her when suddenly there is a whiff of the caricature of the poetic moods of 'old maids' and the fops among the decadents, is vain . . .

The superiority in terms of wit of Vlas's poem in Act Four loses force because it emerges as a protest against the impression created by Kaleri's poems . . .

Vlas's poem cannot destroy the impression of 'the snowball – of dead flowers'. There is just no substance in it.

In a word there is no disguising this rudimentary theatrical clumsiness.

The author cannot quite bring himself to blacken Vlas. This is a splendid character but I am not convinced that he stands head and shoulders above those around him. He is a fine figure of a young man, fair in his denials and he exudes the finest qualities of the finest down-and-outs but when I compare him with all the others I don't think he has the right to cast accusations of being spiteful at them. And Dvoetochie treats him exactly right, I mean that Vlas may turn into a fine person but for the moment he is still 'all adrift'. And so, if I am to take Vlas for a genuine person after the first act then I can only feel deceived later. He too, is no more than a character for a big scene.

His witticisms only pleased me in the bout with Kaleri.

---

1. At the end of Act Three Sonya sings a lullaby.

In order to go on to the other characters I have first to establish the following position.

A year and a half ago, in the finest dramatic work produced in Russian literature for the past 25 years, 'The Lower Depths', the author produced a speech on the necessity for human respect.

Among the Buddhists there is a great and moving custom: when someone is dying they go to the dying man and tell him the good things he did in his life. And these memories comfort the dying man. And as Buddhists believe that the better his life was up to death the lighter his sufferings will be after death, he will meet death more easily as the passage from one life to another.

In this custom, as in Luka's speech which is put into Satin's mouth, there is so much love that it is able to cleanse our souls of all that is base. And as the Buddhist respects his Gottama through this loving ceremony, so Russian audiences hold dear every word their poets utter. And when Gorki read his play he himself was in tears because of his love for people. And that made him a great man, the Gottama of the Russian theatre.

What has happened since? Who has angered him so much that he has written a play in which there is such a level of fury that it is impossible to speak of 'human respect'? It is easy to understand his being angry with life for sending people great tribulation and sufferings that no one needs. But none of this can be seen in the play. Only Marya Lvovna suffers from the tempest of life and that is why I spent so much time on her and her torment. But the author dealt with that quite easily and so it is not life as a vale of tears and grief that excites his spirit . . . Is it society? The people he sees all round him?

Who? And what is it about them that exasperated the author so? Basov? There's nothing there for Gorki to waste his talent on. Let writers of weaker calibre sharpen their pens on him . . .

Basically all the anger falls on four men: Basov, Suslov, Shalimov and Riumin. And from that one can conclude that the author has suddenly become a convinced feminist. So be it. But how did he get there? With Suslov he keeps within artistic bounds and Suslov leaves an impression of a strong and living character. I have spoken of Basov already. But Shalimov and Riumin are so insipid, hackneyed and insignificant they do the play no good . . .

Let me add that the author's setting and staging (the picnic in the wood, the garden and the stage rotunda in front of the house) provide, I am afraid, poor material for an interesting production. I was struck the whole time by the highly critical thought that the mediocrity of the characters is matched by the mediocrity of the theatrical conception. They reinforce each other and deprive the audience of everything which is interesting and artistic in the play.

I will now try and sum up.

'Summerfolk' gives an impression of a total lack of clarity both as a 'play' in the strict sense of the word and in terms of the author's ideas. Probably this springs from a lack of centre in the general picture, a centre both in the sense of the plot, i.e., the external material (or, at least, the strict arrangement of the characters in perspective) and a centre in the sense of inner content.

The author has an inexhaustible, rich treasury of judgements on life. They are scattered throughout the play, given to all the characters but without the author's own clearly resounding voice being heard or with such sermonizing that they are impossible to accept because it is inconceivable that such sermonizing should belong to Gorki.

All this is more like material for a play. The author needs to distinguish precisely those who deserve his sympathy from those who arouse his anger. The author must clear the play of all the mediocre elements he himself cannot believe in. The author needs to take his characters to his heart as an artist and those he cannot feel affection for he must get rid of entirely.

It seems to me that sufficient work of this kind could result in a more interesting play, even in the absence, strictly speaking, of a plot.

But the most important thing is for Gorki to find himself and his sensitive, rewarding, lofty heart!

Nemirovich makes no mention of one reason he disapproved of the play: the evident parody at the end of the first act of Act I of *The Seagull*. For the Art Theatre to stage that scene could only have caused offence, whatever Gorki's intentions. Gorki agreed to look at the play again and give Nemirovich some idea of his progress in mid August. His resentment, however, soon became apparent. He could hardly take kindly to being told that he was dealing in stock characters out of 'women's' literature.

Nemirovich was taken aback by Gorki's reaction to his letter. Over the next few months he attempted to put matters to rights without being entirely sure where the real problem lay. It is characteristic of Nemirovich in all his relationships that when things went wrong it never seriously occurred to him that the real source of difficulties was his own conduct or error of judgement. He looked for an outside cause, usually third parties disrupting a relationship – in this case, Morozov, his *bête noire* and Andreieva.

254 Nemirovich to Gorki

End of June 1904
Neskuchnoe Estate

I've been in the country for six weeks, in the peace and quiet, working
in a very concentrated fashion, and reflecting, and every time I think
about the past season there is a wound in my heart – your relationship to
us recently. 'Us' means the Art Theatre. Your unfriendliness is somehow
linked to a cooling off on Savva Timofeievich's part. How this came
about, because of you, or him or Marya Fedorovna's discontent is
impossible to sort out. But six weeks have passed and I cannot shake off
the feeling of some kind of blindness. Every time I get anxious and ask
myself the question: why?! And every time the answer is a confusion of
thoughts, a bewildering array of exasperated relationships, misunderstood
circumstances, false conclusions, those uneasy impressions which feed
and grow upon unverifiable suspicions. This confusion is locked in my
soul and with all my heart I feel the *injustice* of this burden. In my last
conversation with Savva Timofeievich, without any weeping and wailing I
raised this question several times – why? The conversation lasted several
hours. That should have given me more than enough time to reach an
answer. But instead of an answer there was just confusion.

Recently I have returned more than once to these reminiscences: I am
starting to think more about the coming season. I am thinking, you will
soon be rewriting 'Summerfolk' or starting a new play with brilliant
scenes, characters and ideas in it. The theatre that does this play will have
glorious, living work. But you might not give it to us!

Why?

I feel this may well happen. I could accept this blow as inevitable, I
could even see that it is merited but even in that I cannot trust myself.
When I think back over the theatre's relationship to you I cannot find a
single circumstance that might cast a shadow on our sincerity and
admiration for your talent. And I really am not saying that because I
represent the whole theatre in my own person. What I say goes for
everyone. The energy we brought to your plays, with the exception of
one or two lazy people, is well known to you. The joy people have when
they see you you can observe on everyone's face whenever you come.
You and the Art Theatre should strive towards the same end. Its
importance, worthy of your name, you have never denied, even at the
end of the current season.

You were committed to stay with the theatre and work for it as long as
it did not deviate from its purely artistic path or as long as its behaviour
was not so shameful that you found it personally offensive.

There is only one reason for your coolness towards the theatre and that
is easy to understand. That is because Marya Fedorovna, whom you love,

considers – right or wrongly – that she has been badly treated by this theatre. Hence your irritation which it would be stupid of me not to take into account. But, in the first place M.F., who is sensitive to your work, persuaded you not to sever your connection with the theatre. Secondly let time decide who is right and who is wrong in this dispute. [. . .]

255 Nemirovich to Stanislavski

July 13 1904
Neskuchnoe Estate

[. . .]

I can tell you for certain that my play[1] will not be done in the coming season. I will work all the time but not finish. I want to prepare it sufficiently for it at least to be completed next year. It's a pity but we'll have to accept it. The thing is it would have to be finished by 15-20 August. But I fear that my absence in such a period will ruin the season. And what if the play doesn't come off? It's too risky a game. So I have done some work on 'Rosmersholm' and on 'A Month in the Country' and I am setting up the miniatures. (Still working on my play).

When I went to Anton Pavlovich's funeral I thought we ought to put on 'Ivanov'. I told Luzhski about my idea. He told me that he had received the same suggestion from Vishnievski. And then all round they were saying that we should stage 'Ivanov'. They even said we should start the season with it.

To start the season with it will not work, as we can't oblige Olga Leonardovna to be there at the beginning of rehearsals. Besides it will turn into Chekhov's second funeral and not a show. But I am beginning to form a general idea of the staging . . .

Don't begrudge a few roubles to wire me in Yalta, Hotel 'Rossia' and tell me whether you like the idea . . .

Perhaps we could manage to stage 'Ivanov' and 'Rosmersholm' during the season? The season is long and dangerous. The Gorki might even arrive. I want to write a letter to him.

I have already spoken to Olga Leonardovna about 'Ivanov'. Both she and Marya Petrovna and Ivan Pavlovich [Chekhov's brother] are very happy about it . . .

I am writing to Morozov about 'Ivanov'. [. . .]

---

1. Nemirovich had started on three plays. None was ever finished.

256 Nemirovich to Stanislavski

July 25 1904
Yalta 'Rossia'

[. . .]

Savva Timofeievich is against staging 'Ivanov'. He says 1) That the play is old and has already been done in amateur performances (that's not true, it has never been done with any kind of seriousness). 2) The play isn't suitable because Knipper is too old for Sara (Sara is under 30 and she is ill) and will ruin the role as she ruined Ranevskaya (!). 3) The interest in Chekhov that was aroused by his death will run out before the production of 'Ivanov' (I think that an affection for Chekhov has been revealed in Russian society which we could never have suspected. Never in his lifetime was he set alongside Pushkin and Tolstoi and above Turgenev and now that is almost universally the case). 4) I suggested 'Ivanov' only so that Olga Leonardovna could have a role 'that is very beneficial in her grief but unnecessary for the theatre' . . . (not worth an answer). 5) 'It's an old note for the theatre' (that's absolutely true but contradicts Savva Timofeievich's basic demand to do five productions a year. Surely he's not suggesting five new notes a year?

I think the opinion you express in your telegram[1] is precisely right. If we are to stage 'Ivanov' then it must be now. Or never.

Artistic success will be great, financial success is in doubt. Finally we shall have to put off the question till we have a meeting . . .

But Savva Timofeievich is also against 'Rosmersholm'. But we can't put off decisions about the play one day beyond August 10. I have no hope about Gorki.

You suggest opening with 'Seagull'. With Marya Petrovna? Can she be at rehearsals even in September?

We could also start the season with 'Ivanov'. I think we must get Olga Leonardovna to Moscow as soon as possible. To work. She is just sitting on a stool and weeping all day. She has a strong constitution but she will soon undermine it. And she herself will soon be bursting to start work.

Why do you fear the funereal mood in Maeterlinck? I am counting on this show more than any other in the season and on 'Sketches'.[2]

257 Stanislavski to Nemirovich

Mid July 1904
Contrexéville

Dear Vladimir Ivanovich,
One thing after another and you and I are the whipping-boys.

1. Lost.
2. An evening of short pieces adapted from Chekhov. It opened on December 21 1904.

1. We have lost two dramatists.

2. Savvuchku [Morozov].

3. A useful actress [Andreieva].

4. I think, for a time, an absolutely essential actress (I mean Olga Leonardovna who will need a lot of time to recover).

5. No repertoire.

6. You can't finish your play.

7. My wife is ill and not recovering.

8. Kachalov is looking for fresh woods.

9. Vishnievski is winning laurels in Yessentuki and is artistically outgrowing us.

10. The war and its effect on the coming season.

11. All the plays (Yartsev, Chirikov) are being done by Komissarzhevskaya in Saint-Petersburg and we have nothing to take on tour.

12. We must expect our actors to be called up for the war any minute.

13. I have lost confidence in myself as an actor and my poor health has convinced me that I must accept being in the second rank. [. . .]

There is just one plus to set against all these minuses. The friendly work of those who love and understand our theatre. We are few. So we must do even more to forget everything personal, the struggle to be first, and other weaknesses and petty passions that degrade us and do the impossible to save the season and the theatre.

If that does not happen we will live through our last year.

I picture the season as follows:

Maeterlinck (might have a certain artistic success but in financial terms mediocre) –

        15 performances @ 1300 roubles   20,000

Naidenov and Yartsev (as I am very doubtful whether Chirikov will be allowed) –

        15 performances @ 1300 roubles   20,000

Miniatures, I think, won't go and if they do only at school matinées –

        15 matinées @ 900 roubles   14,000

I won't believe the Chirikov will happen until there is a censored copy.

'Cherry Orchard' (perhaps, because of Chekhov's death the play will finally be understood) –

        15 performances @ 1300 roubles   20,000

'Uncle Vanya' (ditto, because of Anton Pavlovich's death) –

        10 performances @ 1500 roubles   15,000

'Three Sisters' (for the same reason) –

        5 performances @ 1300 roubles   7,000

'Seagull' (revived with a lot of new sets) –

        15 performances @ 1500 roubles   23,000

'Lower Depths' –

        5 performances @ 1300 roubles   7,000

'Pillars' –

     5 performances @ 1200 roubles 6,000

'Fiodor' I hear will be banned.

'Sunken Bell' – no actors.

The rest are sold out or taken out of the repertoire.

So at a rough estimate

     100 performances   132,000

Total performances (say) 180 with a budget of 210-220,000 . . .

We need 80 performances with takings of 78,000, i.e., three plays, or, if the Chirikov is banned, *two*.

The Chirikov is nil in artistic terms but could prove profitable –

     20 performances @ 1300 roubles 26,000

'Ivanov' – must be staged or we lose it forever. I don't think it's profitable but with a good production might succeed

     25 performances @ 1300 roubles 33,000

? some play or other of considerable interest.

If it's yours then the season would be complete (I don't believe in the Gorki however he rewrites it).

You can't find a play that would have 35 performances.

With 15 performances of play? @ 1300 - 20,000.

Then the season is covered financially.

So which play?

In the first place I propose 'Above our Strength' (Björnson) if we can get it past the censor.

Second place – Ibsen's 'Ghosts'.

Third place – Strindberg's 'The Father' as there is much talk about the boldness and audacity of the writer.

Fourth place – 'A Month in the Country' because we do not have the strength to gather motifs and put on the play as we would wish.

I will say nothing about 'Rosmer' as for the present I don't understand the play.

An appalling job – practically impossible. Nonetheless it will have to be done by three or four of us.

Maeterlinck is a new note in the literary sense.

Miniatures also new in the formal sense.

Naidenov and Yartsev are a slight compromise, which gets lost on the rest of the repertoire. The Chirikov (?) the same.

'Ivanov' }
'Seagull' } our debt towards Chekhov.

Björnson, Ibsen, Strindberg – the old but honourable note. To appear reliable.

I have spent a very bad summer as usual and the death of Chekhov has shattered me, travel took up all the rest. I hear you had an unsatisfactory break.

I am troubled by something which none of us is responsible for . . . and no one can in any way correct it. As regards the funeral and other initiatives to immortalize the memory of Chekhov our theatre has been on the sidelines. Nonetheless we must think of something for the coming season. Apart from some kind of series of Chekhov performances (I call them a Chekhov week), apart from a special Chekhov production (I forgot to mention this most important matter earlier) created from miniatures and his *vaudevilles*, e.g., 'Calchas' (never performed), 'Jubilee', 'Marriage', 'The Dangers of Tobacco' . . ., etc.; apart from all that we must think of something; could be a prize for the best play, could be a grant somewhere . . .

I am also concerned abut the following: Chekhov, Nemirovich, Gorki give us their plays for Moscow and Petersburg. Why do young people, like Yartsev and Chirikov, who are absolutely necessary to our theatre, only given us their plays for Moscow? That's disadvantageous not to say impossible for that way we ourselves build the road to Petersburg. Komissarzhevskaya, to crown it all, will steal our production and our role will appear worthy but . . . stupid. I say all this notwithstanding my distaste for monopolies . . .

Then I am very worried about Kachalov. I know he needs more work but I also know that his health won't allow it.

He is playing in 1) 'The Uninvited' (*L'Intruse*) 2) 'Ivanov' 3) the Naidenov or 4) the Yartsev, 5) 'Rosmersholm' or the Strindberg. Isn't that rather a lot? [. . .]

I have read the following out of the miniatures. I enumerate all those which are suitable for the stage and those which, while they cannot be done as they stand, are worth considering. I have put them in three categories:

I – transfer directly, not always profound or significant but full of character, beautiful or new in form;

II – transferable but needing adaptation or reworking by a director or a writer;

III – those we can discuss although they are considerably in doubt.

[Stanislavski lists and categorizes 55 short stories by Tolstoi, Gorki, Turgenev, and Sleptsov]

258 Nemirovich to Stanislavski

After July 26 1904
Yalta

But I, dear Konstantin Sergeievich, have been in rather more cheerful mood and more optimistic in outlook recently.

1. We had already lost Chekhov after 'The Cherry Orchard'. He would

not have written anything more. As regards Gorki, if he writes a play we
shall have it, I am sure of that.

2. We have lost 'Savvuchka' [Morozov] as you call him. We may still
keep him.

3. A useful actress (Andreieva) – yes. But a big 'troublemaker' for us
and our affairs.

4. Olga Leonardovna for the moment? No. Now she will devote herself
to the stage and very quickly. She is bursting to act and to get back to
Moscow. She will return about the middle of August. We must find work
for her.

So Marya Petrova is not making good progress, that's awful. I so
wanted her to act.

Kachalov is not leaving. Vishnievski – can't we really steer him onto
the right path?

The war? You know, having paid great attention to it I am beginning to
believe that by the time our season opens there will be one victory after
another. And that will raise the spirits of society.

Of all those among our actors who could be taken away [into the army]
the only really visible loss would be Gribunin. The rest would not
diminish the theatre's essential flavour and attraction.

You are wrong to lose faith in yourself as an actor and if poor health
keeps you in the second rank you will shine there as though you were in
the first.

There will be friendly work without any doubt. As far as the
'championship' is concerned we are both thoroughly seasoned. Anything
that might be harmful in that sense we have lived through. If we have not
chewed each other up by now then there is no danger. You know, like a
married couple. If we have got through five years we can get through
fifteen. I give all the honour of our stability to you but I profit from what
I have been through.

. . . You also seem pessimistic about the takings.

Maeterlinck 15 @ 1300? Then it wasn't worth taking it. I think, $10 \times
1600$, 5×1400, 5×1300 = about 30 thousand.

Miniatures should give a lot more. You're afraid that they won't go.
I'm afraid too, to speak candidly. But I'm only afraid of the
designers. Simov will live and die as Simov. Only that worries me.

Here's probably what we have to overcome:

1. The number of productions. Very difficult but not impossible.

2. The design department.

We must make a final decision on the whole repertoire in the first half
of August and during August work out the composition of the miniatures.
And then work patiently.

I accept all the plays you suggested to me. The Björnson, 'Ghosts',

'The Father', 'A Month in the Country'. I don't mind which. All I want is parts for everyone. Up till now I simply haven't seen Savitskaya, Vishnievski, Moskvin and you.

Not only have I not finished my play, I haven't even sketched it out. It's maturing nicely. I don't want to mess it up.

There's too much Chekhov in your minatures.

As regards 'Seagull': *either* 'Seagull' *or* 'Ivanov'. Both, more than Chekhov's other plays, are monotonous.

I am refraining from all work so as to gather strength and freshness of reaction.

Don't rush into work (from August 2). Take rehearsals *quietly, cheerfully, not in a scramble*. You can do a lot in three hours a day. Let the actors enjoy themselves during the first rehearsals and don't stop them from doing what they want . . .

Don't lose heart and take from the theatre what gives you *pleasure*. Let Savva Timofeievich say that we 'don't love our business'.

I hope very much to retain an overall confident, active tone. That, in essence, is all my work now. Let there be a smile on every face! If the actors are happy and set to work cheerfully then everything will go well. [. . .]

259 Nemirovich to Gorki

End of July/beginning of August
1904

Most respected Aleksei Maksimovich,

August 15 approaches. At our last meeting you suggested that you would give me news of the state of your new play at about that time . . .

When it comes down to it . . . you write plays and the Art Theatre has the right to decide whether to stage them. That it has earned that right by its work I am ready to defend whenever and wherever you like. That this right is based on a warm and often enthusiastic relationship to you you cannot in any circumstance doubt.

That means, it is possible for me to ask you about you and your play simply in my capacity as manager of the theatre.

However, I take this opportunity to add that if I can be useful to you in the near future concerning things which, as you yourself once said, bind us together professionally, useful by my experience and honesty (you have had many opportunities to be convinced of that) – *since previously* I set everything aside so as to be able to talk to you, I will do so. I want to emphasize a thousand times that my relationship to you, both as a writer and as a person, is absolutely unchanged.

That, I think, goes for everyone at the theatre.

260 Nemirovich to Knipper

August 11 1904

You remember I wrote to you telling you that I had written a letter to Gorki? I asked him what state his new play was in and finally believed that my relations with him were unchanged.

I received the following answer: 'I have decided to rewrite the play from scratch and then anyone who likes can perform it. As for your belief that our relations remain unchanged I can only tell you that it is my relation to other people rather than their relation to me which has always been important and of interest to me. A. Peshkov. [Gorki].'

I find it difficult to take this insult.

261 Nemirovich to Gorki

After August 11 1904

Aleksei Maksimovich!

The time will come when you will realize that you have insulted me, though there was no reason for it on my part, and you will be sorry for it. Or rather I am convinced that you did not realize how deeply hurt I would be by your letter. At this moment I am incapable of setting your insult aside. To demand an explanation – you wouldn't give one and, indeed, it is obvious that right now it would not lead anywhere, but to strike back at you with the kind of words you used to strike at me – that I cannot do.

Vl. Nemirovich-Danchenko.

Since *Summerfolk* was being revised the Art Theatre asked permission to stage *Enemies*.

262 Gorki to Stanislavski

December 2 1904

Telegram

Notwithstanding my personal liking for you, Nemirovich's conduct towards me obliges me to refuse to allow the theatre to produce 'Enemies' and further to decline any kind of connection with the Art Theatre.

Stanislavski began to feel he was getting nowhere in his attempts to shake up his colleagues and force them into some kind of positive action. The problem was that many of his schemes were insufficiently thought through. Hence his increasing reputation for being 'muddle-headed' and 'cranky'. Ideally it needed someone to shape his ideas into practical form. In the view of Stakhovich, Stanislavski's friend and member of the Board, that was the role Nemirovich should have played. However, Nemirovich's sense of the need for stability and for maintaining the present order made him unwilling if not incapable of undertaking such a task.

263 Nemirovich to Stanislavski

1904/5
Moscow

Dear Konstantin Sergeievich,

I wanted to speak to you while my thoughts were still fresh in my mind . . . The third day I started to write, but each time because of a new influx of *these very* thoughts, I put everything aside but still everything comes out as before.

This is what I wanted to say, *dear and beloved* Konstantin Sergeievich.

You are not just. You are not just at all. *You are being unfair.* And because you are neither just nor fair, you find fault, you confuse other people and then get into a terrible state and confuse yourself. You are a great man. But when great men get confused unbelievable chaos ensues.

Concerning me. You think I am in a lazy mood at present. You are greatly mistaken. I am full of energy but I am tactfully deferring to you in everything but you are pushing me around right and left. And at the same time you think I am just being lazy and being a hindrance. You are not just towards the company, not just towards the work, in short, not just towards anything. You are already in a state of nerves. Perhaps you remember what I said at the first discussion on 'Julius Caesar'. I managed to contain you with difficulty and spoke in such a way as to prevent you getting into the kind of state of nerves when you act in such a way as to create confusion all round you.

Your mood gets everyone down, including me, and on the whole there is no laziness but a desire to work on many people's part.

Some means must be found to counter this if the theatre is not to go under.

I think I possess that means.

Don't hold it against me, for the sake of the institution. Marya Petrovna says that you are in a state of torment when you have to accuse me of something. In what way do I accuse you? I don't accuse you, I don't want to accuse you. I merely say that of all the things you insist on having half are impracticable and a quarter absolutely unnecessary. But you insist on things, get upset and find fault.

Don't be angry with me.

Your V. N–D

In April 1905 Meyerhold presented Stanislavski with a plan for a Theatre-Studio, a term he had invented. Seeing that he was making little or no progress in the Art Theatre, Stanislavski set up a small company of young actors under Meyerhold's leadership, at his own expense, taking and converting for them a theatre on Povarskaya Street. This despite the fact that he had always maintained that he had no money available to subsidize the Art Theatre. Nemirovich disliked the whole idea but sent the obligatory telegram of good wishes when the young Studio company began work in Mamontovka, not far from Pushkino where the original company had started its life.

Matters took a much more critical turn when, working on some of the ideas he had discussed with Meyerhold, Stanislavski began to try out new rehearsal techniques, including improvization, on Knut Hamsun's *The Drama of Life*. Gone were the long discussions, the minute preliminary literary analysis. This was anathema to Nemirovich. It flew in the face of everything he held most precious and threatened the whole practice the theatre had carefully built up over a period of five years, a practice in which, nominally at least, literature came first. Nemirovich was faced for the first time with Stanislavski at his most wilful and determined. He was spinning out of control. The whole balance of the agreement reached at the Slavyanski Bazar was in jeopardy. Nemirovich began to wonder if it had been anything more than a passing illusion. He had to bring Stanislavski back into line. His rage, frustration and disappointment were poured into a letter written between June 8 and June 10 which ran to some twenty-eight tightly written manuscript pages. The letter was based on a draft prepared on June 5. As in the case of the breach with Gorki, Nemirovich sought an explanation in malign outside influences. In this case the culprit was Meyerhold. In his attempt to reassert his authority and superiority Nemirovich first sought to discredit Meyerhold by denying him any originality of thought and second to prove to Stanislavski that without a restraining hand he was destined for self-destruction.

264 Nemirovich to Stanislavski

June 1905
Neskuchnoe Estate

Draft

[. . .]

Over the course of so many years we have struggled, worked; every play, in rehearsal, was one long piece of research and experiment for us, we boiled in the crucible of the theatre itself with intense energy, had our quarrels. In the last two years a desire has sprung up in our school for a new movement in the theatre; there were tattered copies of 'The World of Art'[1] strewn all over the stage of the small theatre, unending discussions abut Belkin, Schtuck, Hamsun and d'Annunzio, I dug up 'The Drama of Life' (thanks to Adruska), I discussed my experiences when staging 'At the Monastery' with Meyerhold, said how naturalism was played out, but all that passed you by, it did not touch you. And suddenly it all becomes a revelation on Meyerhold's lips.

That's an insult not only to me but to all the young people. He said: 'We don't need any of these discussions.' I said: it is essential to work out the tone in which the play is to be done; you reply: that's a detail. And then, of course, the first thing you yourself try to discover is precisely that tone. And you discover those very *discussions* which are the result of the vast body of practice we have built up.

Then Meyerhold said that one must go on stage on day four and act the play. And you found that a wonderful idea and when I protested you became angry with me.

In God's name where is the justice in that?

Samarova told me that the whole change in your attitude towards me came from Meyerhold and that he was destined to play the same role between us as Marya Fedorovna played between me and Gorki . . .

Marya Fedorovna wanted to create conflict between you and me, without success. Morozov wanted to force me out of the theatre, without success. Gorki all but laid down conditions for his play – my removal – that didn't happen. Could the least of these people succeed? I am not greatly worried because I never think about it. I mention it because it came up by chance.

But one fact stares us in the face: your relationship to me is now uneasy.
I have done nothing on my side to deserve that!

I could easily hold many things against you this season. But in the end I am always quick to justify you and explain your behaviour because I never doubt that *basically* your attitude to the theatre is deeply beneficial and always most sincere. That is your greatest quality, I want to emulate you. That is why I am writing you this lengthy missive.

1. The magazine of a group founded by Diaghilev in Petersburg.

I am doing everything I can to preserve our relationship, difficult though it is, for the unity of the theatre. I am ready any time you wish to repeat out loud my total respect for you and my love for your talent. But to behave towards me in the way you have behaved these last two months is something that has never happened in all our 7 years together. You do not love me, respect me, I count for very little. I demean myself by speaking of it so directly. Think about this. I do not think I will be able to bring myself to speak of it again. [. . .]

265 Nemirovich to Stanislavski

June 8-10 1905
Neskuchnoe Estate

Letter

Dear Konstantin Sergeievich,

Your attitude towards me has become very strained. I am sure you would wish, with me, to remove this strain?

Because I feel that our relationship is going through a critical period. Not to clarify it now could result in a fatal, a disastrous error.

You relationship to me became incomprehensible not with that ill-fated discussion over 'The Drama of Life' but much earlier. Even in Petersburg I detected a new kind of note. The discussion over 'The Drama of Life' was only the explosion of combustible material that had been building up for a long time. I have been conscientiously going over everything that passed between us this season in my memory to see where I might have been guilty towards you.

I will go through the entire season.

Maeterlinck [Triple Bill]. A flop. Your accusation that I declined to help the production of the Maeterlinck has reached me. I attach no importance to it. Flops always lead to unfairness. People have to blame someone. I have often been unfair to you in similar circumstances. These are trifling considerations which are lost in larger concerns.

But I take this opportunity to emphasize one consequence of all this. I can only be really useful when I think deeply about a play and concentrate on getting to know it properly. When I am alone, and delve into it independently and stir up everything within me that is capable of responding to it. I cannot do this with other people or through discussion. Discussions need time to settle in my mind. If this time is not available however much I am bullied and pressured, even accused of bad faith, I am as much use as a block of wood. I think: yes that's not bad, but that's good too, it could be this or perhaps it could be that. I have no fixed, definite opinion, coming from within.

And this is true not only for directing but for all occasions in life.

You have encountered this trait in me more than once.

But I did not give the Maeterlinck any great thought. It was agreed that during the summer I would write my play (which I had abandoned after Chekhov's death) and in the autumn I was well into 'Ivanov'.

'Ivanov' was put on. In that regard I have nothing with which to reproach myself as far as you are concerned.

You found the production of 'Ivanov' inartistic. That is *not a fault*. The success of 'Ivanov' after the failure of the Maeterlinck upset you very much – I can understand, even sympathize completely with you. Of the whole production of 'Ivanov' I only really felt satisfaction with the 3rd act which flowed from the heart of me. But you, it seems, thought I was proud of my directing in 'Ivanov'. And all too often you tried to make me feel how inartistic the production was. That was unfair and cruel. You didn't want a failure did you?

In fact everything that can be inferred from your charges against me apropos of 'Ivanov' and which, perhaps, was subsequently reflected in your attitude towards me, is unfair. [. . .]

You approved the model for the 1st act. We settled on the right tone for the actors in the 1st act together. Then you had to go to the Crimea to rest. In the meantime I prepared the third act and started on the second. I simply could not be satisfied with the second. It did not work, even the author got it wrong. But I had an idea what would draw an audience in that act. We could not agree on a number of details. But it would have been strange to insist that I stage it in a way I did not feel, even though you hold the right to the artistic veto.

4th act? Could I really not have staged it much better? Just give me time and the means for another set and postpone the production for 10 days. I decided – and I don't regret this at all – that 'Ivanov' wasn't worth it. And in the end I saved the opening of the season and secured its continued existence for two months. Is it really just to reproach me with that?

Of course it would have been much more effective to postpone the opening for two or three weeks, get the 4th act artistically right (which had gone stale because of the actors) and add 15 thousand to the budget.

No, there's no point in dragging it out. You were unfair if you were angry with me over 'Ivanov'. You really were, knowing as you did how essential it was to have a success as quickly as possible, simply a success.

You behaved badly, sending me a telegram in Petersburg. You suspected me of resting on my laurels. While in fact I was not even dressed by 7 in the evening but spent all my time thinking how to carry on with the season. I laboured with triple energy.

I was deeply offended by that telegram but I forgave you as I could feel what an artistically troubled, dissatisfied mood you were in.

Then came the business of the miniatures for you and 'Monastery' for me. We both, i.e., you and I received 'wounds that still have not healed'. Both of us were the victims of the necessity to provide novelties before the holidays. You sacrified your artistic idea, I did mine.

On the other hand though 'Monastery' was a blow for me you never heard it from me.

But first to the miniatures.

Haven't you always blamed me? Wasn't it I, indeed, who in your mind, destroyed your idea?

That would be a fresh injustice.

You haven't forgotten surely that I spent 6-7 days on the whole presentation of the miniatures and convinced you and Suler[zhitski] that you should not put on such a show . . . Then you were convinced that it was more difficult, in practice, to act the miniatures than a complete play, that there was not an Aliosha and Mitya Karamazov or a Snegirev in the company, not enough painters and props men and – most important – no permission from the censor for interesting items (Tolstoi banned). And then Gorki removed an entire item[1]. Why put the blame for a half-baked idea on me? Do you really not understand how unfair that is?

On the other hand isn't it curious that the real artistic dissatisfaction I experienced over 'Monastery' passed you by unnoticed?

You didn't find the right style for Maeterlinck, I wanted to find it for 'Monastery'. Without the least pretension to compete with you – I beg you to believe that – I was motivated only by the desire to break out of a realism we have had enough of and hit upon a new style for new authors, including Ibsen. I wanted to combine subtle, elegant characterization with the voice of lyrical poetry.

And what happened? I only received a fully sympathetic response from the young – Germanova and Petrova. Our 'Pillars' – Knipper, Kachalov and Leonidov not only tried, in a very crude manner, to drag me in a hostile fashion towards a narrow, weak realism but presented my efforts to you, during the intervals in the evenings, in terms of vulgar backstage tittle-tattle. The remaining actors either ridiculed my endeavours (Vishnievski, Luzhski) or were jealous because I saw in Germanova a future juvenile lead (like Knipper, Litovtseva, etc.). My suffering was unendurable but it was aggravated still further by the fact that I could not carry the day. The play did not help the situation, there was not enough time and I couldn't involve you because you were fully occupied with the miniatures . . .

I built a whole repertoire in terms of a search for a new style – 'Lady from the Sea', 'Gioconda', 'Aglavaine et Célisette', perhaps the Przbyszewski. The time will come, and perhaps very soon, when you will experience to the letter all that I experienced at that time. Only then will

---

1. Refers to Gorki's refusal to allow *Enemies* to be staged (see **262**).

you understand as you should, in what real pain a director exists when he is looking for one style in opposition to prejudiced actors trained in another.

Yes, but you do in fact understand what I am saying. You have so often stood alone in such circumstances you can understand perfectly well right now. No one understands better than you. But when they set you against me, your customary nobility of character still helped you not to be swayed entirely.

I cannot forget one conversation after a rehearsal when (as with Sara in 'Ivanov') I wanted very much to stimulate a real, lyrical uplift in Olga Leonardovna and she listened to me, listened, and suddenly said, 'Tomorrow I will rehearse Olga with a cigarette'.

That was disastrous! Disastrous because of its realism!

Or like Kachalov who, at the first performance, without consulting me, played a completely new character, diametrically opposed to what I wanted, making new moves and new cuts in the part. [. . .]

I have had pitched battles with Vishnievski and Moskvin (super-realistic actors) about the necessity to find a new style on stage. At my first meeting with Meyerhold, I spoke of the necessity for a new style in the theatre. That gave him an incentive to offer his services.

Now suddenly Olga Leonardovna – prime enemy of the new style – wants to act in 'Aglavaine et Célisette', is longing to play Knut Hamsun, says she dreams of playing Hedda Gabler and other Ibsen heroines.

It is my profound conviction that such aspirations are disastrous, there is nothing in her that's right for these roles but the fact is the poison has taken.

For her Meyerhold is suddenly revealed as some kind of innovator; he speaks of a new style and new plays as though no one had ever thought of them before.

But you were so remote from my artistic experiments – we didn't even have the time to discuss them – that all this seemed new to you, but coming from the outside, and not from the crucible of our own theatre.

I repeat if the miniatures are an open wound for you, so is the 'Monastery' for me – but infinitely deeper because it is a long time since I have been fired by a genuinely artistic experiment of that kind, because I experienced total failure and because even the fact that I was experimenting passed unnoticed and any originality was attributed to other people.

You have a very jealous attitude to what you are doing. I am infinitely more modest in that respect. In 'Ghosts' I endeavoured once more to enhance the poetic spirit of the work. And my efforts sank into the waters of Lethe a second time. For that reason they don't trust me. Not because they don't trust me in general but because our company is poisoned by realism, which has been reduced to a narrow naturalism. And if 'Iskusstvo', a new magazine, condemns the production of 'Ghosts', it is not entirely wrong. The ruin of our theatre is, I am convinced, not the absence of new forces but the fact that the old forces have no wish to rise above the portrayal of everyday life. Of those participating in 'Ghosts' *only* Savitskaya understood and felt the elevated, symbolic form I wanted.

But knowing Moskvin, Kachalov, Knipper and Vishnievski well as excellent realist actors, I did not insist too hard on poetic characterization in 'Ghosts'. I knew my words would be spoken to the wind.

I am digressing rather. But I profit from this opportunity to state to you my heartfelt conviction, one that has grown over the last two years, that without *really strong* poetic characterization the theatre will fade away and die. Chekhovian, gentle, somewhat lyrical people have had their day. You saw that brilliantly in 'Seagull' . . . I see real poetry in Brand and Agnes, in 'The Lady from the Sea', *undoubtedly* in 'Gioconda', in 'Aglavaine et Célisette', etc. What we must do to revitalize the life of the theatre, what measures to take with the actors, what changes to effect in our directorial *habits and tastes*, where to show courage and conviction in the selection of actors and casting, what to wash our hands of, what to set our hand to to support it, I simply do not know. How best to exploit the old ways, the fixed, confident styles of our older actors for the continuing success of the theatre and when to allow oneself to go forward boldly towards the new, I don't know that either. But, in my opinion, at no time in the last five years have we needed to be as closely and firmly united as now when we both feel the need for renewal and can both display our *experience* in the cause of that renewal.

And this precisely at the moment when our relations are strained! . . .

I think there are too many people around you who spend all their time poisoning our relationship. God forbid, I am not referring to Marya Petrovna [Lilina]. On the contrary I am convinced that she sees an advantage for you in our close relationship. The people I mean are in the theatre. . . And there is one example – I don't want to mention names – when one person quite intentionally poisoned our relations. I am beginning to see that it was to this gentleman's advantage for us not to be too close. Faced with our absolute closeness and confidence in each other he lost every time.

I return to the search for the cause of your change of attitude. We ended the season on good terms. We had kept the theatre alive.

But then something happened. Your attitude towards me became shrouded in fog.

Thinking over the way you have been these last two months I find that you have, as it were, *cast off all restraint*. During the last 4-5 years you agreed to a number of restrictions on your artistic nature. You trusted, as it were, my *reason* and allowed that *reason* to take your nature under control so that our business could really be a success. You saw from experience that with no one to control your nature you destroyed the pearls of your own talent. Left to yourself, you create with one hand and destroy with the other. There has not

been one single production to date, including 'Three Sisters', that would not
have come to nothing had it not been for my intervention in terms of not only
literary but actual artistic control. You will forgive me for saying this. But I
consider the present moment, the present state of our relations to be of the
absolutely utmost importance.

There are no ideal men. The greatest talent is not ideal. Pushkin and
Tolstoi are not ideal and you are not ideal. There is something in your nature
which is inimical to your talent. You often do the exact opposite of what you
want and, contrariwise, you often do things which are the precise opposite of
your natural inclination. In both cases you are unaware of this but out of
stubbornness, despotism or caprice, persist in what is false. To be what I
have been for you over five years is a massive and unrewarding task. A task
without glory, but one demanding thought, and the greatest delicacy and
sensitivity. You may have understood this consciously or not, or simply out
of trust, but you recognized the necessity for that 'control exercised by
artistic reason' if it can be so expressed.

Then suddenly something happened. Suddenly you discovered that all
this was insufferable 'tutelage' and decided to throw it off. Sudenly it
seemed a restriction on you as an artist.

This, it seems to me, is the psychological change in you. It bodes ill for the
future.

Suddenly you began to think that there had only been real art at the
Sporting Club when no one kept your ideas in check. Suddenly you
discovered that real back-stage ethics had only existed in the Society of
amateur art and literature, forgetting the difference between a company of
actors who play every day and a group of amateurs playing when they feel
like it. A colossal difference! Suddenly you began to find that real work had
been done at Pushkino, forgetting those cruelties, bordering on moral
fanaticism, which we had to accept only because were were taking our first
creative steps but which are unacceptable in an organized, public institution.
Suddenly you decided to give freer rein to your own wilfulness, with no
concern for the fact that, with the full force of your temperament behind it, it
might bring everything we have tried to create over the last seven years to
nothing. Your orders, your work plans, your management decisions were all
suddenly to be accepted without discussion. The smallest objection, even
from me, was suddenly seen as tutelage, a brake which was damaging to
what we were doing. You gave free rein to your wilfulness wherever it led
you and did not notice the eyes popping all round you when faced with such
an unaccustomed lack of consistency.

Let us take a small example: the costumes for 'Woe from Wit'.
Unbeknownst to you I told Grigorievna and Pavlova not to go to the meeting
you had called in Morozov's office but to get on with their work in their own
way. As a result you found that the costumes, a separate department, were

more or less ready. And it could be that other areas would benefit if they were not also subject to the despotic vetoes you impose.

You surrender to that feeling with all your strength when you consider that only what you are doing is effective, when you trust no one else, even those who for the moment enjoy your favour. You just won't see that every modest little worker does ten times better on his own responsibility than when he is given no independence whatsoever. Simov, who was able to demonstrate to you with the third act of 'The Lower Depths', some sets for 'Caesar', the first and third acts of 'Ivanov' that if you just gave him a 'directorial brief' he would be able to do well on his own – that same Simov complained to me three times that he had lost your confidence again and that he had made a series of models for which he had no feeling at all.

And I, every morning I come to the office with a great desire to work but simply don't know where I am supposed to begin.

And that was the time when you thought I was simply being lazy. . . . And all this arose from the fact that you can't organize our work and because you don't trust anybody, and above all you don't trust me, not one iota.

Physical resources don't help you because in such circumstances you thrash about and, as you are a powerful man, in all this thrashing about, you abuse all those who stand in your way. I say to you, 'Look, for God's sake, I give you five days to collect material, go and get it but then we must use it.' You reply that you need a couple of weeks at least for the journey, that you have to go to this place and that. All right, go. But next it transpires that you are not going anywhere and that you are already working on the set-models with Simov. I planned meetings for 'Woe from Wit' for *after* the material had been collected and then it turned out that the models (two acts) were ready *prior to* the meeting . . . There are not the physical resources to cope with what you want and pull it all together, because you are so restless and nervy.

That's what it was like all the time in the first two or three years. That made our work disorganized and made everyone tense and exhausted, you especially.

That's what you want to go back to, get rid of 'reason'.

Why? Was it not the case that *my* systematic way of working proved to be right? Because, thanks to some slanderous remarks and accusations you want to be free of my 'yoke'.

I don't understand.

A brick wall!

I return to the matters that have set us at variance. Under the influence of Meyerhold's absurd blabberings about the need to rehearse as the spirit moves, you suddenly felt the desire to exploit a method you claim to have been 'dreaming about for a long time'. That circumstance clearly indicated a yearning to throw off the 'yoke of reason'.

What pleased you most was the fact that there was no need for discussions, for analysis, for psychology. Reason plays such an enormous role in discussions! You wanted the actors to learn a small scene and start to rehearse without any moves, to lark about, caricature, but act *something*. I quoted a whole series of examples where this had been tried before. But your mind was already poisoned against me and whatever I said seemed banal, narrow, not artistic. You stubbornly denied any such thing. No later than 'Ivanov' we rehearsed the same way, without any clear pictures in our heads. In 'Pillars' we simply tried to find the feel of the play. Etc., etc.

But you said, that's not it. You said, the director all the same has some sort of store of inner images [of the characters] but in 'The Drama of Life' there was no such store and the actors had to create them by their own efforts. Later you explained this to me in more detail.

Call me obtuse, conclude that I have lost my artistic sensitivity, consider me old-fashioned but I stand by the following convictions.

I will try to spell out in a few lines my directorial *profession de foi*.

I understand a director who arrives at rehearsal (or at the first discussion, it doesn't matter) with a fully worked-out view of the play, developed in his own, individual soul, under the pressure of his own artistic world view, with those artistic touches he sees in the play, what tones – colours and sounds – have been prompted by his feeling for the play and his theatrical experience. Perhaps he still does not know the staging in detail, where he will have to change his mind under the influence of the actors and designers he will be working with, but he modifies, he does not refuse to have an over-view, an overall tone, he is well aware of *the atmosphere of the play* in which he will envelop the cast, he knows *the colour of the play and its diction* . . .

An actor can be playing and the director can say 'That is nothing like what I want because . . . because . . . but that note in the voice, which I did not anticipate, illustrates my feeling of the play perfectly.'

That's what I will do when it comes to 'When We Dead Awaken' or with 'Pillars of Society'. My imagination may prove to be artistically mediocre, my production plan may be barren, flawed, my discoveries may be modest but I have a very firm sense of what I do and don't want. And if I am listened to, the picture which has developed in my soul based on my observations of life and my feelings, on my experience and most heartfelt emotions will be executed.

That's how you will be when dealing with, let us say, 'The Sunken Bell' or 'Hannele' or 'Merchant' or 'A Law Unto Themselves' . . .

In all these cases, the most important quality the director possesses to make the affair a success is confidence in the unity of tone. One person is more talented, more clever, more inspired, more resourceful, another less so. Out of this difference will come differences in the artistic importance of the results.

An innovator may appear who possesses such confidence. A director whose every touch is new, whose flair creates new methods for actors, designers and props men. That was you with the fourth wall, the pauses, the important role given to stage sound. That was the person who staged 'Seagull', which was created from a mysterious combination of you and me, when one of us (me) felt the atmosphere of the play and its diction and the other (you) succeeded in putting it on stage. I in my domain, you in yours were the confident purveyors of a specific artistic idea.

I also understand a director of another stamp. Who is captured by a play which has unexpected beauties in the conflict, in the characters, in poetically vital scenes, in the passions so that at first he throws up his hands and says: 'I really don't know how to stage this play. The methods I have used up till now are not suitable.' Perhaps he is mistaken, perhaps those methods are just what is needed only rather better defined, improved on, but a love of novelty, a cooling off towards everything that has been tried before leads him to think that everything must be new, a fresh experience and that therefore he should set about this play differently.

What can be done in such a case? For me the answer is quite clear. One must make the play one's own, talk about it left and right, with everyone who can in any degree be useful, with artists, actors, critics, it may be that double, treble the number of *general* artistic discussion are necessary than on previous occasions, not of course, going into any great detail, for that could dry up feelings. You must look at tens, hundreds, thousands of pictures; then in the director's mind all kinds of images, touches, colours, sounds will begin to stir *in response to this particular play* and to him, the director, who is the artist painting.

If these awakening images do not create the whole picture of the production for him, its general feel, they give him some individual bits. And it's good for him to try them out on stage. For example you saw the fair [in *The Drama of Life*] as booths and shadows and you tried it out. You talked to your collaborators: get this ready for me, give me 20 men; to these 20 men you say move like this, light the stage for me this way . . . , etc. *You objectify images already produced in your mind.* [. . .]

The essence is in what I emphasized earlier: the director puts to the test what *he had already felt*; he tries to stage images which *have grown in his imagination*.

Not one member of the company would say a word in contradiction to what I have written, something which, albeit not in these terms, I said in that notorious discussion.

Just remember what you were asking. You wanted the actors to go on stage and act bits of the play *when neither they or the director* had *any kind of images*!! You wanted to draw the material for the production from what they acted without any knowledge of the characters or of the overall tone. So that out of this weird acting by actors, whose gifts and natures you know down to the last detail, you can draw a new original tone for the production! The reading of the play made no impression on the actors; the first group were respectfully bewildered (like Muratova), the second group went to sleep (Luzhski), the third group expressed regret at not being in the play (Kachalov), the fourth group were indifferent and only two or three were enthusiastic.

After a reading like that what should have been done? What I want is this. Start with discussions so as to arouse the enthusiasm of the company, catch them up in the artistic atmosphere with sketches and photos and at the same time evoke in the director a series of stage realizations.

But suddenly the director said: I don't know how to stage the play but one thing I do know, there is no need for discussion. What we need is to go up on the stage and act. In fact it was not the director who said that but a gentleman who risks nothing at all, whatever nonsense he utters, but it makes our eyes blaze with anger.

This is either such genius that we cannot take it into our poor little heads, genius bordering on madness or the empty mumblings of a *tired mind* which can rave as it pleases. Now Meyerhold, whom I have known since his first year as a student, has never shown any signs of genius and now seems to me merely one of those poets of the new art who are in favour of the new simply because they are incapable of doing anything noteworthy in the old and, on the other hand, I saw that you were clutching at something just so as not to lose time but then you turned obstinate, took offence and just followed your own whims, and, as I finally felt that such a method of work would at some moment introduce confusion, unease and waste of time into something well tested, and might even ruin the play completely, I gathered up my energy to protest.

I *had* to do it. I *dared not* act otherwise. You would have done the same in my place. I did not usurp the right to protest, you yourself have, over many years, given me the right to maintain the structure of the theatre as a public institution. And the maintenance of that structure sometimes means restraining you on those occasions when you start to 'destroy with one hand' what you yourself have created.

I don't doubt for a minute that if we were to listen to you the best that would happen would be a waste of time. The worst would be that you would set them against you as Sanin set them against him at Pushkino.

To tell you the truth I never expected that incident to make such a profound impression on you and set you so strongly against me. The end result was worse than if I had not bothered to argue but simply let you do everything you wanted. Perhaps things turned out worse not just for me but for our whole enterprise. And that's what I am writing about.

Why is it that things which in earlier times, and not so very long ago, would have caused only mild irritation have now created such a yawning chasm between us? That means the soil was prepared. By what?

Once again a brick wall. I don't understand.

It is probably just because I find myself faced with a wall that I keep looking for new ways to explain it.

You once said to me: who can decide which way an artist takes, where he starts from, from an image, from a single touch and 'perhaps, from a whim'.

That phrase has stuck in my memory. [. . .]

Why shouldn't the great artist Alekseiev indulge his whims, the man who gathered round him all those who wanted to fulfil his every whim at the Sporting Club.

But Stanislavski did not confine himself to the role of the amateur artist. He felt that he could play a principal role not in modest circles, which had albeit undoubted artistic goals, but in a great, artistic institution, founded – because it is an institution – with a definite system, having within it a large number of people, one which makes every effort to see that the artistic gifts of those people can grow and flourish.

Can the artist-director discover the feel of a play from a whim? He can start from a mistake, yes. He can be wrong in the expression of this or that artistic image which for the moment he cherishes, yes. And in that respect there were few occasions when I or the actors got in your way. We argued with you but finally did not try to stop you.

But to indulge oneself, playing about with time, actors' energy, their self-esteem, using them literally like pawns, that he cannot do.

Yes, and you yourself are capable of making wonderful speeches against such playing about, one of those speeches you know so well how to make, when you speak of the theatre as a matter of great social importance. In your serious moments you reveal yourself as a *teacher* of the ethical view of art, work and the actor's soul. Then you are a great man but not when you give free rein to your whims. [. . .]

When, on stage, you show the actors how to express the deep, all-embracing content of some theatrical image, as for example with Kachalov in 'Ghosts' and a thousand other cases, you are a great director and I admire you with all my artistic soul. That is a Stanislavski worthy of his name.

But when, unbeknown to yourself, because your mind is jaded, because of a slackening of artistic energy, you transform serious matters into a personal plaything or without noticing it, indulge yourself, flatter your pride, as in many rehearsals of 'Pillars', when you worked in French, you are like a talented but naughty boy, busy with trifles. [. . .]

You understand of course I am not talking about times when we are in a happy mood, or about jokes, which are always essential when dealing with serious matters, because without humour there is no life. And I often admire your humour as much as your seriousness. No, I am talking about self-indulgence in serious matters, which you once showed every step of the way but which subsequently has occurred less and less. And the less it occurred the more your authority grew in the company. In the first years you were more feared than respected. Now you are less feared and much more respected, immeasurably more.

Please believe me. [. . .]

I draw to a close. One can't go on writing for ever.

And perhaps my letter will play the same role as my criticism of 'Summerfolk'?!

I have said many disagreeable things!

So be it!

I want things to be clear with you, whatever the price.

I am almost in a sentimental mood. I feel not only that I need your confidence but also that I am extremely fond of you. And as I am fond of you it would be dishonest on my part to hide anything [. . .]

Your V. Nemirovich-Danchenko

266 Stanislavski to Nemirovich

June 1905
Moscow

Dear Vladimir Ivanovich,

I also admire some of your qualities, your talent, intelligence and so on . . . And I am distressed at the deterioration in our relationship . . . I rack my brains over how to improve it.

I expected rather different words from you and so your letter, the good intentions of which I thank you for, has not achieved its desired effect. I don't think our relations can be improved by trying to explain them. That is too painful for my (perhaps difficult) character and dangerous for your dignity and pride . . . Shouldn't we look for some other way? Instead of talk, work. That is your most powerful weapon against me. Believe me, no one admires you more than I when you are in one of your great periods of work. Unfortunately I am reserved by nature and that prevents me from speaking openly and expressing my feelings.

That is one of the reasons I cannot answer your letter point by point. I

assure you, it would not do any good. The main thing is I am not in a fit
state to do so now because my nerves are so tense. I have to forget last
season as quickly as possible, forget the Art Theatre for a time. Without
that I shan't be able to start work on 'The Drama of Life'.

Let us say things are as you write. It's all my fault, my despotism, my
whims, the vestiges of my amateurism. Even if everything in the theatre is
going well.

I only ask you one thing. Make life possible for me in the theatre.
Allow me some kind of satisfaction for without it I cannot go on working.
Don't bring near the time when I shall lose even my love for and faith in
our theatre *forever*.

Understand that at present, like all of us, I am far too concerned about
what is happening in Russia. We will not discuss any kind of professional
jealousy and pride. Dear God, I have done with them for ever, if only
because I have aged considerably. There was never any jealousy in my
work as a director. *It is an activity I do not like* and I do it out of
necessity.

In the field of acting I have surrendered my pride, consistently giving
place to all and saying amen over that side of me. In future I shall only
act so as not to lose the capacity to demonstrate to others.

Give *some* recognition *at least* to the personal effort I have made, to my
victory over myself and don't remind me of my successes as a director, I
spit on them.

I would never have previously given up any role I was right for yet now
I do that with great pain but how easily I *always* do it in the field of
directing.

It costs me nothing to hand over a play I relished to someone else if I
thought he could do it.

Isn't that clear proof that I am an actor and not a director at all by
nature? I cannot refrain from a smile of pleasure when I am praised for
my acting but I laugh when I am praised for directing.

My success as a director is essential to the theatre, not me. And I am
glad in those circumstances *only* for its sake. Don't settle any accounts
with me in that field. Take my name off the posters once and for all. I am
not your rival now. Think rather what it cost me to cede my pride of
place as an actor to Kachalov and others. I did it for the business and my
family and now I have no personal pride at all. On the contrary, I have
become tougher and more jealous with regard to our business from which
I demand even more, given all the things I have crushed in myself. I now
have the right to demand a widespread, public theatre activity throughout
the whole of Russia even . . . and in that direction I won't have to hold
my obstinacy in check. I may come a cropper but perhaps . . . I shall die
in peace.

I can't go into fine details about what kind of person Meyerhold is, great or insignificant, tricky or straight . . . I need him because he works enormously hard. I am glad when he talks intelligently and sorry when he creates a weak set of moves. If you broaden the scope of your concerns to activities of a social and civic nature . . . I shall be grateful to you but if you reduce their scope to the level of a simple business affair I shall stifle and start to fight as befits an obstinate man.

Judge for yourself: can you get anything out of such an obstinate person? By talking? I doubt it. What is needed is superhuman work. If that's what you're asking of me I shall be the most obedient of men.

Let us work as every decent man *should* at this moment.

Do what I did. Kill your pride. Defeat me with theatre and with work. Then you will find no one more faithful than me. Talking won't settle things . . . let us rest and apply ourselves to *real* work.

Affectionately yours,
K. Alekseiev

267 Nemirovich to Stanislavski

June 28 1905
Neskuchnoe Estate [?]

Dear Konstantin Sergeievich,

First, I ask you to forgive me for that part of my last letter in which I spoke of rivalry between us as directors. The idea that I may have caused you even momentary offence weighs heavily on me. I am speaking with absolute sincerity. It looked as though I had incidentally succumbed to stupid and insulting slander.

Very regrettable.

Let's bury it.

So you consider talking doesn't do much good. Fine! To the devil with it. I resort to talking when I feel that our relations may be impaired by really serious misunderstandings. Or out of fear for all the time every misunderstanding consumes.

If communication accentuates radical differences in artistic matters then no kind of talking can help. They can only paper over the cracks which will soon show through again.

As regards differences in artistic matters my own preference is to discuss and analyse them in depth but . . . I am beginning to mistrust my long letters.

The late Morozov told me firmly not to write them. I don't know why he said it but it would appear he was right.

So I will convey only the essentials.

I have asked myself more than once: are there not radical differences between us in artistic matters? Was there not an optical illusion which can be diagrammatically expressed as follows:

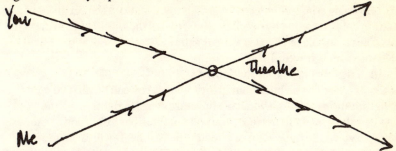

That is, we both developed artistically on our own, *each in his own way*, in a straight line. Our paths seemed to contain a common goal, a serious theatre, an ideal which in all major respects was identical for both of us. We came together and that created the illusion that we had become one. We never thought that, as each of us went his own way, at a certain moment we would separate and that the illusion would be broken.

Perhaps that's rather more starkly put than is just, it's speculation, too cut and dried perhaps. So much the better. But as the thought occurred to me more than once, I put the question: what is to be done if this really is the case?

My answer was: if I am honest, I should acknowledge that you, not I, are the fountainhead of the artistic trends which guided the theatre's first steps and, in essence, laid the foundation of its prosperity. It could well be that I should give way whenever our tastes diverge.

Sometimes, however, either for reasons the necessity of which you too recognized, or out of instinctive stubbornness, which is characteristic of all people with strong convictions, I refused to give way and opposed you. That led to the present situation. That is not good for you or me. You almost came to hate what you had loved and I found myself in the position of, let us say, a modern Russian minister. Hence that morally loaded word 'tutelage'.

You write: 'There is a point in me beyond which intense love turns to hate'.[1]

There's food for thought there!

On a medallion I have there are some Latin verses. Translated direct they read: 'Let him die who knows not love'. (*Pereat qui nescit amore*) and he dies twice who prevents love. We were bound by a common love of the theatre *an und für sich*, the theatre as self-standing, not just as means to an end. For both of us the theatre was precious as much for our love for every part of its intricate mechanism as for what it expressed. This is the warmest, the most

1. These words do not, in fact, occur in Stanislavski's letter.

endearing trait in us, as in all 'men of the theatre' (*les hommes du théâtre*). To poison that love is a real crime. He dies twice who 'turns that love to hate'.

To date my role as regards you has been difficult and unrewarding, now it risks becoming criminal. And the reason is to be found at the very root of the situation created for me by people who entrusted their wellbeing to me. The reason lies in 'tutelage'. That is as clear as day.

No tutelage of any kind!

And things become easier for both of us . . .

I absolutely give you back your artistic veto as you call the first voice in artistic questions. Though you have full and extensive rights to tell me artistic truths straight to my face, you will not often have occasion to exercise your veto when the full weight of directing lies on me. It will fall to me in a friendly way, and sometimes, with great persistence, to give advice and prevent possible mistakes. That isn't tutelage. That is a right and an obligation.

For what I am saying to go beyond the stage of good intentions we must come to an understanding about everything that is essential for well-ordered work.

To do that isn't it finally time for us to listen to *all* those around us, including our wives, and to arrange without fail one morning a week when we meet and distribute our respective work? That is terribly important! It's worth ten rehearsals. Everyone is saying it is important at the tops of their voices. That day they can always rehearse without us. And what if nothing happened that day! Our meeting once a week is our first responsibility. When we have nothing to talk about (O happy day!) we can discuss plays, production plans, look into the future, survey the present, encourage each other's love of the theatre, finally arrange management meetings. Dear God, how many stupid things happen in the theatre just because we are not in agreement!

We must do everything to maintain a close relationship. The work to which you summon me in your letter is splendid but if we have separate thoughts about the same work then we will encounter grounds for disagreement every step of the way. I do twice as well in four rehearsals after one discussion with you than I do in ten by myself. That's because I can be sure of one thing, that we will not disagree. I think it's the same for you.

Yet if this doesn't help, then we will think again!!

I would be very happy if this letter reassured you more than the last.

8-10 [July] I shall be at Kislodovsk with my wife. I intend to work on the 3rd act of 'Woe from Wit' while there.

Your V. Nemirovich-Danchenko

Nemirovich's letter of June 28 1905 calmed the waters and the two men made an effort to re-establish their working relationship. They agreed to collaborate on Griboiedov's 'Woe from Wit' and also on Gorki's *Children of the Sun* which received its première in Petersburg from Vera Komissarzhevskaya, who had also given the première of *Summerfolk*.

Gorki was only persuaded, with difficulty, to allow his play to be performed and did so when Stanislavski explained the difficult situation the theatre was in. As in the theatre's early days, Stanislavski wrote the production plan while Nemirovich took rehearsals which Gorki attended. The situation was by no means an easy one. Stanislavski, moreover, was not present to mediate as he went down to Sevastopol to complete the plan for Act IV. With Gorki came Marya Andreieva for whom Gorki had written the role of Liza. This increased the tension.

268 Nemirovich to Stanislavski

July 14 1905
Neskuchnoe Estate

Dear Konstantin Sergeievich,

It would be desirable in the highest degree for us to start work in August with the reading of Aleksei Maksimovich's play on 7 August. And for all the copies of the play we need to be ready on that day, the parts copied out, etc. And that there should be no delays on the purely office side. To do that *it is essential that Aleksei Maksimovich send the play to Moscow by 1 August and not later* . . . I will put the copying quickly into reliable hands, which will be ready and available.

Best of all would be if Aleksei Maksimovich would read the play himself to the company. Then when other plays are in rehearsal the first few days can be spent in casting, on discussion about the set-models, then we can prepare the *mise-en-scène*, etc.

Please be kind enough to write to Aleksei Maksimovich about this. I would do it but I haven't got his address.

But please be sure to ask for the manuscript by 1 August. Otherwise there will be difficulties afterwards. Perhaps he doesn't realize how long it takes to make copies, part-copies, etc.

So wire him like this: 'Request you send play by 1 August to theatre either Vladimir Ivanovich or Leonid Aleksandrovich von Lessing.[1] We start 7 August with reading of play to actors. Best would be you read play yourself. Need play by 1 August to prepare necessary copies and part-copies.'

I embrace you.

V. Nemirovich-Danchenko

1. Inspector of the Art Theatre.

269 Nemirovich to Gorki

August 2 or 3 1905
Moscow

KUOKKALA
ALEKSEI MAKSIMOVICH PESHKOV-GORKI

Konstantin Sergeievich wired you with a general request from the theatre administration to read the play to the company of artists on August 6. Be kind enough to reply to me at the theatre if you will do it or not or whether you will entrust the play to, say, Kachalov. We are most anxious to start familiarizing the actors with your play. Forgive my enquiry but the whole allocation of work in the theatre depends on your answer.

Nemirovich-Danchenko,
Art Theatre

270 Nemirovich to Stanislavski

September 4 1905
Moscow

Dear Konstantin Sergeievich,

I will try and give you a daily account of what is going on in the theatre.

Yesterday afternoon we rehearsed the first half of the third act.

Gorki was at the rehearsal and sat by me and often voiced his comments. He was very pleased to have an opportunity to do so. He told me, by the way, that when he was with Komissarzhevskaya he had no chance to say anything – devil knows why. It was not arranged.

His comments were, so to speak, psychologico-literary. He has nothing against any kind of inserts or changes in places where it's thin. He only protests *very strongly* against the spray, saying that such cowardice makes Protasov not only ludicrous but absurd.[1] What to replace it with I don't know.

This morning we carry on with the third act. This evening 'Tsar Fiodor'. Tomorrow, 'Children of the Sun', morning and afternoon.

Your V. Nemirovich-Danchenko

At the end of the summer the young members of the Studio returned to Moscow to prepare for the coming season. They encountered more than a little hostility from the other members of the company. In addition to their

1. In Stanislavski's production plan Protasov uses an antiseptic spray on his wife Elena and the objects in the room because he is afraid of cholera.

work on the Studio plays they were expected to perform in the main repertoire. They wrote a joint letter to Stanislavski.

271 Studio to Stanislavski

September 1905
Moscow

In recent times, mainly since we started to work in Moscow, it became clear to all of us individually that our artistic work in the theatre is stuck in an impasse, is not moving forward, that there is inadequate preparation for us to be able to open the theatre.

We are all aware that if we do not find a way out of this intolerable, negative situation our dreams for the theatre will come to naught.

Stanislavski was extremely worried by the strain on Meyerhold who was directing the Studio plays and rehearsing *The Seagull*.

272 Stanislavski to Nemirovich

September 1905
Moscow

Dear Vladimir Ivanovich,

It is a failure of the third act that it can be played in the morning, the evening or even at midday. As you like . . . I see it rather as an overcast, rainy day.

I am firmly convinced that no better ending could be found than yours. Psychology has nothing to do with it. There are a million ways of going mad. The important thing is that this ending should close the act effectively and in an original manner.

I defend it very strongly!

I'm afraid Aleksei Maksimovich will confuse and intimidate Marya Fedorovna but I don't know what attitude to adopt. He created the part for her and now the character is damaged. I'm afraid there will be big arguments and then I shall be blamed for God know what.

I have written half of the 4th act. [. . .]

I am terribly concerned that Meyerhold has no understudy as Treplev.

In the studio everything depends on him and he is already overstretched . . . He is needed at every 'Seagull' rehearsal. There is no one to stand in for him. Still he won't need many rehearsals.

Los can play Medvedenko.

Who is to be the understudy? Without one *there is no way* we can get through.

If work comes to a stop in the Studio we have to postpone the opening and then I am in trouble. That finishes me financially as I have no more than 20,000 in reserve to cover losses. An understudy is essential, particularly in the early period. Later when everything in the studio is underway Meyerhold will have much more free time. I have nothing against his being in 'Seagull', on the contrary. I am very glad for the Art Theatre which does not have a Treplev but I am afraid that in the early period Meyerhold might cut down on the Art Theatre or the Studio. This is what I will do. Medvedenko will be played by Moskvin or Gribunin (he has slimmed down), Los will understudy as Treplev.

Your K. Alekseiev

273 Nemirovich to Stanislavski

September 5 1905
Monday   Moscow

Yesterday morning and this morning we went on and finished the third act and went through it again. Gorki took part in everything. He changed the *mise-en-scène* in places. Cut pauses in places.

Unfortunately I only feel this act *in the evening* – ending with the lamps. (Antonovna can bring one lamp and light another when she is clearing the tea glasses). All those discussions are absurd in the daytime.

The end provoked weird disagreements. Marya Fedorovna is rather edgy: she is visibly edgy about her role and *him* [Gorki]. He's already 'cursing' this role ('God damn her to hell, this Liza!'). He listens to everyone, visibly, agreeably but there's something in Marya Fedorovna, there's something he finds not quite right. He's apparently happy with the others, some more some less so . . .

274 Nemirovich to Stanislavski

September 6 1905
Tuesday   Moscow

I am starting a fourth page!

I just can't put down everything I could say in words.

Yesterday's rehearsal (second act) was one of those when 'you want to take your hat and coat and go, just go, where your eyes can see'.[1] Or when you know that the theatre is just not worth all that effort.

1. Quote from *Three Sisters*.

You wanted to get away from the author's banalities and conceal them under 'the life of the household' and 'breakfasting'. But that would lead to such a maze of over-stretched interpretation and difficulties that it would either require your help to get out of them or a new *mise-en-scène*, i.e., a better one.

The author is being all sweetness and light. I prevailed on him not to come down too hard on things he didn't like. So he didn't. However through his comments, even though they were manifestly tinged with affection for you, he disavowed all the details of the *mise-en-scène*.

Possibly I have too high an opinion of myself. But finding myself caught between his comments, which for the most part I cannot consider reasonable, on the other side a desire not to traduce your *mise-en-scène*, and third a feeling of unease faced with a writer who didn't want to be involved with the play and, finally, mindful of the necessity to make decisions this way and that so as not to lose time, involved in all that, I, it must be said, felt I was indispensable. It's an offensive and stupid situation. The more so since the actors never look you in the eye when they speak, when they are unhappy and lay it all to my account . . .

I shall probably work only on the first and third acts in which I have only diverged from your *mise-en-scène* in trifles. And I shall prepare the two acts in final form. But I'll set the second aside until we meet, read it twice at the table.

Or I may prepare a different *mise-en-scène* and show it to you when you arrive.

Your V. Nemirovich-Danchenko

275 Nemirovich to Stanislavski

	September 8 1905
Thursday	Moscow

Yesterday we ran the 1st act. All the actors say that it is specially good and conscientious. 'Those of us back-stage think that the act "works" ' they said to me. But it me it seemed quite hopeless, uninteresting, so hollow, boring . . . And, most important, so calculated.

I told them as much . . .

Every character must be crystal clear in its features, its living quality, the simplicity of tone. But if the actors can't achieve that then their attempts to come alive, the success or failure of the play, or indeed the whole theatre, are matters of indifference to me.

The highest qualities of our own realist art seem to me to be: simplicity, calm, and newness and clarity of characterization. Our highest art, in my view, is to be found in 'Cherry Orchard' and in the way we played 'Uncle Vanya' once in Petersburg. You, of course, concur. We only differ on the way to get there. You say there is no other way to achieve it except through calculated brilliance but I continue to think that one must approach it with directness and determination. 'Children of the Sun' is undoubtedly written in Chekhovian tones and the only blemish is Gorki the journalist. We can combine that.

Today is 8 September. I'm beginning to get nervous. 8 September and nothing yet. [. . .]

276 Nemirovich to Stanislavski

September 9 1905
Moscow

Yesterday morning there was a heated rehearsal of the first act, in the evening the beginning of the third.

Our actors simply don't know how to work at home. That does them great harm. They not only have to be given their moves and be helped to find the character, you more or less have to show it to them. They are used to being dealt with on stage as though they were working at home. You have to infect them with the director's nerves and energy, as it were invest them with one's own nerves and energy. Alone without you or me they are lost. And it's good that they understand that (or rather, they only do so before their first taste of success, when they feel impotent on being faced with a new role).
[. . .]

The 1905–6 season came to a premature and abrupt end in October. The revival of *The Seagull* excited no interest, despite Stanislavski's completely new interpretation of Trigorin. Two general strikes and then revolution stopped *Woe from Wit* in mid-rehearsal and *The Drama of Life* was abandoned completely. The theatre closed its doors.

Stanislavski was in a highly depressed mood. He decided that he could never again collaborate with Nemirovich on a production; they were now too far apart. Worse, the Studio had proved a complete failure. That was partly his fault. The work he had seen in the country, in a small space, modestly presented, had been encouraging. But it was lost in the vast auditorium he had rented and which, true to his belief that actors must work in dignified surroundings, he had completely redecorated. What he saw on the Studio's opening night was not a new style, a new approach for actors but puppets being manipulated by an extremely clever director. He cut his losses and closed the Studio. Meyerhold left the Art Theatre for good but on good terms with his 'master' for whom he always felt great affection. Stanislavski had, however, shown his openness to experiment with new ideas and received an offer of help from the leading Symbolist critic Valeri Briusov whose ideas on 'superfluous realism' were beginning to exert a strong influence.

The Povarskaya Studio had planted a seed and it was from that experiment that the idea for future studios sprang.

For the moment, however, Stanislavski, faced not only with heavy losses at the theatre but also in his factories, could see little hope anywhere. His despondency was increased when Savva Morozov, himself deeply depressed by the failure of the 1905 revolution, went to Nice and shot himself.

277 Nemirovich to Stanislavski

November 1905

My dear Konstantin Sergeievich,

Stakhovich has told me very painful things about your mood. And among other things that my depressing reflections about recent events and my gloomy resolution on the future, about which I spoke to him quite openly, all served to round off your mood. He acted unwisely.

Can you believe that I, at this moment, am not fretful. I am very fond of you and so ill at ease. Still I am not getting carried away or flattering myself with the thought that it is the prospect of not working with me which depresses you. Your reflections must be deeper and wider. Yet I will still do all that is in my power to support you.

All is but passing, Konstantin Sergeievich! Sorrow before joy, the dark before the dawn. With me or without me, you are always strong in what you do. That thought should uphold you.

And I . . . you can never know how much joy I felt when the whole theatre rejoiced to see the two of us in such close union. And what prevents that, the devil can sort out. Your nature, my suspiciousness, the differences in our tastes, the devil only knows!

At all events, now we are asunder.

Now cheer up, don't be depressed on account of the 'Studio' or any other failure. Good health!

Cheer up.

Your V. Nemirovich-Danchenko

278 Stanislavski to Kotlyarevskaya

November 29 1905
Moscow

[. . .]

The Art Theatre is safe for the moment. It has suffered enormous losses and by the end of the season all its capital will be spent. (This between ourselves).

Business is exceptionally bad. Our entire audience has left Moscow. The budget is exceptionally high. We are under pressure from all sides.

Really. There has been a proposal to merge with the Maly Theatre and found a State theatre. But . . . this business will have to be deferred until a State Duma is summoned. Subsidies, especially large ones, cannot be handed out by officials. To petition for such a subsidy in a period of interregnum is no easy matter. I don't think a merger with the Maly will produce good results.

What we shall be doing next year is uncertain. Probably we shall spend the whole year away on tour abroad where we are in great demand. Perhaps we shall organize the tour during Lent.

The future is full of shadows. Whether art is needed is a big question. Whether a theatre with high prices has a future is another.

I have promised not to spread rumours about the Maly's invitation to us. I only talk about it to family and friends. Don't give me away! The mood is pretty vile. No one wants to work, no one has any use for it at the moment. We feel like clowns . . . a shame . . . 'Woe from Wit' could turn out original and not bad at all. [. . .]

Your devoted,
K. Alekseiev

TEN

THE STRUGGLE FOR CONTROL

In a desperate attempt to keep solvent the Art Theatre decided to accept some of the many invitations it had received for a foreign tour. Stanislavski went to Berlin in late January 1906 to make final details for a tour which included Berlin, Dresden, Leipzig, Prague, Vienna, Frankfurt. Towards the end of the tour a special command performance was given for the Emperor Wilhelm II at Wiesbaden, when Stanislavski and Nemirovich were awarded the order of the Red Eagle, fourth class.

The honour bestowed by the Emperor is symbolic of the impact the Art Theatre made. Critics and public, except in Vienna, were unanimous in their acclaim. Duse, who was in Berlin during the tour, suggested they should go on to Paris. Nemirovich made a flying trip to see Lugné-Poë but could not agree satisfactory financial terms.

It was this first foreign tour which launched the international reputation of the Art Theatre, ironically at a moment when it was in danger of blowing apart.

On their return from Germany the company had to reconstruct the lost 1905 season. *Woe from Wit* would be picked up where they had left off and presented no problems. It was the other two productions, Stanislavski's *The Drama of Life* and Nemirovich's *Brand*, which led the two men once more into conflict. There was the question of which should come first, closely linked to the question of casting. Would Stanislavski play Kareno in the Hamsun or not? Or would Kachalov? The dispute began in July and rumbled on well into the autumn. The company was split down the middle. Nemirovich ostentatiously stayed away from the early dress rehearsals of *The Drama of Life* in February 1907, something which Stanislavski described as 'theatrical filth, revenge'.

Stanislavski confirmed all Nemirovich's worst fears by his first experiments with what was to become the System. He spent the summer of 1906 in Finland drafting notes for a book. He was evidently determined to go his own way and not submit to Nemirovich's 'reason'. Then he added fuel to the flames by engaging Sulerzhitski as his personal assistant, paying him out of his own pocket. Nemirovich made it clear that Sulerzhitski had no status within the company since his engagement had never been discussed, and lost no opportunity of humiliating him.

Nemirovich now came to the conclusion that if the theatre was to survive he had to take complete control of its management. He was afraid that the theatre would become 'Stanislavski's club' as the Society of Art and Literature had once been. A bitter and painful struggle ensued between him and Stanislavski which was not resolved until 1908 when Stanislavski ceased to be a member of the theatre's Board and to exercise any official control over policy.

279 Stanislavski to Vladimir Alekseiev

February-March 1906
Berlin

Dear Volodya,

I have never worked like this before. Not only all day long but all night long too . . . [The first performance] was a triumph the like of which we have never seen in Moscow or in Petersburg. The whole of Berlin: men of letters (Hauptmann, Schnitzler, Sudermann, Halbe, etc.,) scientists (all the famous professors and doctors), financiers . . . Barnay, Duse, all the theatre managers and the 80-year-old Haase who never goes anywhere and the famous critic Kerr . . . The next day we were inundated with articles. There are more than 100 newspapers here with evening editions. All, without exception, brought out huge articles and were wild with delight. I have never seen such reviews. As though we were a revelation. Almost all of them end their articles with the cry: we know the Russians are a hundred years behind politically but dear God how far they are ahead artistically. Recently they have been knocked from Mukden to Tsushima. Today they have had their first significant victory. *Bravo, Russen!* . . .

Everywhere actors and directors are being recommended to come and learn from us. The apogee of (refined) success was reached with 'Uncle Vanya'. Hauptmann howled like a baby and sat in the last act with a handkerchief to his eyes. In the interval he (notorious for his reserve) ran out into the foyer with a great show and shouted to the whole room: 'This is the greatest theatrical experience I have ever had. These are not people acting but artistic gods!' Well done! Of course we were introduced to him and his wife. He has simply fallen in love with us and is staying in Berlin until the end of the tour. After 'Depths' which had a very noisy success (not as refined as 'Uncle Vanya'), Hauptmann told us that he had not slept all night but thought about the play he is going to write for us. [. . .]

In a word, in terms of success we are, as Mamontov used to say, stuffed full.

The financial side by Berlin standards is spectacular and everyone is amazed that we are making 2,500 marks a night. The most popular theatre

here is the Deutsches Theater and that makes the same amount.
Unfortunately it's too little for us, we are hardly covering costs, which, I
repeat, are horrendous. We hoped that we would come home with a tidy
little sum. Everyone was unanimous in saying that you can't make a fortune
in Berlin, that here you get the patent and with this patent you can go to
other cities and make capital. That's true because the best impresarios of the
whole world are gathered here in Berlin like bees round honey. Of various
gentlemen who have not even seen us, some are inviting us to Austria,
others to America. I don't know if we shall be able to draw profit from our
success. [. . .]

There is word that [the Emperor] Wilhelm intends to pay us a visit. That
would be the first time he has ever visited a privately owned theatre. Today
we received a request from the court to send them the week's performance
schedule. [. . .]

How hard it is here to open a newspaper and read what is happening with
you at home. It is especially hard because all our misfortunes at best lead us
towards western culture – that is appalling. That culture isn't worth
tuppence . . . There is no heart here – and that is why the critics above all
praise the heart of Russian man and the absence of any sentimentality. [. . .]

I kiss you affectionately.

Your Kostya

280 Stanislavski to his sister Zinaida

February 1906
Berlin

[. . .]

Today in Berlin something unusual happened. There is a critic here called
Norden. He only writes articles in exceptional circumstances . . . and they
are always blistering. He has never praised anyone. In a short essay today he
wrote roughly the following: 'Berlin saw something of an event. The
Russians came. In every generation one can expect to meet 6-8 great artists.
In this company they are all artists and they are all in one place. That is a
stroke of genius . . . and critics are silenced. Everyone should go to the
theatre to get to know the Russians, not only artists but diplomats,
politicians and those who are convinced this is a ruined country. A country
that can create such art and literture is a great country. They have a culture
but we are not familiar with it. It is not like our own but that does not stop us
getting to know it better.' [. . .]

Recent events had taken their toll on Stanislavski. He now felt artistically sterile. He had fallen into the worst of traps: acting mechanically. While on holiday in Finland in the summer of 1906 he began to look once more for the creative springs of acting and began his first attempt to write what he then called his 'grammar' of acting.

281 Lilina to Knipper

June 3 1906
Finland

[. . .]

Now a few words about our husband. He is happy, he finds the northern air and climate agree with him; he is getting used to it. But, between ourselves, our time is passed very strangely; he doesn't walk at all, or swim, and takes little air: he sits in a half-dark room and writes and smokes the whole day. He is writing what look like interesting things: entitled 'A Draft Manual of Dramatic Art'.

I am very severe in my views about his writing and very blunt but what he read me from his notes I liked. [. . .]

Relations between Stanislavski and Nemirovich were now so bad that they were quarrelling openly about the shape of the season, something that had never happened before. Stanislavski's letter reveals that he recognized Nemirovich as the manager of the theatre.

282 Stanislavski to Nemirovich

September 1906 [prior to the 26th]
Moscow

My dear Vladimir Ivanovich,

We must not quarrel at the present time. Forgive me.

I, more than anyone, detest that tone in myself, which I was not able to restrain yesterday. It insults and demeans me more than anyone.

I am truly sorry for it and once again I ask forgiveness.

There are two reasons which mitigate my guilt.

First One should never demand explanations after a very difficult act from an artist whose nerves are in shreds.

Second I can never reconcile myself to any blunder or unchivalrous behaviour in the theatre. When outsiders take the theatre to task and I know they are right and I cannot oblige them to be silent or expose them as liars, I am more sorry than anyone, as it is very important to me that our theatre should not only be artistic but cultivated and correct in the highest degree. Without that it loses half its value for me.

When it seems to me that you, in your capacity as a manager, are making a mistake I am sorry in the truest sense and cannot sleep all night and am angrier with you than anyone else can be. What is that, a proof of love or ill-will?

I answer you with an example: 'A mother, who beats her child because he has climbed under a trolley-car, shows the highest degree of love not hate.'

I am fond of you, as few people are, and so I am often too demanding, as we only meet to discuss business when there are too many opportunities for conflict.

Forgive me but do not misinterpret my state of nerves. I embrace you and ask forgiveness. I wish very much that all those who were present at yesterday's unfortunate scene could read this letter.

Your K. Alekseiev

I am writing badly but the fault today lies with the second act of 'Woe from Wit'.

283 Nemirovich to L. N. Andreiev

End September 1906

[. . .]

I have finally arranged the season: I am doing 'Brand', Stanislavski, 'The Drama of Life', we are rehearsing independently and separately of each other, completely on our own, I, in the foyer, and he, on stage. When I am on stage, he is in the foyer. This is the first experience of drawing a demarcation line, essential given the continuous artistic differences between us. [. . .]

284 Stakhovich to Knipper

November 2 1906

[. . .]

How tiresome, how sad, how insufferably boring that our two chiefs can't get on together. And how helpful and desirable it would be if the talent, gifts and artistic creativity of the one could join forces with the knowledge, experience and intelligence of the other. But I think that will never happen and that is why the Art Theatre in its present state is not fated to last much longer. It is a hard and bitter thing for me to accept but I no longer have any doubt about it. Were Vladimir Ivanovich less self-absorbed and self-confident, *entiché de sa propre personne*, anxious about his position, if he loved and prized Stanislavski's gifts more then things could come right.

In creative matters, artistic, theatrical intelligence, knowledge and experience must give place to another's talent. But Nemirovich is too fond of himself and is not prepared to sacrifice his own Ego and take pleasure in being Konstantin Sergeievich's visible and invisible helper. To help Stanislavski where he is weaker and contribute even more to his glory goes against the grain for Vladimir Ivanovich and he will never do it.

On November 3, after being asked many times, Nemirovich attended a rehearsal of *The Drama of Life*. He violently disagreed with the staging of the third act, which was largely played in silhouette. He claimed that he had walked out of the rehearsal three times and forced himself to come back. Nemirovich expressed his feelings at a Board meeting that same day. There was a further dispute over casting. The Board decided to take Podgorny out of the key role of Kareno but no agreement could be reached as to who was to replace him. Nemirovich stated that Kachalov was too busy with *Brand* and, much to Stanislavski's bewilderment, suggested he should not take it although he was prepared to play it. Stanislavski, who had no taste for boardroom in-fighting, withdrew to await events.

285 Nemirovich to Stanislavski

> November 4 1906
> Moscow

Dear Konstantin Sergeievich,

No time to talk, I write a few words. I have often detested you heartily but mostly I have loved you much more. And when work was done and we experienced its success or failure I always treated you warmly and *affectionately*. And in the end I have given you and our common endeavour so much of my heart it would be cruel not to part as friends.

That was the reason I intended to speak to you. What can we do so as not to part with bad feeling? Can you not invent a theatre in which I wouldn't feel the nonentity I have for the whole of October, when you stopped thinking of me as one of the owners of the theatre or as a man of letters?

But the moment has come to arrange a more *intelligent* parting, we must save the season. I have already replied to your two accusations. The first, regarding the 3rd act of 'The Drama of Life' I accept, I confess to. I really think I am incorrigible in that respect. I just can't ever keep silent over things which *in my view* are wrong. When *I don't understand* then I can keep silent and even make a real mental effort to understand. But when I am convinced that old, tired mistakes are being repeated then it is hard for me to restrain myself. Then I am not afraid of arguments or of upsetting you. I forge ahead *for the sake of the theatre*. And were I to leave the theatre tomorrow, the day after I would send you a whole essay with the title 'I beg you not to repeat mistakes'. You may regard that as intrigue, as a dishonest atmosphere but I, perhaps, consider it an irrepressible yet passionate, staunch devotion to the theatre. Tactless? Perhaps. But not ignoble. True, honest.

Your second accusation I categorically reject. I believe that if you ask yourself the question, where is Kachalov more important, in 'Brand' or in 'The Drama of Life', *there can be no two opinions*. No *discussion* is needed. 'Brand' is the work of genius of the century and 'The Drama of Life' is a talented question mark.

When I saw that the actors were noisily supporting 'The Drama of Life' because there were parts for them, and you also because it was the play you were doing, and that *no one* was standing up for Ibsen's outpouring of genius – not counting Mosvkin whose views can be suspect – then the whole shareholders' meeting became *repellent and repulsive to me*. Yesterday I despised it to the depths of my soul, despised it because *I considered it humiliating to defend* 'Brand'. Leaving the meeting, I came to the conclusion that there were now profound and creditable reasons for me to leave the theatre. I saw that in this theatre the actors only love the roles they are playing and you, only the work *you* are doing. The theatre lost any kind of attraction for me.

But in order not to damage the things I am currently involved with, today I gathered the supporters of 'Brand' (whose sincerity, I repeat, is suspect to me) and persuaded them to drop Kachalov as Kareno (I also detest Kachalov for having figured in such a problem) and put off 'Brand' for an indefinite period.

So you can see how far I am from having a cunningly executed plan (athough, I admit, I am sorry that is not the case, that would have been more conscientious in relation to 'Brand'. If people don't understand, and if you can't drum into them what's important and what's secondary, then there's nothing left except to leave or to introduce anything of importance into the theatre by guile.)

I go back to the beginning. You see, my relationship to you is even more important than 'Brand'. I offer it up as a sacrifice. I have cancelled tomorrow's rehearsal. Take heart, set aside a passing pain and with God's help get down to work. I will be able to convince the shareholders . . . Better that you should have a quiet mind than neither of us.

Perhaps we may not leave. Then it will be possible to stage 'Brand' with Kachalov, after Kareno.

Your V. Nemirovich-Danchenko

To make clear my mental state at yesterday's meeting, a mental state which you . . . took so badly. I recall the first meeting to discuss Podgorny's playing of Kareno, when I really suffered from the vile attitude towards 'Brand' and ended up with a hysterical outburst, but at home, by myself, I wept, as I told you. Did people really not understand that the next time we met I *just kept quiet*?

What is your view of me if you see cunning in that?

Thank you once again for speaking out and not clamming up. [. . .]

286 Stanislavski to Nemirovich

Saturday

November 4 1906
Moscow

Dear Vladimir Ivanovich,

I cannot answer that part of your letter which concerns me personally.

And so I pass on to the business part.

Here I have to repeat what I said yesterday. I will play Kareno if I must; I will direct those plays which are offered to me.

I can work with energy in an unsullied atmosphere and if that expression is insufficiently clear I am willing to clarify it in the presence of the shareholders. I have considered and still consider it an obligation to defer to all your demands on the literary side. On the artistic side I insist on what was arranged by you this spring in Warsaw.

I have publicly expressed my views on 'Brand'. They are not accurately set out in your letter.

Personally I shall be very happy to let 'Brand' go first as I am very tired. Whether Kachalov can sustain it is a question I addressed more than adequately at the meeting.

I shall be very happy for the theatre's sake to let 'Brand' go first, with Kachalov, as our theatre will gain from it both artistically and financially.

Once more I emphasize that I am agreeable to any arrangement. I take no responsibility on my own account but will accept the joint decision of the shareholders.

It is your function, as chairman, to call them together to take a definite decision.

I think my presence at that meeting would be superfluous and even harmful.

In my capacity as a shareholder, I would ask you to resolve the question as quickly as possible so that we do not lose two days which are free from performances.

I earnestly request you to acquaint the shareholders with the contents of this letter.

I will present myself for work at the theatre as soon as I am notified.

Your K. Alekseiev

287 Nemirovich to Stanislavski

November 4 1906
Moscow

Dear Konstantin Sergeievich,

Since you acknowledge me in your letter as chairman, I will simply ask you to participate in a short meeting of the shareholders, to which I am inviting Z. G. Morozova and Prince Dolgorukov so as to draw up an official minute to that effect. Then I will assume total *responsibility* for the current season and at the same time full *power* as chairman.

Since there will be, in all probability, no obstacles to this, I am assuming the post today without waiting for official confirmation.

In this capacity I am organizing future work in the following manner.

I ask you not to bring any individual to work in the theatre, even in the capacity of your assistant, without my agreement or the agreement of the management if the occasion should arise during the current season.

While acknowledging your unlimited authority as a director in those plays for which you are responsible, I would ask you, nonetheless, in the first instance, to inform me, through your assistants, of *all* your instructions concerning the play, so that I coordinate them with other work in the theatre, or in other circumstances request you to cancel those instructions if my arguments appear sound to you.

Apart from directing those plays for which you are responsible, I must ask you not to give any instructions of any kind without my knowledge. And that applies to the general routine of the theatre and the company, to agreements with authors, activities in the school, as our instructions, yours and mine, often run counter to each other and create conflict.

In that way I think I shall be able to establish a definite regimen as a result of which you, as a director, will find things easier and calmer – that in itself is very important for the plays you are responsible for.

Turning to the present situation, I don't consider it necessary to summon the shareholders to make decisions about what is already in rehearsal. I take entire responsibility for that, for this reason. Those shareholders who are available have already expressed their opinion. But apart from them there are 4 or 5 people absent and I cannot not take their wishes into account. At the same time I have a very clear picture of the way their opinions would incline were they asked. They became shareholders of the Art Theatre and the Art Theatre is indissolubly linked to your name. And naturally they would never be willing to frustrate you in your artistic efforts and experiments, whatever the financial consequences might be.

Therefore I have decided: to proceed immediately with the production of 'The Drama of Life' with Kachalov as Kareno. If you need a few days' rest, take them. Further allocation of work and the repertoire I will work out myself and ask the management, should the case arise, to approve it or, if the management is not here, ask you to discuss it.

Finally, regarding my 'literary' intervention in plays you are directing, since we hold completely dissimilar views on the meaning of the term 'literary' intervention (I see it in immeasurably broader terms than you) and as it always inevitably produces quite serious conflict, I renounce the *right* to that intervention, while recognizing a personal *obligation* when you feel the need to ask for it. And in order to avoid backstage discussions between us taking quite another tone, I will try and speak to you only when it is necessary.

I would ask you to respect the terms of this letter if you are in agreement with all the total statement, as a document for the shareholders.

                                        Your Vl. Nemirovich-Danchenko

Inform me of your agreement as soon as possible.

288 Stanislavski to Nemirovich

November 4 1906
Moscow

Dear Vladimir Ivanovich,

The chairman of the board is the spokesman, leader, executive officer of the board as a whole. The role which you wish to have in our affairs is called the managing director.

I agree to your being granted these powers if the shareholders agree. I do not have the right to decide this matter without a shareholders' meeting.

I did not notify you *officially* concerning my invitation to Mr Sulerzhitski and my private expenditure. You knew about it from private conversations, you saw Sulerzhitski directing at my behest and said nothing to me.

At that time our relations were easier and it seemed strange to me to resort to official procedures. On the official side and even, forgive me, on the ethical side, I am in the wrong and I ask your pardon.

To rectify this mistake I now make official application for you to recognize Mr Sulerzhitski as my assistant. I assume responsibility for his activities and for his financial remuneration.

This question only concerns the management as it now exists. Therefore, in this matter, I give my vote and also Stakhovich's vote, which I am able to confirm with letters I have. I ask for a swift response to this request as I cannot stage 'The Drama of Life' without an assistant, because of daily performances and my responsibilities to the factory and the office.

To date I have tried to inform you of any instructions I issued concerning the plays I was directing. Rehearsals never began on stage without prior discussion with you. As for rehearsals in the foyer they are evident from the book the actors sign.

In my capacity as a manager and a director I am *obliged* to keep an eye on anything untoward which occurs in the theatre. I have the right to introduce any person I think necessary and to answer letters which are addressed to me personally either by private or public persons, even if they are from actors.

I don't imagine you want to deprive me of the right to talk to whom I please or write to whom I please.

As you are aware, I have shown you all the letters from actors. If you can manage to relieve me of the burden of talking to Naidenov, Andreiev, Kosorotov, Asch, Przbyszewski and others who send me their plays I shall be very grateful to you. This passage in your letter is simply not clear to me.

I don't imagine you want to turn me into a sleeping partner. It's not a role I can accept. If the shareholders agree to release me from the onerous role of manager in the middle of the season I will gladly resign and thereafter shut my eyes to everything happening in the theatre, including things which threaten disaster.

In view of the confusion and danger our theatre faces, as a shareholder and a member of the management, I must protest against the fact that the decision concerning the next play was taken by one individual. At the last shareholders' meeting it was decided that 'Brand' should be presented with Kachalov and 'The Drama of Life' with me.

I indicated my agreement and therefore will not take on the responsibility of altering the shareholders' decision.

Naturally you are free to act as you wish on your own individual responsibility. One cannot be guided by the intentions of shareholders who are not present: I am convinced that Stakhovich would not be in favour of 'The Drama of Life' and of 'Brand' with Kachalov. I think Morozov would have said the same.

I take no responsibility for literary matters as I know nothing about them. I will be guided by your advice and demands but ask you to convey them to me privately, as otherwise it is difficult for me to convince the actors to try a new style.

I can start on 'The Drama of Life' but to do that first the question of Sulerzhitski must be settled as I cannot mount any production whatsoever without him.

As regards Hauptmann's play, I am very much in favour of approaching Efros. He could translate it. At least it will be successful.

Yours K. Alekseiev

I earnestly request you to communicate this letter to the directors. As regards the school, I am willing to cease my activity but on condition that you authorize me to tell the pupils I promised to help that it is not my fault I have stopped.

In addition, naturally, I reserve the right to work at home with anyone I like and even elsewhere and in another school, even with Adashev,[1] if he invites me.

289 Nemirovich to Stanislavski

November 4 1906
Moscow

I am endeavouring to write in such a way as not to create further confusion. Decidedly today is the day for letters.

I really do not feel the need to play the monarch in the theatre. But what name to give to the role I wish to play, 'managing director' or 'chairman of the board' – is not what is important as far as I am concerned. Call it 'secretary' if you like. The one thing I do consider essential – and you in this cannot, of course, disagree – is that one individual should hold the reins. For the last year that person appears to have been me. And that is how it has come to be viewed in the theatre. When people have clashed with you they have come to me. During October I more than once found myself in a ridiculous position. *As to your having Sulerzhitski as your assistant I now give my vote*. You say there is a board and that you have a written agreement from Stakhovich concerning Sulerzhitski's entry here and yet I learn of it for the first time when he is already taking rehearsals. Whichever way you look at it, from my point of view that is amazing. What is more, you instruct him to read 'Bluebird' to the cast and he gives a talk on the *interpretation* of this play. By what stretch of the imagination could anyone think that such a 'literary' exposition could take place without my knowledge? I learned of this by chance at lunch with Yurgens, a teacher at the school. I had to make a pretence that it had happened with my knowledge. And moreover, Sulerzhitski is not only your assistant but also what we call the second director, consequently a teacher to our actors. I am the last to know about that too.

At which meeting of the board, the board on which you have now assigned me full powers, did we discuss the question of granting such wide powers to Sulerzhitski? As director I never discussed it. And internally requests from even the youngest actor don't go through without discussion.

Concerning the school. I have *never* dreamed of preventing your taking

1. Private theatre school where some members of the Art Theatre taught.

an interest in the school, I have always told the teachers what joy it was that you should wish to work with them. And as to what you write about going to teach at Adashev's school, I consider that an offensive and unworthy threat.

But to instruct N. G. Aleksandrov to do light comedies without my knowledge at the very moment when I had fixed the studies in the school in a precise manner is inappropriate because it resulted in total confusion in the planning of work-time and rest. And I would like to know how I am to organize the teachers' time if I do not know your instructions . . .

You don't understand my statement about writers? Then I will explain. As many authors who do not get into our theatre consider me the greatest obstacle because I hold the power of veto, it seemed strange to me that you did not pass on the requests you received to me . . . You cannot be unaware that this is somewhat abnormal and puts me in a ridiculous position.

I am mindful of the fact that all this happened three or four weeks ago but that I did not utter a sound either to you or to anyone else because I did not want to disturb you when you were in an energetic mood and working.

But it left a bitter taste behind.

I will not linger over odd details of times when your orders ran counter to mine. All this comes back to the old question: what am I in the theatre, just your assistant in all departments both artistic and administrative? But when, in recent times, people began to turn to me as general manager I was quite lost. I cannot set the tone in any department of the theatre's life as I think best. But at the same time I am supposed to sort out the mess. My lack of authority in the theatre has never been greater. Put yourself in my place and agree, can I feel the energy to do things? Where am I to get it? . . . When there are three of us then there is a board but when there are just the two of us and our views differ you always get your way no matter what – literature, art, administration, the school, back-stage ethics . . .

I wrote to you today of my wish for power, not for power's sake, but to know how things stand, to look to the future and be *responsible* for it. I wrote to you about this today not for my own satisfaction but to find ways of managing the season properly and *to give the strongest possible support to your artistic intentions*. Was that really not clear from the letter? Obviously not because the tone of your reply in no way corresponds to my intentions . . .

To conclude: at today's meeting I propose to establish what I am to be responsible for in the theatre and I will stick strictly to what I am assigned. Up till now the shareholders have only wanted one thing, that you and I should come to terms. I propose this agreement, that you stop making decisions without consulting the shareholders, even, naturally, when you are angry with me. *With all the strength of my soul* I would like *even in the current season* to make our working relationship a good one, so as to support the theatre. Obviously I can't.

290 Stanislavski to Nemirovich

November 5 1906

Sunday   Moscow

Dear Vladimir Ivanovich,

There is no doubt that you are the person to gather the reins of all the different departments in your hands and while you continue to hold them things will go well at the theatre.

I have already presented my excuses over Sulerzhitski, recognizing that I was wrong both in the official and ethical respects. I explained why all this happened. I willingly excuse myself once more for my tactlessness.

I don't see any threat in my giving lessons either at home or for Adashev. On the contrary, it is a request, as without that I would not consider I had the right to talk to Adashev. These last days I have read so many strange and unexpected things that I really have come to believe that my classes are not wanted. So much the better if this is not so.

I am sure that my participation in the school was wanted not so that I could do what other people were doing but so that I could find something new – I settled on light comedy. I could not do it myself so I asked Aleksandrov to do it on his own account (we didn't get around to discussing payment). At that period you were ill and couldn't work and I wanted to keep everyone's spirits up by giving them work. I thought that without this new work, for which he is fully qualified, Aleksandrov would go on a drinking spree. I wanted to combine the pleasurable with the useful. I call your attention to the fact that I stressed that work on light comedy should in no way interfere with normal classes and when I learned from Samarova that students were turning up tired to class I asked Aleksandrov to find another time for his rehearsals.

In a formal sense I was wrong there too and I ask your pardon but it was not done with ulterior motives.

In the future I will ask you to make clear whether I should discontinue these classes. Concerning writers you are absolutely wrong.

It is ludicrous to suspect me because I like to read plays and write comments on them. I write to everyone without exception to say that I am passing them on to be read and will communicate the results.

Kosorotov came to me direct requesting me to say what I thought about the play. So did Asch. So did Pinski. (By the way that play must be returned.) These are private requests which have nothing to do with the theatre or with you. Right now I don't understand how I should behave in such circumstances other than the way I have behaved up till now. I repeat, if you save me from correspondence with writers and with foreign countries I will be infinitely grateful to you as it takes up a lot of my time . . .

I am probably happier than anyone for myself and for the theatre when you are working with great energy. In those moments you do not complain.

When you are not working I strain every last nerve to maintain the company's flagging spirits.

If this protracted correspondence is a sign of a renewal of energy I am the first to rejoice and am probably the first to support you and set an example by my obedience (with the exception of those indiscretions I commit in the heat of the moment, when working, and for which I ask pardon in advance).

I thought and I continue to think that you yourself wanted our theatre to be neither revolutionary not reactionary. It is in that sense that I have acted. I do not want to stir up either the revolutionaries or the reactionaries. Does that mean that we are afraid of them or that we are above all that? When we are attacked we must avoid fighting back so as not to divert attention from the most important thing, that is art. This is not a political but an artistic question.

I bow low and thank you sincerely for the desire you express to support my artistic intentions. I am sorry not to have understood that from your earlier letters.

I wish with all my heart that our relationship was more than merely decent but much bigger, the more so since that creates unease. Let me unburden my heart in just one play and I will do everything, but without that I cannot breathe and, like a starving man, think only of food.

It is shameful in the times we live through to give our time to the things we have been giving them to for the last few days.

Hauptmann is sending us a play. Maeterlinck has agreed a contract with America [for *Bluebird*] on condition the production uses our *mise-en-scène*. Zabel is starting work on a book about our theatre and what of us . . . men of culture whom they take as a example of people who, to a certain extent, bring glory to Russia . . . It's bad, shame on us.

Your K. Alekseiev

Stanislavski's concern with the process of acting made him, like Nemirovich, increasingly impatient with the passive actor who brought nothing to rehearsal. He was himself partly responsible for this situation since for years he had imposed performances on his young actors, demonstrating what he wanted when necessary. Only the really creative, like Meyerhold, rebelled.

291 Stanislavski to Leonidov

November 7 1906
Moscow

Dear Leonid Mironovich,

We Russians love to make infinite sacrifices for the thing we love most with one hand and then destroy it with the other.

That is what is happening in our theatre.

The sacrifices the actors have had to make for the theatre cannot be counted but these same actors, thanks to one or two purely Russian qualities, are breaking that theatre apart. You have probably never given a moment's serious thought to the fact that the directors of this theatre give the best of their hearts and minds to the actors.

And this energy has been expended not only in artistic matters . . .

For example, consider deeply what it costs to maintain the far from perfect order which reigns in the theatre, in rehearsal and backstage.

This order is not maintained by the whole company and the employees *in corpore* as it should be . . . It is maintained by a very small group of people.

If they were to go or to slacken the reins our whole business would become chaotic.

Ask yourself a few questions, for example, do these people represent an adequate support for the company?

Don't a few people pick on every word and action of those who fight for order – and that, in the present time, is everything for us as it is for the whole of Russia.

We, in Russian style, offer sacrifices with one hand and annihilate them with the other.

You will never know, if you have not been through it yourself, how much blood, nervous tension, health and torment of soul and disappointment it costs to sit at your table as a director in rehearsal.

Say, in all conscience, how many actors can you find in the company who can or are able to work independently? Are there many who can bring a character and a creation independently to the stage without the help of the director's imagination?

The following highly comical view has become axiomatic in our theatre: 'it was ever so in our theatre and so it must be'.

It is difficult to find a character for oneself although no one knows his theatrical resources and his inner gifts better than an actor.

It is harder still to find a character for someone else, whose personality the director may not be able to feel.

How then to create a dozen characters and adapt them to a dozen different artistic personalities?

And another thing, will these characters that directors have created for other people be easily absorbed and integrated by the actors?

Aren't most of them concerned to latch onto a few superficial features, or just follow their whims, especially those who do not work at home?

Directors who do the work for the actors have to beg and pray, accept gratefully or simply work over what they themselves have given these actors. Such things are frequent in our theatre and then, as you sit at your director's table, you experience the resentment, the anger, the rancour which a dying man cannot always contain.

One might imagine that in moments of extreme tension when one man is doing the work of few, a certain tolerance might be expected and that if people did not help, they would not hinder. Not so.

Anything that can destroy the director's mood in moments of creative tension (the director cannot take one step without that mood and nervous tension), everything that offends him in the sense of disrespect for his efforts, all this a director gets continuously, every minute as payment for his efforts. And all this is done unconsciously, from Russian habit: to despise other people's efforts.

Creation is possible when there's quiet, a common feeling. Every actor knows that perfectly well yet chatters away. It is possible to create when nerves are very tense but this abnormal condition does not grant the director the right, in the actors' eyes, to an outburst of anger. The director speaks unceasingly and to the whole theatre but this does not prevent the cast from speaking even louder, forcing the director to use all the power of his voice, to outshout the crowd.

The most difficult moment for the director, one which demands sensitivity and imagination at the highest pitch, is when for the first time, for a fleeting second, he sees the stage picture. He has to hit upon this picture so that we can draw the actors and the whole production into it. He has already raised the edge of the curtain, he is ready to understand the whole . . . but he is distracted by some misplaced joke or a search for a missing actor and everything is lost.

Many rehearsals are needed, there has to be another instant of grace for that moment to recur. Imagine what a director feels in that moment.

And the number of moments like that in our working life is endless.

Everything that is said in rehearsal is related to the whole. All the details of the production create the kind of atmosphere in which the actor merges with the author and the other actors and every department of a complex theatrical mechanism.

Is it possible for us to keep an actor in that atmosphere of his own free will? Won't we be told: 'It's inhuman to keep an actor in a rehearsal when he is in the play but not in this act'?

The director is stuck in his seat all the time and that is considered human, but for an actor it's considered impossible.

And so the director is obliged to say the same thing a dozen times to different people and that is not considered inhuman and the director doesn't have the right to lose his temper nor to reproach the actor with his coolness of attitude towards the business in hand.

Don't forget the most important thing.

The director is working with the most sensitive and delicate parts of the organism, which wear out very quickly.

This is a question of health and life. One must not endanger either of them out of wilfulness or the superficiality of others.

To come back to myself, one must remember that up till now I have had all the leading roles and that I have been very busy as an actor, that I have a large business to take care of, that I also have public duties, such as a school and guardianship,[1] that I have a family and that I am a sick man.[2]

I have been doing this work for 20 years, without complaining.

I did it as long as I could.

Now I must take care of myself.

Fortunately I have found a way to do it, that is to discontinue rehearsals whenever they are unworthy of our theatre.

I am happy you have found such a discovery, I will always use it.

In an extremely painful moment for a director I may have been less than polite towards you.

If that is so I willingly ask your pardon. If however you were not quite polite towards me you do not need to be told what to do.

Respectfully K. Alekseiev

292 Nemirovich to Stanislavski

January 1907
Moscow

I have to say once more that I do not like the musical element as it has been introduced into 'The Drama of Life'. It may be excellent per se. But, in the first place, there is too much of it for the drama and that not only does not help the effect but, on the contrary, waters down the depth and strength of the dramatic effect. In works where the dramatic force of the situation is not sufficient to affect the audience this is permissible or even desirable. But in a drama, in which the audience must not be allowed to cool off from scene to scene, music is only good *as background from time to time*. Here, in 'The Drama of Life' it works independently and swamps the impression the actors have built up over the preceding scenes. This creates emotions which are wonderful in themselves but absolutely lethal for the dramatic intention. And, in the second place – I'm sorry but this is important – the character of Satz's music is not compatible with the simplicity and naïveté we expect from roving, country musicians. What, in fact, we have here is the presence

1. Stanislavski was a trustee of a school for foundlings.
2. Stanislavski worked himself to exhaustion and was extremely prone to chills and influenza. He was only seriously ill, however, in 1910, when he contracted typhus and in 1928, when he suffered a double heart attack.

of the kind of excessively virtuoso music which always, everywhere, damages the effect. I do not know *one single* example on stage where the drama gained from music like this. And I have always considered this predilection of yours, as a director, for a plethora of music to be *a fault*–a passion for secondary elements to the detriment of the force and turmoil of the dramatic impetus.

Forgive me for having expressed myself so bluntly.

V. Nemirovich-Danchenko

293 Stanislavski to Stakhovich

February 4/5 1907
Moscow

My dear Aleksei Aleksandrovich,
'The Drama of Life' still hasn't flopped yet because I have been ill and haven't acted for two weeks. I have been going out the last few days and working but the illness has taken away all my energy. I get tired very quickly and so rehearsals are unproductive. We are terribly sick of the play and can't wait for the time when we have done with it. That, it seems, will be in three days' time, i.e., on Thursday. [. . .]

For the rest it's the same old thing at the theatre. Nemirovich is behaving abominably. He has made a great show of not coming to a single dress rehearsal of 'The Drama of Life'. Luzhski too. In the company the attitude towards my experiments is extremely hostile and whenever they can people are sarcastic and obstructive.

Suler[1] during this time has worn himself to shreds. Yesterday there was a great hullabaloo. All obstacles had to be hacked down and today things have improved. Knipper seems to have gone back to her earlier ways somewhat. Moskvin, Vishnievski are working well. I am not expecting a success but a great deal of shock, disputes and hostile criticism. I am thankful for that. 'Brand' is making money like mad. The other plays as well. But my illness will cost dear . . .

Nelidov is offering his services as he is going to leave the imperial theatres. Nemirovich mentioned this to me *en passant* and the matter has been dropped in a bureaucratic manner. The American trip has also been dropped although Nemirovich did have some discussions. [. . .]

1. Sulerzhitski was always known as Suler to his intimates.

294 Stanislavski to Kotlyarevskaya

February 15 1907
Moscow

[. . .]

'The Drama of Life' had the success I hoped for. Half the people hissed, the other half were in raptures. I am satisfied with the results of a number of trials and experiments.

They have opened up many interesting principles to us.

The Decadents are happy,

the realists are outraged,

the bourgeois are resentful.

Many are taken aback and telephone to ask if I am all right.

If a lot of people are spitting venom, what could be better? We worked well and, I think, achieved a lot. [. . .]

The possibility of a merger of the Art Theatre and the Maly, first mooted in 1905, was still a live issue. When it appeared to Stanislavski that such a merger might take place, he immediately decided to leave. Just how difficult this decision was for him is evident from the correspondence. He first drafted a long letter of resignation, which he scrapped, sent a short letter then, the same day, withdrew it.

295 Stanislavski to Nemirovich

February 23 1907
Moscow

Draft in Notebook

Dear Vladimir Ivanovich,

I am writing this letter sooner than I had intended but unforeseen circumstances have arisen which compel me to hurry. I refer to Nelidov's proposals to join us here at the theatre.

I withdraw from any discussions of this question but put before you a statement that may influence a proper response to Nelidov's proposal.

I give you my word I am writing this letter calmly, after proper reflection and with full awareness. Pain, grievances, insults, discontent, hopes, all the elements of internal conflict, are now behind me.

My statement is a friendly request to you. I hope you will enable me to carry it out, if only for the sake of memory of our past good relations and our work together.

By virtue of innumerable circumstances, which are well known to you, next year I shall be obliged to cease to be a member of management and a shareholder but can remain as an investor. Tell me how that can be done without adversely affecting the business. [. . .]

In practical terms the theatre will not suffer from my departure as I am a manager without any responsibilities and a shareholder without influence.

I am needed by the theatre as an actor and a director. I will fulfil these and other responsibilities no better and no worse than in the past. Try to accept this letter in the simple, good spirit in which it is written. [. . .]

My dear friend, release me as a manager and a shareholder.

I will remain as an investor and actor, I will fulfil any commissions. I will work better than I am now and will feel freer and happier. Think what it will mean to you: you will be free and independent.

We don't need any more rehearsals, excruciating for both of us, to satisfy ourselves that we are such different people and that we shall never agree on any item.

Up till now the unique feature of our merger was the respect we had for the efforts we put into the business.

But this too has gone. We have been pulling the business in different directions and are tearing it apart. That is criminal. Married couples can divorce, lovers, friends break off their relationship rather make each others' lives a misery. Can't we (condemned to torture each other all our lives) find some *modus vivendi* which will enable us to avoid the worst possible harm: to ruin another man's very existence.

To create this new relationship we must, above all, part.

I don't want to play on gratitude or be overmodest . . . I should be the one to give in. [. . .] if you quit, the theatre will cease to exist.

I don't have the right to be a shareholder or a member of management because my family, my commercial situation and financial means do not permit me to remain in the false and dangerous position I find myself in at the present moment.

I am one of the few actually solvent members of the association. Do I possess the right to risk what I don't have? The risk is enormous. It threatens my family with total ruin, it is also a threat in that I will not be able to justify the confidence of the stock exchange and will compromise a commercial undertaking that has been renowned for its probity for 150 years. [. . .]

Don't think for a moment that I am trying to avoid my share of the losses in the event of a crash. I am willing to give an undertaking to participate in losses. [. . .]

Shouldn't we change the statutes so that I don't have to take that risk? What should be done? . . .

I can't be a dictator. I don't want to be and I am not capable of it. I don't trust myself in that role. I would go too far. [. . .]

There cannot be a solution until we recognize what is natural and established by the business itself.

Put me into normal conditions and everything will go like clockwork . . .

1. The theatre needs me as an actor in certain parts
2. The theatre needs me as a director for one or two productions
3. Sometimes it needs my tact and acumen in business

This will still obtain in a new role.

If the theatre needs me, call on me; if not I will stay at home (I cannot witness things which are against my nature and with which I will never agree under any circumstances) . . .

As you can see, I accuse no one but rather acknowledge my own guilt. It seems to me that from that it is easy to recognize that I am writing this letter in a good spirit and expect a similar attitude from you. I am indebted to you for many things and am grateful, I have great affection and respect for you. May these things unite us if not with bonds of close friendship then in bonds of grateful memory and respect.

Let us part friends, so that later, an enterprise of world renown may never be broken up by its members.

It is our civic duty to support it.

It would be a barbarous crime to destroy it.

296

Letter

Deeply respected Vladimir Ivanovich,

I bring to your attention and to the attention of the shareholders my intention, with a deeply aching heart, of laying down my responsibilities and title as a manager, as I can no longer fulfil them as conscientiously as I would wish.

Seeing that these responsibilities have been reduced to nothing, the theatre will not suffer any harm from my departure from the board of management.

It goes without saying that I will undertake my remaining duties until the end of the year in the same conscientious way as my attachment to the theatre and to my colleagues still binds me very closely to them.

Respectfully yours,

K. S. Alekseiev

297

Letter

Dear Vladimir Ivanovich,

Consider the situation I am in. Read my letter through once more and find some way for me to retract what I have said.

Your K. Alekseiev

298 Nemirovich to his Wife

April 30 1907
Moscow

At 10 in morning while I was still in bed, a ring at the door and a visiting card – 'V. A. Nelidov' on an important matter. A-ha!

'I have come to ask you to accept the post of principal director of the Maly Theatre. Your conditions are more or less known and will be accepted. If you need to offer jobs to one or two people – actors or artists – it will be done.' . . .

Nelidov went away with this answer: 'I don't say no but I must see Telyakovski for an hour or so with the firm object of getting not just a simple agreement to one or two of my conditions but to a total reform of the Maly Theatre.' . . .

Telyakovski arranged an appointment for four-thirty. He arrived late, at five, not deliberately but simply because he had been talking to K.S. (to whom he said nothing) stayed late and arrived about five . . . We talked until a quarter to seven . . .

'This is a completely analogous moment. Take advantage of it, you can create in Moscow within 25 years the greatest of artistic institutions but if you don't take advantage of it the Maly Theatre will go into terminal decline. Now I can work to bring all the best performing and artistic forces in Moscow into the Maly Theatre and in three years your minister will turn the Maly Theatre over to us just so as to be rid of it . . .

If I join you now I merely paper over the cracks and destroy the Art Theatre . . . I propose something else. You've wasted so many years, be patient a while longer . . . in June I will submit my programme of reforms. In August we will discuss it and make preparations during the winter and after Lent next year I will assume control of the administration of the dramatic company of the Maly Theatre.

My plan, of course, is to use everything that's best in the Maly and Art theatres and not to put people like our own Samarova and Artiom, etc., out on the street and to restore the Maly Theatre to all its brilliance . . .'

Leaving him I went to Alekseiev's house. He was asleep and I didn't disturb him. I told him about it at the theatre that evening.

– I am talking to you first. I have declined the invitation to go to the Maly Theatre but now I have agreed to draw up a plan of reform.

– Why are you doing this?

– I can't turn it down. You can, I can't. You, so to speak, are a free artist. You create and for that you seek good conditions. I haven't created at the Art Theatre, mainly I have founded an institution where people create. If I am told, you have created a theatre now create a state academy, I am obliged to accept and to bring all the best theatrical forces. My attachment to one theatre, even to one of my own creation does not warrant my refusal because that would reduce the forward-looking nature of my activity. It would be like a man refusing to go into parliament because he is a distinguished member of the local council. [. . .]

Nemirovich's negotiations with the Maly convinced Stanislavski that he should reconsider his position within the Art Theatre. He was once again struggling with the stylized allusiveness of Symbolist drama in the form of Andreiev's *The Life of Man*, of which he had no high opinion.

The production, when it opened on December 12 1907, owed its success mainly to the quality of the design, based on Beardsley, and Stanislavski's production tricks. He was no further forward in his attempts to deepen and broaden the actor's inner, psychological technique.

A new source of inspiration came from the modern dancer Isadora Duncan who gave a special series of matinées at the Art Theatre. Isadora decided that Stanislavski and Gordon Craig should work together.

299 Isadora Duncan to Stanislavski

January 4 1908
Petersburg

Dear Friend:

I have just come back from Madame Duse . . .

I danced last night. I thought of you and danced well. I received your cards and today received your telegram. Thank you. How good and thoughtful of you! And how I love you!

I feel a surge of new, extraordinary energy. Today I worked all morning and put many new ideas into my work. Rhythms again. It is you who have given me these ideas. I am so glad I feel like flying to the stars and dancing round the moon. This will be a new dance which I will dedicate to you.

I have written to Gordon Craig. I told him about your theatre and about your own great art. But couldn't you write to him yourself? If he could work with you it would be *ideal* for him. I hope with all my heart that this can be arranged. I will soon write to you again. Thank you once more. I love you. I still work with joy.

Isadora

My tender love to your wife and children.

300 Stanislavski to Isadora

January 1908
Moscow

[Written in French]
Dear Friend!

How happy I am!!!

How proud I am!!!

I have helped a great artist to find the atmosphere she needed!!! And it all happened when we were being delightfully lazy in a cabaret surrounded by vice.

How strange life is! How beautiful it is at times. No! You are good, you are pure, you are noble and within the great, exalted feeling and artistic admiration which I have experienced towards you hitherto I sense the birth of a deep and genuine friendship and affection.

Do you know what you did to me? I have not spoken of it to you so far.

In spite of the great success our theatre has had and the innumerable admirers that surround it, I have always been alone (except for my wife who has supported me in my moments of doubt and disappointment). You are the first to tell me in a few simple and convincing words what is important and fundamental about the art I wished to create. That gave me a fresh burst of energy at a moment when I was about to give up my artistic career.

I thank you, I truly thank you from the bottom of my heart.

Oh how impatiently I waited for your letter and danced when I read it. I was afraid you had misinterpreted my reserve and would take pure feeling for indifference. I was afraid that your feeling of happiness, the energy and strength you took away with you would desert you before you arrived in Saint-Petersburg.

Now you are dancing the Moon dance and I am dancing my own as yet unnamed dance.

I am content, I am more than rewarded. [. . .]

Every free minute at work we talk of the divine nymph who came down from Olympus to bring us joy. We kiss your wonderful hands and will never forget you. I am happy if the new creation was inspired by my love for you. I would like to see this dance . . . When shall I see it? I don't even know your itinerary?!

301 Stanislavski to Isadora

Prior to January 14 1908
Moscow

[Written in French]
Dear Friend and Colleague,

This time I am talking business. It's about your school. The director of all the imperial theatres, Mr Telyakovski (excellency), is in Moscow. The director of the Moscow theatre, Mr Nelidov (the same one who should have been here today but didn't come because of illness), spoke to him about you today.

Mr Telyakovski was interested in the proposal and he wants to know you and discuss your school.

Tomorrow Telyakovski will be coming to the theatre and I will do my best to try and interest him still more. The day after tomorrow, i.e., Tuesday evening, Mr Telyakovsky leaves for Saint-Petersburg. Try to see him on Wednesday. I asked Mr Nelidov to draft a letter for me, that I should send to you. Unfortunately I haven't the time to rewrite and so am sending it as it stands, as I am very anxious to get it off. Forgive me.

I am sending you the draft so that you can know Mr Nelidov's opinions, he knows Telyakovski very well. It's not for me to teach you how to talk to people. Your talent will prompt you better than I.

Still, I take it on myself to advise you:

1. Ask for about 15 thousand roubles a year to open. If you ask for more you risk frightening Telyakovski off.

2. Ask for some amount or other for the removal costs of the school but it would be better at the end of the meeting or at the next discussion.

3. Tell Telyakovski it would be possible for you to return part of the amount if he would make the stage of the Imperial Theatre available to you for some student performances.

4. Above all try to talk to him with your distinctive artistic gifts and talent about the principles of your art (don't be too harsh about old-style ballet). May the gods go with you. [. . .]

302 Stanislavski to Isadora

January 19 1908
Moscow

[. . .]
It is being rumoured that your enchanting children are coming to Saint-Petersburg. Is that true or not?

That means . . . that the business with the school is settled? My dream comes true and your great art will not die with you! You know I am much more enthusiastic about you than about the beautiful Duse. Your dancing said more to me than the usual kind of performance which I saw yesterday evening.

You have shattered my principles. Since your departure I have been trying to discover in my own art the things you created in your own. That is something beautiful, simple, like nature itself. Today I saw the beautiful Duse repeat something which I know already, something I have seen a hundred times. Duse didn't make me forget Duncan!

I beg you, work for the sake of art and believe me, your efforts will bring you joy, the best joy life can offer. [. . .]

Stanislavski's resignation from the Board, when it came, provoked by a letter from Nemirovich which is lost, was undramatic. In fact, he remained a shareholder until 1911.

303 Stanislavski to Nemirovich

February 8 1908
Moscow

Dear Vladimir Ivanovich,

As our ten years of effort have ended with the letter I have just received,[1] any belief in my *infinite* devotion and love for you, the theatre and our association can only be futile.

I ask you to take note that at the end of the current season I shall cease to be a shareholder and a member of management.

As to the future, I offer my services, gratis, as an actor in my old roles and as a director – under conditions of which you are aware.

1. Lost.

ELEVEN

THE THEATRE AND THE SYSTEM

Stanislavski's new status in the company was much as he had envisaged in 1907. The most important feature of the new agreement was his right to stage one production of his own choice a year and in as experimental a manner as he chose. For the rest, he would continue to perform in the roles he had made famous and would accept new roles if they were suitable.

Stanislavski profited from his departure from management by being more outspoken about the company's failings both artistic and ethical. He was particularly concerned about arrogance among the young and the bad example they were being given by senior members of the company whose behaviour he considered at times dissolute. Even allowing for Stanislavski's puritanism, outside reaction would seem to indicate that the company was acquiring a reputation for poor behaviour. He took the opportunity on the occasion of the theatre's tenth anniversary to issue an appeal, *Help!!!* (see letter **309**, page 270).

Against the deep-seated faults in the company he set his own burgeoning System which demanded both artistic and ethical integrity. Few, including his own wife, were convinced that his new approach to acting had anything to offer them or that it was worth the risk abandoning old and tried methods, which had made them stars, for a time-consuming self-examination and a method which was, at the time, crudely expressed in a bizarre vocabulary drawn from various sources including Gogol and Yoga. Stanislavski had to prove his point through successful productions. He elected to stage *A Month in the Country* which demanded subtlety of playing and deep psychological understanding and presented little external action. At the same time he persuaded the Board to invite Gordon Craig to oversee a production of *Hamlet*, which he himself would stage as far as possible according to Craig's concept. If Stanislavski could pull off both productions, using the System, he would have proved his case.

Nemirovich's view of the System was very mixed. He recognized some of its merits and yet it was deeply inimical to him. It relied too much on the actor and his own personality. Nemirovich saw himself, and in one letter explicitly described himself, as someone who 'inspires'. It was the director's vision that motivated the actors. He had, using Tolstoi's term, to 'infect' them with the play's meaning, with the author's inner essence, or, as he put it, his 'inner image'. On the practical side he was disturbed by the amount of rehearsal time the System took. Knowing that open opposition would finally drive Stanislavski out of the theatre, he declared the System the official working method of the Art Theatre with the full intention of jettisoning those aspects of which he did not approve.

Stanislavski, despite the progress he was making with the company, realized that it was to the young that he must turn and began to demand money and resources to enable him to teach his ideas and create the company of the future. Major talents, like Vakhtangov and Michael Chekhov, were joining the theatre. Their gifts had to be developed and protected, as Stanislavski saw it, from the jealousies and failings of the established members. From there it was but one step to revive the idea of the Theatre-Studio. Thus it was that in turn the First, Second, Third and Fourth Studios were created, taking him further and further away from his erstwhile colleagues. This caused Nemirovich great distress.

304 Stanislavski to Kotlyarevskaya

May 5 1908
Petersburg

[. . .]

Here there is a ferment of struggle and life. The first explosion of the revolution has died away and we are adding up the pluses and the minuses. After a great deal of effort we nonetheless managed to shift the company out of the stagnation which everyone would have been happy to stay in so as to collect more laurels. Now it is possible to talk more freely of stylization, of the rhythm of feelings and about everything new that has come into being, though for the moment in distorted form. That's a plus. The actors have understood that this is no time for sleeping and have quite woken up. I myself, looking back over everything that has been done these last two years, can see that nothing of consequence has been discovered. That's a minus.

We have managed to get on the track of new principles. These principles may well stand the psychology of the actor's creative process on its head. I conduct experiments every day on myself and on others and often achieve highly interesting results. I am mostly busy with the rhythm of feelings, the discovery of affective memory and the psychophysiology of the creative process. With the help of these experiments I have managed to achieve much greater simplicity and strength in existing roles and I am able to fortify my creative will to such an extent that even when I am ill, or have a temperature, I forget about my illness and find energy on stage. As a result the company respect these new ideas and have stopped laughing at my experiments and listen to what I have to say with considerable attention . . .

What can I say about us? We have been slaughtered, more than was ever thought possible but the takings are enormous, despite the fact that we've come without any new repertoire. 'The Life of Man' is one big horror, muck, not a play at all. 'Rosmersholm' though very well staged by Nemirovich is not very theatrical. The rest is old stuff . . .

While in Petersburg Isadora had been active as a go-between to and from Craig and Stanislavski. Early in 1908 she wrote to Craig.

305 Isadora to Craig

[early] 1908

Mr Stanislavsky, the régisseur of the Theatre, is a wonderful man – really Beautiful & Great – I talked with him many hours about you – He says he would love to have you come & be régisseur altogether, as he prefers to *act*. The plays for this year are all fixed, but he says if you came next August & prepared a piece Aug. & Sept. to be given in October, then if you liked & all went well you might stay with them. They are all wonderful people & he is Beautiful. So kind & unassuming – *a really great* man – I have never met anyone like him.

He asked if you would write to him. I told him he should write to you first – he seems shy – said he would write you a long letter but that it would take him a couple of weeks to compose it. He wants me to telegraph & ask you only to come & visit them & see if you like them – but I didn't think you'd care to come for anything that was not sure. He says he would give you a perfectly free hand in the Theatre – that the actors would follow your directions as to movements etc. & that you could do what you liked & take all the time you like to do it in –

All the people belonging to the Theatre are so simple & sweet & unassuming. There are 300 pupils in the School. I told him 6,000 gulden for two months. He said he would put it before the directors. He said afterward you could take a troupe from their theatre & go on tour –

He said 'Tell Mr Craig we are very simple people, that we care nothing at all for ourselves but very much for Art & that if he will come we will all be glad to follow his ideas.' I can only repeat that he is great & simple & Beautiful – such a man as one doesn't meet with once in a century –

I showed him your book[1] & he thought it very beautiful – He is very anxious for you to come. He is a bit afraid of your prices – the Theatre is not very rich –

---

1. *On the Art of the Theatre* in a poor German translation.

Stanislavski finally wired Craig suggesting that they meet in Hamburg while he was on holiday.

306 Gordon Craig to Stanislavski

July 10 1908
5, Piazza Donatello,
Studio 9,
Firenze

[. . .]

Alas I cannot come to Hamburg and I cannot come to Moscow in September, if I could *come* to either place I would do so.

I cannot come because I am at work upon four very difficult plays to be produced in Berlin . . . Deutsche Theatre. One of these (King Lear) is to be ready September: as you know 'King Lear' is not very easy.

I wish I could come to see you. I wish I could come.

As I cannot come, I wish to write to you as though I had known you for a long time and as if I understood what you want. By doing so we may perhaps understand each other. I therefore drop the role of 'Régisseur' or 'Stage Reformer' and whatever mask you may think covers the real man and will attempt to show you myself and my wishes . . . Hopes!

Is that right? Clear? Good; then let us proceed.

My wishes first.

1st. I want to work with you: I want to come to Moscow and produce with your help the best thing yet seen on stage in Europe. This must be a play we *know* . . . *n'est-ce pas*.

For my part I am familiar with Hamlet, Macbeth, The Tempest, Midsummer's Night Dream, Ghosts (Ibsen) and *fairly* familiar with Peer Gynt.

Could either of those plays be chosen by you?

2nd. I wish to do this work between October and January for the plain and simple reason that I shall be free then and not free before . . .

3rd. I wish to make money. [. . .]

I am poor . . . always was and always shall be. That is why I can refuse so many small offers to do *small* productions in a small way for a *small* sum.

I am really in love with my Art . . . and with the Theatre, vile and mad as it is I have no other interests in the world than to remain true to the Art, and I am not able to continue a work in a theatre where there is more than one master. I studied under Henry Irving who rules his theatre sternly and justly. I have not had the pleasure of meeting any such ruler since he died. In the European theatre intrigue rules and the director is merely a figurehead. I understand that this is not the case in your theatre. I should be glad of this assurance from you, and in this event glad to work under you.

I would rather remain in Italy than go to any land and produce what has been seen before . . . and so if I must visit Moscow it must be understood that I come there with that purpose and the theatre must be prepared to make things possible.

All *Enthusiasm* has left the hearts of those who work in the theatres of Europe. They work without *playing*. They work without laughing or singing. To me Art is a game . . . a wonderful and exciting game. I hope your workmen would be prepared to play it with me.

And now my best greetings.

Write to me as you would to someone you were inviting to go on a shooting expedition . . . then I shall understand.

Gordon Craig

Stanislavski continued his negotiations with Craig through Maurice Magnus, Craig's friend and associate. Magnus, who was in the Hague, made a quick visit on August 22 1908 to Stanislavski who was staying in Westende les Bains, in Belgium. He then relayed Stanislavski's offer to Craig.

307 Maurice Magnus to Craig   .

August 1908
The Hague

[. . .]

Stanislavsky makes the following proposition: that you come to Moscow October 1 (Russian style) – that is, about the 13th of October, stay there for some weeks, speak to him, see the theatre, the work they are doing and have a talk. He says it is impossible to do things by letter as most of the time that brings confusion and misunderstanding, especially as he writes nothing but Russian and he would not have trusted any one to make a translation, so he did not write. He speaks French and German, but does not write it.[1] He would like you (after you have seen the theatre and Moscow and feel you can stay there and work there) to become engaged to the theatre by the year – that is, they play seven months of the year – he feels it would only be in justice to you. He fears that if you came for only one production, the theatre would unconsciously or consciously have gained impressions from your work which they could not efface; and what they would benefit from that one

---

1. Stanislavski wrote French perfectly well but not German.

production would be unjust to you if you were not there to also draw the benefit. In other words, that your ideas are subject to be taken advantage of, which he decidedly does not want. Besides, he says, if you did one production and you went away and came back again, it would mean starting afresh, as some might have forgotten what they had learnt, and only *constant* training can bring forth the results desired. Now if you came and stayed, and found that the theatre had possibilities and the conditions were not too impossible and you could grow to love it, he would be very glad.

You would not have to be there the seven months at a stretch but could go off, of course, occasionally, when your part of the work was done, etc. They would not expect you to do more than about two productions this first season.

. . . Your trip there will be at his *own* expense, and your preliminary stay. I told him you had no money and he would have to send you a thousand marks for the trip beforehand. This he agreed to do.

. . . It is the best proposition I have yet heard and certainly one which is more dignified that any other, for you to deal with first-class people.

Stanislavski's last production as co-manager with Nemirovich was one of his most celebrated, 'The Bluebird'. In it he finally came to terms with the problems of Symbolist drama, achieving a synthesis between abstraction and the truthful realism he required in characterization. The production stayed in the repertoire until 1938, although it was withdrawn for a short period just after the 1917 Revolution. Such was the fame of the production that Sulerzhitski was despatched to Paris to reproduce it for Réjane, although the changes she made caused a furious Stanislavski to declare his work had been vulgarized. Beerbohm Tree sent his assistant, Stanley Bell, to Moscow to see the production and many of its features were reproduced in the English production at His Majesty's Theatre.

Although a long time in preparation, with just under 130 rehearsals, the final stages proved difficult. Stanislavski complained about the lack of coordination and cooperation back-stage. One evening he vented his rage on Sulerzhitski.

308 Stanislavski to Sulerzhitski

September 26 1908
Moscow

Dear Suler,
I'm writing this while still at the director's table. Forgive me if I was rude to you, it wasn't my intention.

Whether I shouted or not I can't remember but I had been bellowing from 11 in the morning to 11 at night and was vocally and nervously no longer in a position to maintain order . . .

Satz has altered the music and now my imagination is working to fit the movement to the music.

The water [-effect] doesn't work – after one and a half years. People whisper to me that I must give up something I have been thinking of for half a year.

Anyone who has sat at the director's table must forgive a man if, in such moments, while giving his all uncomplainingly, he behaves badly. I am the only one doing any thinking and I impose my will on all the actors, I am living for them all sitting at the table.

Forgive me – perhaps I was wrong but I deserve indulgence.

Your K. Alekseiev

Having drafted an open letter to the company Stanislavski, having no official management status, sent it to the Board, asking for a decision as to whether it should be posted on the bulletin-board or not.

309 Stanislavski

November 28 1908

Letter to Some of my Fellow-Artists
Help!!!

1. The [10th] jubilee honours, the success of our plays, full houses, do not raise the theatre's level of energy but reduce its capacity for work.
2. In the first half of the season the theatre has not staged one *single* new play.
3. The play which was staged after two years' work [*The Bluebird*] and which provides our theatre with its living, no longer evokes affection.
4. It is not the difficulties of the change-over which prevent us from staging plays but the creative apathy of the company.
5. The staging of the best works of our national literature in the jubilee year no longer appears to be an event for our theatre.
6. In the critical moment the theatre is living through actors' hurt pride is not only tolerated but sympathized with.
7. The cancellation of two performances in a week is used for rest and amusement and not more intensive rehearsal.
8. People feel able to absent themselves from Moscow without official leave from the Board.

9. Illness or absence are reported after the beginning of the performance.
10. Neither requests nor reprimands, neither regulations nor a sense of ethical obligation to one's fellows are capable of eliminating lateness or failure to turn up for rehearsal.
11. The behaviour of individual persons which hinders the work of our theatre is no longer capable of provoking a general protest.
12. To speak out strongly against disruption in the general interest of the theatre is considered to be an act of denunciation while concealment of guilt is considered an act of friendship.
13. Fledgelings in our art publicly flaunt an as yet unproved talent and congratulate themselves in advance for successes to come, instead of winning them by work. That is considered amusing.
14. New theories in our art that should be developed through effort are capable of interesting our theatre for no more than two-three weeks.
15. New currents in our art, coming from the west, are not sympathetically received.
16. The enormous efforts of a small group, which represents the soul of our whole enterprise, encounters less sympathy than the feeble rancour of people among us who have in no way proved themselves.
17. The superhuman work of the directors, who give the actors the best part of their artistic souls, is only appreciated in words and not in deeds.
18. The artistic, administrative, ethical and disciplinary aspects of the theatre are maintained by a small group of self-sacrificing hard-working people. Their strength and patience are being exhausted. The time will soon come when they will have to refuse work which is beyond human capacity. Reflect while there is still time!

With best wishes
K. Stanislavski

310 Nemirovich to Stanislavski

November 28-29 1908
Moscow

Rumyantsev presented your appeal at the meeting of the Board ('Help!', that's good).

I proposed that it should be made public without discussion as the Board has no right to assume it can censor your communications to the company. But Rumyantsev read out your letter in which you ask for the trustworthiness of your views to be tested. The Board then went through every point and asked me to convey its thoughts to you. [. . .]

The conclusion of the Board was (I am not expressing my own opinion): yes, something untoward is happening; Konstantin Sergeievich is right about many things, but he deals unfairly with many others, he exaggerates many things for which he himself is guilty (it could be that had I not been there they would have said I was more guilty than anyone), he writes warmly, sincerely, but he will hardly attain good results with such an appeal precisely because not everything in it is firmly substantiated or, rather, well-founded, and sometimes is not worthy of attention. [. . .]

In general the Board cannot be certain of the success of such an appeal. Many will harbour objections in their hearts which will lead them to reject it but which they will not express out loud. Feelings will run high . . . On the other hand, the Board is not trying to dissuade you from posting up your appeal but merely expressing its opinion on the grounds of your letter.

My own personal opinion is rather special. I did not express it to the full at the meeting. That was the reason why, in general, I said little. Your appeal did not excite any strong reaction in me. You can post it for all to read or you can choose not to. I have no feelings on the matter. Not because, in actual fact, it is exaggerated on some points, or ill-founded but because the reasons which lead you to cry help lie not in the apathy of 'a number of fellow-artists' but much, much deeper. And your appeal does not strike home to the place where those reasons lie. And no appeal could hit home – or so it seems to me. The demoralization of our undertaking is rooted in the undertaking itself, and its very essence, in the impossibility of reconciling irreconcilable demands. If we attempt to write down 20, 30, 50, 100 points concerning our wishes, if we attempt to set down on paper clearly everything which, in our opinion should become part of the structure of our enterprise, including every detail on the artistic, financial, ethical and educational side then it is easy to see that one half of these wishes is at odds with the other . . . *And there is no way out! And there won't be!* And all my ingenuity as an administrator consists in advancing some demands at the right moment and suppressing others in time and then letting other needs erupt to the detriment of the first. [. . .]

In our theatre there are three ventures, not one: artistic, commercial and educational in the broadest sense. And there are too few people who are equally committed to all three. Every one of the shareholders or the actors or the members of the Board only cherishes one of them in his heart. In words he loves them all but in truth his heart gravitates only to one or other of them.

And so he will always be among the discontented at times when primacy of place is given to trends which are inimical to him. And besides that there is the fact that the majority of art shows run counter to clear commercial interest . . .

And beneath all that there are the rumblings of the insecure *actor*. The *actor's* psyche. So sharply different from the psyche of any other person. *The actor* with his personal ambitions, his innate view of things, even if he is of no great intelligence, with his impatience, his blindness to his own and other people's qualities, with his *theatrical understanding* not only of literary works but of life itself, with his suspiciousness and mistrust, his egotism, which is always ready to take offence, with his abrupt transitions from bold faith in himself to panic-stricken doubt, with the full stamp of his theatrical *experience* upon him. And the more powerful and talented the actor the more anxious his joys, and the more his discontent with the conflicts among the artistic, commercial and ethical and educational aspects of our enterprise. And the more sharply he understands our directorial and administrative imperatives. And the more basic the actor the dimmer his understanding of our ideas and tasks.

If we want a glittering success we should stage 'The Bluebird'. To stage 'The Bluebird' we need talented actors. But talented actors won't like 'The Bluebird' for very long. If I want to be guided by the actors I settle on 'Rosmersholm'. If I want to stage a play with the actors' strengths in mind, I settle on 'Ivan Mirovich'. To allow them to develop we should stage many plays. But to do that we would have to give a play to Luzhski, but Luzhski doesn't lead the actors in the proper direction. For the theatre to have a future we need to prepare the young members but the young members must be given a chance to perform. And that would be at the expense of the 'veterans' who are already on the way to maturity. To bring all this together we need a budget of 350 thousand. And for a budget of 350 thousand we need to play 'The Bluebird' six times a week and ruin it. And we need subscriptions. But subscriptions limit artistic demands. To maintain the theatre's reputation we need to stage beautiful plays. But beautiful plays demand our participation, yours and mine. If you stage a play I should help you and ought not to get in your way. But if I don't have my own tastes I am not me. And I start to be a hindrance to you. Four plays is not possible. We have to make the most of what there is. And the actors get depressed. An actor has to have an artistic life. But in that there is not much Platonic love for the *enterprise itself.* He needs his own individual work. If there aren't many plays and not much work he gets depressed and looks for an opportunity to leave. You and I plunge headlong into artistic work and don't have time to take general charge of things and we give general charge to Vishnievski and Rumyantsev, to the young – Luzhski, and to beginners – Tatarinova. And we don't satisfy the older ones. And now we want to make use of Craig. Camaraderie in work? Camaraderie is possible either with real beginners or when we are very few, 10-12 people. Create a study group? First of all where do we put the people who are productive in our community? Secondly, which people do we use to create this group? None of the veterans will leave and all of them are far from being worthy to be in the group we could dream of. They preserve the disruptive elements in our affairs. Let's create two groups. We tried that. It did not work. We quarrelled almost to breaking point. What can we hold on to? Unite

everyone around one single person, you, and submit to your inspiration with
the sacrifices it entails. But some new Nemirovich might come along in
combination with some Zimin or Morozov and half, two-thirds of the
company would go over to them. It would just need one Kachalov to go
over. The new Nemirovich would draw them away from you, Stanislavski,
because Stanislavski won't allow them to play 'Rosmersholm' whereas he
does. I really do often think that such a combination of a 2nd Nemirovich
with a 2nd Morozov could occur and take away from us all those with a facile
belief in themselves. [. . .] And they could take away all those who are not
especially attached to you or me. They would let them act more than we do.
And who knows, would that not be better for very many of our actors? They
would act *too much* there. Above their capacity? But there is another
question, is it better to act *too little*? Under one's capacity? That's a real
question. Why do they act so little? Because we put on too few plays. And
why do we put on too few plays? If it is because plays demand a great deal of
work setting up back-stage that is of no interest to actors. Let us find a way to
reduce this side of the production. If it is because we spend a lot of time with
the actors and precisely because we strive to get special results from them,
then, in that case we are both sorely mistaken. And the actors have long
since realized that we are mistaken. They have seen perfectly well that half
our time if not more is spent to no purpose. Absolutely to no purpose. They
have demonstrated to you beyond question that starting with the 5th, the
10th to the 150th performance they act just as they did *when they started
rehearsal*. They have shown you how, having submitted to your despotism,
they only played four performances grudgingly in the way you wanted and
then freed themselves from this violence and played in their own way or
practically in their own way . . . You see too few performances; I see half of
them and know this phenomenon all to well . . . Your blocking, that is what
is great to them. Your blocking and your *first* rehearsals, that is what is dear
to them.

With young people it's another thing. They need your instructions every
step of the way. You can mould them as you wish. But those whose nature
is fixed, they are dry clay. So, when 'The Inspector General' is on, you can
take pride in the Khlestakov you created in the 2nd act and Uralov in what
you provided in five-six rehearsals. You agonized through forty rehearsals
to no purpose. It makes no difference, he will still play as he did after your
fifth-sixth rehearsal. So will Leonidov, and Luzhski and even, of course,
Vishnievski . . .

I wanted to write so much and I have only written a quarter of it. And yet
it's two-thirty in the morning . . . I will try and find time to write further. I
want to add something. About what I see ahead.

                                            Your V. Nemirovich-Danchenko

Craig visited Moscow in October 1908 and saw performances of *The Bluebird* and *An Enemy of the People* and, as he put it, 'Onkel Vanja'. He was impressed by the time, money and energy spent on productions. He was satisfied that he could work there.

On January 19 1901 the Board decided that the new productions for the 1909/10 season would be *A Month in the Country*, directed by Stanislavski and Andreiev's *Anathema* directed by Nemirovich. They also agreed to stage *Hamlet* in the 1910-11 season but decided, given its complexity, to start work on the project immediately.

311 Stanislavski to Isadora

March 20 1909
Moscow

[. . .]

Today we started to work seriously on 'Hamlet' with Gordon Craig, who is now in Moscow, in charge.

Everything he does is beautiful. We try to fulfil his smallest wishes as he seems to be as happy with us as we are with him. The theatre has created two work-rooms especially for him. He works in one of them like a hermit. No one is allowed in. The other houses a huge model as well as an array of props men under Suler's command, who carry out all Craig's fantasies, which are then transferred to the big stage once he has approved them. Tomorrow Craig is putting all the cast into leotards so that he can see their bodies and their movement. I am working separately on scenes from 'Hamlet' with a few actors so as better to understand through this experience what Craig wants. When we have mastered his conception he will go to Florence and we will work alone, without him. We are getting the play ready for August; he will return to Moscow correct our work and give us his final orders. 'Hamlet' must be ready for November this year [. . .]

The whole company is enthusiastic about the new System and so, from the work point of view, the whole year has been interesting and important. You have played a great part in this work without knowing it. You said a great deal to me about the things we have now discovered in our art. I thank you and your genius for that. [. . .]

Nemirovich was anxious to be involved with the *Hamlet* production but Stanislavski continuously kept him at a distance.

312 Nemirovich to Stanislavski

> Between April 4 and May 9 1909
> Moscow

Dear Konstantin Sergeievich,

The more I think about what I saw when I visited Craig the more enchanted I become by the beauty, worth and simplicity of these shapes. And particularly for Shakespeare. I have conceived a number of ideas on how to put them into practice. But we need to have good early discussion before doing anything about it. [. . .]

> Your V. Nemirovich-Danchenko

313 Craig to Martin Shaw

> May 1909
> Moscow

[. . .]

I have been here three weeks – Rehearsals have begun – in a most *orderly* fashion, and nice through and through owing to the really sweet nature of the manager – 'Hamlet' the play – The entire company, taking their lead from the manager, do *everything* I say. It may be a dream, dear old chap, but my God, it's like Heaven after years of Hell. First and foremost, they take time, and nerves are not allowed . . . consideration for every second – every move – every idea –

Again (for it must fade, it can't be real), it may all be a dream. It is nearer those divine Purcell days than anything I have experienced, though I am a *guest* in this case, and receive a nice salary into the bargain. [. . .]

Stanislavski adopted completely new methods for *A Month in the Country*. Whereas Art Theatre rehearsals were normally open, Stanislavski excluded anyone not involved in the production and worked in an intimate manner, probing the psychology of the characters, insisting on the minimum of movement. The process was slow and painstaking. Even after some eighty or ninety rehearsals there was little to show. Nemirovich who attended a reading was appalled at the lack of progress.

A major problem was Knipper. She could not get to grips with the character of Natalya Petrovna. She was essentially an instinctive actress with no technique or method to get her out of trouble when she needed it. She disliked the emerging System and was confused by its terminology. She relied on the character coming together once she got into a make-up and costume. It did not work. At a dress run on November 9 she broke down in Act III. Nemirovich, who was in the back of the auditorium, crept out rather than become involved. The next day Stanislavski sent her flowers and a letter.

314 Stanislavski to Knipper

November 7 1909
Moscow

My dear Olga Leonardovna,

I am staying away from you rather than cause you further trouble. I have become such a nuisance to you that I had better lie low for a while. I am sending flowers in my place. I hope they will convey to you the tender feelings I nourish for your great talent. This enthusiasm makes me very harsh towards anything which might sully the beautiful gift with which nature has endowed you.

At the moment you are going through a difficult period of artistic doubt. Deep feelings of suffering are born of such torment. Do not imagine that I am cold-blooded when it comes to your torment. I suffer with you at a distance and at the same time know that this torment brings forth wonderful fruit.

Let someone else, not me, Moskvin, say, explain to you what nature has given you. I am willing to admire patiently from afar the way in which your talent, having rejected what is unnecessary, will then shake itself free and manifest itself with all the individual force which for the moment is being blocked by the actor's damnable stock-in-trade.

Believe me, all the things which seem so difficult now are really mere details. Have the patience to look into these details, think them through and understand them and you will know the greatest joy a man can know in this world.

Should you need my help I will divide [your role] into sections and promise not to frighten you with scientific terms. That was probably my mistake.

I beg you to be staunch and courageous in the artistic struggle which you must win not only for the sake of your own talent but also for the sake of the whole of our theatre, which represents my whole life's dream . . .

You need to do so little to be the beautiful Natalya Petrovna I have already seen a dozen times. Look at the whole role and decide quite clearly which units it breaks down into.

Here I want to hide my anger; here I want to confide my feelings to someone else; here I am amazed and frightened; here I am trying to convince him that nothing terrible has happened and so become at moments tender, at others capricious, at others I try to be earnest. Then I am once more lost in thought. When Verochka arrives I do not for one moment come out of myself. Finally I understand, I play the part of a lady and try to persuade her that she must marry.

At every point in the role look for certain wishes, yours alone, and banish all trivial wishes – about you and the audience. This psychological work will easily enthrall you. When this happens, you will distance yourself from something which is unworthy of a real artist: a desire to serve or be servile to the audience. [. . .]

You are lucky, you have charm on stage and that makes people listen to you and so it is easy for you to do anything you want.

It is more difficult for the rest of us as, with every new role, we have to calculate, invent that charm without which an actor is like a rose without scent.

Take courage and claim once and for all your royal position in our theatre. I will admire from afar or, if necessary, work for you like an unskilled labourer.

Forgive me for the torment I have caused you but believe me it was inevitable.

Soon you will attain the real joys of art. [. . .]

While the production was a success and Stanislavski and the young Boleslavski were praised, Knipper's performance was considered something of a failure. The System had, however, proved its point. *Hamlet* would confirm it. In the meantime, Stanislavski decided the moment had come for the theatre to support his experimental and reaching work more fully.

315 Stanislavski to the Art Theatre Board

January 19 1910
Moscow

[. . .]

3. Above all I want total freedom for all those who are possessed of a pure and disinterested love of the theatre. Let whoever will make his own trials and experiments. I want the same right for myself.

4. Perhaps I have gone too far but therein lies my strength. Perhaps I am wrong but that is the real way to make progress. I am now persuaded as never before that I am on the right track. It is my belief that soon I will discover simple forms of words that will sum up everything and help the theatre to discover what is most important, that will serve as a compass for many years. Without that compass, I know that the theatre will lose its way

at the precise moment one of its present pilots, who are guiding it between Scylla and Charybdis, goes. I make considerable, perhaps presumptuous demands on myself.

5. I want not only to discover the fundamental principles of the creative process, I want not only to formulate its theory, I want to put it into practice.

6. The man who knows the difficult, uncertain, primitive nature of our art will be aware of the difficulty, scope and importance of this task. Perhaps it is insane arrogance. So be it! Then it will prove to be beyond my strength and I shall get a broken head. And deserve it. But from my broken pieces may there come someone else, or at all events, that without which there can be no theatre, without which it is crippled and depraved, without which it is a thieves' kitchen and not the temple of the human spirit. Perhaps I am a madman and a dreamer but I cannot be and do not wish to be otherwise. At my age your roots are your roots.

7. The task is complicated and long and I am not young in years. Especially if you bear in mind that in my family people die young. At the very most I have ten years' work left in me. Is that time limit important for a plan which is perhaps beyond my powers? Then it's time to think of one's will. After all, every man wants to leave some small mark behind him. That's understandable.

8. I need material for my plan, I need help. It's impossible to count on everyone but there are a few people whom I have prepared with great difficulty or who believe in my dream. Of course I prize their help greatly.

9. The paths of our art are pitted with ruts and holes. They are deep and you can't get past them without falling. In moments like those you should give help and lift up those who have stumbled and not think of them as already dead. Perhaps in the first instance we have over-inflated embryonic talents and then become too quickly disenchanted when they ceased to impress us by doing the unexpected. I learned that not so long ago and have tried to be more patient and steadfast. Otherwise you can't take a single pupil through to the end and I want not only to begin but to complete the education of those who have been put in my hands.

10. The theatre rightly starts afresh with those it has selected for entry, but once that selection has taken place, once those students have been put in my care, I am responsible for them. There was a time when there was not a single young person who was a real hopeful. Now there are such young people and we must, in the first instance, get them to take satisfaction in work, unless they turn out to be something of a miracle, for which there must always be a place in our theatre.

11. Without work there can be no progress. I would like to assert that principle and not make my pupils an exception to it.

12. I would like to forget just for a while many hurtful expressions used in respect of me – 'scatter-brain', 'a bundle of whims' – because they are unjust.

I don't get into a mess all the time, sometimes I pull it off, succeed, and my whims are not always unsuccessful.

13. If these expressions disappear perhaps it will result in greater faith both in me and in the people I have trained to help me. [. . .]

15. It may be that the people I have chosen are failures, or that I have harmed them or that I am a bad teacher. If it is the case then it is better to tell me so straight out and not use hidden weapons against me. [. . .]

17. For my research I need various material, not only what is artistic but also what is flawed. It is more difficult to eradicate faults than simply to develop secure talent. I need both people who are artistically dull, static, somewhat anaemic and weak and also those who are on fire. I can only verify the things I am working on with a range of differing pupils. That is why in my research on the material I devote some time to people who are not members of the theatre. While others are not denied the right to have pupils who are thick, let me also be allowed that privilege.

Craig returned to Moscow in mid February 1910 to resume work with Stanislavski on *Hamlet* and returned to Italy at the end of April. The plan was for Craig to return in August and for the play to open in November. Disaster struck when in August Stanislavski went down with typhoid. The doctors predicted that he would not be able to return to work before the spring of 1911. The production was, therefore, postponed until 1911.

Stanislavski's illness distressed Nemirovich and brought about a kind of reconciliation although in the event this proved more sentimental than real.

The autumn of 1910 was a good period for Nemirovich. He staged his adaptation of *The Brothers Karamazov* which was given over two evenings. Once again he set high hopes on this project, just as he had with *Julius Caesar*. Again he overestimated its potential success. Audiences stayed away, despite a good critical reception. Stanislavski for the first time paid generous tribute to Nemirovich's talent, to this 'genius' – however, from a distance. He endorsed Nemirovich's idea of adapting other novels and even made some suggestions of his own – including *War and Peace*. Yet, at the same time, he was being drawn even further away from a 'literary' theatre.

In December 1910 Gorki invited Stanislavski to join him in Capri to convalesce. Gorki was now interested in the possibility of creating plays through improvisation: a writer working with a company of actors. On December 20 he and Stanislavski went across to Naples to see a company improvising in the manner of the *commedia dell' arte*. This extension of ideas first explored with Meyerhold at the Povaraskaya Theatre-Studio ultimately found its expression in the training methods of the First Studio. Whatever was said in letters, in reality Stanislavski and Nemirovich were further apart than ever.

In Stanislavski's absence Nemirovich continued to work with some of the cast of *Hamlet* using the System which he was convinced he understood, although he had never worked on it directly with Stanislavski himself. In particular he rehearsed Olga Gzovskaya, who had joined the Maly in 1906 at the age of seventeen and left in 1910 to join the Art Theatre with the express intention of studying the System. She was cast as Ophelia. In his letters Nemirovich tried to reassure Stanislavski that all was well. It was Lilina who wrote Stanislavski's letters for him and it was to Lilina that Nemirovich addressed his correspondence.

316 Nemirovich to Lilina

September 5 1910
Moscow

[. . .]

Hitherto I have neither sent wires nor written. Why? Did I do it consciously or unconsciously? I don't know. I couldn't give an answer at the moment. I can't say what there would have been for me to wire or write about. To express sympathy? It was strange because I myself felt in need of sympathy. Of course I can't claim to have the sort of troubles you are experiencing but I often feel that the troubles I am experiencing are no less than yours, if not as acute, at least as deep. And all the deeper, repressed and hidden because I have been far from Konstantin Sergeievich and had to find the strength and courage for demanding work. Who else has a relationship to me to compare with Konstantin Sergeievich?. [. . .]

If my mother or my brother were ill like this it would be more remote to me, would weigh less heavily on me, than the illness of Konst. Serg. Despite everything that has happened between us, all the most important strands of my soul and my life are intertwined with his. And, of course, precisely for that reason there has been so much unfriendliness between us for in him lies all that is most important and vital in my soul. Our ties have long ceased to be purely formal and have far outstripped the ties of birth. I have been my brother's brother and my mother's son for 50 years but I was only spiritually close to them for one year in the way I have been close to K.S. for 10 years. In my life and soul he is as myself. No one else can compare. And there is no known measure of friendship, love and sympathy that can be applied to us. We can despair over each other, we can be hostile towards each other but all the same only death can sunder the ties between us. And not even death can sunder them. All this stood out especially strongly to me when I learned of his illness. And I was so struck by it all that the usual expressions of sympathy and interest seemed petty and trivial to me. Others can express their agitation out loud, I can give vent to it only when I am quite alone. Give vent to it more weightily and profoundly than most others. [. . .]

At the Board meeting of August 6 we decided question number one: whether to stage 'Hamlet' without K.S. or not? Should we summon together Craig and his general forces, Suler and Mardzhanov, and me to stage 'Hamlet'? We decided that we might crush K.S.'s most treasured dreams and rejected the idea. Then I proposed a choice of two plans, one with 'Karamazov' and the other without. We couldn't decide for some time. Then I said, imagine, gentlemen, as realistically as you can that K.S. was here with us and guess what his answer would be. We unanimously decided on the plan with 'Karamazov' . . .

At a general company meeting on August 8 I said that the best support we could give K.S. during his illness was for the whole theatre to work hard and have great success. No one could suspect him of petty ambition, he is not one of those administrators who rejoice when things go down when they are out of his control, on the contrary he feels genuine joy when he knows his children are standing on their own feet and that they are up to their job when he is not there to help.

The whole theatre understood that. Work began as . . . as for our 'cabbage evenings'.[1]

I didn't have an easy time with Gzovskaya. I put myself in her place, she came to the theatre in order to act with K.S. and suddenly the greater part of the season is lost to her. Apart from that I thought: what is to be done for the best? Leave her without anything to play until K.S. is better? Wouldn't it be better, rather, to give her work and help her with all sincerity and to the best of my ability? I asked her to choose for herself. She, of course, with absolute tact and discretion, chose us . . .

I am working with her in the way *I* can . . . I, of course, can't approach the role with her in the way K.S. would but I think that *beyond that* I will give her something of my own . . . She will return to Konstantin Sergeievich with something I have supplied . . .

Each scene is divided into units, into 'wishes',[2] into the search for what I call 'living feelings' (to get rid of clichés). In the first rehearsals perhaps I wore her out too much, reduced her to tears but we simply didn't know each other. Then it all turned out so well, so naturally that she suddenly recouped everything from earlier rehearsals. And Moskvin said that I had managed to arouse a naturalness in her which she had never displayed in all her roles at the Maly.

---

1. 'Cabbage Evenings' were satirical cabarets in which the members of the company poked fun at each other.
2. This is an early version of the terminology for the System. 'Wish' (*khotenie*) was later replaced by 'task' – or 'objective' – (*zadacha*).

317 Nemirovich to Lilina

September 9 1910
Moscow

Dear Marya Petrovna, I am writing further to my letter because when you read it to Konstantin Sergeievich he may well feel a little worried.

It seems to me that *the way* I am working on 'Karamazov' will bring the actors closer to Konstantin Sergeievich's theory. So that that may not sound quite unfounded I can say that even Vasili Vasilievich [Luzhski] (do you understand what that 'even' means?), seeing the way I was proceeding with the others, asked me to explain and, as best we both could, we mapped out the role with K.S.'s new methods in mind all the time . . .

All scenes were divided into units, into *wishes*, then on to feelings and the search for circles [of concentration]. The units ('brackets') are learned first then the words, etc., etc. . . .

I am writing this letter immediately after a conversation with Luzhski, *initiated on his own, personal initiative* – experiencing the feeling of a not inconsiderable victory . . .

After the successful first night of *Karamazov* there was an exchange of telegrams one of which, from Nemirovich, provided a full account of all the actors' performances, and covered six separate forms.

318 Nemirovich to Stanislavski

October 1910
Moscow

[. . .]

You write of my 'triumph'. In actual fact there was no triumph. No real victory. That's to come. But that it will come is beyond doubt. It will come when you return, it will emerge fully and powerfully with the next novel. For the moment, as in the war, we have only taken a key position, Mukden. We have all been going round a giant stockade, looking for a gate, an entrance, even a crack. Then we marked time, instinctively feeling that somewhere there it would be easy to breach the wall. With 'Karamazov' we breached it and when we got to the other side of the wall we saw the broadest of horizons. We hadn't realized how broad and vast they were.

Let me say at once that apart from me and you no one can have even a rough conception of how broad the horizon is. I myself didn't anticipate that such giant vistas would open up. There was no triumph, no victory and yet something enormous happened, there was, in some sort, a colossal, bloodless revolution. During the first performance there were a few people who were in sympathy but they were still not aware that with 'Karamazov' a huge process that had been maturing for ten years had been brought to a conclusion.

What process is that? If, with Chekhov, the theatre extended the limits of the conventions, then with 'Karamazov' these conventions have been destroyed. All the conventions of the theatre as a collective art have collapsed and now nothing is impossible for the theatre. If, with the plays of Chekhov, we gave a downward shove to third-rate and second-rate dramatists but the theatre was still too convention-bound for budding talent, the ground has now been cleared of all the obstacles they found so intimidating.

Of course, I am getting carried away and am overrating events. But discount 50% and how much is left? I think that this revolution will last not 5, not 10 years but a hundred, for ever! This is not a 'new form' but the total destruction of all the theatrical conventions which stand in the way of budding literary talents.

Why have the great novelists not written their great works for the theatre? For the following reasons, grounded in the nature of theatre as an art:

1) because in the theatre what was demanded above all was *action*, movement. Chekhov put an end to that. Yet how much still remains? 2) The novelist says: I cannot set out my images and thoughts in a single evening and 4 hours. Now we can answer, don't restrict yourself, do you need 2-3 evenings? Feel free. The audience will be able to listen and will be grateful to you. 3) The novelist says: I can't divide my work into these 'acts' all of which are supposed to last a certain length of time. We reply that this convention no longer exists. Have 20 acts. One of them will last an hour and a half, another 4 minutes. The novelist is inhibited by the fact that everything must be done in fast-moving dialogue and that long speeches are not allowed. We have demonstrated that actors can speak one after the other for 20-25 or 28 minutes . . . and they are listened to with even greater attention than if they revealed themselves in dialogue. 5) The novelist says that in drama in order to advance the plot you have to introduce characters into the action to report or say something. That is no longer necessary now either. We have the reader. And people listen to him with bated breath . . . He blends into the darkness of the theatre, with the power the theatre has over the crowd. I can foresee 6. which is not made use of. Another novelist will write strong descriptive passages. Hamsun describes the forest wonderfully. But this is not wasted in the theatre. A great artist must create a décor that matches Hamsun and the reader must complement it so that the audience may be intoxicated by seeing the landscape and hearing its description. [. . .]

From reading this do you understand why I am now saying that *every possibility* is now open to the theatre and that it is a revolution?

Theatre will be divided from Ostrovski to Chekhov, from Chekhov to
'Karamazov' and from 'Karamazov' to . . . They will say to Greek tragedy? I
think otherwise: from 'Karamazov' to the Bible. Because if the religious
censorship goes, and it must sooner or later, as it is old and crumbling like a
hollow oak, there is no better subject for a new theatre than the Bible. [. . .]

I haven't managed to say anything at the theatre of the possibilities I see
opening up.

When I think of the construction of a new kind of theatre there are
questions which torment me: where is the place of the reader and how can
we achieve quick scene changes?

And the creation of a beautiful theatre with *previous* goals doesn't interest
me in the least.

Changes will have to be made in the organization of the theatre – at least
considerable additions.

For example, we should start a literary department of some kind side by
side with the directors' committee. At the moment there is not one person or
other dealing with this important matter. [. . .]

Then we must create something which has started a long time ago, an
artists' workshop. At the moment Sapunov, Simov, Luzhski and two or
three young model-makers are working. We need to strengthen them as
artists. They not only made models but soon put all the other ideas into
practice, sketched furniture, went looking for them in Moscow or on country
estates, ordered, sought out objects and brought them into harmony with
what was already to be found on stage . . . Furniture, coverlets, tablecloths,
lampshades, cups, everything on stage was brought into the same style. Just
to stage 5 acts of one play in three sets.

'Karamazov' was staged against a single background. That is too pedantic.
We need to stage some scenes against a background, others naturalistically,
with ceilings and cornices, a third kind almost like tableaux vivants, a fourth
kind like cinema, a fifth as ballet. Let me dwell on that a little. Perhaps
everything I am saying to you is questionable and stems from the fact that I
was in charge of the work and that I am me but I am telling you how things
were.

It seems to me now that if it is good to get into, to emphathize with the
writer's psychology it is altogether important to get into, to empathize with
the novelist's – it is a prime necessity. Almost the most important difference
between the dramatist and the novelist is that the latter provides not only the
outlines but also the 'circles' and 'adaptations'. The approach to him must be
precise with exactness. [. . .] To discover the point where the individuality
of the actor and the individuality of the novelist meet, that is the most
important task. And that takes place entirely at the table. This work requires
enormous concentration, digging deep into the novel and the actor's
soul . . .

I was not afraid for a moment that the actors would lose anything during the transition to the large stage. And *only* Gzovskaya went relatively wrong and Kachalov to a certain extent . . .

In every other case the transition from the New [rehearsal] stage to the Large one required no more than two rehearsals and after them all we needed were dress rehearsals. [. . .]

During rehearsals I spoke in terms of theory but now I maintain quite firmly that if the psychology is grasped truthfully, if the actor lives truthfully, then it will reach the 25th row even if the odd word can't be heard. That is an extremely important observation which neither Vishnievski nor Knipper understands. The person who does not live truthfully but resorts to tricks fails even in the first few rows.

That is the very thing we talked about so passionately two years ago, especially during 'Month in the Country', now, in novels, it becomes of *primary importance* . . .

To be able to experience you have to think yourself onto the psychological plane of the author, that is very, very difficult and God forbid it should be hurried. Everything goes downhill if you don't hit it and then the actor has to find *it* in his own soul. The New stage is quite sufficient. You can go to the Large stage when everything is secure in the soul, and in two rehearsals! . . .

I have been saying this for a long time and now I am definitely convinced it is true. The Large stage should be the province of the scenic designer, the electricians and the props men.

When you stage a novel you can ask me to develop this idea in as much detail as possible. You know all this without me and your whole theory tends in that direction. But I think that in my dealings I am more sure of myself, more audacious than you. As an actor, you are very often concerned with the diversity of the audience and more easily lose courage than I. Moreover the corrective I have introduced into your theory plays an important role in all this. (Again you said you expected a theory from me). In that corrective lies all.

When I began on 'Miserere' I began *in my own way*. I began the search for the *inner image* by means of *infection*. That's what one must *start with*. Once that is achieved you can apply your theory of units and adaptations. Then that proves to be of colossal service to the actor . . . (If of course the role suits him) . . .

In general the production of 'Karamazov' has convinced me of a multitude of methods I could not have anticipated. I venture to think that even for such a greatly experienced director like you there are many proven facts to be found here . . .

319 Stanislavski to Nemirovich

November 16 1910
Kislovodsk

[. . .]

There is no necessity for you to convince me about novels or the Bible or even Plato. (Some time ago we laughed about Craig. Not so long ago I read about Komissarzhevskaya's dream before she died of going out into the wilds and starting a new school. Another one of Craig's ideas).

A new difficulty arises: what to do about the takings. If the public can't fork out for 'Karamazov', which was such a resounding success, it will be even more difficult with other works. You are wise. The books are in your hands.

I can't write anything about 'Karamazov' or the dramatization of novels. I have many plans, drafts, a great number of miniatures and tales have been planned. All that was in theory. Now it has happened in practice. So, above all, we must look at it.

I will touch on what you say about my system. Of course, before you start work on a role you must evaluate it from the literary, psychological, social, day-to-day side. Only then can you start to split it up, beginning with physiological units and then proceeding to psychological units or wishes. I now know the practical way (because it is my job to find a method in every theory before putting it into practice. Theory without practice is not my field and I reject it) to help the actor in the psychological, physiological, day-to-day analysis, even the social evaluation of a work and a role. But the literary side awaits your judgement. You should respond to that not only as a writer, a critic but also as a practitioner. What is needed is a theory backed by practice and rooted in experience.

At the moment I know that before you start work with my system you must: a) stimulate the process of the *will*; b) begin the process of investigation with some literary discussion (your expression) – how to maintain and develop these investigations, that I know; c) how to stimulate the process of lived experience – I know; d) how to help the process of physical characterization I don't yet know in detail but I am aware of the fundamentals and seem to be getting close to the right track; e) the process of *synthesizing* and *influencing* are clear. Now I have to find a way of arousing the actor's imagination in all these processes. This aspect of psychology has received little attention, especially the creative imagination of the actor and the painter. I have not only worked out all the rest but checked it sufficiently carefully. Some things are not written down in the right order. You will agree with me about all of it. At present much that has been conveyed to you by other people has only been understood by them with their heads and not, most likely, with their hearts. That's the main difficulty. It is not difficult to understand and remember; to feel and to test it is difficult. I would like to talk about that at length but where's the time (for you, I'm unemployed) and where's the energy?

Before I was ill I had the following plan for Gzovskaya. First and foremost to get her into the right psychological state before going onto the stage itself. Then teach her to live in a small circle on the large stage (daily exercises so that it would become a habit). After that establish for her our scale for adaptation, i.e., the short one, to her partners, not to the audience . . . We would give her specific objectives for each performance, so that on each entrance, she would be concerned with one aspect of the psychology of the role. Above all we have to teach her how to get rid of clichés . . .

320 Nemirovich to Stanislavski

November 21-22 1910
Moscow

Matinée

[Draft only]

[. . .]

More than anything I think that my work is not limited to the confines of theory. That I am not so much a theoretician as someone who inspires . . .

What one should call the things I am able to achieve I don't know. Let's call it 'the inner image'; but I cannot find any other approach to it than through some kind of *conviction* but your theory, if it is adopted in too primitive a manner, without being gone into, without a proper study of its successive stages, doesn't help me, indeed often hinders me. [. . .] And I am put off the track, confusing, mixing up the psychological line of the inner image, which is complex, precise and often not susceptible to analysis, although easy for me to reproduce, with the technique of 'wishes' which forms a separate stage in theory. I questioned Suler for some time and he gave me a fairly accurate explanation. I took out the chapter you wrote, and which I have, once more . . . In brief I am *really* looking for a synthesis of my own working experience and what I know of your theory. But I am just not succeeding . . .

I try to draw conclusions from practical work. And there I get nearer to you. For example when I have succeeded in establishing with the actors what I call 'the inner image', which is the emotional stage of *pure water* which is completely directionless and yet at the same time is extremely precise in a given role, when I have achieved that, when I see that the actor has been infected or charged up by this image, that he can portray it without words or with words which really respond to the psychology, albeit drawn from his own vocabulary and not from the play, then it is easy to break down the role into units, wishes, etc., etc. *Then* this theory is incredibly all-embracing. So all-embracing that even for those with little stage experience rehearsals go quickly and securely.

But the stimulation of that emotion is the most important and without it one should not rehearse at all. One should not even have models made. Even if models have been ordered and they are imbued with the essentials, which will provide the key to the whole inner image. If the models are shown for their own sake and then the 'literary' work (as you call it) is done for its own sake, 9 times out of 10 things go wrong. [. . .]

What emerges with particular clarity is the fact that one should not take a single step without emotionally experiencing the inner image.[. . .]

If the actor's own individuality doesn't merge with what is most beautiful in the writer's individuality then he can *never* play well. If the border at which such a merger can take place is found then the acting is already passable and can even turn out to be very good. [. . .]

But the first thing is to discover the individual beauties of the work and the border where the individuality of each performer can merge with them. That is undoubtedly the beginning. It is the beginning because only by crossing that border line can the actor come to love *the work and himself*. Only through that can they achieve that artistic joy without which fine acting is impossible. [. . .]

This also occupies first place in your theory. But there's where we differ. You look for this in the first literary discussion. Or from a number of them, as with 'A Month in the Country'. In practice I think that is too little. Especially when we are talking about a play which is new to me . . .

Too little because the relationship among the different stages in the creative process is not a mechanical one. It constitutes the *organic* basis. I follow the path established by your theory and find 'me' in varying degrees.

You write:

a. The process of *the will*. Fine. Independence is always essential.

b. Literary discussion. Yes and probably not just one. But even more important; what one might see as absolutely essential here would be to develop and broaden, even *modify* this in course of all the work, *all* the rehearsals, of everything including the externals of the production, the bow in an actress's hair.

c. How to stimulate the process of experience – that I know.

d. How to help in the process of embodying the character – I am groping for it.

Here that 'me' has to be vigilant lest some attractive stage effect should push aside the essential, the soul, the artistic idea, to one side and also lest the point of contact should not be lost . . .

e. the processes of merging and influencing are clear.

I don't fully understand which merging and which influencing you are talking about. If you are talking about the integration of the mutual adaptations of the actors then my 'me' is on the alert all the time and rearrangements, changes and even a certain increase in depth of intensity might occur in the soul of the work . . .

By the beginning of 1911 Stanislavski was preparing to resume work on *Hamlet*. He needed to agree a timetable with Craig. This proved difficult. Craig had little head for business and interpreted his contract rather differently from the Art Theatre management. He began to demand money which he thought was owing to him, often in a rather peremptory tone. Stanislavski tried to do his best to mediate with the Board and reach a suitable financial arrangement but it was left to Sulerzhitski to negotiate direct with Craig. When it became apparent that Craig was virtually washing his hands of the production Stanislavski seized the opportunity to work on *Hamlet* entirely in accord with the System. A certain incompatibility of approach had already become apparent. Moreover, Stanislavski was dissatisfied with some of Craig's costumes and in October 1910 had already engaged Mstislav Dobuzhinski to make alternative designs.

321 Stanislavski to Sulerzhitski

> January 1-5 1911
> Rome
> Trinita dei Monti
> Hotel Hassler

[. . .]
   Now, to Craig. I hope you know that he is in Paris at the moment. It would be desirable not to say essential to go and see him . . . I can't go to Florence as there's no suitable diet there and that's most important for me . . .
   Where can we see Craig? In Cannes but it's the season and very expensive. In Berlin. That would be better for this reason. In Dresden there's a Dalcroze school of stage-movement and rhythmic dance. I am going there as I am told it's excellent. It should be of interest to Craig. Let's do it this way. On the same day we will leave Cannes or some other place and Craig will leave Paris, we will come to Berlin and go to Dresden. In that time we will discuss the one or two things that need discussing, i.e.:
   1. will he allow us to experiment with the positioning of the screens on the stage itself and not slavishly follow his models.
   2. will he allow us, while preserving the general notion of the king, the court, Ophelia, Laertes, i.e., as caricatures, to portray or present them in a

slightly different form, i.e., more subtly and in consequence less naïvely. You understand that to present 'Hamlet' as Craig wishes is dangerous. It (not Hamlet himself who is wonderful in Craig's version but the treatment of the other roles) will be unacceptable in Moscow in the form Craig wants to convey it. We must do what Craig wants, i.e., the king is Herod, a barbarian, the court is mindless with its absurd etiquette and Ophelia and Laertes are the children of their milieu, but we must show it without using those puppet-like devices Craig has used. Personally speaking that's all I have to talk to him about, the rest is just the simple wish to see him and make arrangements for his coming to Moscow.

Here are my ideas in that respect. I'll be back in Moscow about the 25th February. There'll be a cabbage night on the 28th. Then rehearsals for 'Uncle Vanya' (new sets) – then straight on to 'Hamlet'. So there shall be no delay I have sent my notes to Muratova (for the actors) and to Gzovskaya (for the young ones). They are to read them before we arrive so that we can get straight down to work. The school and colleagues who need not only to have my notes read but explained to them I leave to you; please get on with this as soon as you arrive. You and I will deal with the main characters, i.e., Ophelia, Hamlet, the king, the queen. Polonius and Laertes and Mardzhanov will deal with the rest. We will explain everything to each other beforehand and reach an agreement on analysis, psychological units, wishes, etc.

We will adjust the general features of the staging, lighting and try out this set-up.

Finally costumes.

Clarify with Craig, with this timetable in hand, when it will be convenient for him to come: now or in May?

If he needs to see the action on stage then we'll have to write him in for the 4th, 5th and 6th weeks (Lent starts on February 21). He should bear in mind that perhaps he may have to come to Moscow before then. If you decide on some other time write to me. Write and tell me does Craig want to or does he have to go to Berlin? Of course we'll pay his journey there and back. [. . .]

322 Stanislavski to Sulerzhitski

February 12 1911
Rome

[. . .]

As to Craig this is what has been decided. He is wrong in every respect so advise him not to take a provocative tone with the theatre or he will ruin everything for me. It makes no difference if we have to pay him part rather than the whole. It would be better if he were to come to Moscow about the beginning of the third week in Lent. On his arrival in Moscow, i.e., February 16/19, Stakhovich will send Craig 300-500 roubles. That's what I've asked the theatre to do and I hope it will fulfil my request.

The end in the next letter.

To continue.

Explain to Craig that I can't send him any money from here because I have barely enough for my return journey. Nothing can be done by telegram as things are at breaking point and we have to be careful with the Board. The quickest way is to act through Stakhovich who is leaving for Moscow today.

Explain to Craig that what I am writing is my plan of action and not a promise; he might latch on to it and believe I had made a definite promise. It doesn't prevent Craig from writing as the question of the constume[s] is very important. I don't understand Craig's thinking. Above all get him to bring the *mise-en-scène* for the 5th act as well. [. . .]

323 Stanislavski to Sulerzhitski

February 19 1911
Capri

Dear Suler,

Thank you for your letter. Now that Craig has given up on the whole thing I don't need to meet him. *Say nothing to him about this*. I will spin the whole thing out and then leave as a matter of apparent urgency without having seen him. He is now in a western mood and is only thinking of what he can get out of the theatre without doing anything. Help is there for him if only he would behave with gentleness not vainglory. I don't like him at all as he is at present. *Say nothing to him about this*, but on your own account, as though by chance, say or explain that the theatre has already paid out about 25,000 roubles (for experiments) and seen nothing in return. Could more be demanded from foreigners and strangers? You know foreigners' attitude towards us Russians. If we were to find such generous people abroad as we, the directors of the Moscow Art Theatre, we would cry it aloud and glorify them. Craig should understand that. He needs to . . . Remind him: I arranged a guaranteed annual salary of 6,000 roubles. He went mad and squandered the lot. Now the devil only knows how much he is getting. In the autumn he was ill and couldn't come; he's brushed aside the costumes and the staging. Of course the Board turns to me and asks me to explain what they are paying Craig's salary for. He is starting to get insolent. What am I supposed to do? It will end with the Board dismissing him. Talk as if on your own account, don't cause a quarrel between him and me.

Your K. Alekseiev

In a word things are at breaking point and one false move and they go snap.

324 Sulerzhitski to Stanislavski

February 1911
Paris

Dear Konstantin Sergeievich,

I went to see Craig and here's what he made clear to me:

He doesn't want to go to Dresden, he says that rhythmic dance doesn't interest him and he doesn't think it will prove of interest to you either. He doesn't want to go to Berlin which he hates. He maintains that you summoned him by telegram to Cannes and he is going there at once.

So he wants to meet you in Cannes or in Capri (depending on where you are) and you must send for him by telegram.

His answer to all your questions concerning the staging of 'Hamlet' and the treatment of the roles is that he trusts you to *do everything* so that it *will be good*, you know him best. So do as you think best.

He thinks it best to come to Moscow in May.

Those are the answers to your questions.

To tell you the truth, as far as his coming in May is concerned, I made my views clear. I think it would be better if he came later when something or other will be ready. Otherwise he will get in the way of the work and start making screens of bronze, of oak, etc.

325 Sulerzhitski to Stanislavski

February 21 1911
Paris

[. . .]

I still haven't take Craig to task. He is living in dreadful poverty. He borrowed 20 francs from me yesterday because he hadn't a sou. What does he do with all that money? If I got that much I would be living in my own dacha and working in the theatre as a patron. At all events he has no money and he asked me to wire you so that you can send him something at least from the theatre. He said they told him he would be sent a certain sum twice a year and he agreed, proposing that he should be sent for twice in the course of the year. Now his second trip has been arranged outside the limits of the year for which the agreement was made and so he considers that he should be paid anew for his trip in the new year as the agreement applies only to one year. He is therefore asking for an advance. Obviously he wants to renegotiate his agreement on an annual basis. He is confused and needs money terribly. But perhaps he is saving and putting it aside? It's absolutely incomprehensible what he does with his money living a life like this. [. . .]

Your Suler

Craig has arrived and says that he would have been much happier if we had sent for him for a certain period, had finished the work, paid him and had done with it.

But the work has been dragged out indefinitely, the dates of his trips have been altered and he doesn't know when he will be needed. And of course he would be much happier to have an annual agreement. His family hasn't had a sou for the last two weeks. Neither has he. There is no signed contract, which he and the theatre would have signed; he has nothing against that as long as the theatre sticks to its promises but the theatre is continually altering them!!

Those are his words! . . .

He is now sitting in a chair in a round hat, stroking his chin, looking up at the ceiling, a parchment book under his arm in which a new system has been sketched out, which he will only show to you, and a stick with an ivory handle, he knots his brows, tugs his chin and doesn't know what's to become of him, what to say, where to send a wire and what to do in general.

He is an unhappy lost figure which nonetheless provokes in me both tenderness and a smile.

We must support him. My feelings tell me so. What can one do if he is after all a child and, when all's said, an artist? No contracts are possible with him and with him the whole business side will always be a muddle. Yet, all the same, we must support him. That's my opinion. [. . .]

The apparent reconciliation between Stanislavski and Nemirovich led them to attempt to work together once more. Each would attend the other's rehearsals. Stanislavski would sit in on *The Living Corpse* while Nemirovich would attend *Hamlet* and participate in the exercises. Work began in the first week of August. By the end of three days Nemirovich was distraught. Whatever he had thought the System was about, it was quite different as practised by Stanislavski and he found it torture. In order to avoid a confrontation Nemirovich suddenly declared the System the official working method of the company. This was purely a manoeuvre. He then retired to the Chernigovski Monastery, where there were guest rooms, for the weekend to recover his equilibrium and on Sunday wrote to his wife outlining his strategy.

326 Nemirovich to his wife Ekaterina

August 7 1911
Chernigovski Monastery

[. . .]

The 'Stanislavski-itis', i.e., his awkward side with his persistence, or rather, his obstinacy and absurdity, is not so easy to get rid of. But as, when all's said and done, there is always some underlying artistic purpose, you are carried along. And that's one of the reasons why I came here, to spend some time alone, to find out whether he has not dragged me along too and whether that is not a danger for the future. I have reasons to be suspicious. I already feel it is the case. How I have unwittingly drifted away from the [original] plan. It's time to back-track before it is too late. We are a little off course. We have to go back to the beginning but that means a huge detour . . . I have to agree that what he says is good, right, beautiful . . . The trouble is I can't leave him alone with the actors . . . I spent two days, Thursday and Friday, on something that Stanislavski has no way of refusing – that we apply his system to everything we work on (which is impossible) . . . Keep him within bounds in such a way that he will not notice and rear up, arrange things so that we can take what is useful in his theories. Others will be persuaded by his example. My intention is this, not to do it right away; Stanislavski will be obstructive all winter . . . Better to delay at first so as to proceed calmly later. [. . .]

Nemirovich's strategy broke down as soon as Stanislavski became involved on *The Living Corpse* rehearsals. He was unable to contain his innate hostility.

327 Stanislavski to Lilina

August 11 1911
Moscow

[. . .]

How is work going? . . . In terms of what has actually been accomplished, little. In terms of what has been laid down in the actors in the sense of my system, something has been accomplished. Things are as they always have been. I talked for 2 days and 2 nights, just to the principals in 'Hamlet'. Nemirovich is of the opinion that it is not possible to explain things to the bulk of the characters all at once. In the end Nemirovich did all the exercises and not at all badly. On the third day the whole company was called and Nemirovich himself, in my presence, explained my system. He spoke intelligently but it was ordinary. I think he has only understood bits of it. Nonetheless it was decided that everyone understood the system. Then we marked the 1st scene of 'Hamlet' (2nd Part) and the cast even acted it for me. Of course, it was all thin but the important thing is that they all suddenly came to life. Moreover, all of them suddenly, following the tasks I gave them, played different external images. The Hamletists, it would appear, are convinced by the system and from Vasili Ivanovich [Kachalov] and Luzhski to the latest newcomer, Nelidov, all did the exercises. But since then 'Hamlet' hasn't been rehearsed for a while as after that I had to be in the office, at the factory and to help with 'The Living Corpse'. There things are as they were of old. Vladimir Ivanovich gave a talk. Everyone (especially Moskvin) apparently understood him. It went no further than apparently. For a full hour Nemirovich stated that he had said all this before but that he was far from being in agreement with it all . . . Then in more heated tones – barking like some general – he went on to say that if we applied my system we wouldn't finish analysing the play this year or next year either. I rejoined that it was each individual's responsibility to do this analysis at home and that it was easy. After that I had to endure another barrage. I was told I was a child, and credulous, they all talked nonsense at me . . . In other words out came all the old stereotypes and clichés that have made my life in the theatre a misery. [. . .]

In the spring of 1911 Nemirovich consolidated his position. Under new statutes adopted, as a temporary measure, at a Board meeting on May 7, the power of the Board was greatly reduced and authority concentrated in Nemirovich's hands. However, during earlier discussions Kachalov had made it quite clear that he would resist any attempt to exclude Stanislavski and would if necessary quit the company. This served as a warning to Nemirovich. If Kachalov went, others could follow. The interim statutes were confirmed in 1912 when it became clear that Stanislavski was firm in his resolve not to accept any management position. He was now deeply involved in the creation of the First Studio. He asked for premises to work and perform in. Nemirovich bowed to the inevitable, still hoping that he could draw Stanislavski back eventually into the fold, and rented a flat above the *Cinematograph* (later the *Lux*) cinema.

328 Stanislavski to Nemirovich

July 1912
Moscow

Dear Vladimir Ivanovich,

I am very touched and grateful to you and to the theatre for trusting me this time and for helping me to do something without which, it is my profound opinion, the theatre would stagnate and come to a dead end. Does any of us know what we ought to do now, in which direction to take the actors and which plays to perform? These are hard and difficult times. We must experiment and experiment again . . . On what? I don't know, or rather, just have a feeling about it . . . If nothing comes of these experiments it means that I am too old and it's time to retire and make way for someone else.

The flat looks splendid. I didn't expect such luxury, in terms of dimensions. How shall we settle in? What do we need, what should we be doing in this flat:

1. First and foremost the Molière rehearsals, which take place initially at the table[1] (i.e., they are also possible in the small room) and then can go onto the large stage,

2. Daily exercises for those who know the theory (actors, students). Sometimes with me, sometimes with Suler.

3. Theory for actors and students who are not familiar with it – [Michael] Chekhov, Vyrubov, new students and those among the older actors who are convinced and want to get to know what has already been done). Sometimes me, sometimes Suler.

4. Old and new collaborators – Vakhtangov and, perhaps, someone who wishes to extend his knowledge. All this must be set in motion and placed at the head of the line.

5. Once this has been started, we must consider how those who have completely understood and mastered the system are to apply it. At first in performances for themselves (not for the public). For that we must employ two methods: 1st extracts or miniatures, to test out intellectual understanding in practice (i.e., with me or Suler watching). Independent work on other extracts or miniatures.

Of course, it is desirable to present excercises not once but several times to an audience (internal) and show what has been done. It would be good, therefore, to select extracts with a certain calculation. I have a plan for that but for the moment I will wait before talking about it.

6. We must launch a studio for directors to discover new possibilities for staging, lighting, popular shows for touring companies, Punch-and-Judy, puppets, new theatrical architecture, shows in large halls, circuses, mobile

1. It was the practice at this period of Stanislavski's work to spend a long initial period in rehearsal reading and discussing the script 'at the table'.

theatres, etc., etc. Often this research in various fields is necessary not in order to become actively involved in Punch-and-Judy or popular theatre themselves but in order for us to put out feelers on various sides so as to find new directions for our theatre.

7. Experiments in new ways of writing plays and a new view of art . . . I will say nothing for the moment of other dreams. How can we adapt the flat to these ends?

So we need:

a. A room with a stage and lighting where performances can be given. Rostrums are not necessary. I have explained to Basilievski how to adapt the ceiling and the movable front curtain. In the same room we need a folding table for lectures, two comfortable armchairs and some bentwood chairs. Lighting for those parts of the room where the audience sits (i.e., for the moment the wiring). Stage lighting – hanging, movable lamps. (I have explained to Basilievski).

b. We need a room for Suler's or my activities – work at the table.

c. Ditto for Vakhtangov's activities.

d. For the directors' work.

e. Assembly room.

f. Anteroom.

g. Smokers' corner.

h. A table for business matters.

i. An office for me and Suler. [. . .]

But the most important is to make sure there are three places to rehearse and to install the lighting. Then we can start work on September 1 without loss of time.

What do we need for that?

1. So to arrange things that the three rooms can be used simultaneously. If the walls are thin and let sound through they must be clad with something. If the doors are thin then make canvas curtains for one or both sides.

There's still the question of where to put the watchman and his wife whom we shall probably need. The woman will perhaps come in and out but we will need to find a place for the man (perhaps a camp bed).

Stanislavski and Nemirovich maintained their professional working relationship. Nemirovich continued to consult his former partner on repertoire and scheduling but Stanislavski's main concern was now the Studios. The outbreak of war had added to the theatre's difficulties. There was now a shortage of materials with which to mount productions. But the main problem was the lack of creative energy and renewal inside. With Stanislavski concerned with teaching, and the best of the young talent in the

Studios, the Art Theatre itself was barely ticking over. Indeed, in 1916 the decision was taken not to mount any new productions but to call a halt and take stock of the situation. Little came of this period of reflection.

While Stanislavski relentlessly pursued his own path, Nemirovich was torn between his frustration and anger at his friend's wilful refusal to recognize his own contribution and his desire to see him once more fully integrated into the main company.

329 Nemirovich to Stanislavski

Beginning of 1915
Moscow

Our artistic dispute.

Sometimes I am seized by a growing, and terrifying suspicion that you really don't understand the actor's particular theatrical gift. You find the well-known expression 'an actor by grace of God' a stupid lie, a bright, hollow phrase. In the same way Zola didn't acknowledge dramatic talent and said that any intelligent, talented author could be a dramatist. This theory, which caused a sensation at one time, was then completely destroyed for ever.

Why is it we can't direct plays together?

In the past this was explained by the fact that you went from the outside, from the characteristics, from the 'picture' and I from the inner image, from the psychology, the 'sketch'. But then you moved over to the psychological. At that time I thought that the moment had come when we could direct plays together. In 'The Living Corpse' we suddenly parted company. That means we could still not be as one. Then three years went by. The rehearsals for 'Woe from Wit' showed that we were as far apart as ever we were. And it is worth noting: at that time we were working on a role you yourself were playing (already played by you) – believe me, I had only to utter one word about another role and you shook with outrage.

We were sitting with Benois in the accountant's room and discussing whether there are occasions when a 'demonstrator' director gets something. You said no, I said rarely but cited Famusov as an example. You took great offence and said, sharply, that the success of Famusov could be explained exclusively by your own considerable hard work. Of course, it never entered my head to ascribe that success to myself but I still don't understand how you can deny the evident fact that you not only changed your whole image of Famusov under the influence of the sketch, which I gave you and you took on trust, but that I acted it out for you several times in order to make it clear. You even asked me twice to repeat the 'demonstration'. True, you, as no one else can, grasped the essence. You were able to take what sprang from my own individuality and make it your own but the essentials weren't changed. However, as soon as it was over you denied its significance.

What is it all about? Satanic pride, fear that I might get above myself? But that's not it. [. . .]

Weren't there one or two things in the distant past? Only to mention you personally: Astrov, the whole of the 4th act of 'Enemy', Vershinin – perhaps the memory of Moskvin in 'Tsar Fiodor' has been erased or of Knipper and Savitskaya in 'Three Sisters', whom you and Morozov, in my absence abroad, replaced as useless with Polyanskaya and Pavlovaya, – Knipper as Masha and Savitskaya as Olga! [. . .]

And in all these cases, in the course of the last 16 years I have only followed my own, individual path. Nonetheless, nothing has convinced you, nothing has won your trust. Because of your peculiar capacity only to trust and like what is born of you or of those in your immediate circle, you very soon forgot my achievements and continued to nurture mistrust both towards my methods and my art, suspecting in both a striving for the trite and the banal.

You kept Kachalov away from me as Hamlet and all the other actors you were interested to work with. [. . .]

It is a curious trait in your character that the more impulsively, the more trustingly you once came towards me, the more strongly your trust now cannons off me, like a billiard ball. And when you write to me in one of your more recent letters that you are more closely attached to me than anyone, I read between the lines: and I hate you more than anyone in the world.

I have often said, without exaggeration, that there is not a man alive whom you hate more than me.

And as that is no joke, I devoted a lot of my attention to trying to discern the psychology behind your relationship to me.

I would very much like to be wrong, our theatre would benefit if I were, but this is how I explain it:

1. Your monstrous ambition, which is ostensibly burned out but is not burned out and never will be – intolerance of anyone near you.

Why can't you come to terms with the fact that you aren't God? That you are just a man. And dear to all of us precisely because we know your great, human qualities, for the sake of which we forgive your simple, human faults.

2. You like, you love only what is born in your vicinity and completely mistrust everything outside, however great its achievement as art, even when we worked together. As an artist you can, for a very short time, be carried away by 'other people's work'. You are able, better than anyone, to appraise, in the very first minute, what is valuable in the productions of 'Julius Caesar', 'Ivanov', 'Anathema', 'Ekaterina Ivanovna', 'The Brothers Karamazov', etc. But with the passage of time, very little time, that

appreciation of their value begins to fade in your memory. And not only are your memories of them not happy ones, you recall them as though they were something very bad and even – as far as your honesty allows – spread negative attitudes around you. But, at the same time, you believe Gurevich and Fedorova more than you do me. I can tell you twenty times that Fedorova is a figure completely without sparkle on stage but because she has grown up in your circle and Gurevich praised her, you encounter my objections with suspicion and indignation, scorning my flair and experience in that field over 20 years.

Above all you are terribly obstinate and when you meet with a rebuff from me you once again feel suspicion and hate towards me.

Finally, thirdly, the most important thing in the psychology of your attitude towards me, the most profound and deeply rooted in your mind is that artistic difference I referred to earlier. The completely instinctive which stirs you up against me. The deep and dark things that in my eyes constitute the soul of art but which stir up in you a kind of spontaneous protest. And not only against me now but against all those who nurture this belief. Most harshly against me because I am the most conspicuous proponent of this tendency in our theatre.

As the most important and interesting element in our relationship this has always, of course, concerned me more than anything else. But it has been the least susceptible of analysis. I would even say that if it were completely clear to you or if I could find the words or the time to clarify it then the major misunderstandings between us would come to an end. We would either really become as one or would part forever, as enemies. And if it were necessary for us to work on the same thing then at least we would be fully conscious of our differences.

On this point I said that you shake with outrage when you are present while I am directing. When it's a question of my not being able to endure your directing method it costs me as great an effort as you, but with this difference, that I indulge myself less than you and am more tolerant than you. When you are directing in the area of the 'picture', I watch you with a feeling of real pleasure, I try to learn from you, I am proud of you. Possibly there are times when I am interpreting plays or roles when you experience some sort of artistic joy.

But when I endeavour to penetrate into the very depths of a phenomenon, when I strive with all my might to imbue the actors with a sense of the creative mysteries which I have received from the play or the role, to imbue the actors with the flavour of the author's creation which will not submit to too clear an analysis, that psychology of feeling which you cannot force into any system or subsume under any form of 'roots of feeling', when two times two is not four but God knows what, then you shake with outrage.

And vice versa, when you approach what constitutes the character of an author or a role with 'material' means, then I start to feel, then too, as so many times in the last 15 years, that the theatre is passing by the secrets of art and psychology of the heart and is becoming a crude, manufactured, artificial surrogate.

Then we become enemies. [. . .]

330 Nemirovich to Stanislavski

January 9 1915
Moscow

Most respected Konstantin Sergeievich,
  In a short time I shall be calling a general meeting and will make some proposals to the Committee and then make one or two reports concerning the coming season.
  It may seem to you that I am trying to keep everything between us on a formal level and avoiding preliminary discusssions in person. That is not so. But I think that our discussions can only have essential meaning where there is a certain attitude on your side, one where there is no hostility and suspicion and when people want, in reality, to reach an agreement and bring extreme opinions into some kind of equilibrium and not merely to stress the fact yet again that they hold opposite views in every sense. In such cases it is better to keep things on a formal level and for both to rely on the decisions of the Committee.
  So if you have a real need to have access to my plans, or if you have something to say to me or simply to ask, then please arrange a time and place at your convenience. I will always try to make myself available.

Yours V. Nemirovich-Danchenko

331 Stanislavski to Nemirovich

August 11 1916
Essentuki

[. . .]
  My indifference, etc., has its reasons. I was not always so. There was a time when I was afire. But a radical disagreement exists and there are many other reasons. I and the shareholders have different goals, different paths to tread, different (how shall I put it?) ethics, upbringing, culture, views, habits, nature.
  The financial question. This must be discussed in financial terms. Money can be earned most easily when one has built a lasting, solid, good business,

whose strength consists in the fact that it *primarily* has the permanent
capacity to produce *only good* wares. Moreover it is always *pleasurable,
convenient, agreeable* to do business with it. There strength is used to *enable
and simplify* and not to *hinder and complicate*. There everyone is imbued
with a single thought, to *consolidate* the business, to nurture it. For that
reason every novelty, every innovation is caught on the wing and executed
soon and fast. Things that take decades to catch on in other businesses are
adopted at once. In a business like that there are ideas, plans, ambitions, a
guide-line, that lead upwards. There are profits too.

But there are other kinds of businesses. They are less concerned with
themselves, with continuous improvement, they are afraid of loss of time in
a period of transition so that they concentrate their view not on the far
distance but go no further than the current year of operation. Is it worth
writing any more when everything has been understood and said a hundred
times? Our theatre possesses many advantages in comparison with other
theatres not only in Russia but throughout the world and it is what separates
it from other theatres that holds me to it. But at the point where our goals
and paths divide there is only one solution left to me, to close my eyes, not to
see and pass by as quickly as possible and deliberately develop that
indifference which enables me to work in businesses which have ends other
than mine in view.

There is another reason which reinforces everything that has been said. I
am financially secure, others are not. It is easy for me to take risks, others
not. I, in appearance, take no risks in the business and others, in
appearance, do. In these circumstances I acquire the dangerous label of an
impractical, addle- pated genius, etc. And it is true, as far as the current
season is concerned, I am impractical but I am practical as far as future
profits are concerned. Naturally, in those circumstances, I have no voice
(and seek none, don't imagine this is a hint). Consequently I have
considerable responsibilities in the financial sense, as I am the wealthiest
person with a liability and depend on the bank and the market. For me the
soundness and durability of our business is more important than future
profits. And in that respect our interests and tasks differ radically from those
of all the other shareholders. Above all, I, as a Muscovite born and bred,
surrounded by the traditional prejudices of a certain group of people, on
whom I and my family depend, financially and in other ways, must be
scrupulous in another area, known as public opinion, the '*que dira-t-on*'.
And the ethical side of the theatre is at present very low and more than once
I am pained, embarrassed and get into an appalling state. Nowhere is there
more drinking, more drunkenness than in our theatre, nowhere is there such
conceit and disdain for other people and such insulting outbursts. In state
theatres this is kept down by a bureaucratic system which we, thank God,
don't have but we don't have the civilized traditions of a civilized house

either. And in addition to that Moscow is proud of us and so certain people need to have a thought for their reputation. So we have another set of compromises. Our dark side shows here and there and we must stop up the holes. In Rostov there was a publicity poster which misled the public and the wool-merchants wrote on it: 'Ask Alekseiev why he allows his actors such deceit?' Another conflict. We end up in a stupid situation. 1) In reality I have no rights, no vote, no administrative or ethical authority, no power, I can make requests and make a fuss but it is I who have to answer in the eyes of society and of Moscow. 2) Total lack of time because I am playing and directing and when necessary studying and working for the future (so I am working on two or three fronts) and then when necessary I raise money. 3) I am financially reponsible whatever the lawyers tell you. 4) In the discretionary and objective sense of an agreement I bear no responsibility and so it is awkward for me to give other people orders. 5) When I am useful I am wheeled out and my name is used; when I am not I do not even know what is going on backstage, which things are contrary to my principles, my habits and views. I often conceal what I am struggling against. 6) When a signature is needed at the bank I have to provide it. In a word I must give my name for risks the business takes and to hide them when they are not to my liking. 7) When we are dealing with things which are dear to me, for which I would give my life, then a thousand invisible obstacles impede my every step. That's how it was with the system, that's how it was with the two studios (not now but earlier), that's how it will be with my new plans. What is needful for the future, and which is my concern, is in the majority of cases disadvantageous for the present.

Can all this be reconciled? No! That's impossible. I have either to convince everyone or give up and step aside. I haven't been able to do the first, so I have to do the second. The only possible way out (I repeat) is the following. I will stay at Karietny and have my own studio (a general or independent company). People will come from the theatre and say to me 'Stage this, play that or help with this'. 'Fine. Here are my conditions' (not financial, of course). (You know all these conditions by heart.) A fine play is ready in my studio – splendid! I will bring it to the theatre and play it for 10 seasons. There are actors in the Art Theatre who are free and want to act with me – splendid! 'Such and such a play with such and such in it!' Everything is clear, everyone knows that I am responsible for the studio and *you* for the theatre and there is no false situation. If there's a crash, come to me. If you need actors you come to me.

Summing up. In my opinion you make two mistakes from which all misunderstandings flow:

1. You want forcibly to unite things that cannot be united. Poland and the eastern provinces cannot be united with Russia. Autonomy is necessary for them to come closer together and like each other.

2. You are afraid to let go of power and want to keep a grip on everything big or small.

Time is passing. Call the shareholders together. They must decide for themselves (apart from questions of performances and artistic matters) (approval, of course) and both of us must stand to one side but close together. (Just you and me without a third party). They, i.e., the whole group of people, want to put on a bad play. Let them mount it and show it! If it's worthwhile we will finish it and help them. If not they will learn from their mistakes. First and foremost we must revive a dormant sense of initiative. And we must not be afraid of one thing, a season which is a large write-off. Otherwise it's misery, bankruptcy, which I fear and which I will defend myself against in every way.

I gave an honest warning of this a long time ago. Were it not for the war I would have taken steps.

Reading through this letter I am aware of a hostile tone which I do not tolerate in others or in myself. The tone is somewhat offensive and grouchy. What can I do? It happened against my will. I wanted to write in a friendly, businesslike tone and in a good mood.

I am fond of many people but I don't agree with all of them all of the time. Another misery. That I can't convince people.

As far as the repertoire is concerned let's talk to each other when we see each other, I'll write a few words tomorrow, I'm very tired today.

Your K. Alekseiev

332 Stanislavski to Nemirovich

December 4 1916
Moscow

Dear Vladimir Ivanovich,

It is difficult and distressing for me to declare once again *absolutely and categorically* that under no circumstances will I sign any document, official or legal, binding me to a new association. I have notified you already of this fact repeatedly and with the departure of Stakhovich (and after him all the investors and people who might have been able to share my financial responsibilities) – I do not have *any right at all vis-à-vis* my family and my late father, to whom debts were a moral responsibility – to put the financial wellbeing of my children at risk.

Above all, for me to assume sole responsibility, I would need to have all rights, general support and love. I do not have any legal voice (and seek none), no right and no moral or any other kind of authority.

Under such conditions it is not only frivolous but foolhardy to take on more responsibility than I can manage.

It is distressing that no one is able to help me or understand my position in

this business and that they approach this problem from the point of view of
the theatre's interests. And so the more forceful and categorical is my
refusal. It is yet more distressing if this refusal is taken as a withdrawal from
something I have worked on all my life. That is not the case. I will do
everything in my power, with even greater zeal, to benefit our enterprise and
to ensure the security of our colleagues in these dark days. In financial terms,
in the absence of any legal document, I assume my share of the risk and
losses equally with the other shareholders although I am not one of their
number.

My decision is sufficiently categorical for me to ask you not to return to
this matter again. It is too difficult and painful.

Your K. Alekseiev

I make no secret of this letter but think it would be better if it were not
made too public. I say this not for my sake but for the theatre.

333 Nemirovich to Stanislavski

January 5 1917
Petrograd

Dear Konstantin Sergeievich,

I asked, through Luzhski, for there to be no rehearsals on the 9th and
10th. We need to give everyone a rest from both shows. Three days is not a
lot. It would be good to establish that fact. That's one thing.

Then I have to tell you that, following our last conversations, my
agitation, uncertainty and fears have not abated in the least. The more
energetic my ideas the more they encounter one brick wall or another. For
six days in Moscow (24-29) I wrote and wrote and quarrelled with you and
others about everything. I have the really painful feeling that 'my wings are
clipped'. And you know very well that when 'my wings are clipped' I go limp,
it's worse than if I had none at all. I often fall into a mood when, though it
disgusts and shames me, I feel that the best parts of my soul have been
trampled underfoot and scornfully misunderstood. And so on. That's not
the question at the moment.

But I take wing when I know clearly, philosophically, logically in which
direction to take the theatre and take it there. But take it without ifs or buts.
But I am surrounded by ifs and buts.

When you say, 'there's no need for plans, they will come to nothing anyway'
I am ready to shout! They come to nothing because they haven't been thought
through. And for that reason the theatre lurches first this way then that,
because every week there's a new idea that everyone latches on to, forgetting
all the important tasks that were set previously and are now forgotten.

You say: 'Complete the plan we started'. Marvellous! That's all I ask! I have been putting this programme together in my mind for 14 months. But somehow I am afraid that I won't be allowed to complete it – this is the most important – because you, without knowing it, will play into the hands of much that will prevent the established programme from being completed. You have done it before. That is why I need to talk to you urgently. Right through. Be it for a while, be it for a year. You need to know about me soundly.

1. *I cannot work except in full agreement with you*. I have always considered and still consider you one of the most rewarding people I have encountered in my life. But because of some agonizing traits in your character you yourself know how difficult it can be dealing with you. But on the other hand it has long been clear that the more we separate, the greater the opportunity it is, for 'fishing in troubled waters'. That is sickening, loathsome, repellent to me. I want no more of it. It's disgusting. It stinks to heaven.

2. *I remember very well everything you have said*. I've thought it through 100 times and if I prized you less it would be easier for me to administer our affairs: I would simply take no notice of what I heard you say. And when one thinks about all this and when you yourself are not aware of the flagrant contradictions in your expressed intentions, then my wings droop, one goes limp like a fish. And then it becomes disgusting because it's shameful merely to be the executor of someone else's will.

3. In the past I counted on your enormous confidence but you are manifestly not capable of it now. Perhaps we should get to the bottom of it. I am not afraid to do that. *I am ready for the most radical decisions* – even including leaving the theatre altogether. It is all a question of establishing some agreed compromise between us. But that is clearly difficult to obtain. It may indeed be difficult for us to achieve, it may be we are indeed different in character, we may indeed in some respects go our separate ways but let us fight on the same side.

Or do we admit that full agreement is impossible between us even with a compromise? Perhaps there is such a gulf between us it cannot be bridged. What do we do then? We try to fence ourselves in if only so as not to work with our hands tied. Perhaps for all my wisdom there's something of value I don't understand in our relationship.

This thought has just come into my head: how many times have I tried to negotiate with you, how often have I wanted to know your opinion but has there been one occasion when *you* have said, 'Vladimir Ivanovich, I need to reach an understanding with you'? Even once in 10 or 12 years? You have been satisfied, I'm sorry, with what you heard about me or what you suspected about me. And now we have reached a situation when I am completely aware of your artistic intentions and wishes, when I know your artistic methods and objectives but when – I can say this truthfully – you don't

know me at all. I am frequently aware of this because of *what* you
attribute to me.

Very well. I won't dwell on the matter.

In practical terms:

More than a year ago we decided to call a 'halt' so as to review our
affairs both in the artistic and administrative sense. Then came the time
to draw up the balance and construct a programme on that basis. We had
to, so that the whole company would not have to grope its way forward
but could move with 'transparent action'. But, before calling them
together and announcing the programme, I have to negotiate with you.
They need to see that the programme has been worked out by the two of
us together. Then there will be understanding. For me to acquaint you
with the plan and modify it according to the 'compromises' that may be
necessary will take a lot of time. Not just an hour or two, or, I'm afraid,
not a day or two but more. I have already tried to grasp all the problems
so that we can find short cuts to a common understanding. But we must
talk about a practical programme, not an ideal one.

I don't need a third party present but if you do I have no objection to
someone. Provided there are not unnecessary arguments and discussions
'about this and that'.

I will be in Moscow by the 8th.

I have written what I wanted to write but now various doubts about the
possibility of reaching a new understanding fill my head. So I have to say
this.

Perhaps you, *in all sincerity* consider that, dear God, as you might say,
you have no need to talk and the reason, Vladimir Ivanovich, for your
uncertainty lies simply in your weakness. I add this. Say we don't reach
an agreement. Then we have two ways out:

1. In our last conversation you dropped the remark that you would take
on the administration of our affairs (in the dictatorial sense) 'with
pleasure'. I couldn't see how to reconcile that with your formal refusal to
accept responsibility which we have been talking about for the last six
years. But that is your affair. The first way out of my uncertainty is for
you to take everything in hand and then *tell me what I am to do*. That
would be ideal for me as I could take a long holiday. I would do what I
had to do on the literary side. Then I would be free for the theatre again.

2. The second way out is the absolute opposite. I carry out the
programme as I have conceived it and tell you what I require of you. If I
realize, not later then the 15-20 January that I am not up to it, I will tell
you that I cannot continue in charge of our affairs.

I think I have gone through the possibilities very conscientiously. Only
it would be so much more worthwhile to accomplish the things for the

sake of which we 'called a halt' and to get free of this uncertainty and doubt.

Till we meet again soon,

Your V. Nemirovich-Danchenko

In March 1917 Nemirovich shocked the company by removing Stanislavski from the cast of his own adaptation of Dostoievski's *The Village of Stepanchikovo*. The play had been in rehearsal since January 1916, with Stanislavski and Moskvin directing. In February 1917 Nemirovich realized that it was nowhere near ready and that the season could go by without a new production. Stanislavski, who was overstretched both by his work at the theatre and by industrial disputes at his factory, could not pull the character of Colonel Rostanev together.

Nemirovich took over but demanded that Stanislavski radically revise his interpretation of Rostanev, insisting that his own version of the character was nearer to Dostoievski's original intentions. Stanislavski was unable to reconcile his own work with Nemirovich's new demands. A distresssed company saw him in tears in the wings at a dress rehearsal on March 28 and he was only just able to finish the evening. Immediately after Nemirovich removed him from the cast. He did not protest but stayed away from the theatre until the autumn.

In September Nemirovich got wind of supposed comments that Stanislavski had made and felt the need to justify himself. Both men were soon engulfed in the turbulence of the October Revolution.

334 Stanislavski to Lilina

March 13 1917
Moscow

I may not be able to give birth to Dostoievski's Rostanev but to a son we both produce with many resemblances to both mother and father. But Nemirovich, like all literati, wants mother and father to produce another mother and father in their exact image. What's the purpose if they already exist? I can only give Rostanev/Stanislavski or at the very worst Stanislavski/Rostanev. Literary critics can give one Rostanev. He will be dead, like their critical essays. Let's absolutely not have that but something living. It's better than something that's identical but dead.

335 Nemirovich to Stanislavski

Early September 1917
Moscow

Dear Konstantin Sergeievich,

I am disturbed.

In January I wrote to you from Petersburg in a firm, definite manner about my relationship to you. Since then nothing has changed. That can't last all our lives. However, given your suspiciousness concerning the 'Stepanchikovo' business, the statements I made in January could appear contradictory. I would like you to take a more sensible view of my sad role in this story. No one will be more delighted than I when you get a new, successful role. I assure you, no one.

But I really cannot refrain from telling you when a role isn't working. That is the grievous side of the obligations imposed by 20 years' work together.

The other aspect of this story with 'Stepanchikovo' has to do with directing.

And so, you must understand this, there was nothing I could do. Faced with an 'affair' with a budget of a million, a director's vanities must give way. My concern comes down to this, to preserve intact everything beautiful which you brought to the production and to patch up what you were not able to do. I don't find such a role enviable. There was only one way out to prevent our *personal* relationship being damaged: postpone the production once more. That was impossible given the state of the rehearsals and the cast were horror-struck at the very thought of it.

You know *all this* from your own experience. I am writing only so that you don't yield to the temptation of feeling in any way, even a little, that I am to blame or even to reproach me.

Your Vl. Nemirovich-Danchenko

336 Stanislavski to Nemirovich

September 15 1917
Moscow

Dear Vladimir Ivanovich,

I don't know what provoked your letter. I have done nothing or said anything special to anyone, the more so since I have seen no one. I am going through a difficult time; it is difficult and unbearably boring. But I struggle with what is within me in silence.

As far as my vanity and in particular 'The Village of Stepanchikovo' are concerned the misery is that I am very happy not to be acting and only dream of one thing: to forget all that's happened and to see nothing that is in any way connected with that unfortunate production.

I have no thoughts about future roles, there is nothing more I can do, at least in the Art Theatre. In that respect after the total collapse of my plans my energy has plummeted completely. Maybe I could be reborn in another sphere, another place. I am not talking about other theatres but about the studios – *Othello free* [in English in the text]. . .

Your K. Alekseiev

PART FOUR

THE REVOLUTION AND AFTER

TWELVE

AMERICA

The October Revolution caught the Art Theatre at its lowest ebb. Between September 1917 and April 1920 the Art Theatre presented only one new production, Byron's *Cain*, directed by Stanislavski, which came off after eight performances. Despite Stanislavski's attempts to give the play contemporary significance the new working-class audience found both the text and the staging baffling.

On the other hand, the advocates of a new theatricalized theatre, such as Meyerhold, Mayakovski and Tairov soon established their importance. Meyerhold, while remaining loyal to Stanislavski personally, wanted nothing more than to close the Art Theatre down, while more extreme groups such as the Proletkult demanded nothing less than the abolition of all pre-Revolutionary culture. The perennial mainstay of the Art Theatre repertoire, Chekhov, was no longer seen as relevant. New and influential critics like Vladimir Blum described the theatre as the 'standard-bearer of the bourgeoisie'. Unfortunately for the Art Theatre, Blum later came to occupy an important place in the new system of Soviet censorship, represented by the Central Repertory Committee, the Glavrepertkom. The theatre's strongest support came from the top, from Lenin himself, who stated categorically that the theatre must survive and was himself a frequent visitor, and from Lunacharski, the first People's Commissar for Education.

The theatre was in a poor position to defend itself. At the height of the Civil War, in 1919, most of its leading actors – Kachalov, Knipper – were cut off while on tour in Europe. They did not return to Moscow until 1922 and then only after much persuasion and not in full strength. It took much pleading from Nemirovich to get them back. He had formulated a number of plans, with Lenin's approval, but these were mainly concerned with reorganization; they did not respond to the question of a new repertoire for a radically altered situation and audiences. All the new work was being performed in the Studios, which, much to Stanislavski's consternation, were themselves turning toward the new theatre of Meyerhold and, apparently, forsaking the practices of the Art Theatre.

At the same time Stanislavski and Nemirovich were being diverted into

opera – Stanislavski into a newly created Opera-Studio for young singers at
the Bolshoi and Nemirovich into his own Music Theatre.

A final blow came when at the beginning of 1921, under Lenin's New
Economic Policy, all subsidies were withdrawn and theatres were expected
to survive commercially. The theatre's takings, even with full houses, only
covered half its costs.

By the time the subsidy was restored in the autumn of 1921, the decision
had been taken at the highest level to allow the theatre to accept the offers it
had received from abroad and embark on a foreign tour, notably to Berlin,
Paris and the United States. This would withdraw it from the line of fire and
also enable it to earn foreign currency. The Art Theatre was absent from
September 1922 to May 1924, making two separate tours. The schedule was
gruelling. It was Nemirovich's secretary, Olga Bokshanskaya, on loan to
Stanislavski for the tour, who kept him informed of events. It was she also
who, at Stanislavski's dictation, typed *My Life in Art*.

Despite the enormous theatrical impact of the Art Theatre, in terms of its
own stated objectives, the tour was not a success. It did not make money. On
the contrary, in the summer of 1923, after the first tour, the company was
$25,000 in debt. Far from being removed from open attack it was con-
tinuously accused at home of having sold out on the Revolution, of living a
high life while fellow countrymen starved. Even Nemirovich fell prey to
these suspicions. Stanislavski returned home to the newly created Soviet
Union exhausted and disillusioned.

337 Nemirovich to Kachalov

July 17 1921
Moscow

[. . .]

The Art Theatre either merges with you or it is finished. Perhaps another
will be started but we, the Art Theatre, sink into the waters of Lethe. This
merger can take place either here in Moscow again or abroad.

A year and a half ago I worked out a project for us to go abroad
periodically in groups. The project was adopted by the Centrotheatre and at
first everything went well. Even Lenin expressed sympathy for it. But now
the project has collapsed. Since then the authorities have been very much
against people travelling and at the moment there is little chance of getting
permission. In the summer the First Studio tried and was refused.

However, I haven't given up on this project and think that sooner or later
it will happen. The Art Theatre is slipping but nonetheless it is so strong that
it can (with you) create at least three strong groups from within itself. The
project proposed that one group should play in Moscow, the second in

Petersburg or in the provinces and the third abroad. . . if we don't join our Art Theatre will surely be turned into something else, hence this attempt to get you to return as for the moment the chances of our being able to leave are nil. [. . .]

338 Bokshanskaya to Nemirovich

March 23 1923
New York

[. . .] Here is the as yet unconfirmed performance schedule for our tour:

CHICAGO

APRIL

3rd, Tuesday		Tsar Fiodor	Holy Week
4th, Wednesday		Tsar Fiodor	Holy Week
5th, Thursday	mat.	Tsar Fiodor	Holy Week
	eve.	Tsar Fiodor	Holy Week
6th, Friday		Lower Depths	Holy Week
7th, Saturday	mat.	Lower Depths	Holy Week
	eve.	Lower Depths	Holy Week
8th, Sunday	mat.	Lower Depths	Easter
	eve.	Lower Depths	
9th, Monday		Cherry Orchard	
10th, Tuesday		Cherry Orchard	
11th, Wednesday		Cherry Orchard	
12th, Thursday	mat.	Cherry Orchard	
	eve.	Cherry Orchard	
13th, Friday		Tsar Fiodor	
14th, Saturday	mat.	Tsar Fiodor	
	eve.	Tsar Fiodor	
15th, Sunday	mat.	Tsar Fiodor	
	eve.	Tsar Fiodor	
16th, Monday		Three Sisters	
17th, Tuesday	mat.	Three Sisters	
	eve.	Three Sisters	
18th, Wednesday		Three Sisters	
19th, Thursday	mat.	Three Sisters	
	eve.	Three Sisters	
20th, Friday	mat.	Lower Depths	
	eve.	Lower Depths	
21st, Saturday	mat.	Lower Depths	
	eve.	Lower Depths	

PHILADELPHIA

23rd, Monday		Tsar Fiodor
24th, Tuesday	mat.	Tsar Fiodor
	eve.	Tsar Fiodor
25th, Wednesday		Tsar Fiodor
26th, Thursday	mat.	Tsar Fiodor
	eve.	Tsar Fiodor
27th, Friday		Lower Depths
28th, Saturday	mat.	Lower Depths
	eve.	Lower Depths
29th, Sunday		No performance
30th, Monday	mat.	Lower Depths
	eve.	Lower Depths

MAY

1st, Tuesday	mat.	Lower Depths
	eve.	Lower Depths
2nd, Wednesday		Cherry Orchard
3rd, Thursday	mat.	Cherry Orchard
	eve.	Cherry Orchard
4th, Friday		Three Sisters
5th, Saturday	mat.	Three Sisters
	eve.	Three Sisters

BOSTON

7th, Monday		Tsar Fiodor
8th, Tuesday	mat.	Tsar Fiodor
	eve.	Tsar Fiodor
9th, Wednesday		Tsar Fiodor
10th, Thursday	mat.	Tsar Fiodor
	eve.	Tsar Fiodor
11th, Friday		Lower Depths
12th, Saturday	mat.	Lower Depths
	eve.	Lower Depths
13th, Sunday		No performance
14th, Monday	mat.	Lower Depths
	eve.	Lower Depths
15th, Tuesday	mat.	Lower Depths
	eve.	Lower Depths
16th, Wednesday		Cherry Orchard
17th, Thursday	mat.	Cherry Orchard
	eve.	Cherry Orchard

18th, Friday		Three Sisters
19th, Saturday	mat.	Three Sisters
	eve.	Three Sisters

So from April 3 to May 19 in three cities, 67 performances. As you can see, dear Vladimir Ivanovich, life is not easy for us with 9-10 performances a week, on tour as well in unknown cities. We shall even be playing in Holy Week and the first day of Easter at the same intense tempo. Holidays for us are working days. [. . .]

In the *Novoe Russkoe Slovo*, published in New York, Stanislavski is reputed to have said: 'What was our horror when the workers invaded the theatre with dirty clothes, uncombed, unwashed, with filthy boots, demanding the performance of revolutionary plays.'

This was reported in the magazine *Krokodil* and subsequently in other papers. Nemirovich immediately arranged publication of a rebuttal by Stanislavski.

339 Stanislavski to Pravda

November 24 1923

Telegram

The report of my American interview is lies from beginning to end. Repeatedly, in the presence of hundreds of witnesses, I stated the very opposite about new audiences, boasting about, taking pride in their sensitivity, citing as an example the philosophical tragedy 'Cain' which was splendidly understood by a new audience. I thought that my forty years of activity and my long-standing dream of a people's theatre would have protected me against scurrilous suspicions. I am deeply hurt, cut to the quick.

340 Stanislavski to Nemirovich

December 28 1923
Philadelphia

Moscow accuses us of disloyalty. But we get even blacker looks abroad. France just about let us in. We only managed to get a favourable result by cicumventing French law. In Paris a considerable number of people, both French and Russian, boycotted us because we came from the Soviet Union and therefore were communists. Now they won't let us into Canada, officially declaring us Bolsheviks, and all our plans have collapsed. Who knows how many more difficulties lie ahead of us? You only have to think of recent persecution in the press stirred up in the Boston papers. . .

Here we are attacked by both Russians and Americans for using our theatre to glorify present-day Russia. In Moscow they are slinging mud at us because we are preserving the tradition of bourgeois theatre and because plays by Chekhov and other authors of the 'intelligentsia' are successful with Russian émigrés and American capitalists; they think we are rolling in dollars while in fact we are up to our ears in debt. Believe me it's not for my own pleasure that I am spending almost two years going from place to place, from city to city with absolutely no time for the things I love and dream about and that I am losing what remains of my health. My spirits are low, I'm depressed, I've almost lost heart and at times think of giving it all up. . .

Seeing all the abuse that's heaped on me in Moscow I am refusing all kinds of good offers coming my way from Europe and America and yearn with all my heart for Russia. [. . .]

341 Nemirovich to Bokshanskaya

January 20 1924
Moscow

[. . .]

For the most part, when I consider the way you are living over there, how difficult, boring, monotonous the work you have to do is, I find you are making a profound psychological error: you are concentrating all your attention on dollars and that not only fails to alleviate the difficulty of your current work, it actually increases it. It seems to me that if other items were put on your 'agenda', if these other items assumed the same importance as the question of dollars, if you were to display the same interest in them as in 'dollars' then it would be easier to live and to be more circumspect in your behaviour. And such questions are here, right to hand. . . I mean the political situation in our country and all countries. The ideological mountain that has risen up in our lives. And the most important is *our future*! This question is a *memento mori*. There is not a day, sometimes an hour when I don't go over this question again and again and all the minor questions connected with it. There is not the smallest theatrical event, discussion, meeting that can fail to push us towards new discussions of the enigma of the future. And when one reads all the letters you send, then one is astonished that you seem to have forgotten that soon you will have to return to Moscow and play in 'The Journey of the Art Theatre'. What will you play? With whom will you play? How will you play?, etc.

It seems to me if you were thinking of that then it would be easier to get away from the 'dollars' and the arduous labour of performing would be lighter. . .

I remember in Waren,[1] in the dining-room of the pension, after coffee, saying that every one of you should send his plan for the future in November. Naturally that has been completely forgotten but what are they thinking of when they put this question completely from their minds?!

This is appalling! [. . .]

V. Nemirovich-Danchenko

342 Stanislavski to Nemirovich

February 12 1924
New York

[. . .]

I have read your letter to Olga Sergeievna [Bokshanskaya] and nonetheless take the time to try more or less to correct some of your ideas about our life here and give you an opportunity better to appreciate the facts.

There can be absolutely no talk about making dollars. Our sole concern is to leave here free of the debts incurred in revolutionary Germany and an expensive Paris last summer, which increased our budget five-fold. I also want to be in the clear with Gest and not get him into the red and so keep him on our side in the future. We also have to consider, once we have paid out debts, how and with what money we are to get from London to Moscow and transport 60 people and 8 waggon-loads of belongings safe and sound. Where are we to put these belongings? Where do we get the money to prepare a new repertoire as none of us is prepared to appear in Moscow except in a new play? If that is not possible then personally I propose we should close down the MXT groups temporarily or permanently. [. . .]

Make no mistake about it, a tired, broken, disorganized army is returning to Moscow whose backs cannot be burdened with heavy packs and great loads. Four days a week, a matinée on Sundays given by young people with a minimal participation of selected actors and artists, that is the absolute maximum that can be counted on. For this to happen budgets must be reduced so that perhaps we have to play all new productions in drapes and old costumes and all our hopes for success must be based exclusively on good acting. In America only that, that and nothing else, finds success. That's why in the last performances and the revivals of 'Uncle Vanya' and 'Pazukhin's [Death]' it was an advantage for them to be done in drapes (true, they were cleanly and snugly adapted) because, as a result, the critics and the audience

1. In the late summer of 1923 the company was preparing for the second American tour at Waren, near Berlin.

were able to concentrate on the actors. Indeed a company like that, with such individual personalities does not exist in Russia or anywhere abroad at the present time. But they might be able to discover the things in the art of the future which we are all so avidly seeking. But whether they will try to discover it or rest on their laurels is a question I find worrying. [. . .] It would be sheer folly to count on our company to cover the theatre's incredible expenses. It seems to me that everybody recognizes that fact and would even, albeit with great reluctance, agree to a significant reduction in the lavishness of previous productions and in other things rather than to work which is beyond their strength, for half the company is genuinely ill and some of them are cripples. I am writing you all this to limit any hopes you have of getting the help which, I know, you need badly. We must cut down, be more modest, rely on pure art, technical experience and people of talent – that is the watchword for this group in future . . .

Don't think I have been idle. I have been working unremittingly, working on things which in my opinion are very important, which in this age of charlatanism have been forgotten by everyone, except you. And that gives me strength. We are strong because of other things. The recognition we have had in America. (I'm not counting Europe as we can expect nothing there except success and good notices). America is the only auditorium and the only source of money for subsidies on which we can count. I am of the opinion that we cannot make do without America and almost convinced that America can't now do without us . . . The American people has a feeling for the theatre. They grasp individuality like no one else, seek it out and know how to value it. [. . .]

Your statement that beyond the dollar there is art, that we must think about new ways within it, work, experiment, lay in a store for Moscow, can only, here in our present circumstances, evoke a kindly, indulgent smile. Do you know where we rehearse when we are putting someone new into the cast? In the untidy rooms of our low-grade hotels where we lodge. Are you aware that if we are given some dreadful green-room, or rather the ante-room of some theatre, in five minutes the cleaning-ladies arrive and shamelessly start yelling and shouting and making a racket with the object of demonstrating that an actor's intellectual labours are nothing but that their unskilled work means everything to America. When the stage director, really an amazing, splendid fellow, comes to put up the set, the actor has to give way, clear the stage, double-quick, American-style. But when the actor has to play a delicate, tender two-handed scene in Chekhov or a pause, the stage-hands stomp up and down in the wings, play cards, and if one says the slightest thing to them they just put on their coats to a man and go off to their homes in their cars and we can start swimming for Europe in our underpants.

The idea that we can think about creating something new when we are playing ten shows a week is mad . . . Believe me, if I can manage to bring

back this horde and their belongings, drop them at the Art Theatre and
hand them over I shall be the happiest man alive. And I won't board this
slave-ship a second time, at least not under the conditions we are working
in now.

So forget the idea, and try to persuade our enemies, that we are living
off profits here. We are getting into debt, in the first place with you,
Bertenson, Leonidov (Davydich), Podgorny, Kachalov, me, Gest – for
the sets, transporting them there and back – with no mention at all what
we are to do for money when we get back to Moscow . . . We even
reckon that on our return the whole repertoire, with the exception of
'Pazukhin' and 'Locandiera', will be banned. We have even less idea what
we should play or how we should play it. Realistic sets are now a thing of
the past, there can be no two opinions about that. But what new kinds of
sets we can justify by our inner feelings we can only decide when we see
in which direction you have led our art. Two years is no short period and
so as a director I have first to look around me and learn, adapt myself to
the things I have been working on during this time, things I have dreamed
of, without which I cannot go on working. I have to tell you that I have
given not a little consideration to a total renunciation of the stage and art.
I will certainly do so if I feel too old and if the young have left me behind.
I cannot be a kind of artistic poor relation. I have worked for forty-five
years, I have built up a certain level of inertia which keeps me going but I
can't be content with that. I will study, teach, write if I cannot get my
own way, because I know for certain that it is needed, that people are
waiting for it, that they will never find it without me, just as without you
they will never find what you can give – something essential for the art of
the future. [. . .]

Nemirovich negotiated the theatre's future with Lunacharski, officials of
Narkompros [People's Commissariat for Education] and with Olga
Malinovskaya, who had charge of what were now called the Academic
theatres. The government offered additional premises in the form of the
New Theatre but there was no clear view on how it should be used. A major
consideration was the relationship of the main Art Theatre company to the
Studios which had flourished during the tour.

343 Nemirovich to Bokshanskaya

February 10-15 1924
Moscow

[. . .]

I need the *unconditional* agreement of K.S. and the shareholders to my plan (that is the one I have worked out).

Or everything will be left to chance: to a decision by Narkompros or the authorities, or, if nobody pushes us, we will decide the future in September (!!!) or I will decide here by myself. . . .

Should the 1st Studio take the New Theatre . . . it will be more inclined to be completely independent (2nd Art Theatre?). Especially [Michael] Chekhov. He has his own artistic-ethical line and is afraid of being swamped by other elements. But Chekhov doesn't meet with total sympathy. As he says, one third of the studio treats him 'rather negatively'. And if the 2nd group (the veterans) suddenly start to come together with the former theatre, well then splits might start to appear in the 1st Studio and one or two might be drawn towards us.

The 2nd Studio is in such a state that the authorities are amazed I should defend it. I think I can reform it and retain the core.

The 3rd Studio, although it came a cropper with 'Marriage', still holds together *as a studio*.

The 4th will be left to survive as it wishes. It attracts sympathy. . . .

At all events I would add that by 'unconditional' I mean that not all those who are currently in America may prove to be essential to us in Moscow. I would put it like this, that in the New Art Theatre we have *absolutely no need* of artists (*or staff*) who have proved themselves to be undisciplined, unethical and completely badly behaved. [. . .]

344 Stanislavski to Nemirovich

June 10 1924
Chamonix

[. . .]

I accept and approve the measures you have taken. The 1st Studio – to be independent. This long-standing sickness of my soul requires a definite operation. (A pity that it will be called the 2nd MXT. It has betrayed it in every respect). Privately I call the studio Goneril's Studio.

The 3rd Studio also to separate – I approve. That is Regan's Studio. The Second Studio can be likened to Cordelia. They are nice and there is something better in them but, but . . . you know them better at the moment,

I, at a distance, cannot conceive what they will make of themselves after their Futuristic spree . . .

If it is still possible to save the Art Theatre then only one man can do it, *you*. I am powerless. My edge has gone completely. For two years I've had to shout and swear so much that now I have no authority of any kind while *you*, on the other hand, have acquired more . . .

I agree to play in 'Fiodor' but don't be deceived: Kachalov and I are playing badly. [. . .]

Be the leading personality in the Studio? Fine. I agree and will try to do what I can. But this time you sustain a belief or even some sort of ray of hope in me for the Studio. They have disappointed me so much that I have no more belief in them or good feelings towards them. All the people in the studios are petit bourgeois with tiny, practical, utilitarian spiritual needs. There is a touch of art here and there and a lot of compromises . . .

I am almost incapable of reaching compromises and when I do they credit them to my account, exploit my weakness and abuse it. And when I stand firm they say I am intolerable and run away. Nobody needs what I have to give . . .

345 Nemirovich to Lunacharski

October 14 1924
Moscow

In view of the statement by the Glavrepertkom [Central Repertory Committee] on the necessity for modifications and corrections in the presentation of Maeterlinck's 'The Bluebird' the Management asked Com. Muradreva who is at the Art Theatre to explain the Glavrepertkom's demands in detail. As a result of lengthy consultations Com. Muradreva held with V. I. Blum the cuts and changes in 'The Bluebird' proved so great that the theatre found it impossible to present the play in that form. Suffice it to say that V. I. Blum produced a demand to remove the whole 'Azure Kingdom' scene.

The theatre understands the Glavrepertkom's ideological standpoint which Muradreva explained very clearly. However, in the present case there is a divergence of principle between the theatre and Glavrepertkom. The theatre management does not consider that it has the right to enter into a dispute in the present formal case with a body instituted by Narkompros to control the theatre's repertoire. The more so since this divergence is very profound and has implications for the overall understanding of the influence the theatre has or may have on the audience, even when it is very young. The theatre management considers that its influence certainly does not lie in psychological claptrap in the sense it is understood by the bodies holding powers of censorship. I repeat I find it impossible to raise any objections at the moment. But I have to make it clear that with the cuts V. I. Blum is demanding the play cannot go on for reasons of artistic integrity. The series of changes and cuts proposed by V. I. Blum are accepted in full but to implement them all and in particular to take out the 'Azure Kingdom' means perverting Maeterlinck's artistic intentions to such a degree that it is more honourable to remove the play from the repertoire.

In the meantime the theatre is moving to the edge of the abyss and I, as the manager of MXAT, do not know what measures to take.

> With profound respect and
> devotion
> VI. Nemirovich-Danchenko

The problem the theatre encounted with *The Bluebird* was a foretaste of difficulties to come. While there was as yet no rigid party line on the arts, works which could be classified as 'counter-revolutionary' were banned. It was of the utmost importance for the Art Theatre to establish the fact that it had adapted to changed circumstances and could provide relevant programmes for post-revolutionary audiences.

Nemirovich was absent abroad with his Music Theatre from 1925 to 1927. During that period Stanislavski relaunched the Art Theatre with nine new productions ranging from the classic *Marriage of Figaro* to the revolutionary *Armoured Train* staged to celebrate the tenth anniversary of the October Revolution. The highlight of this period was Bulgakov's *The Days of the Turbins*, adapted from his novel *The White Guard*. It seemed to the theatre, particularly the younger members, that they had found a new Chekhov. Rehearsals recalled the heady atmosphere of Pushkino in the summer of 1898.

But the play proved ideologically contentious. Even the title had to go. The word 'white' was unacceptable. Apart from changes which had to be made to Bulgakov's original script to make it theatrically manageable, there were compromises on ideological grounds, which Bulgakov was only persuaded with difficulty to accept. The play was eventually passed by the Glavrepertkom but an unremitting campaign was mounted to get it banned.

346 Lunacharski to Luzhski

> October 12 1925
> Moscow

I have read the play 'The White Guard'[1] attentively. I find nothing

1. In Bulgakov's first draft.

inadmissible in it from the political point of view but I cannot conceal my own personal opinion. I consider Bulgakov to be a very talented man but this play of his is exceptionally undistinguished except for the one or two lively scenes of the Hetman's departure. All the rest is either the turmoil of war or unusually commonplace, rather stupidly dull scenes of middle-class philistinism of no interest to anyone. There is not one single character, not one engaging situation and the end simply makes one angry with its vagueness and total lack of effect. If certain theatres say that they cannot stage this or that revolutionary play because of their dramatic imperfections then I can say with confidence that the average theatre would not accept this play precisely because of its dullness, the result, probably of the complete dramatic weakness or considerable inexperience of the author.

347 Bulgakov to MXAT Committee and Management

June 4 1926
Moscow

I hereby have the honour to inform you that I am not in agreement with the removal of the Petliura scene from my play 'The White Guard'.

The reason: the Petliura scene is organically related to the play. I am also not in agreement with changing the title of the play to 'Before the End'.

I am also not in agreement with the change from a 4-act to a 3-act play.

I am in complete agreement with the idea of discussing another title for the play 'The White Guard'.

In the event of the theatre's being unable to agree with the points made in this letter, I ask that the play 'The White Guard' be withdrawn as a matter of urgency.

Mikhail Bulgakov

348 Stanislavski to Lunacharski

September 13 1927
Moscow

[. . .]

The banning of 'The Turbins' and 'Uncle Vanya' would destroy the whole of the scheduling for the current season.

The attached information will acquaint you with the sums our losses would amount to should a ban occur. These losses do not cover only the daily drop in the projected takings for 'The Turbins'. We will incur losses on other days thanks to the fact that our repertoire will be much thinner. We shall have to stage old plays several times a week . . .

To increase takings we would have to take swift steps to revive old plays which are not in the repertoire at the moment. That would take a great deal of time when every working hour is precious to us as we have urgently to mount 'The Armoured Train'[1] for the 10th anniversary of the October Revolution. There is an enormous amount of work which demands undivided effort from the whole company. There are a large number of crowd scenes in which the whole company is involved almost without exception. There is a great deal of artistic work on the décor and technical side.

The presence of 'The Turbins' in our current repertoire would act as a guarantee that other new plays would be forthcoming. Now we must either risk not being able to mount a show for the jubilee of the October Revolution or deliberately suffer financial losses.

I would like to inform you that 'The Armoured Train' has still not been finally approved. We need extensive and complicated changes from the author [Ivanov] who is abroad. We have sent him a telegram and all we now await is his arrival.

It is almost impossible to rehearse a much-needed show when there is no final script. Uncertainty is the worst enemy in the theatre, it saps energy and creates difficulties by the minute.

---

1. Adapted from the novella by Vsevolod Ivanov.

THIRTEEN

STALIN

The thirtieth anniversary of the Art Theatre in 1928 marked a turning point in its life. Stanislavski suffered a heart attack during a gala performance of Act One of *Three Sisters* and never appeared on stage again. The last ten years of his life were passed as a semi-invalid. He worked when he could and against the advice of his doctors. He was absent from the theatre from late 1928 to late 1930, during which time his only contribution was to write two-thirds of a production plan for *Othello*.

During his absence the political climate in the Soviet Union changed radically. The Stalinist era dawned and the suppression of artistic freedom and the imposition of orthodoxy began in earnest. Lunacharski who, within limits, had followed a pluralist policy, was sacked. Mayakovski committed suicide. Perhaps no writer suffered more during this period than Bulgakov, whose destiny was inextricably linked for ten years with that of the Art Theatre. His works were consistently banned and subjected to vile abuse. The sole exception was *The Days of the Turbins* which, ironically, was saved by Stalin himself. Having succeeded finally in getting the play taken off during Stanislavski's absence, the zealous ideologues were disconcerted to find that Stalin liked the play and, indeed, had seen it fifteen times. It was quickly restored to the repertoire.

The authorities were beginning to tighten their grip on the theatres. As far as the Art Theatre was concerned this amounted to the appointment of a communist, a 'red' director to the board of management whose task would be to mediate between the government and the company. Stanislavski saw no objection to this. Much more serious was the pressure on the theatre to turn out more productions. Just as the emphasis in the economy was on forced collectivization of agriculture and increased production in heavy industry, so the Art Theatre was being pressed to increase its productivity by doing more contemporary plays more quickly. What was required was an immediate response to issues of the day. This ran counter to everything that Stanislavski and Nemirovich stood for but did find a sympathetic response in younger directors, like Sudakov, and young actors, who felt that they were underemployed in a company which could, for one reason or another, take months or even years to get a play on. Stanislavski and Nemirovich toyed for three or four years with the idea of creating a branch theatre, a 'production' theatre which would give the younger members their head. Such a theatre, while under the control of the Art Theatre, would be distinguished from it. The creation of such a theatre became a distinct possibility in 1933 when the company, thanks mainly to some spirited lobbying by Sudakov, was offered the premises of the Korsh Theatre which had been closed down. But the notion of a divided company was inimical to both Stanislavski and Nemirovich.

The decade 1928-38 was also marked by what might be called the war of succession. Who was to take over the Art Theatre? Both Stanislavski and Nemirovich were absent for long periods alternately: Stanislavski 1929-30, Nemirovich 1931-33, Stanislavski again 1933-34. Younger members such as Sakhovich, Sudakov and Yegorov saw themselves as possible inheritors. The struggle became more acute when the Art Theatre was designated by Stalin as the model for all Soviet theatres. Whoever controlled the Art Theatre would wield immense power artistically and enjoy considerable privilege.

In 1927 Bulgakov wrote *Flight* which the Art Theatre accepted for production. Once again the censors and the Glavrepertkom took the view that the material was sympathetic to White or counter-revolutionary forces. Gorki was strong in his support for the play, maintaining that it satirized the Whites. Nonetheless, after a long discussion, it was banned on October 8 1928. Nemirovich took the view that the satirical humour of the play was lost in a simple reading but would emerge on stage. Stalin's comments to the dramatist Bill-Bielotserkovski may explain the censors' intransigence.

349 Stalin to V. Bill-Bielotserkovski

February 2 1929
Moscow

[. . .]
'Flight' attempts to evoke pity if not actual sympathy for certain elements among anti-Soviet émigrés . . . as regards 'The Days of the Turbins' that is not such a bad work as it does more good than harm. Remember the deep impression the audience receives is favourable to the Bolsheviks. If even people like the Turbins are obliged to lay down their arms and submit to the will of the people and admit what they stand for is lost, the Bolsheviks are invincible. . . 'The Days of the Turbins' demonstrates the almighty power of Bolshevism. [. . .]

During his convalescence abroad Stanislavski relied on his correspondence with Leonidov for news. Leonidov was to play the title role in *Othello* for which Stanislavski was writing the production plan. Their letters dealt with both politics and the interpretation of Othello.

350 Stanislavski to Leonidov

September 15 1929
Badenweiler

[. . .]

The question of a Red member of the Board, as is well known, is not new. It first appeared before Sviderski [Narkompros] but at that time I was on form and management was in the hands of people I considered efficient. Then, as you know, I fell ill. Vladimir Ivanovich was left all alone, business management was pushed aside, Vladimir Ivanovich was not able to deal with administrative-financial matters and these fell into the hands of the current management. I like them very much, they are good actors but where is their business experience? Why should we trust them in this area. How could they take on such complicated matters? Their inexperience and lack of understanding in these matters was all too clear when, as a first step, they got rid of the two experienced and efficient people they should have hung on to given their own inexperience. [. . .]

You understand, at my years I cannot take on the responsibility for management and stand in the dock in my old age because of the inexperience of a young board. I myself, as someone who in my time has started three businesses and dealt with efficient people over a period of thirty years, openly declare that without an efficient board – to be precise Nikolai Vassilievich [Yegorov] and Nikolai Afanassievich [Podgorny], I am fearful of taking on a directorship. I have uttered this sentence before, say it now and will say it in the future. I discussed this with Sviderski when he came to see me during my illness before I came away.

The question automatically arises: what is the way forward? I am ill and cannot work as I used to. Vladimir Ivanovich is overstretched and cannot work because of age but can still hold on to the literary-artistic and production department. But I told Sviderski that the only way out I could see was to nominate a Red board member and even there I hastened to present him with a big 'but'. There are board members and board members. One can bring great benefit, another can wreck everything. To destroy the finely-tuned organization of the Art Theatre irrevocably, for ever, is the matter of a moment, of one stroke of the pen; to create it is a chance event which occurs once in a hundred years. That is why the selection of a Red board member is a question of the continuing existence of the theatre, its life or death. A good director can be an enormous help to the theatre in its present circumstances. I say that from my own personal experience at the Opera Theatre. When questions of a political character arise then we, the non-Communists, cannot speak with authority, we command no respect, but the picture suddenly changes when a Red board member, a Communist, deals with the question, because he does command respect and matters are discussed with him in a different way from us, and he speaks in a completely different way from us. We knew the importance in the theatre of Communists who understand its nature and are careful to defend everything that needs to be lovingly saved and preserved. I am profoundly convinced that what we need is a red board member who understands the nature of theatre or, at least, wants to understand it.

I expressed these thoughts, although somewhat more carefully phrased, to Sviderski when he asked me how we should proceed. Of course I made it clear to him that I was talking about previous years and not about this current season when I was not *au fait* with what was happening in the theatre.

I reported my conversation with Sviderski to Vladimir Ivanovich by telephone as far as a telephone conversation and the medical monitoring of my pulse allowed. If I am not mistaken Vladimir Ivanovich agreed not to a Red board member but to a Red co-director. But that's just playing with words, what is important is not what he is called but that he is a Communist with an official watching-brief over the conduct of affairs. I believe that a Red board member who has directly to do with the directors is better, more useful or – in the case of a bad appointment – less dangerous if only because he is in constant contact with us instead of being far away and because officially he only has one vote while we have two if we manage to come to an agreement. To reach an agreement with an efficient, educated, disciplined Communist who loves our theatre and art is not difficult and I know this from many incidents in my personal experience during recent years. But the most important thing is that an important Communist should be named, someone who is not content merely to be just one member of the board. But what if an insignificant Communist arrives, with no authority who will take not an artistic social line but his own, bureaucratic one? It will prove more difficult with such an official, who is seeking power, than with a man who is educated, intelligent, and who understands and likes the theatre . . .

All that remains is for me to give you the text of the telegram I received from Sviderski and my reply.

Sviderski's telegram of the 29/VIII:

A dissolution of the board of the First MXAT in its present form is projected. Creation of a board and three directors: Stanislavski, Nemirovich and the Communist Heitz, former director of the Board for Moscow Entertainment Enterprises. The division of duties among the directors will be reached by agreement. I consider the project appropriate and Heitz's candidature acceptable. Wire your opinion soonest. I have put the same question to Nemirovich. Glaviskusstvo. Sviderski.

My telegram in reply:

Everything depends on the personality of the director: if he is educated, understands the nature of theatre, I agree, if the opposite, I do not. Apart from the directors a board is needed. In the finance-administrative departments of the board Yegorov and Podgorny urgently needed. Writing. Stanislavski.

Unfortunately my requests and wishes have not been fulfilled . . .

351 Stanislavski to Leonidov

February 10 1930
Menton

[. . .]

Let us establish the circumstances as experienced by Othello. He has been indescribably happy with Desdemona. His honeymoon has been a dream, the ultimate height of passionate love. This ultimate height has been little presented by actors playing 'Othello', the writer himself gives little attention or space to it and yet it is important if we are to show what Othello is losing and what he is saying farewell to . . . This scene marks, in essence, the dividing line. From here on Othello goes downwards. Can a man suddenly renounce the happiness he has known and to which he has become accustomed? Is it easy to acknowledge what one has lost? When a man loses the very thing by which he lives, he is at first bereft, loses equilibrium then begins agonizingly to look for it. Once there was happiness, how can one go on without it? A man going through a crisis goes over his whole life in agony and sleepless nights. He weeps for what he has lost, values it more highly than before, and compares it to the future as he now imagines it. What must a man do to accomplish this huge inward task? He must go deep into himself to review the past and to imagine his future life. Small wonder then that a man in such circumstances does not notice what is going on around him, that he is absent-minded and strange and that when he returns once more from the dream-world to reality he is even more horrified and disturbed and looks for a pretext to pour out the bitterness and pain that has built up while he was deep within himself.

That is Othello's situation in the scene as I see it. And that was the reason for the set. That is why Othello flies to the top of the highest tower, as in this scene . . . to live the moment when he says 'Ha, ha, false to me!' [. . .]

I don't think that Othello is jealous. The petty jealousy with which Othello is usually portrayed belongs more to Iago. The fact is, I now realize, that Iago is basely and vulgarly jealous of Emilia. Othello is an altogether nobler being. He cannot live in the world in the knowledge of the injustice men cause one another, or bear to see the sublime love that lives within him ridiculed or debased with impunity. And that under the mask of an ideal beauty, almost of a goddess of heavenly purity and innocence, of unearthly goodness and tenderness! All these qualities are so cunningly portrayed that you cannot tell them from the real thing!

And so, in relation to this scene, I think it is not a question of jealousy but a pathological disappointment in the ideal of a woman and a man the like of which the world has never seen. It is the most profound pain, unbearable sorrow. Othello sits hour-long in this attitude, eyes staring at a fixed point, delving into his innermost being, trying to comprehend, to believe the possibility that such a satanic lie could exist. And so when Iago comes up from below, cautiously, unseen, like a snake, and says, with unusual gentleness, like a doctor to a patient, 'Why, how now, General! No more of that', Othello begins to tremble in anticipation of the pain this torturer is preparing for him . . . Most actors playing Othello fall into a rage here. In reality it is still the most excruciating pain. It hurts so much that the illusion of joy he had before now appears to him as real joy. He compares this illusion of joy with what is happening now and begins to bid farewell to life. There are only two passions in the world for him: Desdemona and the art of generalship, as with great actors whose life is divided between the love of women and art.

So, 'Farewell the tranquil mind! Farewell content!', etc., is a farewell, a lament, a lament for his second passion and not at all a sentimental panegyric over a life of war, as it is usually played. I will applaud you loudly if you remain in some attitude or other, motionless, oblivious to the things around you, and survey with an inner eye the total picture that is so infinitely dear to a master of the art of war. Sit still, wipe away the tears that are running down your cheeks in great drops, hold on to yourself so as not to sob out loud and speak in a muted voice, as people do when talking of something important and intimate.

This speech might be broken up by long pauses during which he sits there and silently surveys the picture of what he has lost. In other pauses he might bend forward over a stone and sob a long time unheard, shaking his head as though he were saying farewell. This is not emotional enthusiasm for war but the tears shed before impending death. Once he has bound up the wounds of his heart with this farewell, he feels the need to pour out his torment to somebody else. So he begins to reveal his pain to Iago. And when he has grabbed him and well-nigh thrown him off the tower, he takes fright at what he might do and runs up to the stone platform, throws himself down, racked with silent sobs. There he lies, like a boy, in a childlike posture, on this rock, and asks forgiveness and pours out his sorrow to Iago who is standing below him. And at the end of the scene, when it is almost dark and the moon and stars are appearing in the sky, Othello is standing on the upper platform and calls Iago to him and, up there, between heaven and the sea, outraged in his deepest human feelings, he calls the moon that is sinking below the horizon and the stars to witness and performs a terrifying ceremony, i.e., an oath of revenge.

Bulgakov's play [*Molière*] is very interesting. Isn't he giving it to someone else? That would be a pity.

Keep the following in mind: if it's set in Molière's time there is *absolutely* no one in Russia who has a feeling for the XVII century outside Golovin. He is ill and works slowly. If you have decided to do the play next year then it would be a good idea to ask him to do the sets well in advance, the more so since he may be without work at the moment and feeling the pinch.

In 1930 Bulgakov, whose works had been consistently banned or taken off, was driven to make an appeal to the Soviet government. This resulted in a telephone call from Stalin. Both the letter and the telephone call helped to create the erroneous opinion that it was possible to come to a private arrangement with Stalin, who was still seen as a benevolent figure. Some of Stanislavski's later appeals to the authorities were, it is claimed, partly drafted by Bulgakov on that account. It would seem that Bulgakov's entry onto the staff of the Art Theatre was a result of pressure exerted from the Kremlin.

352 Bokshanskaya to Sergei Bertenson

March 7 1930
Moscow

[. . .]

Now we are concentrating all our attention on 'Othello'. Tomorrow there will be a run of the whole play in make-up and costume. The next rehearsal after that will be on the 11th to which the Repertkom of the Art Th. polit. committee have been invited, then on the 14th there is a private performance for some organization or other, dress rehearsal on the 17th and opening night on the 20th. Of course the performance can't achieve those heights under Sudakov that it would under Konstantin Sergeievich. That would have been too much to expect although Konst. Serg. did send us his detailed working out of the staging and the characters. So far, while in Nice, he has managed to complete and send off the first two acts and part of the 3rd. What he has sent us is an amazing creation, you could bring it out as a book, as a work of genius, a model of the director's work. But Sudakov hasn't taken everything from it, he has made some changes of his own and taken another approach with certain characters. [. . .]

The external aspect of the production is our biggest worry as regards the presentation of the show. Vlad. Iv. has done no work on this show at all. He hasn't been to a single rehearsal and has given absolutely convincing arguments for not doing so. He won't be at the dress rehearsal either as he can see no advantage in that either to the play or himself. [. . .]

353 Bulgakov to the Government of the USSR

March 28 1930
Moscow

I address the following letter to the Soviet Government:

1.

After the banning of all my works, voices were raised among citizens to whom I am known as a writer, offering the same piece of advice:

To write a 'Communist play' (I quote) and in particular to compose a letter of repentance to the Soviet Government, which would contain a rejection of my previously held views, as they appear in my literary works, and giving an assurance that in future I shall work as a fellow-travelling writer devoted to the idea of Communism.

The objective: to save myself from persecution, poverty and ultimate inevitable ruin.

I have not taken this advice. I am hardly likely to put myself in a favourable light to the Soviet Government by writing a deceitful letter, which would reveal me as a grubby and what's more a politically naïve time-server as well.

I did not even make an attempt to write a Communist play knowing well that I could not bring off such a play. My growing desire to put an end to my torment as a writer has impelled me to approach the Soviet Government with a truthful letter.

2.

Having proceeded to an analysis of my album of cuttings, I have counted over the ten-year period of my literary activity 301 references to me in the Soviet press. Of these 3 praised me and 298 were hostile and abusive.

These last 298 have proved the mirror-image of my life as a writer.

The hero of my play 'The Days of the Turbins', Aleksei Turbin has been called in print 'A SON OF A BITCH', and the author of the play recommended as 'decrepit OLD DOG'. Of me they have written that I am a 'literary SCAVENGER' rummaging among 'THE PUKE of a dozen guests'.

This is what they wrote:

'. . .MISHKA Bulgakov, my god-father, you are ALSO, EXCUSE THE EXPRESSION, A WRITER, rummaging IN STALE GARBAGE . . . I am a man of taste SO HIT HIM ON THE HEAD WITH A BASIN . . . LET'S WISH THE TURBINS EMPTY BOX-OFFICE AND EMPTY SEATS. ('Zhizn Iskusstva' No 44, 1927).

They wrote, 'Bulgakov was and is a NEO-BOURGEOIS MONSTROSITY spitting venomously but impotently against the working class and its communist ideals.' ('Koms [omolskaya] Pravda'. 14/X 1926).

It is said I like 'THE ATMOSPHERE OF CANINE COUPLING around the red-hot wife of a friend' (A. Lunacharski, 'Izvestiya' 8/X 1926) and that my play 'The Days of the Turbins' gives off a 'STENCH' (Record of an Agitprop meeting in May 1927) and so on and so forth . . .

I hasten to add that I am not by any means offering these quotes to complain about criticism or to enter into any kind of polemic. My object is much more serious.

I wish to demonstrate, documents in hand, that the whole of the Soviet press and all the authorities charged with the control of repertoire, throughout all the years of my literary activities, have unanimously, and WITH EXTRAORDINARY VIRULENCE, demonstrated that the works of Mikhail Bulgakov have no place in the Soviet Union.

And I also maintain that the Soviet press is ABSOLUTELY RIGHT.

3.

The starting-point of this letter as far as I am concerned lies in my lampoon 'The Purple Island'.

All Soviet critics, without exception, greeted this play with the comment that it was 'talentless, toothless, squalid' and that it presented 'a libel on the revolution'.

Unanimity was complete but it was suddenly and completely surprisingly broken.

In No 12 of the 'Repert [ny] Bull [etin] (1928) there appeared an article by P. Novitski in which it was stated that 'The Purple Island' was 'an interesting and witty parody' in which 'the ominous ghost of the Grand Inquisitor rises up who suppresses real artistic creation and nurtures SLAVISH, ABSURDLY BOOT-LICKING CLICHÉS and grinds down the individuality of actors and writers', and that in 'The Purple Island', 'the dark sinister power which nurtures HELOTS, BOOT-LICKERS AND EULOGISTS . . .'

It was stated that 'if such a dark power exists, THE INDIGNATION AND MALEVOLENT WIT OF THIS DRAMATIST, GLORIFIED BY THE BOURGEOISIE, IS JUSTIFIED'.

One may well ask, where is the truth in this?

What, when all is said and done, is 'The Purple Island' – 'A squalid, talentless play' or a 'witty lampoon'?

The truth is contained in Novitski's review. I will not venture to judge how witty my play is but I acknowledge that in the play an ominous ghost does rise up and that is the ghost of the Glavrepertkom. And that it nurtures helots, eulogists and broken-spirited 'lackeys'. And that it is killing creative thinking. It is killing Soviet drama and will soon kill it off for good.

I have not gone around whispering these ideas in corners. I have included them in a dramatic lampoon and put this lampoon on stage. The Soviet press, lending its support to the Glavrepertkom, has written that 'The Purple Island' is a libel on the Revolution. This is absurd nonsense. There is no libel on the Revolution in the play for several reasons of which, for lack of space, I will mention only one: it is IMPOSSIBLE to write a libel on the Revolution because it is such a huge event. A pamphlet is not a libel and the Repertkom is not the Revolution.

But when the German press writes that 'The Purple Island' is 'the first call for freedom of the press in the Soviet Union' ('Molodaya Gardiya' No 1, 1929) it is writing the truth. I acknowledge the fact. To struggle with censorship as it was, or is, whoever may be in power, is my duty as a writer, as is my call for a free press. I am an ardent admirer of that freedom and take the view that if any writer should consider trying to prove that he has no need of it he is like a fish declaring publicly that it has no need of water.

4.

That is just one of the features of my work and it alone is sufficient for my works not to survive in the Soviet Union. But this first feature is linked to all the others which appear in my satirical works; the dark and mystical colours (I am A MYSTICAL WRITER) in which the countless horrors of our daily life are depicted, the poison that fills my tongue, the profound scepticism with regard to the revolutionary process proceding in this backward country of mine and the Great Evolution which is opposed to and preferable to it, and most important of all, the depiction of the terrible aspects of my country, those aspects which, long before the revolution, were a source of such profound suffering to my teacher M. E. Saltykov-Shchedrin.

Needless to say the Soviet press never seriously considered taking note of all that, busy as it has been with making unconvincing declarations that M. Bulgakov's satire is full of 'SLANDER'.

Only once, when I first became notorious, it was noted with a hint of condescending astonishment:

'M. Bulgakov WANTS to be the satirist of our time' ('Knigohosha' No 6, 1925).

Unfortunately the verb 'wants' is wrongly put in the present tense. It should have been in the pluperfect: M. Bulgakov HAD BECOME A SATIRIST just at the time when any real satire (venturing as it does into forbidden areas) was absolutely unthinkable in the Soviet Union.

The honour of expressing that criminal thought in print did not fall to me.

It was expressed with total clarity in an article by V. Blum (No 6, 'Lit. Gaz.') and the thought behind that article can be encapsulated with shining precision in one sentence: EVERY SATIRIST IN THE SOVIET UNION ATTACKS THE SOVIET SYSTEM.

Am I conceivable in the Soviet Union?

5.

And, finally, the last characteristic responsible for the banning of my plays 'The Days of the Turbins', 'Flight' and my novel 'The White Guard': the portrayal of the Russian intelligentsia as the best stratum of our society. In particular, the portrayal of aristocratic families within the intelligentsia thrust, thanks to an immutable historical destiny in the years of the Civil War, into the camp of the White guard, in the tradition of 'War and Peace'. Such a portrayal is completely natural for a writer born and bred in the intelligentsia. But such a form of portrayal in the Soviet Union results in the author, together with his heroes, despite his great efforts TO BE DISPASSIONATE ABOUT THE REDS AND WHITES, receiving the label of a White- guardist and having once received it, as anyone knows, he is a finished man in the Soviet Union.

6.

My literary portrait is now complete; it is also my political portrait. I cannot say what sort of inveterate criminal it reveals but I ask one thing: don't try to discover anything beyond its limits. It has been done with complete honesty.

7.

I am now destroyed.

This destruction has been greeted by Soviet society with absolute delight and called 'AN ACHIEVEMENT'.

R. Pikel, referring to my destruction ('Izv [estiya]', 15/IX 1929), expressed the liberal notion: 'We do not imply by this that the name of Bulgakov has been struck from the list of Soviet dramatists'.

And he consoled the murdered writer with the words 'we are only talking about his previous dramatic works'.

However, life, in the person of the Glavrepertkom has demonstrated that R. Pikel's liberalism was entirely unfounded.

On March 18 1930 I received a paper from the Glavrepertkom which informed me cryptically that not only my previous works but also my play 'The Cabal of Hypocrites' ('Molière') HAD NOT BEEN PASSED FOR PERFORMANCE.

To put it briefly: beneath a couple of lines on official paper lie buried my work in library archives, my imagination, my play which has received innumerable commendations as a brilliant play from qualified theatre specialists.

R. Pikel is under a delusion. It is not only my past works which have been destroyed but my present works and my future works too. And I personally, with my own hands, consigned a draft novel on the devil to the flames, the draft of a comedy and the start of a second novel 'Theatre'.

There is no hope for anything of mine.

8.

I ask the Soviet Government to bear in mind that I am not a political activist but a man of letters and that my entire output has been devoted to the Soviet theatre.

I would like to draw its attention to the two following comments about me in the Soviet press.

Both come from men who are inexorable enemies of my works and are therefore very valuable.

In 1925 the following was written:

'A writer has appeared, WHO DOES NOT EVEN DISGUISE HIMSELF AS A FELLOW TRAVELLER'. (L. Auerbach, 'Izv [estiya]', 20/IX 1925).

And in 1929:

'His talent is as evident as the socially reactionary nature of his works'. (R. Pikel, 'Izv'., 15/IX 1929).

I ask you to bear in mind that, for me, not to be able to write is like being buried alive.

9.

I ASK THE SOVIET GOVERNMENT TO INSTRUCT ME AS A MATTER OF URGENCY TO QUIT THE BORDERS OF THE USSR ACCOMPANIED BY MY WIFE LIUBOV EVGENEVA BULGAKOVA.

10.

I appeal to the humanitarianism of the Soviet authorities and ask that I, a writer, who can be of no use to himself or to his country, be generously allowed to leave it for freedom.

11.

But what I have written is not convincing and I am condemned to lifelong silence in the Soviet Union, I ask the Soviet Government to give me work within my own specialist field and to place me for work in a theatre as a staff director.

I ask in the most precise, exact and emphatic terms FOR A CATEGORICAL ORDER, A DIRECTIVE as all my efforts to find work in the one field where I could be of use to the Soviet Union, as an exceptionally well-qualified specialist, have proved a fiasco. My name has become so odious that proposals for work coming from me have encountered ALARM, despite the fact that in Moscow a great number of actors and directors and also theatre managements are perfectly aware of my virtuoso knowledge of the stage.

I put myself forward to the Soviet Union in perfect honesty, without a hint of sabotage, as a specialist director and actor, who undertakes to stage and play conscientiously, from Shakespeare down to the most recent plays of our time.

I ask to be appointed as an assistant director at the 1st Art Theatre, the best school, which is headed by the masters K. S. Stanislavski and V. I. Nemirovich-Danchenko.

If I am not appointed as a director I ask to be employed as an extra on a regular basis. If I cannot be an extra then I ask to be employed as a stage-hand.

If even this is impossible I ask the Soviet Government to deal with me as it thinks fit but to do something because, as the author of 5 plays which are well known in the USSR and abroad, I am faced AT THIS VERY MOMENT with poverty, the street and ruin.

M. Bulgakov

The result of this letter was a telephone call from Stalin, reported by Bulgakov's wife, Elena:

' "Yes, this is Stalin, speaking. Hallo, Comrade Bulgakov!" (or Mikhail Afanasievich, I don't remember exactly).

"Hallo Iossif Vissarionovich."

"We received your letter. I and my comrades read it. You'll receive a welcome answer . . . Is it really true that you want permission to go abroad? That we have been such trouble to you?. . ."

"I have given a lot of thought recently to whether a Russian writer can live outside his own country. It seems to me he can't."

"You're right. That's what I think too. Where is it you want to work? At the Art Theatre?"

"Yes, I would. But I mentioned it and they turned me down."

"Put in an application. I think they will agree. We need to meet and talk, you and I."

"Yes, yes! I need to talk to you very badly, Iossif Vissarionovich."

"We need to find time and talk, without fail. And now I wish you all the best." '

Bulgakov followed up Stalin's telephone call by a letter to the Art Theatre requesting employment.

354 Bulgakov to the Art Theatre

May 10 1930
Moscow

To the Management of the Moscow State Art Theatre [sic]
from Mikhail Bulgakov

I request the management of the M.S.A.T to take me onto the staff of the theatre in the post of a director.

As Stalin had indicated, Bulgakov's application was successful. Stanislavski learned of the appointment while still abroad convalescing and immediately sent a warm letter of welcome.

355 Stanislavski to Bulgakov

September 4 1930
Badenweiler

Dear Mikhail Afanasievich,

You cannot imagine how happy I am that you are joining our theatre!

I had the opportunity of working with you during a number of rehearsals for 'The Turbins' and then I sensed the director in you (and perhaps the actor?!).

Molière and many others combined this profession with that of literature!

I welcome you with all my heart and believe in a successful outcome and look forward to working with you as soon as possible. [. . .]

Stanislavski had been deeply shocked in March 1930 when he learned that *Othello*, for which he was still writing the production plan, had been rushed on after only three or four months' rehearsals and that his whole concept, as well as the sets, had been modified by Sudakov. Outraged, he demanded that his name be taken off the posters. He attributed this indecent haste to artistic ineptitude. It was only on his return that he realized the political pressure that was being exerted on the theatre. Mikhail Heitz had been appointed as the 'red' director but instead of being the cultivated, understanding person Stanislavski had wanted, he proved an advocate of the policy: produce more faster.

Prior to Stanislavski's return Nemirovich registered a polite protest. A year later Stanislavski followed this up with a broadside.

356 Nemirovich to M. S. Heitz

July 24 1930
Geneva

[. . .]

You have reached the end of the season . . .

All's well that ends well but there were many bad patches in the season. When I think back over what has happened (I always do that at the end of the season) I feel there are a few matters over which we should pause. Of course, not matters of detail but those which are characteristic of 'the stage'. The direction we should take. The question is not where we are being taken, because people are trying to take us somewhere we should not go, but of the direction the truth of life itself indicates to us, namely the psychology of present-day audiences. Should we not abandon pot-boilers? Is not the first principle of the old Art Theatre – do everything at our absolute best – proved every step of the way? Financial worries are weaknesses and, after a limited period, things of the past. Everything is in its proper place when you do everything at the absolute best. And then what a difference there is between declarations made at the table with a glass of tea when one's vanity is cosily and comfortably gratified by thinking beautiful thoughts and reality when tense nerves summon up all that is petty, bad and bestial from 'the depths of the soul'. And this too: demagogy is such a tedious, annoying thing but it holds no fears when people of great talent dismiss it. And now we need to love and cherish talent in our business! It has first place. [. . .]

357 Nemirovich to Sergei Bertenson

November 10 1930
Moscow

[. . .]
Stanislavski fell ill during the jubilee performance at MXAT. At the end of the performance, a heart attack. That would not have been so bad but another attack occurred a few days later under normal conditions. It was diagnosed as angina pectoris. I don't know exactly but I think it's that and that K.S. will probably be out of action for the whole winter. They'll probably take him to the south of France. But I remember I wrote to you about that. But I didn't tell you that as well as the heart disease there is also catarrhal inflammation of the lung. However his temperature is almost down to normal and K.S. feels well. But the jubilee performance can't be repeated of course. I am now completely taken up with 'Blockade'. Then comes the revival of 'Brothers Karamazov' (although Leonidov is ill too).

358 Stanislavski to the Government

Summer–Autumn 1931

[from various drafts]
If the artistic-political advisory body has as its educational objectives the

furtherance of the artistic enlightenment of those members of the proletariat who are interested in such things, so as to keep them up to date with developments in the world of the arts and to enable theatres to make contact with them, thus improving mutual relations and understanding, then it cannot but be welcomed in its present form, and the theatres themselves, and those serving on the artistic-political advisory boards, should be given new directors, consistent with those aims.

If, however, these advisory boards are to continue issuing orders, even of the most general kind, concerning the artistic life of the theatre which they do not and, indeed, cannot understand without lengthy specialized study, then in logical and practical terms it must be understood that these committees will not only fail to produce results but will cause damage to institutions, impeding the work the theatres are doing and encouraging superficial attitudes among those who know absolutely nothing of what we do. [. . .]

They are trying to make us offer the audience potboilers and imagine that in that way we can educate new audiences. No, that's false. Audiences cannot be educated through potboilers any more than actors can be educated by them and be responsible towards an audience. [. . .]

In America they contrive to perform the same play three times a day. No need to tell you the negative results this churning out of performances leads to. Nonetheless, it must be admitted that such work is possible using the usual, standard clichés, though not without considerable damage to health.

But it is not possible to play not only every day but twice a day three times a week, thus grinding out 750 performances in 260 days, as we did at MXT in the 1930–31 season.

This facile hack-work is beyond the capacity of the art of the MXT, which depends on the artists' nerves being at key-pitch. Their work is not to be compared with performing artists going through the motions or with a navvy's work. And so the excessive demands made on us, the artists of MXT must inevitably lead to *catastrophe* and premature death . . .

I am sounding the alarm because I see terrible dangers. I am an old hand in the theatre and I know where danger lies. I would be happy if the government were to heed the warning I utter and, having taken the rudder from my hands, would allow me, perhaps, on the eve of my death, to steer my vessel into the hope and quiet of the harbour of socialism . . .

At the present time the theatre has ceased to be artistic in the strict sense of the word. More than that, it is manifestly on its way to perdition. It can be saved from catastrophe only by:

1. the establishment of precise governmental and party directives concerning its place in the contemporary situation as a theatre of classical drama and of the best, artistically significant plays in the contemporary repertoire;

2. its exemption from tasks demanding above all hasty work or an inordinate dissipation of energies in guest appearances;

3. the recognition of its right to compete with other theatres not in the quantity of contemporary plays produced but in the qu: lity of its presentations.

In 1931 Gorki recommended Nikolai Erdman's play *The Suicide* to Stanislavski. Meyerhold intended to direct it but Gorki was afraid he would turn it into a farce. Stanislavski said he laughed so much he nearly fell over when he read it. However, the play was banned. Encouraged to a certain extent by Bulgakov's example Stanislavski decided on a direct approach to Stalin.

359 Stanislavski to Stalin

October 29 1931
Moscow

Deeply respected Iossif Vissarionovich,

Knowing your long-standing interest in the Art Theatre, I turn to you with the following question.

You will have learned from Aleksei Maksimovich Gorki that the theatre is profoundly interested in Nikolai Erdman's play 'The Suicide' which the Theatre considers one of the outstanding works of our time. In our view N[ikolai] Erdman has managed to lay bare the various outward signs and the inner core of the petit bourgeoisie who set themselves against the construction of our country. The means the author uses to show real-life petit-bourgeois and their abnormality is totally novel and yet completely in accord with Russian realism and its best representatives like Gogol and Shchedrin and is close to the direction our own theatre takes.

Therefore, after the author had finished the play, it seemed important to the Art Theatre to employ its skill to reveal the social ideas and artistic truth of this comedy. However, at the present time this play is under the censor's ban. I would like to ask your permission to start work on the comedy 'The Suicide' in the hope that you will not forbid us to show it until it has been presented in the interpretation our actors give. The fate of this comedy could be decided after such a showing. Naturally the Art Theatre will not involve you in any expense prior to the showing.

360 Stalin to Stanislavski

November 9 1931

Most respected Konstantin Sergeievich,

I do not have a very high opinion of the play 'The Suicide'. My immediate comrades consider that it is fatuous and possibly harmful. You may learn the opinions (and motives) of the Repertkom from the enclosed documents. It seems to me that the judgement of the Repertkom is not far from the case. Nonetheless I have no objection to the Art Theatre's making an experiment and showing its skill. It may well be that it will achieve its end. The Kultprop of the Central Committee of our party (Com. Stenski) will help you in this matter. Comrades more versed in artistic matters will arbitrate. I am an amateur in such things.

Greetings!
I. Stalin

Stanislavski's letter to the goverment of 1931 produced its effect. Heitz was removed and the Art Theatre was made totally autonomous and, unlike any other theatre, responsible directly to the government. It became the Moscow Art Academic Theatre of the USSR. This was the beginning of the process, of which Stanislavski was not aware, by which the Art Theatre became a national monument, a part of the Stalinist establishment.

This however did not resolve the problem of the underemployment and resultant frustration of much of the company or of the demand to do more productions. The assured status of the company led, on the other hand, to a certain complacency and a disinclination to work and develop.

Three weeks before the opening of Afinogenov's play *Fear* Stanislavski took Olga Knipper out of the cast. Afinogenov was a leading member of the so-called literary 'left' which constantly attacked Stanislavski and the System on the grounds that they were philosophically 'idealist'. Knipper, who felt that she had been offerered very few new roles of significance since the Revolution, was too lightweight in the role of Clara. Stanislavski replaced her with Sokolovskaya but obviously tried to soften the blow as much as possible.

361 Knipper to Sergei Bertenson

January 9 1932
Moscow

[. . .]
'Fear' is on and is having a great success, especially Leonidov, he is
excellent. I am not playing at the moment. K.S. advised me to avoid all the
hullabaloo of the opening as they will forgive Sokolovskaya things they
won't forgive me. She is the ideal type, ready-made, whereas I have to 'do'
the part. It was an unhappy time to go through but it's probably for the best.
The role is of a very specific kind. Pity, though, they didn't let me do just one
dress rehearsal, I always get there at dress rehearsal. Vladimir Ivanovich
kept out of things. I feel like writing to him as I can't pull my thoughts
together. [. . .]

362 Stanislavski to Gorki

January 6 1933
Moscow

[. . .]
I am very sorry that I wasn't able to see you during your last visit to Moscow
but I came back from abroad after your departure. I would have liked to discuss
a whole range of problems with you which have the highest degree of
importance for the theatre. At the present moment they have become so acute
that they demand a clear, unequivocal and categorical decision. At their root
lies a single quintessential problem concerning how we see the role of MXAT in
the present time, the way we see its special specific art, which distinguishes it
from other theatres. Inside the theatre we define it as a question of 'breadth' or
'depth'. That is to say, should we devote all our strength to understanding, to
deepening, to developing our art, without too much concern for the number of
performances, or should we – following the example of other theatres – attempt
to give a swift and therefore transient response to present-day problems
without too much thought for giving our art greater depth? It would be naïve to
think that I would cut myself off from the exigencies of the current situation
when faced with such a question; on the contrary, I believe that MXAT is
obliged to respond to current events in depth and not superficially; to look into
the heart of things and not their outer shell. I want a theatre of *ideas* and not a
theatre of carefully recorded facts. In all justice I must say I do not see another
role for myself in our time – I want to devote the rest of my days to the
education of actors, the enrichment of the actor's craft so that it is capable of
conveying the deepest and strongest feelings and thoughts of the men of our
time.

I had the impression that your position with regard to MXAT coincided with my views. You were not mistaken when you defined the position of MXAT as a theatre academy.

There are, however, many obstacles to this growth in 'depth'. In the last few years the theatre has greatly increased in 'breadth' – it has a corpus of more than 120 actors of whom many claim work which we are not in a position to give and which MXAT is not able to bear; there have been productions in which the art of MXAT has not been maintained at the required standard; dissatisfaction and depression have arisen. The result has been the creation of a group which opposes a striving for 'breadth' to the 'depth' solution – the swift output of the largest number of plays and a new conception of the actor. I see no alternative to the division of the theatre, so that the basic MXAT can pursue its chosen line in a consistent manner. I consider it essential to concentrate all our forces in a *single* theatre without any kind of branch theatre and I hope to achieve the required results with this single company which shares a common view of art. It seems to me that the seriousness, the acuteness of the situation, which threatens MXAT with disaster, will not be properly appreciated outside the theatre if the measures I have suggested are not adopted quickly. I have sent two papers to [the government]. (I will send you copies) with a request for a decision. I hope you will help us in this critical moment in the theatre's life. [. . .]

363 Nemirovich to Sergei Bertenson

February 22 1934

[. . .]

I'm single-handed here at the Art Th. Konstantin Sergeievich still isn't back from abroad. By tradition he should do the same as I, i.e., not exceed two years. As you know, my heart is really with the Musical [Theatre]. But things have got so low at the Art [Theatre], i.e., just on the artistic side, that it was essential to pull everything together and gather strength. That was why the showing of [Gorki's] 'Yegor Bulichov',[1] which you didn't care for, was such an important event. It's a very good play. I was carried away by it when I read it abroad. I have concentrated all my efforts on the actors' technique which has attained considerable heights. Nothing like it for a long time. On the whole the production has been very well received.

Afinogenov's play 'The Lie' which I had also been working on with great interest was taken out of the repertoire halfway through rehearsals. At the moment we are simultaneously rehearsing 'The Storm'. . . Gorki's 'Enemies', Bulgakov's 'Molière' and Kirshon's play 'The Pickwick Club'. Five productions! Any day now I'll be starting on 'Woe from Wit.' [. . .]

---

1. Opened February 10 1934.

364 Bokshanskaya to Sergei Bertenson

April 4 1934
Moscow

[. . .]

'Molière' is a wonderful play, I am inordinately fond of it and the fact that
we haven't yet put it on can be entirely explained by the fact that Gorchakov
has been put in charge of the production and he is just not interested in doing
the job or is too busy combining jobs in other theatres when he is up to his
ears in work at MXAT and doesn't react at all as a director when actors are
taken away from him, no matter what the play. Another complication is the
fact that Moskvin has long been 'humming and hahing' about the title role:
he wants to play it but it worries him. At the moment the role is officially
considered to be his but it is being rehearsed by Stanitsin and, by all
accounts, very well. According to the schedule it should be done in the first
half of next season and go on to the end, probably. They showed the first two
acts to Vladimir Ivanovich in the foyer. It's being done out of order first,
probably, because of Gorchakov and his total indifference (although he goes
around looking aggrieved because nothing's being done to get the play on
but we know what value to put on statements like that), secondly because
when Sudakov directs a play nothing else matters and his energy is simply
astounding. That's what's happening with 'The Storm', and third because it
was suggested that we should stage Gorki's 'Enemies' which is being done in
two other Moscow theatres, the Maly and MOSPS and we have to get it on as
soon as possible . . . And 'Molière', which has no political role to play in
terms of repertoire has naturally been put back and finally carried over to
next season. The fact that the play is considered to be one Konstantin
Sergeievich should do has also played a part in all this. He isn't back yet but
will return, probably, in the summer and start work in the autumn. [. . .]

Nemirovich profited from the occasion of the theatre's 35th anniversary
celebrations that same year to try and call the company to order. In an
address he reminded them of the unique status the theatre enjoyed not only
in the Soviet Union but in the world: unlimited subsidy, time to rehearse,
freedom owing to MXAT's special status from the pressure to throw on
shows, provided that what they finally produced was of some benefit to an
audience. The total staff of the theatre was now 975. At the time of *Julius
Caesar* in 1903 it had been 250. Yet where now was the drive and
enthusiasm? Energy was simply being wasted.

The Days of the Turbins, which reentered the repertoire in 1932 at the
government's request, continued to be one of the Art Theatre's most

popular productions. The theatre was now engaged in preparing *Molière*. This had originally been accepted for production in October 1931. It was to be directed by Gorchakov, although supervised by Stanislavski. Stanislavski's illness between 1932 and 1934 brought rehearsals to a halt and work did not resume until the autumn of 1934.

Serious disagreements soon emerged between Stanislavski and Bulgakov over the nature of the play. Stanislavski wanted a play about a Great Man. Bulgakov resisted. Stanislavski asked for many rewrites but when Bulgakov learned that he was making changes and moving dialogue around he issued an ultimatum similar to the one he had issued over *The Days of the Turbins*.

365 Sakhnovski to Bulgakov

June 20 1934
Moscow

Dear Mikhaïl Afanasievich,

Today is the FIVE HUNDREDTH performance of your play. You know how the theatre and all our audiences in Moscow and Leningrad love 'The Days of the Turbins'. 'The Turbins' was another 'Seagull' for the new generation of the Art Theatre. You yourself not long ago in Leningrad were a witness to the way the audience received your play and the theatre and especially the young generation, perhaps, defends no play as much as 'The Turbins'.

You have long been made aware by Konstantin Sergeievich and Vladimir Ivanovich that they consider you 'one of them' in the Art Theatre, 'one of them' because you are creatively close and for that reason, on the day of the FIVE HUNDREDTH performance, allow me in the name of the theatre to congratulate you as 'one of us' and not just as a dramatist. And from me without quote marks to embrace you warmly, remembering the friendly work we have done over three years on another of your plays.

For the Management of the MXAT of the USSR in the name of Gorki,

honoured Artist of the Republic,
V. G. Sakhnovski.

Bokshanskaya's letter of October 28 1934 graphically describes the complexity of the internal politics of the Art Theatre: the unresolved conflict between Stanislavski and Nemirovich and the jockeying for position among the younger members of the company. She repeats the allegation against Stanislavski, previously voiced by both Meyerhold and Nemirovich, that Stanislavski was rather too ready to accept second-hand opinions and act on them.

366 Bokshanskaya to Bertenson

October 28 1934
Moscow

Dear Sergei Lvovich,

If you only knew the number of quarrels of every kind we have had at the beginning of the season. I'll try and summarize the whole thing for you. There have been substantial changes in the management of the theatre about which I learned on my return. So I found myself in a criss-cross of complex relationships. Already last year, when Konst. Serg. was away and Vlad. Iv. was in sole charge, strong differences were beginning to emerge between two of the management, Sakhnovski and Yegorov. The main thing was the prickly relationship that developed between Yegorov and the assistant manager he had invited in to help in on the business and financial side, Leont'ev . . . The result was an almost automatic division into two camps, two 'cabinets', the upper (Sakhnovski, Leontev, Markov) and the lower (Yegorov). Poor Vlad. Iv. often had to listen to long discussions, stories and complaints. But despite the fact that he often found the lower cabinet to be in the wrong he didn't demonstrate any opposition to it as he didn't want to fall out with Konst. Serg. who had placed Yegorov in an exceptionally privileged position but tried to smooth out all differences. We all thought that when Konst. Serg. returned, well briefed by our letters, the storm would break. However, at first Konst. Serg. was quite affable towards Sakhnovski and Leontev. Then, suddenly, in the last few days of August, Leontev received notification from Konst. Serg. that the management thanked him for his hard work but in future would dispense with his services. Then events moved very fast. It emerged that a new management structure had been worked out in the lower cabinet. Sakhnovski was removed from his post as acting senior manager. Under the new structure there was to be one deputy manager for the administrative, financial and business departments – Yegorov. There was to be no deputy for artistic matters as it was considered this would be Konst. Serg.'s responsibility. He would have three heads of department under him: Sudakov in charge of production management, Kedrov in charge of the creative side and Podgorny in charge of the company. As there could be no question of making any criticism of Zheni (Kaluzhski) as far as his work was concerned, Konst. Serg. told him privately that he had to appoint Nik. Afanasievich (Podgorny) to this post because times were such in the theatre that they needed a cold fish, a careerist with a desire for power, to be in charge of the company. Why Konst. Serg. had to insult Nik. Afanasievich in this way I just don't understand. I think it's in his nature suddenly to come out with something bad even about someone who is close to him. All this was decided while Vlad. Iv. was away in Yalta. I kept Vlad. Iv. *au fait* with the whole thing. He was in absolute disagreement with the new arrangements Konst. Serg. had informed him about in a wire and wrote a long and eminently sensible letter. But even in a telegram he stated that there were aspects of the matter that could be harmful to the working atmosphere of the theatre. He handed over sole responsibility for the introduction of these reforms to Konst. Serg. and took a firm decision to stand aside from all artistic, administrative matters as he considered his position at MXAT to be that of principal director, responsible for staging his own shows, reserving managerial rights (at least as far as his own productions were concerned). And indeed in the two weeks he has been back he has stuck rigidly to his decision. He has expressed his opinion of the changes, and his attitude to them, both to Konst. Serg. and separately to the Government Commission which is responsible for us. It seems to me that the machinery Konst. Serg. had set up is very unwieldy, awkward and too diffuse for the theatre . . . And to imagine that Konst. Serg. can take charge of the artistic side and run it from home is idealism of the first water. Of course he can run it but he will see it through other people's eyes, because to administer a complex mechanism like our theatre you have to be there all day . . . poke in every nook and corner, every aspect of the theatre's life. People go to his home and report back, mostly those who are close to him, and he manages the theatre on that basis and that's absolutely impossible. If there is any vestige of morale left in the theatre it is because the dress rehearsals for two plays are coming up, 'The Storm' on the new stage and 'Pickwick Papers' at the annexe.

I think Vlad. Iv. has made a wonderful evening out of 'The Storm'.[1]

367 Bulgakov to Stanislavski

April 22 1935
Moscow

Much respected Konstantin Sergeievich,

Today I received an extract from the stenographic record of the 'Molière' rehearsals of the 17.IV. 35 which the theatre sent me.

Having familiarized myself with it I am obliged categorically to reject the changes made to my play 'Molière' as they are indicated in the record relating to the scene of the Cabal and also to the textual changes indicated earlier in other scenes because ultimately I am satisfied that they violate my artistic intentions and tend towards the composition of a play I am not able to write, since I do not agree with its essentials. If 'Molière' does not suit the Art Theatre as it stands, although the Theatre accepted it and has

---

1. The production in fact enjoyed only very moderate success.

been rehearsing it for some years in that form, I ask you to withdraw
'Molière' and return it to me.

Respectfully yours,
M. Bulgakov

Following this letter Stanislavski informed the company that the play must
be done as Bulgakov had written it. He later withdrew from the production
leaving Gorchakov to complete it. The production was bitterly attacked and
taken off after seven performances.

The internal difficulties of the Art Theatre, which Stanislavski and
Nemirovich had recognized in 1933, had still not been resolved. Relations
between the two men were so bad that they would not even contact each
other direct but used Bokshanskaya as a go-between. This negotiation at
one remove proved futile and Stanislavski decided, probably with
Nemirovich's agreement, to make a direct appeal to Stalin to save the
theatre. Part of the solution – despite the unhappy experience with Heitz –
was the introduction of a suitable official to mediate between himself and
Nemirovich.

368 Stanislavski to Stalin

Autumn 1935

[. . .]

Our theatre can and must be the most advanced theatre in the country in
its representation of the fullness of the inner spiritual life of working people
who have been made masters of the soil. The theatre is in a state of
stagnation throughout the world. The traditions of centuries are being lost.

But, happily, the USSR at the present time is proving to be the successor
to the best traditions both of Europe and of all that was good in the old
traditions of Russian theatre. We must succeed in passing on what is most
valuable to the rising generation and, together with them, not merely hold
on to those traditions but also consolidate and develop them further. One
major concern of us, the leaders of contemporary theatre, must above all be
the preservation of the seeds of age-old theatrical achievements and their
development into new forms of artistic beauty. They can only be preserved
by a theatre of the highest culture and the highest technical mastery. Such a
theatre must represent the heights to which other theatres must raise
themselves. In other times the Maly was such a theatre, and after that the
Art Theatre. Now there are no such heights. The Art Theatre is slipping and

is becoming at the very best a decent theatre turning out plays, but the spiritual needs of the people are growing and may outstrip it.

I want to devote all my experience, all my knowledge, all my time and health, my final years, to the creation of a genuinely creative theatre. In my search for ways of creating such a theatre I have turned to the young and a few months ago founded an Opera-Dramatic Studio to this end and am working on my second book in which I want to pass on all my experience and all my knowledge. However, one of the most important ways forward is the preservation and development of the creative riches accumulated by the Art Theatre. A certain section of the company treats these riches in an offhand manner; for them greater creativity, which places greater demands on them as people and artists, is an unnecessary nuisance. This entire struggle between high aspirations and trivial, transient concerns is in progress at the present time inside the Moscow Art Theatre and is dividing it in two. Creative experience and the aspiration towards the great in art is to be found on the side of the surviving 'veterans' and some of those who are up and coming. On the other side considerable energy is being applied to trivial, facile tasks.

The struggle is hard and help is needed in good time if the two chiefs, despite our declining age, the differences in our creative principles and the tangled state of our 40-year-old relationship, are to lead the theatre out of its present position . . .

We need an experienced, cultivated communist director, who would assist V. I. Nemirovich-Danchenko and myself to repair our relationship for the sake of the creative management of the theatre . . .

In addition, we need to strengthen the party organization of the theatre with a cultivated and qualified manager . . .

A thoroughgoing, rigorous review and reappraisal of the theatre's whole creative collective is essential so as to appoint people who are suited to important, creative, experimental work, able to produce genuine theatre. We must oblige those working in the theatre quickly to raise their qualifications to the level of real mastery of their art, having established to that end bonus payments.

The theatre must throw out the slogan 'speed in increase of the actor's skill' since the speed of theatrical production is something which increases of its own accord.

Those people who are unable to enter the collective of qualified actors should continue to work under touring conditions in the branch theatre run by MXAT, and will join the ranks of new actors who are creating a production theatre.

MXAT must be transformed into a beacon of theatre art.

Knowing your affection for the theatre I hope you will help.

Stanislavski's letter provoked an official response and also a more personal one from Nemirovich. In the past Nemirovich had been too inclined perhaps to blame outsiders for the rift between himself and Stanislavski but on this occasion he was not mistaken. For the last few years of his life Stanislavski was virtually house-bound, surrounded by what was called his 'inner cabinet', who fed him whatever information they thought fit. He had no other source of information except what was filtered through to him by people who were far from disinterested.

369 Nemirovich to Stanislavski

January 24 1936

You must be aware, as I am, that the principal directive of the Committee for Arts runs: these two men must be reconciled. It is disgraceful that two such men, with the eyes of the whole world upon them, (that's what was said to me at least) cannot come to an agreement in their own theatre.

You used almost exactly the same words to me two months ago. And I have expressed the same idea to you in these words many times over the years.

The fact is that there is more than enough good will for there to be no misunderstandings between you and me. Although you yourself have often expressed the view that there is such a web of all possible circumstances dividing us that no one would have the strength to unravel it.

It seems to me we are both concerned with trifles and minor arguments with far, far less passion than we once were. We have both achieved such maturity in important questions of art that we can now easily identify what it is that prevents us from complete unanimity.

For me, for example, it is absolutely clear, as I have already told you, that it is odious for you to place Yegorov between me and you. And when you express sorrow to somebody that I have distanced myself from the theatre and do so even more, then I answer quite firmly and emphasize it, that the reason for my coolness is explained by the fact that you have placed Yegorov between you and me.

You deny that because, obviously, you don't know the tenth part of the way Yegorov behaves at the theatre. You don't know first because you are not told, second because for years I have avoided embroiling you in all this sordid business, to spare your peace and quiet.

All the differences between us take two forms: artistic and administrative. You yourself recognize that differences with me on the artistic side cannot be detrimental to the theatre. You have often said that if there are two such important methods of work, like yours and mine, then the theatre can only be the richer for it. [. . .]

But if we cannot agree on anything that doesn't prevent us from working in the same theatre with the same actors. [. . .]

It is easier to divide us in our administrative relationship. That's how it always was when I was up against Stakhovich, Vishnievski and the like. But it has become easier now that you and I don't meet and now that you no longer come to the theatre and can't even leave your apartment because of your illness . . .

I am beginning to lose my energy too. I think it is more needed for work with actors than anything else. And indeed I have less and less energy.

But I venture to remind you that at all decisive, important, disastrous moments in the life of the theatre you and our colleagues always invested me with dictatorial powers. Of course, I won't dwell on that now.

I also venture to remind you that you and those colleagues who founded the theatre with us always acknowledged a preference for my administrative abilities over yours. I don't consider that any special kind of merit on my part but consider it simply as a consequence of elements in your character. You are more emotional than I and your emotional nature is the opposite of my own. You always gave yourself heart and soul to every new enthusiasm your imagination produced. That made you prejudiced towards people, and more merciless towards things your new ideas were blasted off against.

I remind you of that only so [that] you perhaps 'a priori' might trust me a little more and, to be exact, on the administrative matter over which we differ, i.e., the odious role played by Yegorov.

I wrote above and repeat: I am convinced you don't know a tenth of all the harm he has done by being so widely seen as your representative. I made something of a joke by saying he was not 'the director's deputy' but 'Stanislavski's deputy'. And in your absence he has stated openly, quite unabashed, 'I am a director on the same footing as Vladimir Ivanovich'.

I want to say that over the past three years I have done the maximum that can be done to preserve our relationship.

I took over responsibility for the organization when there were two deputy managers, Sakhovski on the artistic side and Yegorov on the administrative side. I headed the organization in your absence. It was not at all easy for me to limit Sakhovski's powers, it was not easy to combat Sudakov's intrigues. And I often found it absolutely insufferable when I had to counter Yegorov's disgraceful behaviour.

If I were the man I was fifteen years ago I would probably have taken decisive measures to reorganize the structure of the theatre's management. But only to preserve our relationship and keep everything safe until your return.

You came back, accepted everything that Yegorov told you, credited the slander he heaped on people who prevented him from playing the lead role and created a new structure in my absence . . .

All my objections aroused the fury of the members of the theatre and encountered one single response: 'None of this must get back to Konstantin Sergeievich or it might affect his health.'

What was there left for me except to busy myself with another theatre [Musical Theatre]? [. . .]

On January 8 1938 Meyerhold's theatre was closed down, as the Second Art Theatre had been a year previously. Both were tainted with Formalism, the ultimate term of ideological abuse under the doctrine of Socialist Realism. Meyerhold did not attempt to contact Stanislavski for fear of compromising him. It was a chance meeting with Stanislavski's granddaughter, Cyrilla, that put him in touch with his old master once again. Despite their disagreements Stanislavski saw Meyerhold as his artistic successor. Although he could not introduce him into the Art Theatre he could work with him in his own Opera-Dramatic Studio which he ran at his own flat at 6, Leontievski Lane. It was Meyerhold who completed Stanislavski's long projected production of *Rigoletto*.

370 Meyerhold to Stanislavski

January 18 1938
Moscow

Dear Konstantin Sergeievich,

When describing one of the incidents in one of his short stories, and experiencing difficulty in expressing on paper what had just occurred in his story, N. V. Gogol suddenly stopped and explained, 'No!. . . I can't! Give me another pen! My pen is sluggish, dead, it has too narrow a slit for this scene!'

Starting this letter to you on your birthday, I am in the same situation as Nikolai Vasilievich.

My feelings towards you, my dear teacher, are such that any pen would appear sluggish and dead when it comes to expressing them on paper.

How can I tell you how much I love you?!

How can I tell you of my enormous gratitude for what you taught me about that most difficult of things, the art of being a director?!

If I can manage to surmount the obstacles that have been put in my way by the events of the past few months, I will come and see you and you will read in my eyes my joy to see that you have recovered from your illness, that you are once more healthy and happy, that you have started work again for the good of the country.

I warmly clasp your hand. I embrace you.

Greetings to all in your home. Special greetings to Marya Petrovna. Affectionate greetings to your granddaughter[1], who touched me with her tears of sympathy towards me when I enquired after you.

> Affectionately yours,
> Vl. Meyerhold

The death of Nemirovich's wife prompted a final exchange of letters.

371 Stanislavski to Nemirovich

> February 27 1938
> Moscow

My dear Vladimir Ivanovich,

There have been many misunderstandings between us in recent years.

The great grief you have suffered has aroused in me thoughts of the past which is so closely linked with the dear departed. I think of her and I think of our earlier, good relationship. These memories have prompted me to write to you. About what?. . .

I cannot pretend to be able to comfort you where there is no comfort for your sorrow; there is nothing special I want to write about . . .

At this tragic moment I want to, I must write a few sincere and simple words, as I used in former times. I think Ekaterina Nikolaievna would have liked that.

I want, as a friend, to say that I feel for you sincerely and profoundly and am looking for ways to help you.

It may be that this friendly, heartfelt impulse of mine will give you the strength, be it ever so little, to come through this heavy trial.

> Sincerely and affectionately
> yours,
> K. Stanislavski

372 Nemirovich to Stanislavski

> March 11 1938
> 'Barvikha' Sanatorium

Dear Konstantin Sergeievich,

I was not able to reply to your affectionate letter straight away, I had not

1. Cyrilla Falk, whom Meyerhold met in a flower shop.

the strength to write. You must understand that even now it is not easy for me to put my thoughts in order . . .

Of course, above all, *people* complicated our good relationship. Some because it was of advantage to them, others out of envy. But we created fruitful soil in which they could sow enmity. To begin with the difference in our artistic method and then, obviously, certain character traits in us which we were not able to overcome and which placed us in a guilt-ridden relationship to each other. And we didn't want to rectify these faults. And these differences and faults assumed such mountainous proportions that it needed a catastrophe such as the death of my dear Ekaterina Nikolaievna for us to be able to see beyond them.

Our relationship has lasted 41 years. A historian, some theatrical Nestor, not without humour, will say: 'Can you imagine! These people, they themselves and the people round them, destroyed this relationship, fought over it and history will find all this a complete mystery.'

I thank you so very much for your sudden impulse and please convey my heartfelt greetings to Marya Petrovna.

I wish you health and strength with all my heart.

Vl. Nemirovich-Danchenko

Stanislavski died in August 1938 at the age of 75. Meyerhold was arrested in June 1939 and executed in February 1940 at the age of 66. Nemirovich died in 1943 at the age of 84.

BIOGRAPHICAL INDEX

The following is an alphabetical list mainly of Russian names which appear most frequently in the text, accompanied by brief biographical details. Where the name is a stage name, a surname is given in square brackets. See Index for text references.

ADASHEV, Aleksandr Ivanovich (1871–1934), actor, teacher, member of the Art Theatre company 1898–1913, created private theatre school 1906.

ALEKSEIEV, Konstantin Sergeievich. See STANISLAVSKI.

ALEKSEIEV, Vladimir Sergeievich (Volodya) (1861–1939), Stanislavski's brother, director and teacher. Musical director of the Opera Studio and Stanislavski Opera Theatre 1918–1939.

ALEKSEIEVA, Anna Sergeievna (1866–1936), married name Shteker, member of the Art Theatre company 1899–1903.

ANDREIEV, Leonid Nikolaievich (1871–1919), writer and dramatist. His plays *Anathema*, *The Life of Man*, produced at the Art Theatre.

ANDREIEVA, Marya Fedorovna [Zhelyabuzhskaya] (1868–1953), member of the Art Theatre 1898–1904, 1905–1906, Maksim Gorki's second wife.

ARKHIPOV, Nikolai Nikolaievich [Arbatov] (1869–1926), member of Stanislavski's Society of Art and Literature. First rehearsals for the Art Theatre took place on his estate at Puskino near Moscow.

ARTIOM, Aleksandr Rodionovich (1842–1914), drawing master and engraver, founder member of the Art Theatre.

BALMONT, Konstantin Dmitrievich (1867–1942), author and translator. Translated three one act plays by Maeterlinck, *Les Aveugles*, *L'Intruse*, *Interieurs*, for the Art Theatre.

BARANOV, Nikolai Aleksandrovich (no dates), student and member of the Art Theatre company 1899–1903.

BENOIS, Aleksandr Nikolaievich (1870–1960), designer, critic and art historian. Member of the World of Art group. Designer and director at the Art Theatre 1913–1915.

BERTENSON, Sergei Lvovich (1885–1962), administrator at the Art Theatre 1918–1928. Emigrated. Died in Hollywood.

BJÖRNSON, Björnstjerne (1832–1910), Norwegian poet and politician.

BLUM, Vladimir Ivanovich (1877–1941), theatre critic, writing under the name 'Sadko'. In 1921 appointed head of the musical-theatrical section of the Principal Repertory Committee (GLAVREPERTKOM).

BOKSHANSKAYA, Olga (no dates), secretary to Nemirovich and Stanislavski, took down the text of *My Life in Art* at Stanislavski's dictation.

BOLESLAVSKI, Richard Valentinovich (1887–1937), actor, director, 1908–1920 at the Art Theatre and its studios. Emigrated to USA.

BRIUSOV, Valeri Jakovlievich (1883–1940), poet, translator, theorist.

BULGAKOV, Mikhail Afanasievich (1891–1940), dramatist, novelist, assistant director at the Art Theatre 1930–1936. *The Days of the Turbins, Flight, Molière* presented at the Art Theatre.

BURDZHALOV, Georgi Sergeievich (1869–1924), actor and director at the Art Theatre.

CHEKHOV, Anton Pavlovich (1860–1904), author, dramatist.

CHEKHOV, Michael [Mikhail Aleksandrovich] (1891–1955), nephew of Anton, actor, director, teacher, member of the Art Theatre company and the studios 1913–1919. Emigrated 1928.

CHEKHOVA, Marya Pavlovna (1863–1957), sister of Anton.

CRAIG, Edward Gordon (1872–1966), British actor, director, designer, theorist.

DARSKI, Mikhail Egorovich [Psarov] (1865–1930), well-known provincial actor, member of the Art Theatre company for the first season.

DIAGHILEV, Sergei Pavlovich (1872–1929), impresario, founded the World of Art (Mir Iskusstva) group with Aleksandr Benois in 1898. Creator of the Ballets Russes.

DUNCAN, Isadora (1878–1927), British creator of 'free dance'. Visited Russia 1908, resident 1921–1924.

DUSE, Eleonora (1859–1924), Italian actress. On tour in Russia 1908.

EFROS, Nikolai Efimovich (1867–1923), critic, author of a number of monographs on Art Theatre productions, the first monograph on Stanislavski (1918) and a history of the Art Theatre 1923.

ERDMAN, Nikolai Robertovich (1902–1970), dramatist, author of *The Mandate, The Suicide*.

ERMOLOVA, Marya Nikolaievna (1853–1928), leading actress at the Maly Theatre 1871–1921.

FEDOTOVA, Glikeria Nikolaievna (1846–1925), actress, teacher. 1862–1905 leading actress at the Maly Theatre. Taught Stanislavski.

GERMANOVA, Marya Nikolaievna (1884–1940), member of the Art Theatre company 1902–1919.

GEST, Morris (1881–1942), American impresario, organiser of the Art Theatre tours to the US 1923, 1924.

GORKI, Maksim [Aleksei Maksimovich Pechkov] (1868–1936), author and dramatist.

GRIBUNIN, Vladimir Fiodorovich (1873–1933), actor, founder member of the Art Theatre.

GRIGORIEVA, Marya Petrovna [Nikolaieva] (1869–1941), member of the Art Theatre company 1898–1925, head of the costume department.

GROMOV, M. A. (d. 1918), actor.

GUREVICH, Liubov Yakovlievna (1866–1940), writer, critic and historian, Stanislavski's close friend and literary adviser.

GZOVSKAYA, Olga Vladimirovich (1889–1962), actress at the Art Theatre 1910–1914 and 1915–1917, member of the Maly Theatre company 1906–1910, 1917–1919.

HAMSUN, Knut (1859–1952), Norwegian writer and dramatist.

HAUPTMANN, Gerhart (1862–1946), German dramatist.

HEITZ, Mikhail Sergeievich (no dates), a political appointment to the board of the Art Theatre in 1929. Dismissed 1931.

IVANOV, Vsevolod Viacheslavovich (1895–1963), writer, dramatist. His short story *The Armoured Train 18–69* was adapted for the Art Theatre in 1927.

KACHALOV, Vasili Ivanovich [Shverubov] (1875–1948), joined the Art Theatre 1900. Its leading actor after Stanislavski.

KEDROV, Mikhail Nikolaievich (1893–1972), director, actor, joined the Second Studio 1922 and the main Art Theatre company 1924, artistic director 1946–1955.

KERR, Alfred (1867–1948), eminent German critic.

KNIPPER-CHEKHOVA, Olga Leonardovna (1868–1959), pupil of Nemirovich-Danchenko at the Philharmonic School in Moscow, founder member of the Art Theatre. Married Anton Chekhov 1900.

KOMISSARZHEVSKAYA, Vera Fiodorovona (1864–1910), actress. 1896–1904 member of the company at the Aleksandrinski Theatre in Petersburg. Founded own company in 1904. Was associated for a short period with Meyerhold.

KORSH, Fiodor Adamovich (1852–1923), dramatist, critic, impresario, created the Korsh Theatre in 1882.

KOTLYAREVSKAYA, Vera Vasilievna [Pushkariova] (d. 1942), actress at the Aleksandrinski Theatre, Petersburg 1898–1918. Wife of Kotlyarevski.

LEONIDOV, Leonid Mironovich (1873–1941), actor, director, joined the Art Theatre 1903.

LILINA, Marya Petrovna [Alekseieva] (1866–1943), Stanislavski's wife.

LITOVTSIEVA, Nina Nikolaievna [Lewenstamm] (1878–1956), joined the Art Theatre in 1901, later worked in the Second Studio. Married to Kachalov.

LUNACHARSKI, Anatoli Vasilievich (1875–1933), politician, journalist, critic, literary historian, dramatist, People's Commissar for Education 1917–1929.

LUZHSKI, Vasili Vasilievich [Kaluzhski] (1869–1931), actor, founder member of the Art Theatre.

MAMONTOV, Savva Ivanovich (1841–1918), Stanislavski's cousin by marriage. Industrialist, banker and patron of the arts. Founded the Moscow Russian Private Opera 1885. Encouraged young painters and designers. Advanced the career of Chaliapin.

MANASIEVICH, Aleksandr Fiodorovich (no dates), administrator at the Art Theatre 1898.

MARDZHANOV, Konstantin Aleksandrovich [Mardshanishvili] (1872–1933), director at the Art Theatre 1910–1913.

MARKOV, Pavel Aleksandrovich (b. 1897), critic, director, theatre historian. Chief dramaturg at the Art Theatre 1925–1949, director 1955–1962.

MEYERHOLD, Vsevolod Emilievich (1874–1940), pupil of Nemirovich-Danchenko at the Philharmonic School, Moscow, director, actor, member of the Art Theatre company 1898–1902, returned 1904–5.

MOROZOV, Savva Timofeievich (1862–1905), industrialist, co-director of the Art Theatre with Stanislavski and Nemirovich-Danchenko from 1900. Subsidized the Art Theatre and financed the construction of the new building. Committed suicide in 1905.

MOSKVIN, Ivan Mikhailovich (1874–1946), pupil of Nemirovich-Danchenko at the Philharmonic School, Moscow, founder member of the Art Theatre.

MUNT, Ekaterina Mikhailovna (1975–1954), pupil of Nemirovich-Danchenko at the Philharmonic School Moscow, member of the Art Theatre company 1898–1902. Meyerhold's sister-in-law.

MURATOVA, Elena Pavlovna (1974–1921), actress, member of the Art Theatre company 1901–1921.

NELIDOV, Vladimir Aleksandrovich (1892–1911), administrator of the Moscow Imperial Theatre, the Maly.

NEMIROVICH-DANCHENKO, Vladimir Ivanovich (1858–1943), writer, dramatist, director, co-founder with Stanislavski of the Moscow Art Theatre.

PODGORNY, Nikolai Afanasievich (1879–1947), actor, teacher, joined the Art Theatre 1903, became member of the management team 1919.

ROKSANOVA, Marya Liudomirova [Petrovskaya] (1874–1958), actress, member of the Art Theatre company 1898–1902.

RUMYANTSEV, N. A. (1874–1948), actor, head of the finance department of the Art Theatre 1902–1925.

SALTYKOV-SHCHEDRIN, Mikhail Evgrafovich (1826–1889), writer.

SAMAROVA, Marya Aleksandrovna (1852–1919), actress, member of Art Theatre company 1898.

SANIN, Aleksandr Akimovich [Schoenberg] (1869–1956), actor and director at the Art Theatre 1898–1902.

SCHOENBERG. See SANIN.

SIMOV, Viktor Andreievich (1858–1935), designer, worked at the Art Theatre 1898–1912, 1925–35.

STAKHOVICH, Aleksei Aleksandrovich (1856–1919), shareholder of the Art Theatre 1902–1919, member of the board and actor 1907–1919.

STANISLAVSKI, Konstantin Sergeievich [Alekseiev] (1863–1938), actor, director, teacher, co-founder with Nemirovich-Danchenko of the Moscow Art Theatre, creator of the 'System'.

SUDAKOV, Ilya Yakovlievich (1890–1969), actor, director, joined the Second Studio 1916, joined the Art Theatre company 1924.

SUDBININ, Serafim Nikolaievich (1867–1944), sculptor and actor, member of the Art Theatre company 1889–1904.

SULERZHITSKI, Leopold Antonovich (1872–1916), known to his intimates as Suler, writer, painter, director, disciple of Tolstoi, friend to Chekhov, joined the Art Theatre as Stanislavski's unofficial assistant 1905.

SUMBATOV. See YUZHIN.

SUVORIN, Aleksei Sergeievich (1834–1912), journalist, theatre critic, dramatist in Petersburg.

TAÏROV, Aleksandr Yakovlievich (1885–1950), director, founder of the Free Theatre and the Kamerny Theatre.

TELYAKOVSKI, Vladimir Arkadievich (1861–1924), in charge of the Moscow office of the Imperial Theatres 1889–1901, head of the Imperial Theatres 1901–1917.

TIKHOMIROV, Iossafat Aleksandrovich (1872–1908), pupil of Nemirovich-Danchenko at the Philharmonic School Moscow, actor and director at the Art Theatre 1898–1904.

TOLSTOI, Aleksei Konstantinovich (1817–1875), poet and dramatist.

TOLSTOI, Lev Nikolaievich (1828–1910), author, dramatist.

VAKHTANGOV, Evgeni Bagrationovich (1883–1922), actor, director, joined the Art Theatre 1911, entered First Studio 1912, created the Vakhtangov Studio 1913.

VASILIEV, Leonid Sergeievich (no dates), chorus master engaged for the production of *The Snow Maiden*.

VISHNIEVSKI, Aleksandr Leonidovich (1861–1943), actor, founder member of the Art Theatre.

VYRUBOV, A. A. (no dates), actor.

YEGOROV, Nikolai Vasilievich (1873–1955), Deputy Director of the Art Theatre 1926–1929, 1931–1950.

YUZHIN, Aleksandr Ivanovich [Sumbatov] (1857–1927), actor, dramatist, at Maly Theatre 1882–1927.

ZABEL, Eugen (1851–1924), German writer and theatre critic.

ZHELYABUZHSKAYA. See ANDREIEVA.

INDEX

(See also Biographical Index)

Abessalomov, Aleksandr Vasilievich, 123

Above Our Strength (Björnson), 205, 207

Academic theatres, Soviet, 323

Acosta (Gutskov), 23, 24

Adashev's theatre school, 248 &n, 249, 250

Adurskaya, Antonina Fedorovna, 114, 115

Afinogenov, Aleksandr, 346–7, 348; *see also Fear; The Lie*

Aglavaine et Célisette, (Maeterlinck) 215, 216, 217

Aleksandrinski Theatre, Petersburg, 13–14, 34n

Aleksandrov, N.G., 40, 122, 154, 173, 175–6, 249, 250

Alekseiev, Georgi, 14

Alekseiev, Konstantin S. *see* Stanislavski

Alekseiev, Vladimir Sergeievich, 238

Alekseieva, Anna Sergeievna (Shteker), 47, 51 &n, 63, 98

Alekseieva, Zinaïda, 239

Anathema (Andreiev), 275, 300

Andreiev, Leonid Nikolaievich, 137, 154, 241, 247; *see also Anathema; The Governor; The Life of Man*

Andreieva, Marya Fedorovna (Zhelyabuzhskaya), 45, 46, 77, 91, 98, 103, 115, 119, 122, 136, 143, 149, 173, 176, 179, 180, 188, 189, 200, 201–2, 204, 207, 212, 229, 231, 232, 301

Antigone (Sophocles), 20, 22, 23, 24, 26, 28, 29, 31, 40, 53, 54, 136

Arkhipov, Nikolai (Arbatov), 19, 22

The Armoured Train (Ivanov), 326, 328 &n

Artiom, Aleksandr Rodionovich, 39, 59, 60–1, 64, 66, 88, 91, 99, 105, 114, 115, 122, 128, 175, 182, 259

Asch, Sholem, 247, 250

The Assumption of Hannele (Hauptmann), 8, 15, 20, 22, 23, 25, 29, 30, 31, 41, 220

At the Monastery (Yartsev), 194, 212, 215, 216

Auerbach, L., 340

Les Aveugles (Maeterlinck), 193

Balmont, Konstantin Dmitrievich, 106–7, 108

Baranov, Nikolai Aleksandrovich, 117, 119, 150, 167

Barnay, Ludwig, 7

Basilievski, W.P., 298

Beardsley, Aubrey, 260

Beerbohm Tree, Sir Herbert, 269

Before Sunrise (Hauptmann), 77–8

Belkin, Arnold, 212

Bell, Stanley, 269

Benois, Aleksandr, 299

Berlin, 237, 238–9, 267, 290, 316

Bertenson, Sergei Lvovich, 323, 335–6, 343, 348, 349, 351–2

Bill-Bielotserkovski, V., 330

Björnson, Björnstjerne, 205, 207

The Bluebird (Maeterlinck), 248, 251, 269–70, 273, 275, 325–6

Blum, Vladimir Ivanovich, 315, 325, 326, 339

Bokshanskaya, Olga Sergeievna, 316, 317–19, 320–1, 324, 335–6, 349, 351–2, 353

Boleslavski, Richard Valentinovich, 278

Boston (USA), MXAT tour of, 318–19, 320

Brand (Ibsen), 237, 241, 242, 243, 244, 247, 257

Briusov, Valeri Jakovlievich, 235

The Brothers Karamazov (Dostoievski), 280, 282, 283–6, 287, 300, 343

Bulgakov, Mikhail Afanasievich, xiv, 326–7, 329, 330, 335, 336–42, 345, 350; appointed director at Art Theatre, 341–2; *letters:* 327, 336–41, 342, 350, 352–3; Stalin's phone call to, 341; *see also The Days of the Turbins; Flight; Molière; The Purple Island*

Bulgakova, Liubov Elena, 342, 343

Burdzhalov,Georgi Sergeievich, 19, 22, 40, 143, 154

'Cabbage Evenings', 282 &n, 291

Cain (Byron), 315

Calchas (Chekhov), 206

Canada, 319–20

censorship, 29, 124–5, 126, 315, 325–6, 327, 329, 330, 335, 336–9, 345

Chalyapin, Fiodor Ivanovich, 107, 142–3

Chekhov, Anton Pavlovich, xiii, xiv, 13–14, 15, 41, 48, 60–1, 72, 102, 131, 152, 155, 165, 170, 193, 205, 206–7, 208, 284, 285, 315, 320, 322; anger at Efros article, 152, 163, 170, 176, 177; death and funeral (1904), 193, 202, 203, 204, 205, 206, 214; enforced 'exile' in Yalta, xiv, 70, 72; invited to be shareholder in Art Theatre, 113, 119, 142; at Liubimova with Olga, 127, 128; marriage to Olga Knipper, 49; tuberculosis, 72, 114, 116, 170, 193; *letters*: Gorki, 70–1, 82, 85, 103, 105–6, 127–8; Ivan Iordanov, 42; Knipper, 54–6, 57–8, 65–6, 67, 70, 76, 77, 78, 79, 80, 82, 83–4, 85–7, 88–90, 92, 93–6, 99, 100, 102–4, 106–9, 110–16, 118–19, 122–3, 125–7, 138, 142, 146, 161, 168–9, 177, 179–80, 182, 185, 186, 189, 190; Komissarzhevskaya, 79–80, 85; Kuprin, 190; Lilina, 147, 181, 186; Marya Chekhova, 44, 46–7, 48, 50, 66, 67, 74, 100–1, 159; Meyerhold, 55,

56–7, 58–9, 72, 77–8, 81, 83; Morozov, 122–3; Nemirovich, 16–18, 31–2, 35–6, 42–4, 48–50, 63–4, 68–9, 73–4, 76, 84, 87, 92–3, 97–9, 109–10, 124, 143–4, 145–7, 148–9, 157–8, 160, 163, 172–3, 175–6, 178–9, 189–90; Stanislavski, 87, 89, 91–2, 94, 114, 116–18, 144–5, 158–9, 160, 161–2, 171, 174–5, 177–8, 180–1, 182, 185, 186; Sulerzhitski, 184, 186; Tikhomirov, 93; Vishnievski, 94, 99; *see also The Cherry Orchard; Ivanov; The Seagull; Three Sisters; Uncle Vanya; The Wood Demon*

Chekhov, Ivan Pavlovich, 202

Chekhov, Michael, 5, 265, 297, 324

Chekhova, Marya Pavlovna, 16, 48, 65, 72, 73; *letters:* to Chekhov, 44, 46–7, 48, 50, 66, 67, 74, 100–1, 159

Cherepanov's company, 7

Chernigovski Monastery, 294–5

The Cherry Orchard (Chekhov), 72, 127, 145, 148, 152, 159–63, 165, 169, 170–90, 193, 204, 234, 317, 318

Chigago (USA), tour of (1923), 317

Children of the Sun (Gorki), 193, 229, 230, 234

Chirikov, Evgeni Nikolaievich, 137, 204, 205, 206

Chronegk, Ludwig, 151, 154

Civil War (1919), 315

commedia dell'arte, 280

Coquelin, Constant-Benoît, 7

Craig, Edward Gordon, xiii, 260, 264, 266–9, 273, 276, 287; *On the Art of the Theatre*, 266 &n; production of *Hamlet*, 275–6, 280, 282, 290–4

Dalcroze School, Dresden, 290, 293

The Dangers of Tobacco (Chekhov), 206

D'Annunzio, Gabriele, 212

Darski, Mikhail Egorovich, 20, 21, 25–7

Davidov, Vladimir Nikolaievich, 34, 35

The Days of the Turbins (Bulgakov), 326–7, 331, 332, 338, 341, 351, 352

The Death of Ivan the Terrible (Aleksei Tolstoi), 49, 53, 54, 57, 58, 68, 74, 78, 83, 136, 158

Deutsches Theater, Berlin, 239, 267

Diaghilev, Sergei Pavlovich, 212n
Dimitri the Pretender (Khromiakov), 145
Diuzhikova, Antonina Mikhailovna, 34
Dobuzhinski, Mstislav, 290
Dolgorukov, Prince, 245
A Doll's House (Ibsen), 25
Dostoievski, Fyodor M., 309; *see also*
  *Brothers Karamazov; The Village of
  Stepanchikovo*
The Drama of Life (Hamsun), 211, 212,
  213, 220, 221, 225, 234, 237, 241,
  242–3, 246, 247, 254–5, 256
Drayman Henschel (Hauptmann), 49, 50–
  1 &n, 53, 54, 57, 62
Duncan, Isadora, 260–3, 266–7, 275
Duse, Eleanora, 237, 238, 260, 263

Efros, Nikolai Efimovich, 52, 81, 110,
  152, 156–7, 163, 170, 172, 177–8, 247
Ekaterina Ivanovna, 300
Enemies (Gorki), 209, 348, 349
An Enemy of the People (Ibsen), 74, 77, 78,
  79, 110, 124–5, 136, 275, 300
Enough Stupidity in Every Wise Man
  (Ostrovski), 145, 146
Erdman, Nikolai Robertovich, 345
Ermolova, Marya Nikolaievna, 196

The Father (Strindberg), 205, 206, 208
Faust (Goethe), 145
Fear (Afinogenov), 346–7
Fedotov, Aleksandr Aleksandrovich, 107
Fedotova, Glikeria Nikolaievna, 47, 50,
  89–90, 116
Les Femmes Savantes (Molière), 20
Finland, Stanislavski's holiday in, 237,
  240
Flight (Bulgakov), 330, 339
Les Fourberies de Scapin (Molière), 68n
The Fruits of Enlightenment (Lev Tolstoi),
  125, 126, 145

Gandurina, Natalya Andreievna, 39
Gennert, Ivan Ivanovich, 40
Germanova, Marya Nikolaievna, 215
Gest, Morris, 321, 323 &n
Ghosts (Ibsen), 25, 145, 205, 207, 216–
  17, 223, 267

Gioconda, 215, 217
Glaviskusstvo, 333
Glavrepertkom/Repertkom, 315, 325,
  335, 338, 339, 346
Gogol, Nikolai Vasilievich, 264, 345, 357;
  see also The Inspector-General; Marriage
Goldoni, Carolo, 42, 323
Golovin, Aleksandr Yakovlievich, 335
Gorchakov, Nikolai, 349, 350, 353
Gorki, Maksim, xiii, xiv, 49, 72, 81, 82,
  83, 102, 107, 108, 110, 111–12, 114,
  115, 116, 118, 124, 126, 127, 131, 137,
  138, 142–4, 145, 148, 176 &n, 188–9,
  193, 202, 203, 206, 207, 209, 212, 215,
  229, 232, 234, 345; breaks with Art
  Theatre, 193, 209, 211; love affair
  with Andreieva, 188, 189, 201–2;
  Memoir, 72; Nemirovich's criticism of
  Summerfolk, 193, 194–200; People's
  Theatre venture, 176 &n, 193;
  Stanislavski stays in Capri with, 280;
  letters: Chekhov, 70–1, 82, 85, 103,
  105–6, 127–8; Nemirovich, 193, 194–
  202, 208–9, 230; Stanislaviski, 347–8;
  *see also Children of the Sun; Enemies;
  Yegor Bulichov; The Lower Depths; Small
  People; Summerfolk*
'Gorkiad' (group of young writers), 128,
  137, 138, 148, 193
Goslavski, Evgeni Petrovich, 68, 74 &n,
  137
The Governor (Andreyev), 26, 28, 145
Grechnaninov, Aleksandr Tikhonovich,
  81
Griboiedov, Alexander, 229; *see also Woe
  from Wit*
Griboiedov prize, 3
Gribunin, Vladimir, 82, 88, 91, 143,
  149, 171, 173, 175, 207, 232
Grigorieva, Marya Petrovna
  [Nikolaieva], 40, 218
Gromov, M.A., 88, 99, 167, 176
Gurevich, Liubov Yakovlievna, 301
Gzovskaya, Olga Vladimirovich, 281,
  284, 288, 291

Haasa, Friedrich, 238
Halbe, Max, 238
Hamlet (Shakespeare), 264, 267, 275–6,
  278, 280, 281, 282, 290–4, 295–6

Hamsun, Knut, 211, 212, 216, 237; *see also The Drama of Life*

Hauptmann, Gerhart, 8, 13, 25, 30, 42, 49, 50–1, 55, 72, 106, 145, 238, 247, 251; *see also The Assumption of Hannele; Before Sunrise; Drayman Henschel; Lonely People; Michael Kramer; The Sunken Bell; The Triumph of Compromise*

The Heart is not a Stone (Ostrovski), 74 &n

Hedda Gabler (Ibsen), 45–6, 53, 68, 136, 216

Heitz, Mikhail Sergeievich, 332–3, 342–3, 346

Hermitage Theatre, Moscow, 15, 42

Hugo, Victor, 146

Ibsen, Henrik, 13, 18, 25, 31, 45–6, 51, 74, 77, 78, 80 &n, 85, 144, 216, 243; *see also Brand; A Doll's House; An Enemy of the People; Ghosts; Hedda Gabler; The Lady from the Sea; Peer Gynt; Pillars of Society; Rosmersholm; When We Dead Awaken; The Wild Duck*

Ilinski, 40

In Dreams (Nemirovich), 102, 104, 106, 107, 108, 109, 110–11, 131

In the Meantime (Rovette), 13, 19, 20, 23, 29

The Inspector-General (Gogol), 125, 145, 146, 147, 195, 274

Irving, Henry, 267

Ivan Mirovich, 273

Ivanov, Ivan Ivanovich, 36, 50

Ivanov, Vsevolod Viacheslavovich, 328 &n

Ivanov (Chekhov), 15, 16, 32, 104, 108, 155, 160, 193, 202, 203, 205, 206, 208, 214, 216, 219, 220, 300

Jubilee (Chekhov), 206

Julius Caesar (Shakespeare), 15, 136, 145, 146, 147, 151–5, 156–8, 159, 163, 164, 165, 166, 167, 169, 171, 178, 180, 183, 184, 210, 219, 280, 300, 349

Kachalov, Vasili Ivanovich, 78–9, 82, 88, 89, 91, 98, 99, 110, 111, 122, 125, 128, 143, 149, 150, 155, 173, 182, 184, 186, 204, 206, 207, 215, 216, 217, 222, 223, 225, 230, 237, 242, 243, 244, 246, 247, 284, 296, 300, 315, 316–17, 323, 325

Kalinnikov, Vasili Sergeievich, 40

Kaluzhski, Vasili *see* Luzhski

Kaluzhski, Zheni, 351

Kataiev, Valentin Petrovich, 126

Kazanski, accountant, 40

Kedrov, Mikhail Nikolaievich, 353

Kerr, Alfred, 238

Khaliutina, Sofya Vasilievna, 175

Kharlamov, Aleksei Petrovich, 143, 150

Khromiakov, 145

King Lear (Shakespeare), 267

Kirshon, Vladimir Mikhailovich, 348

Knipper-Chekhova, Olga Leonardovna, xiii, xiv, 14, 26, 27, 36, 38, 40, 43, 44, 47, 59, 61, 62, 63, 64, 66, 71, 72, 77, 82, 88, 91, 98, 100–1, 102, 116, 127, 144, 145, 148, 150, 152, 155, 159, 172, 173, 174, 175, 202, 203, 207, 215, 216, 217, 255, 286, 300, 315; Chekhov's marriage to, 49; and death of Chekhov, 202, 204; illness (1902), 127, 128; at Liubimovska with Chekhov, 127, 128; removed from cast of *Fear*, 346–7; and the System, 276–8; *letters:* Bertenson, 347; Chekhov, 54–6, 57–8, 65–6, 67, 70, 76, 77, 78, 79, 80, 82, 83–4, 85–7, 88–90, 92, 93–6, 99, 100, 102–4, 106–9, 110–16, 118–19, 122–3, 125–7, 138, 142, 146, 161, 168–9, 171, 177, 179–80, 182, 185, 186, 189, 190; Lilina, 240; Nemirovich, 62–3, 80–1, 128–31, 186–7, 209; Stakhovich, 241–2; Stanislavski, 51, 138–40, 277–8

Komissarzhevskaya, Vera Fiodorovona, 34, 35, 63, 79–80, 85, 204, 206, 229, 287

Korsh, Fiodor Adamovich, 51

Korsh Theatre, 51n, 330

Kosheverov, Aleksandr Sergeievich, 8

Kosheverova, Marya Vasilievna, 38

Kosorotov, Aleksandr Ivanovich, 247, 250

Kotlyarevskaya, Vera Vasilievna, 236, 256, 265–6

Krokodil, 319
Kulturprop, 346
Kupichskaya, 19
Kuprin, Aleksandr Ivanovich, 190
Kuznetsov, Pavel Verfolomeievich, 28

The Lady from the Sea (Ibsen), 18, 25, 31,
  145, 147, 155, 215, 217
Lanskoi, Vladimir, 22, 26, 27, 28
A Law Unto Themselves (Pisemski), 26,
  27, 28, 30, 31, 42, 220
Lenin, V.I., 315, 316
Leningrad *see* Petersburg
Lenski, Aleksandr Pavlovich, 15, 34
Leonidov, Leonid Mironovich, 173, 176,
  179, 187–8, 215, 251–4, 274, 323,
  331–5, 343
Leontev, Yakov Leontievich, 351
Lermontov, Mikhail Yurevich, 145
Lessing, Leonid Aleksandrovich von,
  229
Lessing Theatre Company, Berlin, 7
Levina, N.A., 36n, 38
Lianovski Theatre, Moscow, 128
The Lie (Afinogenov), 350
The Life of Man (Andreiev), 260, 266
Lilina, Marya Petrovna Alekseieva, 36n,
  44, 54, 57, 59, 66 &n, 80, 86, 88, 95,
  100, 106, 110, 111, 112, 114, 116, 117,
  119, 122, 126, 145, 161, 170, 172, 173,
  175, 176, 179, 180, 202, 204, 207, 217,
  261, 264, 358; *letters*: Chekhov, 147,
  181, 188; Knipper, 240; Nemirovich,
  259–60, 281–3; Stanislavski, 40–1,
  295–6, 309
Lisanov's theatre, 119
Litovtsieva, Nina Nikolaievna, 126, 173,
  215
Little Russian Theatre, 7
Litvinov, Ivan Mikhailovich, 29
Liubimovka, Stanislavski's country
  house, 3, 4, 127, 128–9
The Living Corpse (Tolstoi), 294, 295,
  296, 299
La Locandiera (Goldoni), 42, 323
Lodgers (Naidenov), 145
Lonely People (Hauptmann), 49, 52, 54,
  55, 56–7, 58, 67n, 68, 70, 72, 73, 74,
  83, 102, 136, 158, 172, 179

The Lower Depths (Gorki), 102, 127–8,
  131, 138, 141, 142–4, 145, 147, 149–
  50, 163, 164, 166–7, 171, 176, 195,
  199, 204, 219, 238, 317, 318
Lugné-Poë, Aurélien-Marie, 237
Lunacharski, Anatoli Vasilievich, 315,
  323, 325–8, 331
Luzhski, Vasili Vasilievich (Kaluzhski),
  19, 32, 36, 38, 39, 40, 52, 57, 64, 66,
  77, 79, 88, 91, 95, 98, 112, 114, 115,
  117, 118, 119, 122, 126, 131, 132, 145,
  149, 169, 173, 175, 179, 202, 215, 222,
  255, 273, 274, 283, 285, 296, 306,
  326–7
Macbeth (Shakespeare), 145, 267
Maeterlinck, Maurice, 193, 203, 204,
  205, 213, 214, 215, 325–6; *see also*
  *Aglavaine et Célisette; Les Aveugles; The
  Bluebird; Miniatures; The Uninvited*
Magnus, Maurice, 268–9
Maksimovich, Aleksandr, 117, 229–30,
  231
Malinovskaya, Olga, 323
Maly Theatre, Moscow, 3, 13, 15, 34,
  44, 48, 49, 50, 51 &n, 68, 71, 110,
  133, 141, 145, 164, 195, 236, 281, 349,
  353; proposal to merge with Moscow
  Art Theatre, 236, 256, 259–60
Mamontov, Savva Ivanovich, 9–10, 238
Manasievich, Aleksandr Fiodorovich,
  28–9
Mardzhanov, Konstantin
  Aleksandrovich, 282, 291
Markov, Pavel, Aleksandrovich, 351
Marriage (Chekhov), 206
Marriage (Gogol), 146, 147, 324
Marriage of Figaro (Beaumarchais), 326
Marya Fedorovna *see* Andreieva
Marya Petrovna *see* Lilina
Masquerade (Lermontov), 145
Mayakovski, Vladimir, 315, 329
The Mayor, 74
Meininger company, 151
The Merchant of Venice (Shakespeare), 15,
  20, 22, 23, 24, 25–6, 27–8, 29, 31, 41,
  42, 220
Meyerhold, Vsevolod Emilievich, xiii,
  xiv, 5, 14, 21, 26, 27, 33, 36, 38, 44–5,
  52, 57, 68, 70, 77, 79, 88, 90, 91, 93,

95, 98, 103, 104, 105, 114, 115, 116, 118, 126, 212, 216, 219, 222, 226, 231, 251, 315, 345, 350, 355; arrested and executed (1939), 359; direction of Studio by, 211, 231, 232, 280; excluded as shareholder in Art Theatre, 113, 123, 124; leaves Art Theatre, 123 &n, 124, 135; returns from provinces, 194; works in Opera-Dramatic Studio, 357; *letters*: Chekhov, 55, 56–7, 58–9, 77–8, 81, 83; Nemirovich, 45–6; Olga (wife), 14, 21–2, 25–6, 28–31; Stanislavski, 115, 119–21, 357–8

Michael Kramer (Hauptmann), 106, 107

A Midsummer Night's Dream (Shakespeare), 267

Mikhailovski, Nikolai Konstantinovich, 111

'Miniatures' (evenings of short stories), 193–4, 204, 205, 206, 207, 208, 215, 216

Miniatures (Maeterlinck), 146

Mirabeau, Octave, 145

Molière, Jean-Baptiste Poquelin, 20, 24, 25, 68n, 297, 342; *see also Les Femmes Savantes; Les Fourberies de Scapin; Tartuffe*

Molière (Bulgakov), 335, 339, 348, 349, 350, 352–3

Monastery, 215

A Month in the Country (Turgenev), 126, 136, 145, 146, 147, 164, 202, 205, 208, 264, 275, 276–8, 286, 289

Morozov, Savva Timofeievich, 4, 73, 74, 75–6, 115, 135, 138–9, 140n, 149, 166, 169, 202, 203, 204, 208, 212, 218, 226, 247, 274, 300; and actor-shareholders scheme, 113, 119, 122–3, 124 &n, 142; financial support for Moscow Art Theatre, 73; Nemirovich's hostility towards, 73, 74, 75–6, 128–9, 130, 151, 164–5, 179, 200, 201; shoots himself (1905), 235; withdraws financial support, 193, 207

Morozova, Zinaïda Grigorieva, 137, 165, 245

Moscow Art Theatre (MXAT): actors' collective, 113, 119, 122–3, 124 &n, 142; becomes Moscow Art Academic Theatre of the USSR (1931), 346; Bulgakov appointed director at, 341–2; Bulgakov's letter to Committee, 327; censorship, 29, 124–5, 126, 315, 325–6, 327, 329, 330, 335, 336–9, 345; death of Chekhov (1904), 193, 206; first performance success of *The Seagull* (1898), 42–5, 46–7, 48; first season (1898–9), 13–47; foreign tours, 237, 238–9, 315, 316, 317–23; Gordon Craig and production of *Hamlet*, 275–6, 278, 280, 282, 290–4, 295–6; Gorki breaks with, 193, 209; Heitz appointed as 'Red' director to Board, 329, 331–3, 342; Isadora Duncan dances at, 260; merger with Maly proposal, 236, 256–60; Morozov financially supports, 73, 75–6; and withdraws support, 193; Nemirovich negotiates future of, 321–3; October Revolution (1917), 315–16; Omon Theatre acquired (1902), 109, 117 &n, 138–9, 140n; Petersburg tours, 102–3, 124–8, 130; rehearsals in Pushkino (summer 1898), 14, 19–22, 25–6, 28, 29–31, 129, 211, 218, 222, 326; relaunched by Stanislavski (1925–7), 326; Stanislavski's letter to Board (1910), 278–80; Stanislavski's new agreement with (1908), 238, 264; Stanislavski's resignation from Board of Directors, xv, 238, 263; struggle for control of (1928–38), 330; under Soviet Regime, 315–28; and under Stalinism, xiii, 329–59; *see also* Studios; the System

Moskvin, Ivan Mikhailovich, 21 &n, 22, 26, 27–8, 29, 36, 40, 41, 82, 88, 100, 111, 114, 122, 141, 145, 150, 155, 171, 173, 175, 176, 208, 216, 217, 232, 243, 255, 277, 296, 300, 309

Much Ado About Nothing (Shakespeare), 24

Munt, Katya (Ekaterina Mikhailovna), 22, 30, 111, 123

Muradreva, Com., 325

Muratova, Elena Pavlovna, 114, 115, 123n, 143, 173, 175, 179, 180, 182, 222, 291

Music Theatre, Nemirovich's, 316, 326, 348, 357

MXT Association, Nemirovich's letter to members of, 133–4

Naidenov, Sergei Aleksandrovich, 145, 204, 205, 206

Narkompros (People's Commissariat for Education), 323, 324, 325

Nelidov, Vladimir Aleksandrovich, 255 &n, 256, 257, 259, 262

Nemirovich, Ekaterina Nikolaevna, 295; death of (1938), 360–1

Nemirovich-Danchenko, Vladimir Ivanovich, xiii, xiv-xv, 22, 48–9, 50, 51, 54, 55, 65, 78, 89, 90, 92, 93–4, 95, 104, 107, 111, 113, 118, 119, 122, 144, 170, 315–16, 329–30, 332, 333, 341; consolidates position of authority (1911), 296; criticism of *Summerfolk* and break with Gorki, 193, 194–200, 211; differences/rift between Stanislavski and, xiv, 5, 59–62, 75–6, 113, 132–3, 151–2, 163–9, 212–29, 237–8, 240–51, 254–8, 280, 281, 295–6, 299–311, 350, 351–2, 354, 355–7; death (1943), 359; death of his wife (1938), 358–9; first foreign tour (1906), 237, 238; his view of the System, 264–5, 281, 288, 294; hostility towards Morozov, 73, 74, 75–6, 128–9, 130, 151, 164–5, 179, 200, 201; *In Dreams* (play), 102, 104, 106, 107, 108, 109, 110–11; *Julius Caesar* produced by, 151–8, 164–5, 169, 184; Music Theatre of, 316, 326, 348, 357; *My Life in the Russian Theatre*, xv; negotiates future of Art Theatre with Soviets, 323–5; proposal to merge Art Theatre with Maly, 256–60; removes Stanislavski from cast of *Stepanchikovo* (1917), 309–11; Slavyanski Bazar meeting with Stanislavski (1897), 3–4, 5, 6; *letters*: Andreiev, 241; Bertenson, 345, 350; Bokshanskaya, 317–19, 320–1, 324; Chalyapin, 142–3; Chekhov, 16–18, 31–2, 35–6, 42–4, 49, 63–4, 68–9, 73–4, 76, 84, 87, 92–3, 97–9, 109–10, 124, 143–4, 145–7,

148–9, 157–8, 160, 163, 172–3, 175–6, 178–9, 189–90; Efros, 156–7; Gorki, 193, 194–202, 208–9, 230; Heitz, 344–5; Kachalov, 316–17; Knipper, 62–3, 80–1, 128–31, 186–7, 209; Leonidov, 187–8; Lilina, 259–60, 281–3; Lunacharski, 325–6; Meyerhold, 45–6; MXT Association members, 133–4; Stanislavski, 6–10, 13, 14–16, 18–21, 23–9, 32–5, 37–40, 52–4, 59–62, 74–7, 79, 130, 131–8, 140–2, 149–50, 153–6, 163–9, 188–9, 202–8, 210–35, 238–9, 240–1, 242–51, 254–5, 256–8, 263, 271–5, 276, 283–90, 297–309, 310–11, 319–20, 321–3, 324–5, 355–7, 358–9; wife, Ekaterina, 295

New Economic Policy (1921–9), xiv, 316

New Theatre, Soviet, 323, 324

New York, tour of (1924), 321

Nizhni-Novgorod, Gorki's People's Theatre venture in, 176 &n, 193

Norden, Berlin critic, 239

Novitski, P., 339

Novoe Russkoe Slovo, Stanislavski's interview in, 319

Novosti Dnya, 152, 156, 163, 170, 176, 177–8

October Revolution (1917), xiv, 269, 309, 315–16, 326, 328

Olga Leonardovna *see* Knipper

Omon Theatre, Moscow, 109, 117–18 &n, 138–9, 140n

Opera-Dramatic Studio (1936), 354, 357

Opera-Studio (1918), 316

Orlov, Dr Ivan, 48, 50

Ostrovski, Aleksandr Nikolaievich, 15, 74 &n, 145, 146, 285; *see also Enough Stupidity. . .; The Heart is not a Stone; Snowmaiden*

Othello (Shakespeare), 329, 331, 332, 333–6

Paradiz Theatre, Moscow, 7, 8

Paris, 316, 319, 321

Pavlova, Anna, 218

Pazukhin's Death, 321, 323

Peer Gynt (Ibsen), 267

Petersburg, 13–14, 34n, 69, 145, 206, 213, 229, 262, 265–6, 317, 350; Art Theatre tours of, 102–3, 124–5, 126–7, 128, 130

Petrov, Colonel, 95, 99

Petrovskaya, 8

Philadelphia, tour of (1923), 318, 319–20

Philharmonic School, 3, 14, 15, 73 &n

The Pickwick Club (Kirshon), 348

Pickwick Papers, 352

Pikel, R., 339, 340

The Pillars of Society (Ibsen), 51, 126, 131, 132, 136, 145, 147, 148, 149, 150, 151, 155, 163, 164, 167, 169, 171, 205, 220, 224

Pinski, 250

Pisemsky, Aleksei, 42; *see also A Law Unto Themselves*

Platonov, Aleksandr, 26, 29, 38, 39

Podgorny, Nikolai Afanasievich, 242, 244, 323, 331, 333, 351

Pogozhev, 29

Pomyalova, 173, 175

Poor Heinrich, 145

Povarskaya Street Theatre-Studio, 211, 220–1, 232, 234–5, 280

The Power of Darkness (Tolstoi), 131, 132, 139–40, 163, 167

Pravda, Stanislavski's letter to, 319

Proletkult, 315

Przbyszewski, Stanislaw, 215, 247

The Purple Island (Bulgakov), 337–8

Pushkin, Aleksandr Sergeievich, 203, 218

Pushkino (summer 1898), 14, 19–22, 129, 211, 218, 222, 326; Meyerhold's letters to wife Olga from, 14, 21–2, 25–6, 28, 29–31

Rachmaninov, Sergius Vasilievich, 143

Raevskaya, Evgenia Mikhailovna, 36, 64, 123, 125

RAPP (Revolutionary Association of Proletarian Writers) theatre, xiii

Réjane, Gabrielle, 7, 269

Rigoletto (Verdi), 357

Rimski-Korsakov, Nikolai, 81

Roksanova, Marya Liudomirova (Petrovskaya), 36, 38, 40, 47, 51n, 104, 108, 114, 115, 118, 123 &n

Rokshanin, Nikolai Osipovich, 110

Rosmersholm (Ibsen), 145, 155, 202, 203, 205, 206, 266, 273, 274

Rostand, Edmond, 24

Rovetta *see In the Meantime*

Rumyantsev, N.A., 271, 273

Sakhnovski, V.G., 350, 351, 356

Sakhovich, Vasili Grigorievich, 330

Saltykov-Shchedrin, Mikhail Evgrafovich, 338, 345

Samarova, Marya Aleksandrovna, 60–1, 64, 91, 98, 110, 111, 119, 122, 128, 143, 212, 250, 259

Sanin, Aleksandr Akimovich (Schoenberg), 19, 26, 27, 39–40, 52, 88, 89, 90, 91, 93, 98, 100, 102–3, 104, 106, 111, 114, 115, 123, 132, 222

Sapunov, 285

Sardou, Victorien, 24

Savitskaya, M.G., 21–2, 82, 88, 91, 98, 100, 114, 155, 173, 208, 217, 300

Saxe-Meiningen, Duke of, 25 &n

Sazonov, N.F., 34, 35

Schnitzler, Arthur, 238

Schoenberg *see* Sanin.

Schtuck, Franz, 212

Schultz, Vladimir Nikolaievich, 7

The Seagull (Chekhov), 13–14, 15, 16–18, 31–8, 39, 42–4, 46–7, 48, 49, 50, 53, 54, 59, 62, 65, 69&n, 83, 86, 108, 118, 136, 145, 155, 160, 162, 181, 194, 200, 204, 205, 208, 217, 221, 231, 232, 234

Second Moscow Art Theatre, xiii, 357

Senelick, Laurence, 'Foundations of the Moscow Art Theatre', 23n

Shakespeare, William, 13, 15, 20, 23, 24–5, 42, 49, 81, 156–7, 267; *see also Hamlet; Julius Caesar; King Lear; Macbeth; The Merchant of Venice; Othello; Twelfth Night*

Shakovski, Prince, 125, 126

Shaw, Martin, Craig's letter to, 276

Shchedrin *see* Saltykov-Shchedrin

Shchepkin, Mikhail, 3

Shchukin, Boris Vasilievich, 40

Shchukin Theatre, Moscow, 40

Shidlovska, Evgenia Viktopovna, 167

Shpazhinski, Ippolit Vasilievich, 117

Simon, composer, 30

Simov, Viktor Andreievich, 20, 25, 40, 122, 151, 153, 172, 175, 179, 182, 207, 219, 285

'Sketches' (evening of short pieces adapted from Chekhov, 1904), 203 &n

Skitalets, Stepan Gavrilovich, 137

Slavyanski Bazar meeting (1897), 3–4, 5, 6, 211

Sleptsov, Vasili Alekseievich, 206

Small People (Gorki), 84 &n, 102, 105–6, 107, 108, 109, 111–121, 113–14, 115, 116, 117, 118, 124, 126–7, 131, 158

Snowmaiden (Ostrovski), 74, 78, 81, 82, 83, 84, 158, 164, 167, 169

Sobinov, Leonid Vitalievich, 107

Society of Art and Literature, 4, 14, 15, 75, 238

Society for the Establishment of an Open Theatre in Moscow, 13, 17, 38

Sokolovskaya, 346–7

Sokolovski, Nikolai Nikolaievich, 65

Soloviova, Vera Vasilievna, 149

Sonenthal, Matkovski, 7

Sophocles, 13; *see also* Antigone

Sporting Club, Moscow, 8, 41, 218, 223

Stakhovich, Aleksei Aleksandrovich, 123, 128–9, 136, 137, 210, 235, 241–2, 246, 247, 248, 255, 292, 305, 356

Stalin, Iossif, xiii, xv, 329, 330, 335, 341, 345–6, 353–5

Stanislavski, Konstantin Sergeievich Alekseiev, xiii, xiv-xv, 22, 30, 36, 44, 48, 49, 50, 59, 63, 66, 69, 71, 78, 79, 95, 96, 97, 98, 99, 102, 104, 105, 106, 107, 108, 111, 112, 115, 116, 118, 122, 124, 127, 147, 151, 152, 158, 170, 173, 175, 315–16; Bulgakov's disagreements with, 350, 352–3; *Complete Works*, xv; convalescence in Capri with Gorki (1910), 280; death (1938), 359; differences/rift between Nemirovich and, xiv, xv, 5, 59–62, 75–6, 113, 132–3, 151–2, 163–9, 211–29, 237–8, 240–51, 254–8, 280, 281, 295–6, 299–311, 350, 351–2, 354, 355–7; 'A Draft Manual of Dramatic Art', 240; foreign tours, 237, 238–9, 316, 319–23; Gordon Craig and production of *Hamlet*, 260, 266–9, 275–6, 278, 280, 287, 290–4; heart attack, 329, 343; and illnesses, 58 &n, 85, 254 &n, 255, 280–2, 329, 331, 343, 350; and Isadora Duncan, 260–3, 266; last production as co-manager (*The Bluebird*) 269–70; last years spent as semi-invalid, 329, 355; merger of Art Theatre with Maly proposal, 236, 256–8, 260; *My Life in Art*, xiii, xv, 316; new agreement with company (1908), 238, 264; new rehearsal techniques, 211; Opera-Studio, 316, 354, 357; *Othello* production plan of, 329, 331, 332, 333–6; relaunches Art Theatre (1925–7), 326; removed from cast of *Stepanchikovo*, 309–11; resignation from Board of Directors (1908), xv, 238, 263; Slavyanski Bazar meeting with Nemirovich (1897), 3–4, 5, 6, 211; Sulerzhitski becomes personal assistant to (1905), 115, 237, 246, 247, 248, 250; Studios, xiv, 265, 280, 296–9, 315, 316, 324–5; summer 1906 in Finland, 237, 240; Systems of, 237, 264–5, 275, 276–8, 281, 282, 283, 287–90, 294, 296–82; Theatre Studio in Povarskaya Street, (1905), 211, 230–1, 232, 234–5, 280; typhoid contracted by, (1910), 280–1, 282; *letters*: Art Theatre Board, 278–80; Bulgakov, 342, 352–3; Chekhov, 87, 89, 91–2, 94, 114, 116–18, 144–5, 158–9, 160, 161–2, 171, 174–5, 177–8, 180–1, 182, 185, 186; Gordon Craig, 267–8; Gorki, 209, 349–50; Government, 343–5; Isadora Duncan, 260–3, 275; Knipper, 51, 138–40, 277–8; Kotlyarevskaya, 236, 256, 265–6; Lilina, 40–1, 295–6, 309; Leonidov, 251–4, 331–5; Lunacharski, 327–8; Meyerhold, 115, 119–21, 357–8; Nemirovich, 6–10, 13, 14–16, 18–21, 23–5, 26–9, 32–5, 37–40, 52–4, 59–62, 74–7, 79, 130, 131–3, 134–8,

140–2, 149–50, 153–6, 163–9, 188–9,
202–8, 210–35, 238–9, 240–1, 242–51,
254–5, 256–8, 263, 271–5, 276, 283–
90, 297–309, 310–11, 319–25, 355–7,
358–9; open letter to company, 270–1;
Pravda, 319; Stakhovich, 255; Stalin,
345–6, 353–5; Sulerzhitski, 183–4,
269–70, 290–4; Zinaida Alekseieva,
239
Stanislavski, Mme *see* Lilina
Stanitsin, Viktor Yakovlievich, 349
The Storm, 348, 349, 352
Strindberg, August, 205, 206
Studios, Moscow Art Theatre, xiv, 265,
296–9, 304, 315, 323, 324–5; First,
265, 280, 296–8, 316, 324; Second,
265, 324; Third, 265, 324; Fourth,
265, 324; Opera-Dramatic Studio,
354, 357; Opera-Studio, 316;
Povarskaya Street, 211, 230–1, 232,
234–5, 280
Sudakov, Ilya Yakovlievich, 329, 330,
335–6, 332, 349, 356
Sudbinin, Serafim Nikolaievich, 21, 85,
86, 88, 91, 98, 114, 115, 116, 118, 123
Sudermann, Hermann, 238
The Suicide (Erdman), 345–6
Sulerzhitski, Leopold Antonovich, 5,
115–16, 183–4, 186, 215, 237, 246,
247, 248, 250, 255, 269–70, 275, 282,
288, 290–4, 297, 298
Sumbatov, Aleksandr Ivanovich
Yuzhin, 15, 34, 35, 36
Summerfolk (Gorki), 188–9, 193, 194–200,
201, 205, 209, 224, 229
The Sunken Bell (Hauptmann), 8, 25, 37,
42, 53, 74, 146, 155, 205, 220
Surennianets, designer, 145
Suvorin, Aleksei Sergeievich, 39, 41
Sviderski, Aleksei Ivanovich, 331, 332,
333
Symbolists, 193, 235, 269
System, Stanislavski's, xiii, xv, 237,
264–5, 275, 276–8, 281, 282 &n, 283,
287–90, 294, 296, 297–8, 348

Taïrov, Aleksandr Yakovlievich, 315
The Taming of the Shrew (Shakespeare),
24

Tatarinova, Fanni Karlovna, 273
Teleshov, Leonid Andreiev, 108
Telyakovski, Vladimir Arkadievich, 48,
259, 262
The Tempest (Shakespeare), 267
Three Sisters (Chekhov), 68, 72, 81–2,
84–101, 103, 111, 141, 145, 152, 159,
161, 163, 195, 204, 218, 300, 317, 318,
319, 329
Tikhomirov, Iossafat Aleksandrovich,
61, 91, 93, 111, 115, 117, 132, 137,
154, 168
Timkovski, Nikolai Ivanovich, 137
Tipolt, Marya Nikolaevna, 40
Tolstoi, Aleksei Konstantinovich, 13,
44; *see also The Death of Ivan the Terrible*
Tolstoi, Lev Nikolaievich, 87, 115, 139,
203, 206, 218, 264; *War and Peace*, 280;
Who Is Right?, 87; *see also The Fruits of
Enlightenment; The Living Corpse; The
Powers of Darkness; Tsar Fiodor*
Tolstoya, Countess Sofya Andreievna,
87, 88, 89, 91, 148 &n
The Triumph of Compromise (Hauptmann),
145
Tsar Fiodor Ioannovich (Tolstoi), 19, 20–1,
23, 24, 25, 26, 27, 29, 36, 38 &n, 39,
40, 41, 42, 48, 53, 54, 74, 100, 136,
158, 205, 230, 300, 317, 318, 325
Turgenev, Ivan Sergeievich, 148, 155,
175, 203, 206; *see also A Month in the
Country*
Twelfth Night (Shakespeare), 24–5, 49,
53, 54

Uncle Vanya (Chekhov), 32, 48–50, 51,
53, 54–6, 57–67, 68, 69, 70–1, 72, 83–
4, 94, 96, 102, 103, 117, 160, 204, 234,
238, 275, 291, 321, 327
The Uninvited (L'Intruse: Maeterlinck),
206
United States, tour of, 316, 317–23

Vakhtangov, Evgeni Bagrationovich, 5,
265, 297, 298
Varlamov, Konstantin Aleksandrovich,
34, 35
Vasiliev, Leonid Sergeievich, 40
Die Veschwörung des Fiesko, 145

Veselovski, Aleksei Nikolaievich, 50
The Village of Stepanchikovo (Dostoievski), 309, 310–11
Vishnievski, Aleksandr Leonidovich, 36, 38, 39, 40, 46, 47, 59, 64, 66 &n, 71, 77, 88–9, 91, 94, 96, 99, 116, 119, 122, 127, 128, 131, 137, 143–4, 149, 154, 169, 171, 173, 175, 181, 202, 204, 207, 208, 215, 216, 217, 257, 273, 274, 286, 356
Vyrubov, A.A., 297

When We Dead Awaken (Ibsen), 77, 78, 80 &n, 85, 136, 220
The White Guard (Bulgakov), 326–7, 339
The Wild Duck (Ibsen), 158
Wilhelm II, Emperor, 237, 239
Woe from Wit (Griboiedov), 146, 147, 218, 219, 228, 229, 234, 237, 299, 348

The Wood Demon (Chekhov), 67n, 72
The World of Art, magazine, 212 &n

Yakunchikov, Marya Fedorovna, 137
Yakunchikovis, members of the Yakunchikov family, 136
Yartsev, 204, 205, 206; *see also At the Monastery*
Yegor Bulichov (Gorki), 348 &n
Yegorev, Nikolai Vasilievich, 332, 333, 335, 351, 356–7
Young Oaf, 145
Yuzhin, Aleksandr *see* Sumbatov

Zabel, Eugen, 251
Zagarov, Aleksandr Leonidovich, 143
Zola, Emile, 78, 299
Zolotov, Khristofor Stepanovich, 40
Zhelyabuzhskaya *see* Andreieva